DISCARDED

Contents

List of Illustrations

54. Dr John Nolan, NUI Registrar (1987–2004) (NUI Archives).
55. Eamon de Valera's first visit to NUI as President of Ireland (courtesy of UCD Archives).
56. National College of Art and Design (courtesy of National College of Art and Design).
57. Royal College of Surgeons in Ireland (courtesy of Royal College of Surgeons in Ireland).
58. Shannon College of Hotel Management (courtesy of Shannon College of Hotel Management).
59. Milltown Institute of Theology and Philosophy (courtesy of the Milltown Institute of Theology and Philosophy).
60. Institute of Public Administration (courtesy of the Institute of Public Administration).
61. Chancellor Garret FitzGerald with Mrs Linda O'Shea Farren, Chairperson of Convocation (2006–present) (courtesy of Mrs Linda O'Shea Farren).
62. Michael Francis Cox (NUI Archives).
63. Eamon de Valera, Chancellor of the NUI with members of the Committee of Convocation (19 November 1921) (NUI Archives).
64. A copy of the University Education (Ireland) Act 1879 (NUI Archives).
65. A copy of the Royal Charter issued to the Royal University of Ireland in 1880 (NUI Archives).
66. The Royal Charter issued to the Royal University of Ireland in 1880 (NUI Archives).
67. The box containing the Royal Charter and seal of the RUI (NUI Archives).
68. The Royal University of Ireland Roll of Senate and Graduates, Vol. 1 (NUI Archives).

Between pages 228 and 229
69. Reginald Brabazon, 12th Earl of Meath (1841–1929) (NUI Archives).
70. Thomas Kettle (1880–1916) (courtesy of UCD Archives).
71. The Prince of Wales, later King Edward VII (1841–1910) (NUI Archives).
72. The Princess of Wales, later Queen Alexandra (1844–1925) (NUI Archives).
73. Conferring of Honorary Degrees on the Prince and Princess of Wales, 1885 (NUI Archives).
74. The Royal Charter issued to the National University of Ireland on 2 December 1908 (NUI Archives).
75. The NUI Senate Minute Book, Vol. 1 (NUI Archives).
76. The Coat of Arms of the National University of Ireland (NUI Archives).

⌈ x ⌉

Foreword The Chancellor GARRET FITZGERALD

T HE HISTORY OF the National University of Ireland is closely linked with and to an extent mirrors the evolution of the Irish state in the twentieth century. The decision of the Senate of the University to mark the centenary of its establishment by commissioning this book was well justified, and has, moreover, been confirmed by the quality of the contributions penned by those who have collaborated in its preparation.

In writing a foreword to this volume I feel it is appropriate at the outset to try to set the emergence of the National University of Ireland against the historical background of the late eighteenth and nineteenth centuries. I feel this is necessary because the recent secularisation of our society has obscured for many people the extent to which so many of our institutions, especially in the education sector, owe their present shape to the particular way in which from the late eighteenth century to the first quarter of the twentieth British governments of varying compositions sought, with variable success, to disentangle the situation that had been created by the monopoly of Irish institutions established in the seventeenth century by the controlling 15 per cent of the population who belonged to the Anglican Church of Ireland.

The first such British intervention was the foundation of the Royal College of St Patrick's, Maynooth, in 1795, financed by the British government with a view to enabling Roman Catholic priests to be educated in Ireland rather than in revolutionary France. That college's attempt to extend its role to the education of Catholic laymen as well as future priests met, however, with government disapproval, as threatening the higher education monopoly enjoyed by the Anglican Dublin University with its single Trinity College. The attendance of lay students was terminated in 1807.

Next, in 1831, the British government initiated a system of state-financed primary schools in Ireland – decades before doing so in Britain. This move was motivated by concerns about the way in which in recent decades the earlier 'hedge schools' had blossomed very rapidly into some 10,000 largely lay fee-paying private primary schools, run by Catholics, which, perhaps uniquely in Europe, were by 1824 educating about one third – and in urban areas up to two thirds – of Catholic children throughout the island. Most of these schools were described by the comprehensive 1824 Parliamentary Survey of Irish Education as being carried on in 'miserable thatched mud cabins'.

What became known as the 'national schools' initiative by the British government had been promoted by a Catholic Unionist MP for Waterford, Thomas Wyse, one of the earliest beneficiaries of Catholic Emancipation, and seems to have been inspired by a concern that these fee-paying lay private schools might encourage subversion.

Within two decades these new national schools had replaced many of the private schools and had been 'colonised' by the Roman Catholic and Presbyterian Churches, which were both determined that Anglicans should not, through their long-established school system, retain a monopoly of confessional primary education.

Next, in an effort to end the Anglican monopoly of university education, the British government established in the 1840s a non-denominational Queen's University with three colleges – not in Dublin, where such an institution would have challenged the TCD local monopoly, but in Belfast, Cork and Galway. These new university colleges were, however, denounced as 'godless' by the Catholic hierarchy, which greatly limited the attendance in Cork and Galway.

The decades that followed saw a huge expansion in the number of Roman Catholic secondary schools, which had begun to emerge in a few cities and towns in the late eighteenth century. The fact that these schools lacked public finance, of the kind available to Anglicans through the land endowments of the Church of Ireland in earlier centuries, led the British government in 1878 to launch a system of support for secondary education by means of payments made to all schools on the basis of the results of examinations – which still survive in the form of the Junior and Leaving Certificate examinations.

Meanwhile Gladstone in 1873 attempted to merge Queen's University with Dublin University, which under his scheme was to have four colleges: TCD, the Catholic University founded by Newman, and the Queen's Colleges of Belfast and Cork. Galway was omitted from this scheme. But Gladstone's bill was defeated, and his government fell. All that could be agreed in the years immediately following was the establishment of an examining body known as the Royal University, which replaced the Queen's University and gave degrees to third-level students other than those studying at TCD.

Further efforts to resolve the university problem, some along lines similar to those Gladstone had proposed, were suggested at various points during the following 35 years, but persistent opposition from TCD to any change involving other colleges joining it within Dublin University eventually forced the Liberal government to establish two new universities, the National University of Ireland and a revived Queen's University in Belfast – both of which were required to be non-denominational. The non-denominational status of the National University was resented by most of the Catholic hierarchy but was acceptable to the Catholic Archbishop of Dublin, Dr William Walsh, who became its first Chancellor and presided over its fortunes for the first decade of its existence.

For its part, the creation of Queen's as a separate university in Belfast, combined with the British government's decision that the new federal university would be called 'The National University of Ireland', can be seen as foreshadowing the partitioning of Ireland as a provisional measure in the 1914 Home Rule Act, which was given full effect by the Government of Ireland Act 1920.

That decision of the British government about the name of the federal university appears a remarkable concession to Irish nationalism, although the word 'National' may not at that time have had quite the same connotation of 'nationalist' that it later developed. And it is also interesting that the title of the university in Irish, presumably chosen by the university itself, did not incorporate the Irish word 'náisiúnta'. The NUI in Irish is 'Ollscoil na hÉireann'.

Looking back over the nineteenth and early twentieth centuries it is interesting to reflect on the contrary ways in which the seventeenth- and eighteenth-century Anglican educational monopoly came to affect the three educational tiers. At primary and secondary level this monopoly provoked Catholics – and to a degree also Presbyterians – to replicate the confessional character of the Anglican system. But at third level, TCD's determination to hold itself apart from the rest of an emerging university system at a time when that system was being shaped by a British Liberal government had the opposite effect – leading to the emergence of two non-denominational universities.

And of course TCD itself gradually evolved towards a similar non-denomi-national character as the twentieth century advanced. One way or the other the whole shape of Irish education came to be determined, and remains shaped today, by nineteenth- or early twentieth-century reactions to the seventeenth- and eighteenth-century Anglican monopoly of Irish education.

The federal NUI has at times experienced certain tensions, centring mainly on three issues: at the outset, a campaign to make the Irish language an essential subject for matriculation; next, reactions within the institutions to Catholic Church attempts informally to weaken their non-denominational character; and, finally, fluctuating pressures for independence of the NUI emanating from several of its colleges, later universities.

As Gearóid Ó Tuathaigh records in chapter 3 of this book, the campaign by Conradh na Gaeilge to have Irish made a required subject for NUI matriculation succeeded when a number of county councils voted to with-hold scholarships unless and until the University Senate voted (in the event by 21 votes to 12) in favour of this requirement. Official education reports show that the percentage of students taking Irish in the Leaving Certificate examination jumped from 27 per cent in 1907 to 58 per cent in 1913, presum-ably because of this NUI requirement.

A second, largely submerged, source of tensions in the NUI system derived from efforts by some members of the Catholic hierarchy, backed by some university presidents, to modify in practice the non-denominational character of the constituent colleges laid down by the 1908 Act. These efforts had an alienating effect on some academics and many students – a phenomenon which has endured long after such attempts have ceased; institutional memory can be long-enduring in academic institutions.

This has made it difficult to secure acceptance within NUI universities of theology and related subjects, even if free from Roman Catholic ecclesiastical control and after legal restrictions in the 1908 Act were removed by the 1997 legislation, and after doubts about the constitutional permissibility of grants for students taking such subjects had also been removed. This has resulted in TCD still being the only university to offer degrees in theology on its own cam-pus, though NUI now awards degrees in theology at its Recognised College Milltown Institute and there are higher diplomas in religious studies in University College Dublin and University College Cork.

Another area where tensions have arisen at various stages throughout the past century has been the existence of fissiparous pressures within the NUI, emanating mainly from two of its constituent colleges, later universities, UCC and UCD. Although the President of Queen's College Cork, Bertram Windle, eventually accepted the federal NUI structure that he had earlier opposed, by 1910 he had reverted to a negative stance on this matter, as John A. Murphy records in chapter 4 on UCC. Windle's attempt to break away in 1919 failed, and his successor, Patrick Merriman, President from 1919 to 1943 was comfortable with the NUI structure as, despite some rhetoric, was the next President, Alfred O'Rahilly, and as also were his successors.

Under Michael Tierney as President it was UCD that sought to become an independent university, and the 1960–7 Commission on Higher Education recommended the dissolution of the NUI and the establishment of independent universities in Dublin, Cork and Galway. But the Fianna Fáil government in which Donogh O'Malley was Minister for Education decided instead that a new Dublin university combining UCD and TCD as two separate colleges should instead be created. This was opposed by TCD, and when the UCD President J. J. Hogan sought to use this initiative to secure the emergence of a single university in which UCD staff would dominate every department, it met with strong opposition within UCD by academics – of whom I was one. We vigorously opposed the extinction of TCD's identity that this would entail.

That project ran into the ground, as eventually did proposals by a subsequent National Coalition government, of which I was a member, for Cork and Galway to combine in a new university, or in a modified proposal, each together with UCD to become independent universities. As Donal McCartney explains in chapter 6 on UCD, 'after seven years of hectic consideration, the merger proposals fizzled out, with NUI still intact and precious little rationalisation between the two Dublin colleges'.

Finally in 1997 legislation transformed the NUI by constituting its colleges – including the Recognised College of Maynooth – into universities within the National University of Ireland, with delegation to each of them of most of the functions formerly exercised by the Senate of the NUI, including the appointment of their presidents, professors and lecturers. The four universities were empowered to award degrees of the National University of Ireland while the Senate retained the power to award degrees and remained the awarding body for the NUI Recognised Colleges. The Senate was given continuing statutory responsibilities in relation to matriculation and the appointment of extern examiners. Because in that year the Rainbow Coalition lacked a majority in Seanad Éireann, the university senators were able to mobilise the Opposition to help secure important guarantees of university autonomy.

During most of the period after 1997, despite the fact that UCC and UCD have tended to play down their participation in the NUI, the Senate of the NUI worked successfully with the new universities within the new devolved structure, proposing a new and more integrated framework of NUI qualifications with increased opportunities for progression; strengthening the extern examiner system; undertaking more systematic analysis of extern examiner reports and examination results; introducing revised bands of marks for the classification of degrees with accompanying descriptors of each of the degree classifications; increasing the value and extending the range of NUI awards to include post-doctoral fellowships; and providing significant support for publications by staff of the NUI institutions.

In 2005 and 2006 some fresh tensions arose, in particular with UCD and UCC, and after clarification of the legal role of the NUI Senate, as modified by the somewhat confused wording of the 1997 Act, a Senate committee, which included the Chancellor and Registrar of the NUI, the four Constituent University Registrars and other members chosen by the Senate, reported on the future role of the Senate and of the federal university. The committee's report outlined a new basis for the operation of the Senate and its relationship with the constituent universities together with new arrangements committing the four constituent universities voluntarily to work together under the aegis of the Senate towards maintaining comparably high standards in the NUI degrees which each university is empowered to award.

It will be for the Senate elected at the end of 2007 to determine whether these proposals provide a satisfactory basis for the continued existence of the NUI past its centenary in 2008.

There is, I believe, no doubt that the creation of the NUI a century ago led to favourable conditions for the development of university education within what was soon to become an independent state. Throughout the twentieth century it ensured the maintenance of high standards in universities which, even after the emergence of two new university institutions late in the century, continued to provide the vast bulk of the state's graduates and PhDs.

It was greatly assisted in this task by the character of its first three chancellors. Archbishop Walsh must have initiated the practice of chancellors presiding personally at Senate meetings – a practice for which there does not seem to have been a British precedent. He steered the new federal university skilfully through its first decade, apparently making no effort to challenge its non-denominational character.

Eamon de Valera was a hugely popular choice to succeed Archbishop Walsh and was chosen as Chancellor unanimously just 10 days after the Truce had brought about what turned out to be the end of the Anglo-Irish War. But, although a reception was held in his honour in UCD in November 1921, because of the Treaty split he was not really in a position during the next three years to follow Archbishop Walsh in the Senate chair. Indeed the only NUI functions Eamon de Valera was able to attend after the November reception were a Dante commemoration in the Mansion House on the evening of 7 December and his first Senate meeting in the chair on 19 December 1921 when he formally received the Members of Senate and later had lunch with the Senate. He was not to attend another meeting of Senate until 5 December 1924.

On his way into the Mansion House function on 7 December 1921, Eamon de Valera was handed by signatory Eamon Duggan and by my father, Desmond FitzGerald, Director of Publicity of the Dáil government, a copy of the Articles of Agreement that had been signed early that morning in London, which they had brought back by the day mail boat. His grim demeanour at that encounter foreshadowed the tragic events that were to follow.

However, from the time he presided at Senate meeting following his release from prison late in 1924 until his last Senate meeting in July 1975, 51 years later, he fulfilled his role as Chancellor with dignity and skill, never so far as I am aware allowing political considerations to influence his handling of issues. Such at least was my impression, as a member of the last Senate over which he presided.

The Senate was equally fortunate in his successor, T. K. Whitaker, who was punctilious in carrying out his duties with fairness and skill, and who helped to steer the Senate through the difficult discussions with government that led to the 1997 Act. It has taken the ten years since I became Chancellor for the full legal meaning of that Act to be clarified. We have come to understand that the National University of Ireland now comprises five universities: the original university established under the 1908 Act, joined now by four constituent universities which are fully autonomous entities, linked in a loose federation and all awarding NUI degrees.

At the start of the twentieth century when the National University of Ireland was established, few could have predicted quite how strongly it would flourish and how influential it and its member institutions would be in the development of the nation and in its educational, cultural and economic life over the course of a century. It has been an honour for me as Chancellor to have been head of the University and to have presided over its Senate. At the start of this new century, the National University of Ireland faces new changes and challenges and a future which will be determined by its continuing capacity to adapt and respond in a climate where continual change has come to be the norm for Irish society and its institutions.

Acknowledgements

THE EDITORS ARE GRATEFUL to the contributors for their courtesy and professionalism; to the NUI staff, particularly Attracta Halpin, who has driven the project, to Nóirín Moynihan for archival assistance and to Andrea Durnin, who pulled it all together and sourced the illustrations; and to Barbara Mennell and Noelle Moran of UCD Press for their enthusiasm and expertise.

Contributors to this Volume

JOHN COOLAHAN is Professor Emeritus of Education at NUI Maynooth and a former member of the NUI Senate. Widely published, he has acted as consultant to the Department of Education, the European Commission, the Council of Europe, OECD, and the World Bank on educational policy.

TOM DUNNE, a former member of the NUI Senate, is Professor Emeritus of History at University College Cork, where he served as Dean of Arts and on Governing Body.

RONAN FANNING is Professor Emeritus of Modern History, University College Dublin, and the author of *The Irish Department of Finance 1922–58* (1978) and joint editor of *Documents on Irish Foreign Policy* and the *Dictionary of Irish Biography*. He is a member of the NUI Senate.

ATTRACTA HALPIN has been Registrar of the National University of Ireland since 2004, having previously been Assistant Registrar. She is a graduate of UCD, TCD and the University of London.

DÁIRE KEOGH lectures in the Department of History at St Patrick's College, Drumcondra. He is currently IRCHSS Government of Ireland Senior Research Fellow.

DONAL MCCARTNEY, Professor Emeritus of Modern Irish History, University College Dublin; formerly Dean of Arts, member of Governing Body, UCD, and of the NUI Senate. He is author of *UCD: A National Idea* (1999).

SÉAMUS MAC MATHÚNA is Secretary for Academic Affairs at NUI Galway and also Secretary of the University.

MAURICE MANNING taught Politics at University College Dublin and is now President of the Human Rights Commission. He was a member of the

CONTRIBUTORS TO THIS VOLUME

Oireachtas for 21 years, serving in both Dáil and Senate. He has been a member of the NUI Senate since 1982.

NÓIRÍN MOYNIHAN is a Senior Administrative Officer in the NUI. Her responsibilities include the Archives.

JOHN A. MURPHY is Professor Emeritus of Irish History at University College Cork and has served as a member of the both the NUI Senate and Seanad Éireann. Among his publications are several books on the history of UCC, most recently, *Where Finbarr Taught: A Concise History of Queen's/ University College Cork* (2007).

JOHN NOLAN, Registrar of the National University of Ireland, 1987–2004, formerly a primary teacher at St Patrick's National School, Drumcondra and Registrar of Carysfort Training College, 1973–87. He represented the Conference of Heads of Irish Universities at the Confederation of EU Rectors' Conferences, 1989 to 1997.

LINDA O'SHEA FARREN is a solicitor in her own legal practice. She is a member of the NUI Senate and Chairman of NUI Convocation. She has also been an investment banker, adviser at the Department of Justice and director of the Irish Wheelchair Association, campaigner on issues of disability, music education, teaching of foreign languages in primary schools, Irish language, and shareholder rights.

GEARÓID Ó TUATHAIGH is a Professor of History at NUI Galway, where he has served as Vice-President and on the Governing Body. He is a former member of the NUI Senate.

SENIA PAŠETA is a Fellow in Modern History at St Hugh's College, Oxford. She has published widely on aspects of the social and political history of modern Ireland.

W. J. (SÉAMUS) SMYTH was appointed to the Chair of Geography in Maynooth in 1978 and following subsequent periods as Dean of Arts and Vice-President he was appointed Master, later President, of NUI Maynooth.

In 2004, having completed a ten-year term in this headship role he resumed his research in the historical geography of the Irish in nineteenth- and early twentieth-century Canada. He currently also serves as chairman of the Higher Education and Training Awards Council.

JOHN WALSH is a contract researcher with the Centre for Contemporary Irish History, Trinity College Dublin; he lectures in modern Irish history and history of educational ideas. He is the author of *The Politics of Expansion: Irish Educational Policy 1957–72*, to be published by Manchester University Press in 2009.

Abbreviations

ASTI	Association of Secondary Teachers, Ireland
BA	Bachelor of Arts
BAE	Bachelor of Educational Art
BAO	Bachelor in Obstetrics and Gynaecology
BBS	Bachelor of Business Studies
BCh	Bachelor of Surgery
BCL	Bachelor of Company Law
BCS	Bachelor of Computer Science
BDS	Bachelor of Dental Surgery
BEd	Bachelor of Education
BEdSc	Bachelor of Educational Science
BPP	British Parliamentary Papers
BSc	Bachelor of Science
BTech	Bachelor of Technology
BW	Bertram Windle
CAO	Central Applications Office
CCM	College Council Minutes
CDVEC	City of Dublin Vocational Education Committee
CE	*Cork Examiner*
CHE	Commission on Higher Education
CHIU	Conference of Heads of Irish Universities
CNAA	Council for National Academic Awards (UK)
CUR	*Cork University Record*
DDA	Dublin Diocesan Archives
DEconSc	Doctor of Economic Science
DES	Department of Education and Science
DIT	Dublin Institute of Technology
EEC	European Economic Community
ESF	European Social Fund

EUA	European Universities Association
FETAC	Further Education and Training Awards Council
FJ	*Freeman's Journal*
GB	Governing Body
GBS	General Board of Studies
GPO	General Post Office
HC	House of Commons
HEA	Higher Education Authority
HETAC	Higher Education and Training Awards Council
IAWGCG	Irish Association of Women Graduates and Candidate Graduates
ICT	Information and Communications Technology
IFUT	Irish Federation of University Teachers
INTO	Irish National Teachers' Organisation
IPA	Institute of Public Administration
IRCHSS	Irish Research Council for the Humanities and Social Sciences
IRCSET	Irish Council for Science, Engineering and Technology
IT	*Irish Times*
IUA	Irish Universities Association
IUQB	Irish Universities Quality Board
MAE	Master of Educational Art
MB	Bachelor of Medicine
MD	Doctor of Medicine
MEd	Master of Education
MRIA	Member of the Royal Irish Academy
MUP	Munster University Pamphlets
NAI	National Archives of Ireland
NCAD	National College of Art and Design
NCEA	National Council for Educational Awards
NEC	National Education Convention
NIHE	National Institute for Higher Education
NIHEL	National Institute for Higher Education, Limerick
NQAI	National Qualifications Authority of Ireland
NUI	National University of Ireland
NUIA	National University of Ireland Archives
NUIG	National University of Ireland, Galway
NUIM	National University of Ireland, Maynooth

NUWGA   National University Women's Graduate Association
OECD   Organisation for Economic Co-operation and Development
PR   President's Report
PRTLI   Programme for Research in Third-Level Institutions
QCC   Queen's College Cork
QCG   Queen's College Galway
QUB   Queen's University of Belfast
RCSI   Royal College of Surgeons in Ireland
RTC   Regional Technical College
RUI   Royal University of Ireland
SCHM   Shannon College of Hotel Management
SÉ   Seanad Éireann
SFI   Science Foundation Ireland
SM   Senate Minutes
SPIL   Society for the Preservation of the Irish Language
TCD   Trinity College Dublin
TD   Teachta Dála
TEA   Tertiary Education Authority
UCC   University College Cork
UCD   University College Dublin
UCDA   University College Dublin Archives
UCG   University College Galway
UGC   University Grants Committee (UK)
VEC   Vocational Education Committee

1908   1918   1928   1938   1948   1958

1968   1978   1988   1998   *2008*

Early History

CHAPTER 1 *From Royal University to National University,*
1879–1908 JOHN COOLAHAN

T HE IRISH UNIVERSITY QUESTION was one of the three great issues
in Anglo-Irish relations, the others being the land question and home
rule, in the late nineteenth and early twentieth centuries. While the number
of people directly affected by university education was very small, with only
3,259 university students out of a population of four and a half million in
1901, the university issue was a highly significant one in public debate and its
satisfactory resolution proved to be prolonged and complex. Efforts by prime
ministers such as Gladstone, Disraeli and Arthur Balfour, as well as chief
secretaries for Ireland such as Sir Michael Hicks-Beach, George Wyndham
and James Bryce, failed to resolve the problems. The university question was
never purely an educational issue; it was interpenetrated by political, religious
and economic considerations. John Redmond referred to it as 'the most
thorny and difficult of all Irish problems, the problem on which there was
most difference of opinion amongst different classes of people in Ireland'.[1]

Up to the middle of the nineteenth century Ireland had only one university, the University of Dublin with its single college, Trinity College, which
had been established by Queen Elizabeth I in 1592, as part of her efforts to
further the spread of Protestantism and English language and culture. In
1845, the English government took the initiative of establishing the Queen's
University, with its three constituent colleges at Belfast, Cork and Galway.
These, as non-denominational institutions, were condemned by the Catholic
hierarchy at the Synod of Thurles in 1850 as unsuitable for Catholics. As a
counter measure, the hierarchy established the Catholic University in 1854,
but it never benefited from a charter or government endowment. Neither
the Queen's University nor the Catholic University achieved the aspirations
envisaged for it.

The census of 1871 highlighted the unfavourable position of the majority Catholic population with regard to educational participation, and the Catholic Church authorities became more assertive in pushing for educational provision acceptable on a denominational basis. In 1873, Gladstone introduced a university bill which envisaged the abolition of the Queen's University and the restructuring of the University of Dublin so as to incorporate the Queen's colleges of Belfast and Cork, and the Catholic University, as well as Trinity College. It was envisaged as a new national teaching and examining university with limitations placed on the teaching of theology, moral philosophy and modern history. The reaction and opposition to the bill re-emphasised the political sensitivities attaching to university education. The bill was defeated by three votes in parliament and led to the fall of the Gladstone government.

Five years later, in 1878, a bill to support the development of intermediate or secondary education was more successful and became law as the Intermediate Education Act. This Act provided grants to the managers of intermediate schools on the principle of 'payment by results', whereby the managers received state payments on the basis of the performance of their school pupils on a newly introduced public examination system. From the point of view of the churches, the scheme had the great merit of providing state support for secondary education, without interfering with the denominational character of the schools. At the time, there was a great belief in the value of public examinations and their presumed role in promoting a meritocracy with access to public service appointments. One impact of the Intermediate Education Act was to signal an increase in the number of intermediate school students, some of whom would require access to university education. The question arose as to whether a payment by results model might also be applied with benefit to the problematic university education question. In 1879, the O'Conor Don, MP for Roscommon, in consultation with some of the Irish bishops, introduced a bill to establish a national examining university, with affiliated colleges, which would be eligible for results fees.

This was not proceeded with, however, when the government indicated that it was to introduce a measure of its own, which became the University Act of 1879.[2] According to this Act, the Queen's University was to be abolished and a new institution, the Royal University, established. This latter would be a purely examining body which had the power to award degrees to

Hulton Archive/Getty Images

1. Augustine Birrell was Chief Secretary for Ireland from 1907 to 1916 and was responsible for the establishment of the National University of Ireland in 1908.

2. Sir Joseph McGrath, Joint Secretary of the RUI and first Registrar of the National University of Ireland (1908–23).

3. Princess Louise Margaret (1860–1917), Duchess of Connaught, receiving an Honorary DMus from the Royal University of Ireland, 1904.

SPECTACLED "BLUE STOCKINGS" SUPERSEDED BY PRETTY GIRL GRADUATES.

Miss Boyle, B.A.

Miss Coghlan, B.Sc.

Miss J. Kelly, M.A.

Miss M. Hogan, B.A.

Miss E. Maione, M.A.

Miss Hogan, B.A.

Not many years ago people were laughing at cultured women, and calling them "goggle-eyed blue stockings" and many such insulting things as that. But the above series of photographs of girl graduates, on whom the Senate of the National University of Ireland conferred degrees at Dublin last week, will show that it is no longer necessary for a woman to be plain in order to be clever. All the girls' photographs—and they are chosen at random—show that the originals are typically charming Irish ladies whose looks are not exceeded by their brains.

Lafayette, Dublin.

4. The National University was based in Earlsfort Terrace (above) from its establishment in 1908 until 1912 when it set up offices in 49 Merrion Square where it remains today.

5. From 'goggle-eyed blue stockings' to 'Pretty girl graduates'. NUI women graduates, 1913.

above l. 6. James Joyce was conferred with a BA from the RUI at the University College, Dublin, 1902. From 1908, RUI graduates were eligible to be graduates of the NUI.

above r. 7. Mary Hayden (Máire ní Eideáin), Professor of Modern Irish History, UCD, 1911–38, a founding member of the Women's Graduate Association and Member of the NUI Senate 1908–24.

below l. 8. Alice Perry (1885–1969) (QCG) was the first woman to graduate with a Bachelor of Engineering degree in Ireland or Great Britain.

below r. 9. Mary Ryan, Professor of Romance Languages, UCC, 1910–38, was the first woman professor in Ireland and the United Kingdom.

10. Rev.William Delany SJ, President, University College, St Stephen's Green, Dublin, 1883–7 and 1897–1909, member of NUI Senate 1908–19.

opposite 11. Douglas Hyde, First Professor of Modern Irish, UCD, 1909–32, Member of NUI Senate 1908–19, First President of Ireland, 1938–45.

above 12. Eoin MacNeill, founding member of the Gaelic League and first Professor of Early Irish History, UCD, 1908–1941. This photo was taken in the Accountant General's Office, Four Courts, October 1909.

13. Cardinal Tomás Ó Fiaich, President, St Patrick's College, Maynooth, 1974–7 and Pro-Vice-Chancellor of the NUI 1974–7. Primate of All Ireland from 1979 until his death in 1990.

14. *Éigse: A Journal of Irish Studies*, first published in the spring of 1939. There have been 35 volumes to date and the journal is now available on CD.

ÉIGSE

A JOURNAL OF IRISH STUDIES

·

EDITED BY PÁDRAIG A. BREATNACH

VOLUME XXXIV

PUBLISHED BY THE NATIONAL UNIVERSITY OF IRELAND

2004

matriculated candidates successful in its examinations. It did not have constituent colleges, and students from any college could sit for its examinations. However, enrolment at colleges was not essential for candidates, who could prepare for the examinations on a private basis if they so wished. Results payments were not made to the managers of colleges, but colleges could benefit from state-funded university teaching fellowships, of which up to 29 were authorised. As was the case with the Intermediate Act, the most successful students in the examinations could benefit from scholarships and bursaries. In the event, the Catholic University benefited from 13 fellowships, amounting to an endowment of about £6,000 per annum. This was a significant boost to that institution whose title was changed to University College Dublin in 1882, and which was placed under the management of the Jesuits in 1883.

While the Royal University had many shortcomings when viewed from the traditional concept of a university, as an examining board it fulfilled its duties with efficiency and effectiveness. The new system of competitive public examinations enabled young men and women to attain university entrance, and the non-residential requirement for degrees kept costs to a minimum. The common university matriculation examination for degrees set a national standard and was linked to the new intermediate examination framework. The matriculation examination was broad, consisting of five subjects – English, Latin, mathematics, one foreign language and experimental physics. Women, in particular, benefited from the Royal's arrangements, so that by 1900 of the total of 2,173 graduates 501 were women, 43 of whom had continued on MA courses.[3] The University introduced innovations in its curriculum and offered not only bachelor's degrees, but also master's degrees in medicine, engineering and music. Students from all denominations and from every part of Ireland could present themselves for the same examinations and competed for valuable exhibitions, prizes and scholarships. It was particularly useful to Catholic students who were inhibited from access to university degrees under the circumstances which had hitherto prevailed. The university maintained exceptionally high standards for both pass and honours examinations.[4] All degree examinations took place at the Royal University's building in Earlsfort Terrace where the examination halls and laboratories were impressive. The building also contained a fine senate room and a great hall where conferring ceremonies were held.

The Senate of the Royal University was divided equally between Catholic and Protestant representatives, each of whom had 18 members. The Senate held its first meeting on 24 June 1880, the charter of the university having been issued on 13 April 1880.

On 22 August 1881 royal assent was received for the sum of £20,000 to be devoted to the teaching fellowships. The results of the first matriculation examinations of the Royal University were announced in January 1882. The opposition of supporters of the Queen's University to its abolition proved unavailing, and its final commencements also took place in January 1882, with the Queen's University formally abolished on 3 February 1882. Provision was made to protect the rights of students and graduates of the Queen's University on the transfer of arrangements to the Royal University.

While the Queen's colleges benefited from the allocation of new fellowships by the Senate of the Royal University, they experienced a loss of status as constituent colleges of the old Queen's University. Furthermore, they experienced a decline in student numbers owing to the non-residential requirements of the Royal University examination regulations. The Revd Dr William Walsh, then president of Maynooth College and Dr Leebody of Magee College, however, publicly criticised the more favoured circumstances which students in the Queen's colleges still enjoyed vis-à-vis students in other colleges such as University College Dublin and Magee College. Dr Walsh issued a 68-page pamphlet on the issue early in 1883, and also highlighted the relatively poor performances of the Queen's College students of the Cork and Galway colleges.[5] His arguments for the need for equality of treatment between the Queen's colleges and Catholic colleges proved influential.

Eventually, in May 1884, a Royal Commission comprising five members was established 'to inquire into certain matters affecting the well-being and efficiency of the Queen's colleges'. When the commission report was published in 1885, it consisted of a majority report by three members and a minority report by two members. While suggesting some improvements, the majority report was generally favourable, while the minority report by the two Catholic commissioners was highly critical, except in the case of standards achieved by the Belfast College.[6] While the commission gave witness to the unsettled and disputatious context of Irish university education, it gave rise to no fundamental changes at the time.

Yet it was clear that the Royal University was not regarded as a satisfactory solution to the Irish university problem by any of the key parties. The Queen's University and the Queen's colleges' supporters were greatly opposed to it. The President of Queen's College Belfast, Dr Porter, initiated a campaign from the mid-1880s for an independent university in Belfast. The Catholics considered that the Royal University fell far short of their demands for equality of treatment regarding university education. Trinity College, the longest established, best positioned and endowed university remained aloof from the debate, enjoying its privileged status. However, it was clear that the Royal University could be only a stopgap solution and that agitation for a more acceptable outcome would continue.

A key protagonist of the case for equality of treatment for Catholics was Dr William Walsh, who was consecrated as Archbishop of Dublin in 1885. He had a track record of taking a keen and informed interest in educational affairs, an interest which remained with him throughout his lifetime. He initiated discussions with the Chief Secretary, Sir Michael Hicks-Beach in November 1886, seeking the establishment of a government-endowed Catholic university college. Despite some signs of progress, these negotiations terminated on the resignation of Hicks-Beach in March 1887.[7] In 1887 Walsh prepared a long pamphlet, *Memorandum on the Irish Education Question*, which he distributed for the information of Irish parliamentarians, among others. Walsh also drafted a resolution adopted by the bishops in June 1889, on the demands for a Catholic university with state endowment. In response to pressure in parliament from the Irish MPs, Charles Stewart Parnell and Thomas Sexton, Chief Secretary Arthur Balfour stated that the experiment of undenominational higher education in Ireland had 'failed to meet the wants and wishes of the Catholic population. The government, he said, had no alternative but to try and devise some new scheme by which the wants of the Catholic population shall be met.'[8] This signal of a new policy approach was quickly abandoned owing to the political opposition which emerged. Nothing daunted, Walsh published his *Chief Grievances of Irish Catholics in the Matter of Education* in 1890. In the course of this he set out three possible options to settle the university question. One was the reconstitution of the University of Dublin with several colleges including an endowed Catholic college in Dublin. The second option involved two universities for Ireland, one the University of Dublin, comprising Trinity College and a great Catholic college, and the other a restructured Royal University. The third policy option envisaged three universities – one of which would be the current University of Dublin unaltered, the second a Catholic university with linked colleges, and the third a university for 'the Presbyterians and Dissenters generally, located in Belfast'.[9] This latter proposal had some of the elements of the final resolution of 18 years later. However, various political developments, including the Parnell split in 1890, put the resolution of the university question on the back burner for a number of years, with no government initiative from 1891 to 1897.

During the intervening years, Walsh kept the issue before the public in various speeches and newspaper letters. In 1896, he took the initiative of organising a Declaration of the Catholic Laity on university education signed by 1,059 distinguished people – peers, privy councillors, MPs, justices of the peace, and members of the professions. In June 1897 Walsh published *The Irish University Question: The Catholic Case*, which he circulated widely.[10]

In June 1897, in response to questions raised in parliament, the Catholic bishops issued a conciliatory statement in which they accepted that a new Catholic university could have a majority of laymen in its governing body, and accepted that the role of such a university would be 'mainly to teach secular knowledge to lay students', and that chairs of Theology would not be endowed out of public funds. It was also agreed that the appointment and removal of professors could be subject to the control of an independent board of visitors.[11] This was a significant shift in policy by the bishops, and should have been helpful to a solution.

In October 1898, a Liberal MP, R. B. (later 1st Viscount) Haldane, with an interest in university education came to Ireland, with the approval of Arthur Balfour, to confidentially probe the opinions of interested parties on a potential solution which would set up two new universities, and leave the University of Dublin undisturbed. Haldane had a draft bill with him, envisaging the establishment of two teaching universities, one in Belfast and one in Dublin, both to be formally non-denominational, but to be de facto acceptable to Catholics and to Protestants or Dissenters. There would be no public endowment of Philosophy, Theology or Modern History and no tests of religious belief would apply.[12] From his meetings with church leaders, politicians and academics, Haldane formed the view that there was a good deal of support in evidence for the plan. While both Arthur and his brother

Gerald Balfour, now chief secretary, favoured the measure, they were unable to secure the approval of cabinet due to fears of splits in their unionist constituencies on the issue. On 23 January 1899 Arthur Balfour decided to test the political climate by publishing a letter to a Manchester constituent, setting forth the key elements of the planned measure. The letter produced a storm of anti-Catholic protest. In the light of this, the government decided not to proceed with the bill.[13] It should be noted that the measure contained key elements of the solution arrived at by the later 1908 legislation. It helped to sow the seeds of a possible way forward. However, the outcome dashed the confidence of Irish people that a unionist dominated British parliament would ever concede university legislation acceptable to the majority Catholic population. The outcome helped to solidify relationships between a more united Irish parliamentary party and the Catholic hierarchy.

Despite the conciliatory statement on the university question issued by the Catholic bishops in June 1897, there were significant divisions among their ranks as to the most desirable solution. Archbishop Walsh, prompted by his concern for equality, favoured the establishment within the University of Dublin of a college acceptable to Catholics as Trinity College was to Protestants and benefiting from the same scale of endowments as Trinity College. Bishop Healy of Clonfert and Dr William Delany, the president of University College Dublin, favoured a restructuring of the Royal University with an endowed Catholic teaching college within it. Delany had led his college to become a flourishing institution which, though limited in resources, proved highly successful in the examinations and prizes of the Royal University. Some of its students took leading parts in the cultural nationalist movement, and became increasingly opposed to the imperial trappings associated with commencement ceremonies of the Royal University. Bishop O'Dwyer of Limerick, who also spoke and published a great deal on the university question, favoured the establishment of a fully endowed separate Catholic University on which the bishops would have significant control. Archbishop Walsh, while having his favoured view, was open to explore other possible solutions and was on the alert to probe potential advantage points. While his voice was the most influential, the differences of opinion fostered tensions among the hierarchy which emerged at times of serious negotiation, including the forthcoming formal investigations into university education.

Dissatisfaction with the Royal University solution found remarkable expression when a motion to the Senate of that university, by Senator O'Connor Don on 2 February 1899, was passed unanimously. It read 'In the opinion of the Senate, the present provisions for university education in Ireland are not satisfactory, and we therefore recommend the subject to the early attention of the government.'[14] This was followed shortly afterwards by a resolution of the governing body of Queen's College, Belfast, expressing dissatisfaction with the Royal University and calling for the re-establishment of the Queen's University in Belfast. In February 1901, the Senate of the Royal University passed another resolution calling for a royal commission to inquire into its own ability as an educational body. In June 1901, the government conceded to the establishment of a Royal Commission comprising 12 members and chaired by Lord Robertson, a Scottish Lord of Appeal. The terms of reference were:

> To inquire into the present conditions of the higher, general and technical education available in Ireland, outside Trinity College Dublin, and report as to what reforms, if any, are desirable in order to render that education adequate to the needs of Irish people.[15]

The exclusion of Trinity College from its remit was significant and deliberate and a source of dissatisfaction to Archbishop Walsh and Irish Party members. Walsh did not give evidence to the commission but Bishop O'Dwyer and Dr Delany, both senators of the Royal University, gave extensive evidence, each favouring his preferred outcome, in the case of O'Dwyer for a separate endowed Catholic university, and in Delany's case for a restructured Royal University with an endowed Catholic college within it. Walsh still had his eyes on a solution involving the University of Dublin and while the Commission was sitting, issued a pamphlet in April 1902, *Trinity College and the University of Dublin*, in which he argued that Trinity College and the University of Dublin were juridicially distinct institutions.[16]

The Robertson Commission's report was published in March 1903. It recommended the reconstitution of the Royal University as a federal teaching university with four constituent colleges, including 'a new College for Roman Catholics to be established in Dublin', endowed 'on a scale required by a University College of the first rank'. The Queen's colleges were to be remodelled and attendance at lectures would be required of all candidates for examination, without distinction of sex. The Robertson report was signed by 11 of the 12 members, but the impact of the Report was undermined in that each of the signatories recorded reservations.[17] It came to be regarded as a makeshift solution which was not pursued actively by politicians and, thus, was a failure.

Meanwhile, the Chief Secretary, George Wyndham and Under-Secretary Sir Anthony MacDonnell were planning a more comprehensive solution to the university question, of which Archbishop Walsh was aware, involving the inclusion of the University of Dublin. The introduction of Wyndham's Land Bill in March 1903, which became law in August 1903, dominated political activity for that period. However, on 10 October, MacDonnell sent a detailed draft of his proposals to Archbishop Walsh, which envisaged the University of Dublin as a national university with three colleges – Trinity College, Queen's College Belfast, and a new college acceptable to Catholics.[18] In the political climate of the time, the method chosen by Wyndham and MacDonnell for the presentation of their scheme was a letter in the public press signed by Lord Dunraven, Wyndham's cousin, who had been influential in the success of the land act. This appeared in *The Independent*, on 4 January 1904. It proposed the establishment within the University of Dublin of two additional colleges (to Trinity College) – Queen's College Belfast and a King's College established in Dublin, which would be 'well equipped financially, and should be autonomous and residential, with governing bodies selected exclusively on academic grounds. A senate would be set up to maintain standards, and a visiting body would be entrusted with excluding any instruction repugnant to the faith and morals of students.'[19]

Despite the opposition of Bishop O'Dwyer, the Irish bishops at a meeting on 12 January 1904 agreed that 'a satisfactory settlement of the university question can be arrived at on the lines indicated in his Lordship's (Dunraven's) letter. But if, from the attitude of Trinity College or any other cause, the Government are not prepared to give legislative effect to the proposals of Lord Dunraven we then call on them to adopt the alternative scheme (as proposed in the Robertson Report).'[20] However, it quickly became clear that the chief secretary could not deliver the cabinet in support of the measure and it was aborted. This experience had the effect of contributing to a lack of faith among Catholics of a resolution being achieved under the existing parliamentary system. It also led to a distancing of the Irish

Parliamentary Party from the hierarchy, as they considered that the latter's private negotiations with the administration excluded them from their rightful role, and that a resolution of the university question on the hierarchy's terms could weaken the momentum towards home rule. Wyndham resigned office in March 1905 and the Conservative government, containing serious internal divisions, took no further initiative on the university question.

Trinity College continued to oppose any interference with its inherited position within the University of Dublin, and had succeeded in being excluded from the purview of the Robertson Commission (1901–3). However, in 1905 and in 1906 Archbishop Walsh engaged in a public critique of the examination processes in Trinity College which did not employ external examiners, and was particularly critical of its medical school. This helped to create a climate where inquiring into Trinity College was seen as legitimate. When the Liberals achieved a major electoral victory with the support of the Irish Party in January 1906, the political climate changed and the Liberals committed themselves to a step-by-step policy on home rule. James Bryce was appointed as chief secretary and agreed to reopen the university question. Channels of co-operative communication were re-established between the Irish Party and the bishops.

Following discussions with key parties, Chief Secretary Bryce established a royal commission on 5 June 1906. Its terms of reference were:

> To inquire into and report upon the present state of Trinity College Dublin, and of the University of Dublin, including the revenues of the college, the method of government, the system of instruction, the system of university examinations and the provision made for post-graduate study: and also to inquire and report upon the place which Trinity College Dublin and the University of Dublin now hold as organs of the highest education in Ireland, and the steps proper to be taken to increase their usefulness to the country.[21]

These comprehensive terms of reference firmly put the focus on the operation and role of Trinity College. The nine members of the commission were chaired by Sir Edward Fry, Lord Justice of Appeal. The Commission reported on 12 January 1907 and, on the university provision issue, eight of the nine commissioners called for the establishment in Dublin of a college acceptable to Catholics. As to which university the new college should be attached, the commissioners were very divided. Five favoured a solution on the Dunraven lines of its inclusion in a restructured University of Dublin; three favoured its incorporation within a reconstituted Royal University, on Robertson lines. The latter three members stated that they had been influenced greatly by the evidence of Dr Delany, the views of Bishop Healy in the Senate of the Royal University and a written submission by Monsignor Molloy, all of whom favoured the Robertson scheme, and were opposed to a Catholic college within the University of Dublin. The deep division among the Fry Commissioners severely lessened the political impact of the report.

Meanwhile, Bryce and MacDonnell, who had been apprised of the report's findings prior to publication, were planning their own scheme which involved the reconstitution and extension of the University of Dublin, on the lines of the Dunraven 1904 scheme. Within two weeks of the publication of the Fry Commission Report, on 25 January 1907, Chief Secretary Bryce announced that it was the government's intention to establish three additional colleges within the University of Dublin – the Belfast and Cork Queen's colleges and a new college in Dublin, mainly for Catholics, but open to other denominations. The possibility was mentioned of the Galway, Magee and Maynooth colleges being affiliated in the future.[22] While motions of support for the proposals emerged from a number of bodies, including a favourable holding statement from the Senate of the Royal University, a defence committee was established in Trinity College, chaired by Provost Traill. Adopting the slogan 'Hands off Trinity', it organised protest petitions from its graduates, and enlisted the support of universities in England, orchestrating a strong public campaign of opposition. Unionist and anti-Catholic feelings were aroused in opposition to the plan. The Catholic bishops issued no formal statement on the measure at that time and focussed their attention on the contemporaneous government plan of an Irish council devolution bill. While MacDonnell prepared a bill on the Bryce Scheme, Bryce himself was appointed Ambassador to the United States, and Augustine Birrell replaced him in late January as chief secretary.

In April 1907, the bishops, while not committing themselves to the Bryce scheme *per se*, indicated a favourable attitude to the government's efforts to resolve the issue. However, the opposition of the bishops to the educational components of the Irish council bill was a major aspect of its downfall in early June 1907. This bill, as well as the university bill had been largely drafted by Under-Secretary MacDonnell. Birrell had now become disenchanted with

Sir Anthony and decided to plough his own furrow. The defeat of the Irish Council Bill put home rule on the long finger. It remained to be seen what Birrell could achieve on the university question.

In the light of the defeat of the bill, Birrell was keen to make progress on the university issue and, it was hoped, improve relations with the Irish Parliamentary Party and the bishops. Having reflected on the issue, he formed the view that the inclusion of Trinity College as part of an overall settlement, as envisaged by Bryce/MacDonnell, was not politically feasible. He took the approach of making private soundings with key personnel before formulating his scheme. Birrell was on record as stating his view 'that it is simply a disgrace to the Government of the United Kingdom that it should so long have failed to deal with a question of such imperative importance (as the university question)'.[23] It was clear that a resolution along non-denominational lines was needed if it was to win the necessary political support. Haldane was now a colleague in cabinet, as Secretary for War, and he drew Birrell's attention to his plan of 1898 for which he had a good deal of support from Irish interests at the time. Birrell considered that this approach had a great deal of merit and began adapting it. In August 1907, he held a meeting with Provost Traill and, having assured him that he did not intend to interfere with the University of Dublin or Trinity College in his university planning, won the support of the Provost, who saw that 'Hands off Trinity' was prevailing. He held interviews with the presidents of the Queen's colleges, with Queen's College Belfast declaring for an independent endowed university in Belfast. Discussions were held with Archbishop Walsh in November, and a close working relationship developed between the two men. During December, Birrell conducted enquiries on the situation as regards staff, students and funding of the various colleges. He also visited Cardinal Logue in Armagh in December. Thus, it is clear that Birrell was preparing the ground carefully. Before approaching the Treasury on financial aspects he wanted to be assured that his scheme had widespread support.

The main elements of Birrell's scheme were approved by the cabinet committee in January 1908 and it also received the general support of the Standing Committee of the Catholic Bishops on 21 January.[24] Birrell introduced the Irish Universities Bill on 31 March into the House of Commons. Haldane associated himself with the measure and obtained the personal support of the Conservative leader Balfour, who had favoured such an approach back in 1899. The bill proposed to establish two new universities in Ireland, one in Belfast and one with headquarters in Dublin. The latter was on the federal model with three constituent colleges: Cork, Galway and Dublin, the last being a reconstituted University College Dublin. The two universities were to be state funded and be non-denominational, 'with no tests whatsoever of religious beliefs' for appointments. The Royal University was to be abolished and its income of £20,000 per annum divided equally between the two new universities. In addition, Belfast was to receive £18,000 a year, Dublin £32,000, Cork £18,000, and Galway £12,000. Capital building grants of £60,000 were to go to Belfast and £150,000 to be shared by University College Dublin and the headquarters of the new National University. The bill allowed for the affiliation of colleges which were 'deemed to have a standard satisfactory by the university' as 'recognised', but not constituent colleges of the new universities. The senates of the new universities were to be academic bodies with the power to appoint and dismiss professors. No money was provided for the building of any denominational place of worship in the institutions, and there was no public finance for the teaching of Theology. The university's opportunities were to be open to women and men on the same terms. No provision was made for residential accommodation, but as the universities were teaching institutions, attendance at lectures was necessary for students to be eligible for examinations. The members of the first Senate and governing bodies of the new institutions were to be nominated by the government for the first five-year term.

The main opposition to the bill came from the Ulster unionists who interpreted the scheme as one designed to placate the demands of the Catholic hierarchy, and although Belfast was to gain a university of its own, it was at the price of what they regarded as a separate university for Catholics. Leave to introduce the bill was granted on a vote of 307 to 24 votes. Now that the bill was in process through parliament, increased attention was paid to its contents by interested parties. Among these were the Standing Committee of Bishops who, at a meeting on 5 May 1908, sought *ex-officio* representation by two bishops on the Senate of the federal university and written guarantees regarding the affiliation of Maynooth College. They were also concerned about the lack of provision of student residences in the planned legislation.[25] These requests caused concern to Birrell who considered that their inclusion at this stage would greatly imperil the bill, and he did not act on them. On 11 May, the second reading of the bill was passed by the House of Commons by 344 votes to 31. While the unionists continued their opposition, it was significant that the unionist MP for Trinity College, Sir Edward Carson, strongly supported the measure. In the course of his address he stated 'I believe that it is the duty of every Irishman, of whatever creed or politics, to wish God-speed to these universities and to do his best, in a spirit of noble generosity, to make them a great success.'[26]

The bill went into committee stage on 20 May 1908. The affiliation of Maynooth proved to be one of the contentious issues in committee. The bishops at their June meeting passed a resolution which declared the bill 'to be constructed on a plan which is suited to the educational needs of the country and likely to lead to finality on the University question'.[27] This significant statement was communicated to the Commons committee by John Redmond on 16 June and proved influential to its deliberations. On 19 June Birrell's amendment on the affiliation issue was passed in Committee on a vote of 25 votes to 6. It read:

> On the passing of the Act, before the powers of the Commissioners determine, the Royal College of Surgeons in Ireland, the Royal College of Science, Maynooth College and Magee College may be affiliated to one or other of the two new universities subject to the provisions of the charter and to the statutes and regulations of the university.[28]

The final reading of the bill in the House of Commons took place on 25 July and was carried by 207 votes to 19. On the same day it received its first reading in the House of Lords. The bill was signed into law as the Irish Universities Act on 1 August 1908.[29] Public reaction to the act was unreservedly enthusiastic. Newspaper comment praised the efforts in parliament of Birrell and the Irish Party in helping to achieve a satisfactory outcome to a problem whose solution was so complex and so prolonged. Mr Birrell had achieved success within 18 months of assuming office. However, the ground had been well prepared through all the earlier initiatives and a general political concern to reach a resolution of a problem was recognised by all.

The Act did not specify the names of the two new universities, whose designation was stated to be the king's prerogative. It was expected that the university in Belfast would be called Queen's University. It was also rumoured that the Dublin-based university would have the name of the King's University of

Ireland, which drew the wrath of Dr Walsh who threatened not to take his seat on the Dublin commissioners if this were to be the title. In the event, the title which emerged in the letters patent, which were signed on 4 December 1908, was the National University of Ireland, which won general approval.

The Dublin commissioners began their work on 22 October 1908. The charter of the National University was issued on 2 December 1908. The first meeting of the Senate of the National University of Ireland took place in the senate room of the Old Royal University in Earlsfort Terrace on 17 December 1908, with 39 senators present. At this meeting, the Senate unanimously chose Archbishop Walsh to be Chancellor of the National University. Among the congratulations received by the Archbishop was a telegram from Lord Castletown who had been Chancellor of the Royal University. This succinctly stated: 'The Chancellor of the Royal sends hearty congratulations to the Chancellor of the National.'[30] The baton had been passed. The Royal University was formally dissolved on 31 October 1909. The Dublin commissioners worked intensively on the statutes and regulations for the new university and completed their work on 31 July 1911. The senate and the governing bodies of the three constituent colleges then assumed their full powers. In accordance with the federal structure of the university, the Senate approved the statutes of the individual colleges and appointed the presidents, professors and statutory lecturers in each college. The Senate of the National University had responsibility for maintaining course standards and awarding degrees, including honorary degrees. In July 1909, Maynooth College applied for affiliation as a recognised college and this was granted by the Senate on 25 February 1910 for a period of four years in the Faculties of Arts, Philosophy and Celtic Studies. At the end of the four years recognition was granted *in perpetuum* to these faculties and also to a Faculty of Science. The Jesuits ended their stewardship of University College in 1909 and it formed the nucleus of the new constituent college, University College Dublin. The site of the Royal University in Earlsfort Terrace became the main locus of this college, which also benefited from a building grant of £110,000. The Catholic University's medical school in Cecilia Street became incorporated in University College Dublin.

As teaching institutions, both the National University of Ireland and the Queen's University provided new momentum of a qualitative character for university education in Ireland. The senates and relevant governing bodies took their duties of setting and maintaining standards seriously. The injection of improved financial resources gave a valuable impetus to the work of the institutions. Denominational problems did not arise, no religious tests were employed, and every professor on taking office was required to sign a declaration 'securing the respectful treatment of the religious opinions of any of his classes'. The institutions were open to students of any or no religion, and to men and women on equal terms – all very advanced in comparison to international norms. As might be expected, the ethos and general culture of the institutions reflected the character of the populations they served. Greater participation in higher education was encouraged by the empowering of county councils and boroughs, and the Intermediate Education Board to provide university scholarships.

The 1908 Act left Ireland with three universities, each representing a different model. The University of Dublin, with its single college, Trinity College, had been modelled on the Oxbridge tradition and was associated in the public mind with the ascendancy and Church of Ireland culture. Queen's University Belfast could be seen as representing the modern, 'red-brick', non-residential and non-denominational university albeit, if not quite accurately, associated with the Presbyterian tradition. The National University of Ireland was on the model of a non-denominational, federal university, which because of location, student population and cultural tradition reflected a Catholic and nationalist ethos. The existence of the three universities represented the abandonment of the concept of a single, embracing national university, accommodating a variety of colleges on the island in favour of the recognition of the divergent local, political and religious pressures which existed in Ireland at that time. T. W. Moody has aptly commented: 'The university settlement of 1908 so tenaciously resisted by Ulster unionists, was in a profoundly significant sense the prelude to the partition of Ireland in 1921.'[32] Throughout the long-drawn-out debates on the Irish university question, it is clear that political, religious, and to some extent economic considerations predominated over educational ones.

The provisions of the 1908 Irish Universities Act have stood the test of time and Birrell's aspirations when concluding the debate on the bill, 'that these universities we are founding today, which will last long years after every one of us has crumbled into dust, will have before them years of usefulness, and pride and distinction and glory', have been realised.[33]

CHAPTER 2 *Achieving Equality: Women and the Foundation of the University* SENIA PAŠETA

T HE ESTABLISHMENT OF the National University of Ireland marked the end of a long and often bitter dispute which had begun in earnest in the 1850s. Known as the Irish university question, the issue of how best Ireland's third-level system could be reformed in order to attract growing numbers of middle-class students was predicated on the assumption that the potential beneficiary of any such change would almost certainly be Catholic and he would unquestionably be male. Higher education for women was very much a side issue in the wider debate and only began to enter into the public consciousness in the 1870s. The aims and priorities of the women's education campaign changed markedly over the late nineteenth and early twentieth centuries, and this had as much as to do with broader intellectual and political trends as it did with the radicalisation of activists themselves. The need for women to earn a living and to receive an education which would prepare them to do so was a cornerstone of the campaign from the outset. But while many early campaigners argued in primarily practical terms for the necessity of higher education, later feminists framed their arguments more stridently, presenting education and professional life for women as a right rather than a privilege.

As in the rest of the British Isles, the campaign to extend educational opportunities for women began with improving secondary education. Irish pioneers ran a two-pronged crusade by founding schools for women and establishing lobby groups staffed by sharp-eyed and often well-connected activists. Secondary education of most kinds was expensive and consequently restricted to the fortunate few. This was true for men and women, but daughters tended to be less well educated than their brothers who were expected to earn a living and to support their own families in due course.

There were, of course, few such expectations for women and superior education for girls was thus seen by most families as an unnecessary luxury at best, unnatural at worst. Nevertheless, increasing concern with the plight of the unmarried or otherwise unsupported women who were compelled to earn their own living acted as a spur to both the education campaign and what was to become the women's campaign more generally.

The pioneers of the women's education movement were mainly middle class, urban and Protestant. Their geographical and social background is unsurprising, but their confessional allegiance bears further analysis. Why did so few Catholic women become involved in the campaign – at least in a public way – in the early years? The answer lies partly in the way secondary education itself was organised. Most of the education of middle-class Catholic girls was undertaken by teaching orders of nuns, and nuns did not on the whole express any opinions they may have had on the matter publicly. Cohorts of Catholic activists emerged after the first generation of Catholic women had passed through the university system, and were thus more willing and more able to speak out on behalf of their particular constituency. But the articulation of their grievances was principally limited because the aims of Catholic men lay at the heart of the broader university question. Given that the only universities in Ireland until 1879 were the University of Dublin and the Queen's University and that neither was acceptable to the Catholic hierarchy, there was little chance that the women's cause would be taken up. Arguing for female access to university was in any case illogical as there was no approved university for them to go to, even if they were qualified to do so. For most Catholics, therefore, any consideration of female demands would merely further muddy the waters of an already complex debate.

We cannot know for sure whether or not Catholic Ireland was on the whole less sympathetic to women's education than were Irish Protestants, but the evidence suggests that it probably was. This was no doubt partly because Irish Protestants were more genuinely connected to the advances of their English and Scottish co-religionists and Irish Catholics had no equivalent models. This meant, for example, that Protestant women were able to attract the support of individuals who not only approved of women's education, but had had experience of it in England. Richard Chenevix Trench, for example, taught at the pioneering Queen's College, London, before becoming Archbishop of Dublin and a founder of Alexandra College, one of Ireland's first truly academic schools for girls. Finally, it is worth noting that what existed of a nascent Irish feminist movement was dominated by Protestants, some of whom saw women's education as a crucial part of a wider campaign to improve the opportunities and rights of women. A number of early campaigners were involved with or went on to become involved in the married women's property campaign, women's suffrage and even the opposition to the Contagious Diseases Acts. The shift in the confessional composition of the broader women's education campaign was, as we shall see, an important factor in its growth and success.

The culture of academic institutions for mainly middle-class girls grew apace in the last quarter of the nineteenth century and it received an enormous boost with the establishment of the Intermediate Education System in 1878 and the Royal University of Ireland in the following year. The former was a new system of secondary education, open to all Irish students, male or female, whose achievements were to be measured exclusively through examinations. The latter was an examining body only, modelled on London University, and intended primarily to allow for the education of Catholic men in an institution which was neither Protestant like Trinity College, nor non-denominational like the Queen's colleges. The last point is the important one. Neither initiative was designed with women in mind, nor introduced in order to allow for improvements in women's education. Women were in fact left out of the Intermediate Education Draft Bill, and only included after the intervention of a group of women led by the prominent Irish educationalists Isabella Tod and Margaret Byers.[1] They were better prepared the following year, monitoring the inclusion of women in the new university through their recently established Society for School and University Education of Women in Ireland.[2]

The establishment of the Royal University served as a real catalyst for the transformation of secondary education, especially for Catholic girls. Irish Protestants had by 1879 established a number of genuinely academic girls' schools, the most prominent being the Ladies Collegiate School (later named Victoria College) in 1859, Alexandra College (1866) and the Ladies Institute in Belfast (1867). These schools were in the vanguard of the next stage of the women's education battle – the entrance of women to the universities. These and other institutions adapted as best they could to the new university, taking advantage of the Royal University's status as an examining body only, but the fact that the Royal was not a collegiate institution was the source of bitter complaint and undoubtedly one of its real weaknesses. It was, however, something of a blessing for women who were as yet barred from attending the other Irish universities and the Royal was their only Irish option. In common with the boys' schools and colleges which prepared students for university examinations, some of the women's institutions became *de facto* university colleges with separate university classes and a clear distinction made between the secondary students and the university women. Unlike a number of the men's colleges, however – notably University College Dublin (UCD) and the Queen's colleges at Belfast, Cork and Galway – the women's colleges received no formal recognition from the Royal University in the form of university fellowships.

Catholic women were initially much less well served, despite the fact that the expanding Catholic middle class was increasingly open to women's education. A number of convent boarding schools, many of them run by French orders, catered to the social aspirations of this class by providing training in 'polite' subjects including music, French, and art and literature. There were some day schools which provided a basic academic education, but genuinely academic and Catholic schools for girls did not exist, while Catholic boys were much better served by a number of schools. Some ambitious Catholic families voted with their feet by sending their daughters to Protestant schools, especially Alexandra, making it plain that they would continue to do so if comparable Catholic institutions were not provided.[3] Mary Hayden was one such woman and her experiences well demonstrate both the possibilities and limitations which governed the career of an aspiring female Catholic university student. Her diaries reveal an ambitious and clearly intellectual disposition which was not satisfied at her initial convent secondary school. She complained in her diary about her convent schooldays: 'we had little bits of lots of things, some not very useful: while really useful things like Latin and Greek were entirely omitted. Then in respect to reading we were badly treated.'[4] Hayden went on to combine lessons at the Dominican Convent in Eccles Street with classes at Alexandra, eventually winning a scholarship in modern languages and taking a BA with honours at the Royal University in 1885. As we shall see, she was to become one of the most active of all women's education campaigners and, as first professor of modern Irish history in UCD, a true pioneer in the National University.

Despite disadvantages, female students availed themselves of the opportunity to acquire higher education to such an extent that, by 1899, the numbers of girls taking intermediate examinations had grown by 300 per cent, compared with a 190 per cent growth in the number of male candidates.[5] In 1884, only nine women graduated from the Royal with a BA; by 1909, the figure was 70. The women's colleges remained central to this endeavour, the good results gained by the Protestant schools acting as real incentives to an initially reluctant Catholic hierarchy. Increasing numbers of Catholic schools prepared girls for intermediate examinations and while such schools continued to lag behind in the provision of university preparation for women, the establishment or expansion of several colleges – including Loreto College, Dublin, St Angela's, Cork and the Dominican St Mary's in Dublin – improved opportunities for Catholic women enormously.

Perhaps more importantly, the Queen's colleges in Belfast, Cork and Galway began to accept women in the 1880s. Women had attended lectures in some of these institutions well before they were formally admitted and campaigns to force the colleges to accept women had begun in the mid-1870s – before the establishment of the Royal University. The eventual capitulation of college authorities was crucial because the old Queen's colleges were likely to be incorporated in any university settlement, and the admission of women set a precedent which was going to be difficult to undo.

It is clear, however, that experiences varied greatly between the institutions. Belfast admitted women in 1882 and it regularly attracted many more women than the other two colleges. This was almost certainly a reflection of Protestant society's more liberal attitude towards women's education, an attitude held also by many college fellows and naturally more obvious in the northern institution. Thomas Hamilton, president of Queen's Belfast, told a 1902 Royal Commission that he was proud of his college's progressive view on to women students.[6] The other provincial colleges were not initially as obliging: Cork opened its doors to women in 1886 and Galway followed suit in 1888, the latter in the face of fierce opposition from the local Catholic Bishop. Catholic women who hoped to go to any of the Queen's colleges faced the double disadvantage of their sex and their religion. In common with their male counterparts, Catholic women came under strong clerical pressure not to attend the allegedly 'godless' Queen's colleges, and this religious stipulation had a clear effect on overall numbers as well as on the lives of individual women. Mary Aherne, for example, one of the first Catholic women at Cork, withdrew from the college under pressure from the local bishop. Having won a scholarship to the college as a schoolgirl at St Angela's, she returned to her convent school upon her withdrawal, completing her university studies there.[7] The fact that the numbers of women at Cork increased rapidly after its inclusion in the new National University surely owed as much to clerical approval of the new university as it did to changing opinions about women's education.[8]

Despite these difficulties, all three Queen's colleges developed lively, if small, communities of women students. Only five women registered at Cork in the first two years after admission, but by 1896 the number had grown to 30.[9] A real breakthrough was achieved when two women graduated in medicine in 1896, helping to shatter the commonly held belief that the attainment of an Arts degree represented the pinnacle of women's abilities. A separate dissecting room was provided for women in 1907, but some Cork professors nonetheless continued to refuse to admit women to their classes.[10] Women in fact made some significant advances in the sciences. Alice Perry, for example, took a first-class engineering degree from Galway in 1906, thus becoming the first qualified female engineer in the United Kingdom and possibly the world.[11] Her progress was followed closely by her fellow students who applauded her mastery of what had hitherto been considered a 'masculine' subject and noted with approval her involvement in the college's Literary and Debating Society.[12] Perry was quite remarkably one of five sisters to graduate from Queen's Galway and all seem to have been involved in the women's education movement. But change came to Galway slowly, especially in the sciences and mathematics. In the 1950s, for example, when one woman took the honours courses in maths, she became known not by her given name, but as 'Honours maths'.[13]

The Queen's College journals featured contributions by women students, but they were on the whole fairly frivolous pieces, especially in the early days. Most student newspapers were relatively short lived and it seems that their editors were closely watched by college authorities. This may explain why the contents of the 'ladies columns' tended to be superficial, at least in the early editions. The recollections of a number of graduates suggest that the female pioneers lived as though in a gilded cage, enjoying their status as university women, but always conscious of the fact that their existence was as strictly monitored as it was closely watched. Frances Moffett, for example, claimed that she was very conscious 'as a woman student . . . of the restrictions, often trivial' imposed at UCG, and recalled being summoned to see the Lady Superintendent who censured her for not having 'put up' her hair correctly and for daring to wear a ribbon.[14] This, it should be noted, referred to the years after the Great War; it is fair to assume that the first women were even more strictly watched. The small number of women in Galway did, however, have their compensations as they were in great demand at college dances. One male student, for example, recollected that women were so few and far between that the men were forced to 'ration our dances among the men, half a dance to one man, and half to another' at the college's much-anticipated annual social.[15]

The Queen's colleges clearly had their weaknesses, but they offered at least some form of collegiate life for women. The lack of facilities for female students in the capital was a direct product of the need for the girls' schools to become poor imitations of university colleges and this was itself necessary because of the stubborn refusal of the leading men's colleges to open their doors to women. As in Britain, almost all Irish colleges and universities had been persuaded to admit women by the turn of the twentieth century. Only two major institutions held out: TCD and UCD. Even the Cecilia Street Medical School – a remnant of the old Catholic University and affiliated to UCD – admitted women in 1896, but the others held firm until 1904 when Trinity finally capitulated. This news was greeted with great delight by all feminist campaigners, but Catholic women felt even more aggrieved than they had before this date: if they wished to stay true to the teaching of the Church, they would be forced to remain at inadequate women's colleges while Protestant women – who could already attend the Queen's colleges without clerical disapproval – now had the opportunity to attend one of the greatest and oldest universities in the British Isles.

The experiences of Margaret Tierney Downes, one of the first two women to enrol at Cork in 1885–6, highlighted some of these problems. Her own time at Cork had been disappointing and she concluded that Catholic women in particular were being badly served. Claiming that Catholic women at Queen's had met with a reception of 'unfavourable character',[16] she wrote a number of letters to the College Council in early 1889, arguing that she had been persecuted by fellow students and her professor because of her religion.[17] Along with Mary Hayden, she attempted to urge the Royal University Senate to force the colleges allied to the university via its fellowships to offer the same teaching to women as they did to men. She and 12 other 'Catholic lady graduates and undergraduates' sent a memorial to the Senate, arguing that they suffered a severe educational disability because 'they had been refused permission to attend the lectures in University College', and asking the Senate to intervene on their behalf.[18] The Senate replied that it could not interfere in the workings of UCD, but this petition became merely the first of many exchanges in a drawn-out battle between UCD and the feminists who were determined to force the institution to open its doors to women.

In 1886, the UCD Rector, Fr William Delany, allowed some college fellows to repeat their lectures to female students in the buildings of the Royal University, and several fellows also began to lecture in the Loreto College. This unsatisfactory arrangement was replaced in 1902 by the admission of women to some classes in UCD's Aula Maxima, but not all could attend and membership of the College remained only partial. Opposition to UCD's policy was led by the Irish Association of Women Graduates and Candidate Graduates (IAWGCG), an organisation formed in 1902. Its members insisted that they were 'non-sectarian, non-political . . . thoroughly representative, and free from every kind of party bias'.[19] They also refused to take sides on the contentious university question, arguing that their aim was to 'obtain the best advantages possible for the women-graduates'.[20] This signalled them out as almost unique in a context of bitter religious division over university education. By 1907, the IAWGCG claimed about 150 members, and it continued to profess its status as 'widely representative of women's interests'.[21]

The development of the IAWGCG was significant because it signalled the end of an old era in feminist education agitation and the beginning of a new, more modern and more genuinely pluralist campaign. The new generation of activists was led by exceptional women including Mary Hayden, Agnes O'Farrelly and Alice Oldham, all Royal University graduates with personal experience of discrimination in the university and teaching fields. They were old hands in the campaign, but they attracted a large number of younger university women who were affiliated to regional groups in Belfast, Cork, Derry and Dublin. This was especially significant for Catholic women whose interests had hitherto been largely represented by clerics or – by default – by the largely Protestant lobby groups, when they had been represented at all. The evolution of this group coincided with a new wave of activity on the university question, much of it focused on UCD.

UCD was in a difficult situation. Having evolved from the old Catholic University, it had been restructured in 1882 and had passed into Jesuit control in the following year. In the absence of any real rival, it quickly became the centre of Catholic university life in Ireland and its Stephen's Green 'campus' attracted what was known as the 'cream of Catholic ability', but it struggled because of its lack of space, facilities and money. Yet, while the College struggled under almost constant financial hardship, both its lineage and its attainment of between nine and 15 of the Royal's prized fellowships guaranteed its reputation at a serious academic establishment. Moreover, the College boasted an exceptionally lively social and political student culture, described by the prominent student, Arthur Clery, as 'undescribably brilliant and interesting'.[22] Catholic women – unsurprisingly – wanted to share in its collegiate life and although many were clearly involved in UCD's extra-curricula activities, they were not permitted to become formal students of the college. Catholic women had to remain content with their old secondary schools and their patience with the stubborn college authorities grew thinner and thinner, especially after TCD had given in.

Much of this was reflected in *St Stephen's*, the lively UCD student journal, which featured regular columns for university women – another indication of how women made their informal presence felt in the college. The 'Girl Graduates' Chat' column in *St Stephen's* appeared at times to be rather trivial, but it in fact served as an important forum for the women who wished to enter UCD, and was supportive above all of the Women's Graduates Association.[23] Its alleged 'flippancy' was criticised by Francis Sheehy Skeffington,[24] but it may well have been the involvement of men in the early columns which made them appear occasionally glib.[25] Female journalists in fact used the columns to air their grievances, educational in the main, but also professional and political. Most were from Alexandra College or the Loreto and Dominican colleges in Dublin, and they noted, for example, that no women were appointed as commissioners at the Royal Commission into University Education in Ireland and that women were not permitted entry to the Royal University convocation.[26]

Fr Delany, the rector of UCD, explained to activists that he could not agree to admit women because the college lacked space and facilities. This was undoubtedly true, though it is worth noting that Delany had in 1885 told a Commission on Educational Endowments that 'the people do not view with approval among Catholics, especially Catholic ecclesiastics who have the direction of a certain extent of the teaching, some of the subjects of the Intermediate Education Board's examinations as suitable for girls' education'. He added that the schools of which he approved did not present themselves for examinations.[27] It is possible that he had undergone a conversion by the early years of the twentieth century, but it is difficult not to conclude that Delany was suspicious at best of higher education for women and especially wary of the co-education of men and women. He came under increasing pressure from the IAWGCG, particularly in 1904, when the women's group organised two memorials to UCD and one to the Royal University's Senate. Delany and his Academic Council claimed that they had done as much as they could for women, but this point was strongly disputed by none other than the College's own Registrar, Francis Sheehy Skeffington.

Sheehy Skeffington was a well-known supporter of women's rights, married of course to Hannah Sheehy Skeffington, who along with her sisters was a Royal University student and IAWGCG member. They had all signed the 1904 memorials, but Francis Sheehy Skeffington had also solicited signatures from outside the college. Having been admonished for this by Delany, Sheehy Skeffington resigned from his post as Registrar, explaining in a letter to the Rector that he was motivated by his concern about 'the disabilities of Irish Catholic women in respect of higher education, in as much as, while disbarred from attending the Queen's colleges and Trinity College they find no provision made for their instruction in the ordinary university courses given at University College.'[28]

Skeffington's letter contained a list of supporting signatures, including those of Thomas Kettle and Hugh Kennedy, but we should be careful not to ascribe too much benevolence to the male students and graduates of UCD. Hanna Sheehy Skeffington argued forcefully that 'the men were reluctant to stand aside and allow women to enter upon their ground',[29] and her sentiments were supported by fellow activists who declared that they were capable of articulating their own educational needs and objecting to 'superior youths' attempting to do this on their behalf.[30] This was typical of a number similar comments made by women who rejected male dominance in student political and intellectual life.

The IAWGCG further made its presence felt at the Royal Commission on University Education in Ireland in 1902. Annie McElderry, a teacher at the Protestant Rutland School, and Agnes O'Farrelly, who taught at both the Loreto Convent and Alexandra College, represented the Association at the Commission. Their argument that women and men should be educated together – even in medical schools – that women's halls and residences should be established and, most shocking of all, that qualified women should teach male students, was radical and hardly calculated to soothe Delany's ruffled feathers.[31] The Commissioners recommended that any new university settlement should include the full equality of men and women, but no final settlement or solution was enforced. The women's case was weakened, however, by the belief among some female educationalists that while women students should have equality with men, they would be best educated in women's colleges which would be affiliated to the universities. The IAWGCG feared that women's degrees would be less valuable if they were educated separately from men and the organisation's witnesses told the 1902 Commission in no uncertain terms that they did not want 'women shut up in Women's Colleges'.[32]

Many of the leading women's colleges, Protestant and Catholic, opposed the IAWGCG on this issue, no doubt believing that their own institutions would be severely limited by the full inclusion of women in the universities and colleges. The fact that the IAWGCG opposed them on this reflected the widening gap between the younger and more radical women of the IAWGCG and the older generation of women activists. A Royal Commission on the University of Dublin held in 1906–7 heard similarly opposing views on this issue by advocates from both sides, and the commissioners themselves finally supported the recognition of women's colleges, particularly the recognition of Alexandra College as a constituent college of the University of Dublin. This was not done in the University of Dublin, but the possibility of the affiliation of Catholic women's colleges with any new university remained, and seemed in fact to have won support over the years. It was an issue plaguing educational campaigners even after the establishment of the National University.

The first attempt of the St Mary's Dominican and the Loreto Convent colleges to gain affiliation to the new university were rejected, igniting a very public debate, often between former members of the colleges. The alumni of these and a number of other celebrated Catholic women's colleges led the campaign against their association, largely through the IAWGCG which maintained its vigilance on the matter well after the establishment of the new university.[33] The organisation lobbied UCD's governing body and the NUI Senate, and individual members – notably Mary Hayden and Hanna Sheehy Skeffington – expressed their views in no uncertain terms.[34] The IAWGCG stepped up its campaign, arguing that teaching in such recognised women's colleges would be inferior and that the existence of external institutions would lower the tone of the new university.[35] These early applications were rejected, but subsequent submissions in 1911 were actually accepted by UCD.[36] They were finally rejected by the NUI Senate on the advice of its Board of Studies. The IAWGCG had once more lobbied the Senate,[37] and it is safe to assume that Mary Hayden, present at the Senate meetings when the question was debated and decided, felt a small sense of triumph. Her views and those of her fellow campaigners had finally been vindicated.

Women had become almost fully involved in UCD life before 1908, but the establishment of NUI finally guaranteed them the full academic and employment equality for which they had been campaigning for over 40 years. Some women had already made headway as academics in the colleges, but only as lecturers and teaching assistants such as the female demonstrators in education and mineralogy appointed respectively in 1905 and 1907 at UCC.[38] But the reorganisation of the colleges saw a number of formidable women appointed, many of them veterans of the women's education campaign. Mary Ryan was appointed Professor of Romance Languages at Cork in 1910 having been told the previous year, she claimed: 'there is no one else to do it. Will you try?'[39] She described the 'rather grim room' in which women students were housed at UCC, noting that the first women members of staff were expected to fill all manner of positions including 'general whipper-in to the Woman's Sodality'.[40] Other trail blazers included Rosalind Clarke, the daughter of a Presbyterian minister, who went to UCG as a 16-year-old in 1900. Having spent time in Germany and teaching at a girls' school, she was finally appointed to the college's staff in 1908, remaining there until her retirement in 1942. A fellow Galway pioneer was Mary Donovan-Sullivan, elected to UCG's Governing Body in 1913 and appointed Professor of History in 1914.

The most prominent new appointee was of course the redoubtable Mary Hayden, appointed Lecturer in Modern Irish History at UCD in 1909, and promoted to Professor in 1911. She was also the only woman appointed to the National University Senate, surely a vindication for a woman who had felt so bitter about the Royal University's failure to award her a Fellowship after she won a University Junior Fellowship in English and History in 1895.[41] In recognition of her contribution to the National University, she was awarded an honorary DLitt in 1935. Her friend, former Gaelic League and women's education activist, Agnes O'Farrelly, lectured in Modern Irish from 1909 and was finally appointed Professor of Modern Poetry in 1932, after the retirement of Douglas Hyde. Both served on UCD's new governing body.

Both women had of course been involved in a number of political campaigns and this was not uncommon among their feminist contemporaries. Donovan-Sullivan, for example, was one of several prominent UCG women's suffrage supporters, many of whom joined the Connaught Women's Franchise League when it was formed in 1913.[42] She herself wrote a strident piece on this issue in 1913, explaining why working women should support women's suffrage.[43] It is important to note too that the link between women's education campaigners, the early generations of university women and feminist politics did not end when educational equality was legally gained. Not only were many members of the IAWGCG prominent in the women's suffrage movement, the organisation remained resolute in its support of women's issues. Renamed the National University of Ireland Graduates' Association in 1914, when the women allied to the three Irish universities established separate organisations, it remained active in feminist politics long after many other women's organisations had faded from public view. They lobbied de Valera about the abolition of the Senate, the Criminal Law Amendment Act and women's position in the Irish civil service, but their most vocal campaign was launched in response to the publication of a draft version of the new constitution in 1937. Their opposition to the potential watering down of women's citizenship and employment rights was striking not only because of its vigour, but also because the list of names of the women who were involved read like a 'who's who' of the early education campaign. Mary Hayden, Mary Kettle and Hanna Sheehy Skeffington were again to the fore, suggesting once more that the early twentieth-century women's education movement had generated an exceptionally activist and altruistic feminism.[44]

The National University has of course changed almost beyond recognition since women first began to demand admission. Although fewer women than men completed secondary schooling and enrolled at university for much of the first half of the twentieth century, this pattern was largely reversed by the 1980s. Women now make up just over half of all undergraduate and postgraduate students in Irish universities and their participation in the traditionally male fields of medicine, law and accountancy is particularly striking as it has had now reached or exceeded 50 per cent. However, the proportion of female staff members, particularly at the higher level, has not grown at anywhere near the same rate. In Cork, for example, it actually became worse over the twentieth century.[45] The scarcity of women in senior posts within the National University should remind us all that the battle begun well over one hundred years ago continues.

GEARÓID Ó TUATHAIGH

A S A POLITICAL ISSUE, the 'university question' in Ireland throughout the nineteenth century was essentially an issue of religious rights, symbolic as well as substantial. It was a debate about the entitlements of different religious denominations to state support for university education on terms acceptable to their own religious principles and scruples. In effect, as a political issue, this centred on the challenge faced by successive governments in Westminster, in seeking to devise structures for state-endowed university education in Ireland that would be acceptable to an increasingly assertive Catholic middle-class leadership, and in particular to the Catholic hierarchy. The succession of initiatives – from the Queen's Colleges of 1845 to the Royal University – all conceived in some degree or other as part of political strategies for constructing a stable base of Catholic unionism while also conciliating Presbyterian ambitions in Ulster, had not succeeded in meeting fully the demands of the leaders of the aggrieved denominations and their communities. The difficulties encountered by the Catholic initiative of 'Newman's university' from the 1850s served to further sharpen Catholic resentment at the lack of adequate state support for a demonstrably Catholic university in Dublin, in contrast to the historically well-endowed Trinity College (TCD), the bastion of Irish Protestantism.[1] Indeed, the intensity of Catholic resentment at the privileged position of Trinity, and the insistent demands for equality of treatment, had the predictable effect of inspiring Trinity's supporters to steadfastly defend its essentially Protestant character and ethos, and, of course, its resources.

From the later nineteenth century – in the high noon of late-Victorian constructive unionism – further efforts were made to resolve Ireland's university question. A number of Royal Commissions were established, and successive chief secretaries for Ireland summoned up the interest to attempt a solution to the question. The political 'balancing' act demanded that a substantial concession be made to the aggrieved parties (especially the

Catholic bishops and lay leaders), while not provoking the ire of those in possession of the field (and status) – TCD. It was only with the return to office of the Liberals in 1906 – and with no immediate prospect of their bringing forward Irish Home Rule – that Augustine Birrell became the latest chief secretary to search for an answer to the Irish university question. The outcome was the Irish Universities Act of 1908, establishing two new universities: the National University of Ireland, with its constituent colleges in Cork, Dublin and Galway, and the Queen's University, Belfast (an early acknowledgement of the confessional and cultural distinctiveness and demands of Ulster unionism which would soon take constitutional form in the partition of 1920).

Yet, strangely, in this final phase of the Irish university question, the most acrimonious public controversy that marked the establishment of the National University of Ireland (NUI) was not at all related to religious sensitivities and demands (where the relevant vested interests were broadly satisfied), but centred, rather, on the issue of language as an essential marker of 'national' identity. Specifically, the role of the Irish language in the new NUI was to provide an unexpectedly explosive and divisive debate on cultural identity within nationalist Ireland in the period leading up to and immediately following the establishment of the new national university. It was a debate that was to echo, at regular intervals, in discussions of the National University and its role in Irish society down the decades.[2]

The controversy can only be understood in the wider context of the debate on Irish cultural identity which reached a point of particular intensity in the final quarter of the nineteenth and the early years of the twentieth century. But, at the heart of the controversy was the question of whether religion or language (or, for a more rarefied cohort of intellectuals, an elusive 'Celtic spirit') should constitute the defining characteristic of 'Irishness'.[3] The accelerating, and seemingly irreversible decline of the Irish language as a vernacular in the decades following the famine finally prompted the establishment in 1878 of an organisation, The Society for the Preservation of the Irish Language (SPIL), dedicated to halting this decline.[4] SPIL was soon followed by the Gaelic Union (which launched Irisleabhar na Gaeilge), and in 1893 was founded the most enduring and influential of all the Irish language revival organisations, The Gaelic League (Conradh na Gaeilge). The novel feature of these new organisations was their concern with the preservation and, in time, the revival of Irish as a living vernacular; that is, with halting and, so far as possible, reversing the historic 'language shift' of recent centuries.[5]

Interest in the Irish language from an antiquarian perspective had sustained a succession of short-lived societies, concerned with collecting manuscripts, publishing texts and generally investigating and bringing to the attention of scholars and the learned public a sense of the rich cultural resources of ancient Ireland, principally encoded in Gaelic manuscripts. Vindicating the honour of Ireland and the antiquity of its claims to being considered the home of a civilised people was increasingly present as a strong, if not always a primary motive for many individual scholars and cultural societies promoting scholarly research, manuscript collection and preservation, and occasional publications relating to the 'reliques' of Gaelic Ireland.[6] This respect for ancient Gaelic learning and culture (and its residual legacy in Irish 'folklore') was also present among scholars and intellectuals with an interest in Irish during the later nineteenth century, particularly as philological scholarship (most influentially of continental European provenance) quickened interest in – and enhanced the claims to scholarly attention of – the Celtic languages in general.

But the new impulse of Irish-language societies of the later nineteenth century lay in their objective of ensuring that Irish, seemingly in rapid and terminal decline, should survive as a living language. The Gaelic League's declared aim was 'preserving and extending the use of the spoken tongue'. For the language revival movement, the sphere of education was, from the outset, identified as a vital battleground in determining if Irish was to have a future as a living language. As Tomás Ó Fiaich wrote in 1972: 'it became a primary objective of the League to ensure that the teaching of Irish would find a place in the normal educational system of the country, at both primary and secondary level, and if possible a university level as well'.[7] Given the structures and the presiding spirit of the formal education system in late nineteenth-century Ireland, the task facing the language revivalists was daunting. Yet, within a generation their efforts were to effect a remarkable transformation in the status of Irish at all levels of Irish education.

In the state-supported system of elementary schools (the 'National' schools) Irish was completely excluded, as a subject to be taught or as a medium of instruction, until the late 1870s, when the lobbying of SPIL resulted in the teaching of Irish being permitted as an extra subject, outside normal school hours. Few schools availed themselved of this option; by the early 1890s less than a thousand pupils were presenting annually for examination in Irish at elementary level. The situation improved in response to Gaelic League propaganda and pressure. In 1900 the teaching of Irish was permitted during normal school hours, and soon thereafter a Bilingual Programme was sanctioned for schools in Irish-speaking districts (Gaeltacht), allowing for the use of Irish as a medium of instruction in these schools. Again, a shortage of teachers and inherited prejudices affected take-up of the programme. Roughly half the schools in the Gaeltacht were operating the Bilingual Programme by 1922, but elsewhere throughout the country less than a quarter of the 'National' schools were teaching any Irish at all by that date.[8]

If progress was modest, and slow, at primary level, the challenge faced by the League was, perhaps, even more daunting in the private (and largely religious-controlled) sector of secondary education. In establishing the Board of Intermediate Education in 1878 (through which Irish secondary schools could receive state money on a pay-by-examination-results basis), the government had agreed that 'Celtic' (with its softer, Arnoldian nuance, in contrast to the starkly definitive 'Irish language') should be included among the classical and modern languages in which students could take the examinations of the Board. However, the marks allocation for 'Celtic' was lower than the allocation for French and German, and considerably lower than that for Greek, Latin and English. This relatively low valuation for examination purposes, together with a shortage of teachers and parental indifference, depressed the numbers taking Celtic for examination in secondary schools (less than five per cent of all students taking examinations of the Intermediate Board presented in Celtic during the 1890s). Public interest in the matter seemed negligible. That is, until in 1899, in evidence given publicly to a Royal Commission enquiring into the Intermediate system, a senior Trinity don, John Pentland Mahaffy (Professor of Ancient History) demanded (citing, among others, his colleague Dr Atkinson's professional opinion as a scholar-editor of Celtic manuscripts) that Celtic be removed altogether from the Intermediate curriculum, on the grounds that it was unworthy of academic study, a patois fit only for the most rudimentary communication with illiterate peasants; and, as for the 'glories' of the surviving texts of its ancient literature , 'I am told by a much better authority . . . that it is almost impossible to get hold of a text in Irish which is not religious or which is not silly or indecent.'[9]

The President of the Gaelic League, Douglas Hyde (a Trinity graduate himself, and an accomplished Gaelic scholar) organised a major counterblast against Mahaffy and his supporters, in a campaign which excited considerable public controversy.[10] Evidence was gathered for presentation to the Commission from a galaxy of continental and British scholars, decisively refuting Mahaffy's ill-informed opinions, and making the case for an enhanced position for the study of Celtic/Irish within the Irish education system as a whole. The timing of this controversy was crucial. Nationalist sentiment was sharpened by the 1798 centenary commemoration, and by the advent of 'democratic' local government in 1899. Nationalist sensitivities were also becoming more pronounced. The facetiousness of Mahaffy's pronouncements and his tone of contempt were singularly ill judged. The controversy amplified a public debate on 'Irish identity' (within competing 'essentialist' and 'inclusivist' poles) in which writers and intellectuals, journalists and cultural activists were already trading heavy blows. The controversy on 'Celtic' in the Intermediate system was taken up in the popular press as well as in the literary and mosquito journals.[11]

The direct outcome of the controversy was that under the Education Act of 1900 the status of Irish in the secondary curriculum was enhanced, with immediate impact on numbers studying the language. By 1904 almost 30 per cent of all secondary students taking examinations took Irish for examination; by 1908 this had risen to almost 50 per cent.[12] In the wider ideological context, however, the controversy had given an enormous fillip to the public standing and the morale of the Gaelic League, and it had emboldened the more 'advanced' activists to press ahead with the revivalist strategy on all fronts, confident that the resurgent mood of nationalist pride (for which D. P. Moran's writings provide the most aggressive witness) was broadly supportive of the League's programme. That the League had the public support of leading figures in the political leadership of the Irish Parliamentary Party, and of a broad spectrum of the Catholic clergy (including bishops) was a further boost to its confidence. Challenges remained, relating to the supply of qualified teachers and of texts, standardised grammar and spelling, and the continuing effort to influence parental attitudes – the battle for hearts and minds. But, it is worth noting that by the early twentieth century the British state itself was increasingly permissive in acknowledging (and, within limits, accommodating) the particular contribution of the peoples of the

Celtic fringe to the cultural mosaic of an overwhelmingly Anglophone world empire.[13] By the early years of the twentieth century, then, the Irish language revivalists were not without real grounds for optimism, at least so far as the education system was concerned.

This confident mood is important in any consideration of how the Gaelic League responded to the decision to establish a National University of Ireland in 1908. Already in 1902 Hyde had informed the Robertson Commission of the League's understanding of the concept of a national university:

> We believe that the only hope of a new university doing good to Ireland will be to have it frankly and robustly national, in a spiritual and intellectual sense, from the very outset . . . We want a university whose aim shall be to give an Irish education to suit Irish needs . . . We want an intellectual headquarters for Irish Ireland . . . that shall be Irish in the same sense that Oxford and Cambridge are English.[14]

So far as the position of Irish in the new university was concerned, the initial concern of those charged with establishing the new institution was with ensuring that appropriate provision be made (in terms of finance and academic appointments) for Irish/Celtic studies as an academic discipline of the university. This they accomplished. The determination to secure for Irish a position of respect in the curriculum of the new national university reflected the enhanced academic credentials of Irish/Celtic, not least in international philology, and the heightened sensitivity towards its scholarly and cultural value generated by the public controversies of the previous decade.

What precisely the Gaelic League meant by ensuring that the new university would be 'an intellectual headquarters for Irish Ireland' became starkly clear in 1908, when the League declared that it was in favour of competence in Irish being a matriculation requirement for all students entering the new National University of Ireland. Immediately, nationalist opinion in Ireland divided publicly on this policy. Many who had been prominent in support of the League's earlier campaigns (especially the 1899 controversy) now opposed the line taken by the League on Irish in the new university. These included the Standing Committee of the Irish Catholic Bishops, newspaper editors, politicians and others who were generally supportive of the overall aims of the language revival movement.[15]

Among the constituency of Catholic clergy who were unhappy with the

League's demand, a particularly influential figure was Fr William Delany, SJ, President of the Catholic University College (soon to be absorbed into the new NUI), and a long-time supporter of the Gaelic League.[16] As a priest, he declared that he could not support a policy which would have the effect of excluding young Irish Catholics (without Irish) from the new university, and forcing them to seek admission to Trinity. But as an educationalist, he also questioned whether the language had yet been sufficiently developed at primary and secondary level (in terms of numbers taking Irish and in relation to the development of the subject itself) to justify such a drastic demand as that now being made by the Gaelic League. Talk of Irish not being yet sufficiently developed hit a raw nerve with many of the League's most earnest supporters. The public debate on the issue was rancorous and divisive. Being largely a 'family' row within the nationalist community, it left a bitter taste.

The League's policy was strongly defended by Hyde, and elegantly argued by the historian and Celtic scholar Eoin MacNeill in his pamphlet, *Irish in the National University of Ireland.*[17] But it was Fr Michael O'Hickey, Professor of Irish in Maynooth, who proved to be the most trenchant public advocate of the League's policy, and the most abrasive scourge of those who dissented from it. His tongue and pen did not spare those fellow priests and bishops who were now, as he saw it, wilting in their support for the revival, some of whom, indeed, may never have been fully convinced supporters. In December 1908, a meeting in Dublin held to support the League's demand heard a letter from O'Hickey read out which gives a flavour of the terms and the tone (in the manner of D. P. Moran) in which he denounced the dissenters: 'If we tolerate this thing we are still a race of helots, deserving the contempt and scorn of mankind . . . To be opposed by the colonists is a thing we are accustomed to; to be opposed by a section of our own, no matter how worthless and degenerate, is not to be endured'. [18] There was much more in that vein. Among the 'section of our own' who in late December announced (in terms of gentle regret) their opposition to the League's policy on Irish for matriculation was the Standing Committee of the Irish Catholic Bishops. Public denunciation by O'Hickey could not be ignored. Having urged him discreetly, but to no avail, to curb his language, the bishops dismissed O'Hickey from his Maynooth post, and students of the college who had declared public support for his stand were disciplined. But, for all their political influence, the bishops and their allies were unable to prevail against the remarkable propaganda blitz of the Gaelic League. Resolutions and meetings kept up the pressure on the members of Senate of the NUI, of which Hyde and MacNeill were also members. Perhaps the decisive turn in the controversy came when a number of county councils, galvanised by the League, resolved that their scholarships for students entering the new university would be conditional on the university's adopting the Irish for matriculation requirement demanded by the League. On 23 June the Senate of the NUI adopted by 21 votes to 12 Douglas Hyde's resolution that Irish be essential for matriculation to the new university.

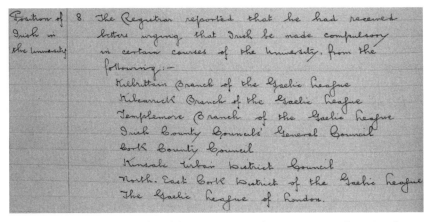

Figure 1 **The first Senate meeting of the NUI, 17 December 1908: excerpt from the minutes concerning the position of Irish within the new university.**

The League had secured another remarkable victory in its campaign to reinstate Irish at the centre of the Irish 'national' educational system. But this victory came at a price. Bitter words had been spoken and written; the 'broad church' of patriotic sentiment which had been gathering around the Gaelic League standard for more than a decade had been severely damaged; resignations and recriminations would leave wounds that would not be easily healed. A century after its foundation, however, the *cause célèbre* of obligatory Irish for matriculation in the National University of Ireland – Ollscoil na hÉireann – merits recall as a remarkable episode in the cultural history of modern Ireland. In the *Kulturkampf* of early twentieth-century Ireland, the decision of the Senate of the NUI on this issue was probably the only occasion in recent Irish history on which the force of a significant volume of public opinion ensured that language trumped religion as the key marker of Irish cultural identity within the nationalist community in Ireland.

Following the establishment of the NUI, the academic study and teaching of Irish became a core commitment in each of the constituent colleges of the university, with senior academic appointments having responsibility for the teaching of the Irish language and literature, from the oldest records of Irish to the contemporary living language (usually as the basis for a broad academic programme in Celtic languages and civilisation). The teaching of Irish as a university discipline was accompanied by active postgraduate research and scholarly publications in all aspects of the Irish language and literature. The NUI, for its part, in addition to grant-aiding scholarly publications of individual works of scholarship, supported a dedicated journal for the publication of scholarly work on Irish: initially as *Lia Fáil*, and from the 1930s under the title *Éigse*. A curious link between the campaign for making Irish an essential subject for matriculation and the support of scholarly work on Irish as an academic discipline within the university is the Adam Boyd Simpson bequest. This Birmingham-based doctor left a sum in his will for the National University on condition that Irish/Gaelic be a required subject for matriculation to the university. It is the Adam Boyd Simpson bequest that was later devoted to the support of the journal of Irish studies, *Éigse*.[19]

The bitter divisions which had marked the controversy on the designation of Irish as compulsory for matriculation were to leave their mark. Those who had opposed the demand of the Gaelic League in the fateful debate largely remained unreconciled to the outcome of the decision; that is to say, they continued to insist that the requirement caused resentment and poisoned attitudes towards Irish among a significant segment of the more casually nationalist Catholic bourgeoisie, and that it prevented otherwise suitable and academically qualified candidates from entering the National University (thereby 'forcing' them in the direction of Trinity). In more general terms, they contended that a universal requirement of competence in Irish for students entering all faculties of the university simply took no account of the actual patterns of language use operating in the wider society. The passage of time did not assuage this sense of grievance or remove this opposition among sections of the academic and wider Catholic community to compulsory Irish for matriculation in the NUI. The injunctions of Catholic bishops against young Catholics going to Trinity may have rested on doctrinal or pastoral grounds, but the 'hurdle' of compulsory Irish for the entry of young Irish Catholics to 'their own' university, must have added an extra coat of irritation to episcopal anxieties.[20]

For their part, committed supporters of the language revival movement continued to see the status gained for Irish in the NUI in 1908 as of immense symbolic and practical importance for the overall prospects of the survival and revival of Irish. They saw the requirement as conferring status on Irish, providing an incentive for students in Irish secondary schools to become competent in the language, and guaranteeing that at least a sizeable cohort of Irish graduates (including those destined for the main professions) would be likely to have some basic proficiency in Irish. In broader ideological terms, the necessity of Irish for entry to the 'National' university seemed to endorse the view that the Irish language was indeed an indispensable marker of Irish national identity. These considerations continued to hold persuasive force for many Irish revivalists in the early decades of the new Irish state after 1922.[21]

The transformation of the institutional and cultural landscape of higher education in Ireland from the 1960s inevitably posed new questions regarding the special status of Irish within the NUI. This was an aspect of wider reappraisals, as more general cultural, including educational, changes at all levels of Irish society increasingly affected state policy – and public attitudes – towards the role of Irish in Irish society as a whole. The global communications revolution, the transformation of the structure, orientation and performance of Ireland's economy, and the Irish experience in Europe, are only the more obvious cultural forces which have transformed the terms of debate on the nature of Irish society, and its future direction, since the 1970s. Specifically, in the sphere of education, the remarkable growth in the numbers participating in higher education in Ireland from the later 1960s, together with the proliferation of new third-level institutions (initially the NIHEs and the RTCs,[22] followed later by private colleges offering various third-level qualifications), and the progressive diversification of the background of entrants to TCD, has created a new, increasingly competitive 'market' for students in Ireland in recent decades. There has been an increasing mobility of young Irish people, between universities in both parts of Ireland, and between Ireland, Britain and continental Europe, part of a wider dynamic of student choice and mobility, to which the constituent colleges (since 1997, the constituent universities) of the NUI are not immune. The fact that the legislative regime under which the impressive suite of new third-level institutions was established did not include any obligatory competence in Irish for entry to the new institutions (in the main, any references to Irish were of a simple exhortatory kind) has, inevitably, prompted renewed concern among sections of academic leadership within the NUI that the obligatory Irish requirement for matriculation, unique to the NUI, may be placing the NUI constituent universities at a disadvantage in the more competitive and expanded market for students now operating in Ireland. Moreover, the growing number of applicants for entry to the NUI seeking – and securing – exemption from the Irish requirement, on grounds that their earlier education (outside the Irish system) did not provide them with the opportunity of acquiring competence in Irish, serves to further underline the uniqueness of the NUI requirement for students educated in Irish secondary schools.

It is unlikely that the issue of obligatory Irish as a requirement for entry to the NUI will cease to be a subject of debate; indeed, it is likely to assume a new urgency in the years ahead. This is so, not only because it has practical implications for the opportunities in higher education open to the growing number of new immigrants settling in Ireland early in the twenty-first century, but also because of the wider debate that has already begun on what constitutes 'Irishness' in an increasingly multicultural society, and what role the education system should play in forming a sense of Irish identity, for natives and newcomers alike. This debate on 'national' identity in an Ireland now attracting large numbers of new immigrants will, no doubt, rehearse issues familiar to many modern states – competing concepts of 'national identity' as a function of citizenship or as an ethnic construct defined in more cultural terms. The new political accommodations in Northern Ireland are at once a reflection of, and a stimulus to a more pluralistic understanding of 'Irishness'. The cultural condition of Ireland is very different in 2008 from what it was a century ago. The future role of the Irish language within the NUI – perhaps even the very concept of a 'national' university – will ultimately be determined by the direction of public opinion on the precise role of the Irish language in any new construction of 'Irishness', calculated to inculcate in its citizens loyalty to an Irish state, and calculated also to effect an acceptable level of cohesiveness and social solidarity within Irish society as a whole.

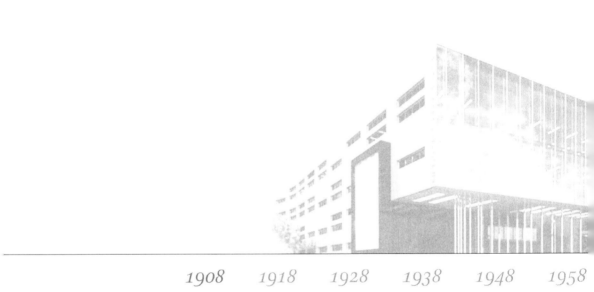

1908　　1918　　1928　　1938　　1948　　1958

1968   1978   1988   1998   *2008*

Constituent Colleges
to Constituent Universities

CHAPTER 4 *University College Cork* JOHN A. MURPHY

WHEN BERTRAM WINDLE was appointed president of Queen's College Cork (QCC) in 1904, his urgent task was to reform 'a derelict institution', poorly attended, meagrely endowed, suffering from low staff morale, publicly perceived as alien and still under ecclesiastical disapproval. Though a vigorous presidency improved matters internally, the absence of a satisfactory university dimension was a major factor in the College's malaise.[1]

By his pieces in the press and his speeches on public platforms in the years before 1908, Windle stimulated and orchestrated the demand for an independent 'university of Munster' while at the same time keeping in touch with impending legislation. As the Irish Universities Bill made its way through the House of Commons in the spring of 1908, he was reasonably optimistic: 'The Universities Bill promises, I think, well. It does not give us all we want here, but it is a decided advance and will put me in a position to make a really big thing of this place, as I hope to do if I live and remain here.' In the Commons debate, Augustine Birrell (Irish chief secretary, and architect of the university settlement) was full of good will, at least, towards regional aspirations: 'I wish to heaven Cork and Galway were strong enough to support universities of their own.'[2]

Windle conducted a dual strategy – continuing to make the case for a separate university while pragmatically concerned to ensure a smooth transition to the new federal dispensation, secure adequate funding, an acceptable governing body and continuity of tenure for his existing academic staff. He developed these views for an enthusiastic public audience in Cork City Hall on 25 April 1908. While not yielding on his chief objective, he welcomed the bill as a 'great step forward'. 'Cork students would be examined in Cork by their Cork teachers with the supervision of external examiners provided by the University', and there would be 'some measure . . . of control over the subjects we are going to teach'. Optimistically, he did not believe 'that we are going to be hampered and harassed by the Dublin members' of the new Senate. The meeting supportively hoped that Cork would have 'adequate representation' in the Senate.[3] Windle later told *Cork Examiner* readers that there was nothing in the draft charter which could prevent the evolution of University College Cork (UCC) into a full university. The president's proactive role earned the trust of the civic and academic communities. This was evident in the College Council's request that he should stay in London to monitor the progress of the Bill in its later stage.[4]

As one of the commissioners responsible for drafting the statutes for the National University of Ireland (NUI) and the constituent colleges, Windle was extremely busy in this founding-father role in 1908–9, the hardest working period of his life. When the statutes were published on 17 May 1909, he permitted himself a jubilant entry in his diary, less a celebration of the new university than of the new college. '12.15. CORK signed: then Dublin, Galway and lastly the university. The meeting broke up in great amity and I caught the 3 pm train home.'

At a time when the College needed his constant presence, Windle was the first UCC president to experience a physically disagreeable aspect of the federal system – the expenditure of time and energy (unconscionable in early twentieth-century conditions) spent in return travel to Dublin for Senate and various other university meetings.[5] This burden borne by successive UCC presidents and officers was perhaps never fully appreciated by their Dublin-based counterparts whose travels to 49 Merrion Square from leafy suburbs involved no more than pleasant brief trips by bus or tram.

In the admittedly exceptional year of 1909, Windle paid an unbelievable 112 visits to Dublin. Over the whole period of his presidency, the number of annual trips to the capital averaged one third of the phenomenal 1909 peak. Overall, the taxing travel experience provided Windle with another powerful argument for an independent university of Cork.

His experience of NUI proceedings in the first few years did nothing to convert him to the federal dimension. In his view, eminently sensible Cork proposals were overruled by the Senate – in effect by Dublin's built-in majority. These proposals included limiting the holding of examinations for external students,[6] confining the term of office of the Board of Studies to one year,[7] and rotating Senate meetings to Cork and Galway, which would have enhanced the sense of federal identity. This interesting motion was withdrawn in the light of legal opinion.[8]

Windle was suspicious of what he saw as a dominant Dublin group. For example, he very much hoped that Archbishop William Walsh would accept the office of Chancellor but 'at this distance I do not hear anything of what is being discussed and I suppose the Dublin people will settle this matter among themselves'.[9] He resisted pressure to have 'Dublin medicine men' as external examiners in Cork: the academic council and governing body had already decided against it, and 'after all, the NUI was not brought to birth for the purpose of affording [easy] positions for a number of Dublin medical men'.[10]

It is extraordinary that someone who helped build the foundations of the NUI was so intent on quickly ending UCC's participation in the enterprise, and on loudly announcing this to his university colleagues and all who would listen. Windle hoped for 'divorce' and 'oh, may it be soon'.[11] 'There has never been any concealment of our intention here to get out of the National University at the first possible moment and to that task I intend to devote all my energies which are left over from the necessary business of the University and the College' though he hoped the parting would be marked by 'unbroken friendship'.[12]

The first meeting of the NUI in Cork on 25 May 1910, to confer degrees was noted by the *Cork Examiner* in an extensive report as truly historic. It was the first such university gathering, said Windle grandly, in the expected ritual tribute to the genius loci, 'at least since the time of St Finbarr'. (Truth to tell, it was a numerically small occasion – five MBs were conferred, one in absentia, and one MD – all men.) Windle chose to use the event (inappropriately, some might say) to sound the clarion call yet again for 'our own independent university'. There were at least two compelling reasons why 'educational Home Rule for Cork' was essential – the inconvenient and 'cumbrous system of boards' and the Dublin-centred nature of the NUI. The system whereby 'Dublin has a large and absolute majority' in the Senate was 'undignified', 'educationally indefensible' and a 'source of danger'. It was up to the people of Cork and Munster to demand that the College be enabled 'to work out our own salvation' – that full university status to which UCC was entitled by virtue of its growing student numbers, its expanding courses and its physical enlargement.[13]

The students present lustily cheered Windle's speech (conferrings were to be a form of indoor rag entertainment for the next few decades), especially the passages demanding 'an independent university of Munster'. Later on, in March 1912, UCC students participated in the great Home Rule demonstration in Dublin, a supportive *Cork Examiner* pointing out that a college seeking home rule for itself was in duty bound to support the wider cause.[14]

In matters of nomenclature, Windle approved of the widespread local usage of 'Cork university', prophetically, he hoped. But he deplored the newspaper practice of calling University College Dublin the 'National University'. Decades afterwards, President Alfred O'Rahilly was similarly annoyed by the conflation of UCD and 'National'. He saw this as insufferable metropolitan arrogance, though in the Dublin context of making a colloquial distinction between UCD and Trinity College it was understandable enough, as well as subtly suggesting the superior 'national' credentials of UCD.

In regard to Cork's relations with its sister colleges, when UCC's exemption status in respect of rateable valuation was confirmed after a lengthy and complex legal process, the southern college felt its victory had also benefited Queen's University Belfast, UCD and UCG. It is of interest that, at about this time, the *Cork Constitution* expressed the view that Galway's weakness and inability to stand alone would frustrate Cork's aspiration to independence.[15]

At this point, it has to be said that UCC's great progress after 1909 was inextricably bound up with the transformation wrought by the Irish Universities Act 1908 and would have been unthinkable outside the federal framework of the NUI. However reluctant Windle was to admit it, a moribund QCC could not have progressed on its own to a vigorous UCC. In one vitally important respect alone, the withdrawal of Catholic episcopal disapproval (and the consequent valuable Honan endowment) could never have happened in a purely provincial and unilateral context. All Windle's arguments to the contrary were disingenuous and unconvincing.

*   *   *

Though Windle never let up on his tireless campaign,[16] a second phase is clearly discernible in 1918–19, and in a radically changed political context. 'This agitation for an independent university for Cork which I am now [Easter 1918] carrying on is just about enough of a job for any man.' The renewed campaign appealed to Cork pride and sentiment: Windle played to the gallery of anti-Dublin feeling. Because of the size of UCD's representation on the NUI Senate, Windle claimed, Dublin could block Cork initiatives. 'Whatever Dublin desires, it can have: whatever Cork desires, it can have only if Dublin will permit it.'[17] There was also a widespread view that the 1908 settlement had failed to deliver 'the poor man's university', a goal which might yet be achieved through full academic independence at Cork.

Windle believed that his case had been greatly strengthened by his experience of the workings of the federal system over ten years. In 1918–19, in newspaper articles, governing body resolutions, pamphlets and at public rallies, the familiar arguments against the federal link were developed *ad nauseam*.[18] For example, the expenditure incurred in frequent and fatiguing visits to Dublin by UCC officers and Senate members might be better diverted towards funding badly needed lectureships.

A governing body supportive pamphlet (written by Windle), issued in March 1918, made the important point that the ostensible reasons for refusing Cork independence in 1908 – low student numbers, absence of popular backing, and little financial support – no longer held true, in the light of UCC's vigorous development in the interim (for example a 530-strong student body, compared to QUB's 390 at independence). The governing body petition for independence was widely supported in Cork. It claimed that the federal system did not allow for regional dissimilarities and this prevented the development of the College in ways which would be beneficial for Munster. A fully independent university would promote industrial development, especially in the context of hoped-for post-war regional economic expansion.[19]

Unfortunately for Windle, his grand design became entangled in the politics of resurgent nationalism.[20] Sinn Féin, ably represented within UCC by Windle's *bête noire*, Alfred O'Rahilly, vigorously opposed the independent university project as unacceptable at that particular time and as an attempt to consolidate pro-British control of UCC. Whereas the political winds of change were likely to favour an early and strong nationalist presence in the Senate, the UCC governing body, with only four of the 28 members elected by graduates, a triennial election deferred, and an unrevised graduates' register, seemed set to retain its conservative complexion and its loyalty to Windle. So the Sinn Féin argument ran. The president's opponents claimed that this was the real reason for his attempted unilateral declaration of independence. Moreover, at a time when the First Dáil was receiving wide-spread pledges of allegiance in the spring of 1919, Windle's petitioning London on the university issue was branded as disloyalty to the nation. Of course, Sinn Féin did not want to be seen as opposing the widely popular 'independent university' demand but they claimed it should be deferred pending widespread discussion, a Convocation referendum and, perhaps, the attainment of national independence itself.

O'Rahilly mobilised student and graduate opinion and received the support of the Gaelic League in Cork and of the 19 recently elected TDs in Munster, all of whom made representations to the Senate.[21] Windle and his associates became the object of vituperative Sinn Féin abuse for 'trying to turn Cork into a crown university'. For good measure, a strong rumour circulated in Sinn Féin circles that a Windle university would scrap compulsory Irish.[22]

For a while, it seemed that Windle was undaunted by this concentrated opposition and he continued to lobby vigorously in Dublin and London. His possessive obsessiveness now verged on the self-delusional. Writing of his 'gigantic struggle for *my* Cork university', he was prepared to wager his own future in '*my* college' on the outcome of the campaign.[23] Writing to a presumably bemused Joseph McGrath, NUI registrar, on 5 March 1919, Windle was already confidently regarding 'this university' as a 'foregone conclusion'. Dublin and Galway must calmly accept the inevitable and make adjustments accordingly. And 'no amount of resolutions passed by that august body of ineptitudes, Convocation, will have the slightest effect upon our action'.[24]

Reality soon asserted itself. Apart altogether from Sinn Féin machinations, the NUI was not going to agree to being reduced to a rump. The Chancellor, Archbishop William Walsh, made some sympathetic noises out of politeness,[25] but the Senate became alarmed at an early stage when they heard about UCC's plans 'from information appearing in the public press'.[26] Windle was informed by Sir Plunket Waldron that UCD President Denis Coffey was 'bitterly – savagely – opposed to it and . . . his policy is procrastination'.[27] That delaying strategy was applied under the direction of Eoin MacNeill and Fr Timothy Corcoran when the draft University Bill was forwarded to the Senate in April 1919.[28]

At a special meeting on 21 May 1919, it was resolved unanimously that the Senate of the National University of Ireland deprecates the hasty introduction of legislation that will destroy the constitution of a university the foundation of which was accepted a few years ago as a settlement of the University question, and it claims that sufficient time be given to set forth its reasoned opinion on the subject.

Convocation discussed the issue at length on 6 June 1919,[29] one pious sentiment being expressed that 'it would certainly be a great loss to the National University to lose the genius of the people of Cork'. But Windle had lost heart by then – 'if I do not get the university this year, I think I must resign'. The end came on 6 June 1919 when the British government made it clear they were dropping the bill in response to intense academic and political opposition. Windle seized an escape-hatch opportunity when he accepted an invitation from St Michael's Catholic College in the University of Toronto to take up a philosophy professorship.[30] When he informed the Senate of his impending retirement as UCC President, the members unanimously expressed their appreciation of his great services,[31] accompanied doubtless by inner sighs of relief.

His exaggerated view of the collapse of the 'Munster University Scheme' was that of 'a calamity for the south of Ireland'. His report to the governing body suggested the government had never been in earnest all along, and the governing body blamed the dominance of the UCD camp in the Senate. Windle's final president's report (1918–19) fired parting shots at the federal system. The Senate had refused UCC's request for a deferral of examinations (the great flu had closed the college for a month and five students had died). It was also guilty of intolerable foot dragging on the question of recognising the Cork Technical Institute which had admitted UCC engineering students to its courses. Windle might also have mentioned the Senate's overruling of the governing body decision to establish (Statute ix) a statutory lectureship in Russian language and literature.[32]

Windle further vented his anti-NUI spleen when he wrote in the English *Catholic Times* that 'we have a sort of a university but a very poor sort', not at all comparable to TCD and QUB – 'almost a *université pour rire*'. It was an ill-judged piece (particularly the disparaging French phrase) even when allowances are made for his sense of bitter frustration at the time. It caused much offence to his former NUI colleagues, all the more so because he was maligning the NUI in an *English* paper.[33]

In more mellow mood, shortly before leaving to begin his new life in Canada, he mused philosophically that, though Cork must continue 'to inhabit the house of bondage' (a melodramatic image of the federal framework), the NUI 'is a mere incident' in the history of the Cork college.[34] UCC's attempt to break free of the federal frame is a very curious (if not bizarre) episode in the early history of the NUI. Cork assertiveness, and resentment

[53]

of perceived Dublin dominance, form part of the explanation as does the very real experience of inconveniences, delays and expenditure of money, time and energy as unavoidable aspects of the federal system. The government's willingness to humour Cork ambition up to a late stage remains puzzling, especially so soon after a reasonably successful outcome of the long-standing and complicated university question. First and last, however, the instigator of the failed initiative was Bertram Windle. His obsessive pursuit of the will-'o-the-wisp of university independence smacked of hubris, locked him into a confrontation leading to inevitable defeat and disillusion and prematurely ended a great UCC presidency. He grievously underestimated the obstacles in his path and he tragically failed to understand the revolutionary forces operating against him.

* * *

After the debacle of the secession attempt, UCC settled down to dwelling in 'the house of bondage'. Since Windle had been a 'bridging' QCC–UCC President, UCC Registrar Patrick J. Merriman was the first *elected* UCC head within the federal system. After a tight vote in a controversial special governing body election meeting, Merriman ran out an easy winner at the Senate. It may have helped that he was a UCD graduate to begin with. The Sinn Féin faction in UCC and its extra-mural followers reacted with considerable chagrin to the appointment, claiming that, on the first occasion a president was supposed to be elected 'democratically', the Merriman clique in the governing body had used 'Tammany tactics' to exclude Professor William Magennis of UCD from consideration. Magennis, Sinn Féin's favourite, unsuccessfully tried to get the Senate to postpone the UCC appointment and to set up a visitation process of inquiry. (A year later, the UCC students' council, backed by NUI Convocation, tried to get the Senate to act against a pro-British UCC professor for writing an allegedly anti-NUI article. What is interesting here is that the Senate seems to have been viewed by these petitioners as a court of appeal.)

Given the comfortable circumstances of his appointment and his lack of a crusading temperament, Merriman was likely to be genially disposed to the federal link. Indeed during his long presidency (1919–43), his critics alleged he became adept at manipulating the levers of power at governing body and NUI Senate levels to ensure the appointments of those he favoured.[35] This was not widely regarded at the time as a reprehensible abuse of academic power. But it does raise the question as to what extent the federal framework was a guarantee of impartial appointments, as some UCC reformist academics rather naively appeared to believe. It is true, of course, that the Senate was less influenced (at least, in non-Dublin cases) by local favouritism and nepotism than the governing bodies of constituent colleges. But the Senate was also a governing body writ large, with correspondingly greater scope for canvassing. The matter was further complicated by the presence of party politics in both assemblies. The real guarantee of high standards in making academic appointments was the acceptance, in time, by the academic bodies of the recommendations of independent assessors' boards. But even after the introduction of the assessors system, there were cases, admittedly rare, where old-style majority voting overruled the recommendations of impartial boards.[36]

Even before he became president in 1943, Registrar Alfred O'Rahilly was the most robust voice in the UCC/NUI relationship. He was keenly aware that a Cork audience would always rise enthusiastically to the anti-Dublin rhetoric which was a stock piece of his repertoire. Thus, he claimed vaguely that the college should be liberated from Dublin control, he complained that the three NUI TDs (before the 1937 Constitution, graduates' representatives sat in the Dáil, not the Seanad) were all Dubliners, and 'Cork University College' was subordinated to, and hampered by, the 'so-called' NUI.[37] Ironically, UCC could be accused of practising its own form of imperialism – protecting its Munster catchment area against possible challenges from Limerick and Waterford. In 1945, Professor M. D. McCarthy (a future UCC president) provided statistics to bolster O'Rahilly's argument that agitations for a university in the other two cities were unsustainable.[38]

O'Rahilly came to believe, however, that the National University's independence of the state was of much greater importance than any aspiration UCC might have to be formally independent of the NUI. He shared the contemporary Catholic phobia of state interference and therefore felt it was essential to defend the federal status quo lest any tampering with the 1908 settlement might open up academic matters to political debate and control, to the detriment of the NUI and, in particular, to O'Rahilly's cherished Catholic ethos in UCC.

All things considered, in O'Rahilly's view, the admittedly imperfect 1908 settlement must be upheld. Had not UCC virtual independence since the outset? (And, he might have added, was he not the man to deal with any niggling federal constraints?)

> This College is an autonomous academic institution and it means to retain its independence . . . Having won our cultural freedom, we mean to keep it, for thereby we can best serve the causes of liberty, truth and religion against the growing menace of statolatry.[39]

And besides, the federal system was not all that bad:

> It is in many ways a great advantage to have a central body for academic appointments and standards. And there is increasing recognition of the different needs and outlook of the College. It cannot be maintained that the functioning of a common Senate impedes our progress or individuality. On the contrary, the existence of such a joint body is of great help towards maintaining academic autonomy. This last point is the most important consideration which makes many of us soft-pedal local patriotism. The University which has a Charter (so has each of the Colleges) provides a practical (if not ideal) solution of a delicate and difficult religious problem. We are not anxious to put this again into the melting pot.[40]

And towards the end of his presidency in 1954, in a succinct summing-up of his position, O'Rahilly reminded Archbishop J. C. McQuaid of Dublin: 'I have always sacrificed Cork interests (separate university for Cork) to what I believe to be the Catholic interest (Charter: protected autonomy).'[41]

Alfred O'Rahilly's picture of UCC as a virtually autonomous institution was in part a propagandist projection but it reflected the feelings of Cork people – students, staff and citizens – throughout the whole federal period. In some respects, admittedly, the NUI was perceived as 'our' university, as against the 'Protestant' and 'alien' Trinity College. Some graduates (particularly if they worked outside Ireland) appreciated the international brand of a 'National' degree, and others added, for public display, the university acronym to the degree awarded, notably BDS (NUI). Cork was also smugly satisfied that its star students won more than their proportional share of Travelling Studentships and other NUI prizes.

But that was about the extent of the awareness of the federal dimension. For the average student, the Registrar, NUI, 49 Merrion Square, Dublin 2, was a remote and faceless personage to whom certain forms and fees had to be sent from time to time. But UCC was the 'Uni', the living reality of the university experience. Support and allegiance – in athletic, debating and other competitions – were all about the college and its colours and symbols, not about a wider abstraction. Later on, NUI graduates' clubs were formed but they were mostly concerned with the constituent college where they were located. In UCC, it was only some staff members who appreciated the quasi-theological subtleties of the federal system. The citizens – and the media – couldn't be bothered with fine college–university distinctions. On conferring days, degrees, whether ordinary or honorary, were seen as being conferred 'by UCC' and that was that.

*   *   *

The first major proposals of third-level reform and reorganisation were contained in the Reports of the Commission on Higher Education (CHE) in 1967. In recommending that UCD, UCC and UCG should become independent universities, the CHE rejected the notion of an unnatural Cork–Galway coupling in a rump NUI. Such an arrangement, it pointed out, would be weakly defensive, perpetuate the same disabilities characterising the status quo and simply postpone the day of inevitable independence. Both colleges had the inherent strength to succeed on their own and could be given explicit guarantees on whatever reservations they might have.

The Commission reported that while UCD wanted dissolution of the federal arrangement and UCG strongly favoured retention, UCC's preference was 'less clear-cut'. Perhaps this caution reflected the unadventurous presidencies of H. St J. Atkins (1954–63) and J. J. McHenry (1964–7). The commission referred to the 'unease' of Cork and Galway in their relationship with Dublin. In his submission to the Commission, Atkins (then retired) said UCC opinion favoured retention 'subject to certain changes' but in oral evidence he added cautiously that there would be 'no objection' to independence if safeguards could be provided for making appointments, a process which would otherwise – and Galway shared Cork's apprehensions on this point – be subject to 'undue internal local pressures'.[42] (This was in the pre-assessors days.)

Education Minister Donogh O'Malley's proposal in April 1967 for a TCD–UCD 'merger' (with independence for Cork and Galway) was, in general, opposed by academic opinion. An NUI–TCD working party presented an alternative plan to the Higher Education Authority (HEA) on 7 April 1970, urging the establishment of four independent universities. This was favoured in the HEA report[43] which wistfully called for 'a quick and lasting solution'.

This hope was confounded by the decision of Richard Burke (education minister in the 1973–7 Fine Gael-led coalition) to ignore previous positions and announce that Cork and Galway would constitute a reduced two-unit NUI.[44] Fortunately, this egregious proposal never saw the light of law.

Meanwhile in UCC, President M. D. McCarthy (1967–78) directed the Cork response to these confusing signals. He was the first UCC head since Windle to actively favour independence, though in a level-headed way. In the mid-1970s, there was a general anticipation of independence and much UCC energy was spent in drawing up provisional plans for the inevitable event. A governing body-approved co-ordinating committee rejected the Burke proposal and pointed out that 'a full university' for Cork had been recommended in the 1967 CHE Report, the July 1972 HEA Document, the NUI–TCD 1970 agreement and by the previous government in 1968. All these recommendations had been based on rational considerations.

The Committee took Dr Garret FitzGerald to task for his contribution to a Dáil debate (11–12 February 1975) on third-level education. (FitzGerald was minister for foreign affairs but in this instance was wearing his hat as an authority on education). In attempting to defend the Burke proposal, FitzGerald warned against a 'proliferation of universities' in the Republic which would undermine confidence abroad in our university system. In rebutting this statement in great detail, the Committee revealed UCC's (and particularly McCarthy's) thinking on federalism, existing and proposed. It exposed the Cork–Galway 'rump' proposal as the nonsense the 1967 Commission on Higher Education Report had shown it to be. It emphasised the Report's passages on the deficiencies of the NUI federal system – an appointments procedure 'slow and cumbersome'; in regard to courses and examinations 'the university function has tended to wither'. The Committee added that even the residual formalities were tedious. Besides, if the colleges were now running their own affairs by and large, 'what does the university then do and what is the point in having it?' – a very central question, perhaps even more relevant in the post-1997 situation. Finally, quoting an earlier opinion of Dr FitzGerald (that a 4,000-strong student body was the minimum viability level for a university in Cork or Galway) against him, the Committee pointed out triumphantly that UCC 'now (June 1975) has over 4,500 students'.[45]

The coalition government changed its mind again in July 1976, now favouring independent status for Cork, Galway and Maynooth. (The NUI Senate, at a meeting on 26 November 1976, seemed prepared for dissolution.) When Fianna Fáil returned to power in 1977, it said it would legislate for four independent universities. But all this ineffectual confusion of proposals succumbed to the traditional low priority of educational change in government policies, and the interest dribbled away. By the spring of 1985, the NUI registrar could confidently claim that 'the continuance of the NUI was not in question'.[46]

Though President Tadhg Ó Ciardha (1978–88) in his previous position as registrar had apparently helped persuade Minister Richard Burke to drop the Cork–Galway proposal,[47] he was quite content with the NUI status quo and was in no way 'driven' to push for UCC independence. By and large, a fairly comfortable consensus prevailed in the NUI for much of the 1980s, as the colleges tended to accommodate one another's needs, unlike the Dublin dominance of Windle's time. That is certainly the impression of this writer who served on the Senate and its committees from 1983. The *modus vivendi* was helped by the close friendly relationship of presidents Ó Ciardha (UCC), Tom Murphy (UCD) and Colm Ó h-Eocha (UCG), which greatly helped the amicable dispatch of business. But as new presidents came to the fore, the consensus was modified and UCD tended to assert the clout it derived from its size and location.

Michael P. Mortell, as UCC registrar, 1979–89, and as president, 1989–99, had 20 years front-line knowledge of the workings of the NUI. In his view, only those UCC academics who had no direct experience of the University could complain unconvincingly about its restrictiveness, or use this as an excuse to prevent a particular course of action at UCC.[48] For Mortell, the most important thing about the federal link was the international standing of NUI degrees, a point he emphasised at the outset of his presidency to an RTÉ interviewer who brought up the possibility of an imminent break-up of the University.

In his president's report for 1991–2, Mortell could not be described as longing for liberation from Windle's 'house of bondage'. He believed institutional restraints had not hindered 'the development of UCC from its original position as a small constituent college of the National University to its present position as a de facto vibrant university'. In other words, the college was already enjoying quasi-university status: the NUI generally respected decisions made in Cork, it monitored and guaranteed standards

in appointments and degrees, and, if it occasionally delayed Cork proposals, this was not necessarily a bad thing. (Emeritus Professor of Music,
Aloys Fleischmann, was a stout defender of the federal status quo. In the
1970s he had campaigned for an independent appointments process but
he still – perhaps naively – saw the NUI Senate as the ultimate guarantor
of academic integrity. Shortly before his death, he expressed concern at
talk of impending change: 'it would be disastrous if the governing body,
as at present constituted' had the final say in appointments.[49])

But change was now unstoppable. An anxious NUI Senate, aware of
Trinity's moves to defend its 'more favourable position' and of media speculation on the demise of the National University, set up a committee to
monitor developments in the progress of the Universities Bill.[50] Subsequent meetings continued to observe the process but the Senate, like the
UCC governing body,[51] was an interested bystander rather than an active
influence on legislation. As well as fearing an 'invasion of the legitimate
management freedom of a university',[52] by the HEA and the education minister, the Senate, like an apprehensive parent, worried about its future treatment at the hands of its soon-to-be-liberated colleges. It urged them 'to
accept the value of the principles of commonality, in helping to preserve
and present a distinctive NUI identity', and it hoped the individual presidents would 'lead . . . in developing a sense of NUI membership' in the
interests of its continuing role in higher education.[53]

Meanwhile, the university senators brought considerable influence to
bear on the shape of the Universities Bill as it was debated in the upper house
in the spring of 1997.[54] Fortunately for those senators and the universities
they represented, the government, unusually, did not have a majority in
the Seanad so that the minister was compelled to take university apprehensions into consideration. Generally speaking, the university senators were
concerned to redress what they believed to be bureaucratic, political-control
bias in favour of more academic autonomy and collegiality. Nevertheless, a
new business/corporate mentality was reflected in the bill as passed,[55] 'the
chief officer', for example, being called 'President' or 'Provost' as a secondary
or consequential description.

As far as the NUI was concerned, the central provision of the Act was the
transformation of the constituent colleges into independent constituent
universities, and the question of nomenclature arose in this connection.
During the Seanad debate, the minister made it clear,[56] that each university

could decide on its own naming usage. The Act itself, while setting out the 'formal' name in the Second Schedules (National University of Ireland, Cork: Ollscoil na hÉireann, Corcaigh) also stated that the minister 'may at the request of the governing authority', provide for a constituent university to extend its name to indicate continuity or succession from its previous description.

Well before the passage of the Act, there was some popular unease in Cork when it was thought the new name of UCC might be National University of Cork (NUC)[57] – hardly a euphonious acronym. Students, and especially ex-patriate graduates, would strongly object to this, just as their predecessors had strenuously protested 90 years before at the replacement of 'Queen's College' by 'University College'. In the event, however, there was to be no name change at all in Cork. The governing body indulged in some indecision and unnecessary consultation but in the end availed itself of the permissive provision of the Act to retain 'University College Cork' as the working name of the institution. Thus the new legal name was 'University College Cork – National University of Ireland, Cork', together with the obligatory and ritual Irish language equivalent. UCD made a similar decision, though UCG was happy with 'NUI, Galway' and Maynooth, pleased at last to transcend its subordinate status, was proud to style itself 'NUI, Maynooth'.

To some Cork observers, the retention of 'University *College*' seemed perverse, given the fulfilment, at last, of an aspiration to full university status, cherished from Windle's time (1904–19) down to McCarthy's (1967–78). But its advocates justified the retention not so much on grounds of sentiment and tradition as on the practical basis of recognition of the 'brand name', UCC. In any event, 'the College', would continue to be the familiar description on the lips of academics, students and citizens alike.

The Universities Act 1997 was a landmark, for Cork as well as for the other NUI institutions, second only in importance to the Irish Universities Act 1908. As a fully independent constituent university of the NUI, Cork was now master of its own destiny, subject only to the requirements of the 1997 Act, deciding its own courses and examination standards, taking its own policy initiatives, choosing its own governing authority, and appointing its own staff from the presidency downwards. As late as 1989, the Senate was the final appointment body for presidents, and candidates still canvassed at that level, but after the 1997 Act an independent assessment system at Cork would apply to presidential appointments.

[61]

With the devolution of full powers to the constituent universities, the 1997 Act diminished the role of the central NUI organ, and cast doubt on its long-term usefulness, not to say survival. In 2002 the Senate reviewed its residual role and function after 1997, and issued its findings as an information document circulated to the constituent universities. It was regretfully noted that in the case of Dublin and Cork 'the name of the National University of Ireland has been diminished or sometimes omitted'. A rather pathetic plea was added that Dublin and Cork should give 'reasonable prominence' to the NUI in their titles and make 'appropriate reference' to it in 'their promotional literature and websites': this would be 'helpful towards consolidating the identity' of the university.[58]

Developments since the publication of the 2002 review suggest that the residual attachment of UCC and UCD to the NUI has further diminished. The new-breed presidents in both universities have shown indifference or disregard, and certainly little *pietas*, towards 49 Merrion Square. UCD's unilateral conferring of honorary degrees in the summer of 2006 was, to say the least, a flagrant defiance of NUI protocol. For its part, UCC, consciously or otherwise, has constantly downplayed the remaining federal dimension. 'University College Cork' tends to be the sole name description in college documents, with a diminishing use, in bottom-page small print, of an 'appropriate reference' to the NUI.

When the vacant UCC presidency was being widely advertised in September 2006, the prominence of the institution and the significance of the office were duly emphasised. But there was no reference whatsoever to the NUI. When the portrait of retiring President Gerry Wrixon was unveiled on the gallery wall in the Aula Maxima UCC, on 31 January 2007, it showed an informal pose and an absence of academicals. The NUI Vice-Chancellor's gown which had been a prominent feature of all the preceding portraits since P. J. Merriman (1919–43) was conspicuously absent. Not even a ghostly NUI presence remained. Bertram Windle could rest at last. The liberation from 'the house of bondage' was complete.

CHAPTER 5 *National University of Ireland, Galway*

SÉAMUS MAC MATHÚNA

I N A CONTRIBUTION of this kind to the history of the National University of Ireland, the main difficulty is in selecting from among the multitude of topics which could appropriately be covered. In the limited space available here, and even at the risk of being seen to attempt too selective and partial a historical survey, I have felt it more useful to concentrate on certain aspects of University College Galway's evolution, over the first two decades of the NUI's existence, which will be less familiar to the modern reader. Those developments provide a context for consideration of the dynamics of the relationship between the college and the NUI and for the evolution towards university status of the college.

Those aspects concern first the college's struggle for its very survival and, second, the process which led to the identification, in negotiation with the Free State government, of a new and unique institutional mission for it, consistent with the broader cultural agenda of the new State. That mission both ensured its immediate survival and influenced the development of the institution since then; and indeed its continued presence as part of the ethos of the modern university has in recent times received renewed legislative recognition in an amended form appropriate to changed circumstances.

The economic difficulties in which the college found itself may be traced back to the establishment in 1880 of the Royal University of Ireland, as a purely examining body, and the associated dissolution of the Queen's University in 1882. Up to then, no degree in arts, medicine, law or engineering could be granted in Ireland except by the University of Dublin and the Queen's University, and for degrees in the Queen's University attendance at one of the Queen's Colleges was required. The consequence of the new arrangement that all degrees outside the University of Dublin would depend merely on examinations was a dramatic drop in attendance at the Queen's Colleges.

In Galway, total annual enrolment dropped from an average of 86 in the decade 1872–81 to 34 in the decade 1882–91. As the remuneration of the professors consisted of a fixed stipend together with an amount equivalent to the class fees paid by the students attending the particular professor's classes, a significant reduction in professors' income resulted.

More immediately, however, the main grievance was that, whereas QCC and QCG had enjoyed the same level of state endowment, the 1908 Act provided an endowment of £12,000 for Galway as against £18,000 for Cork. As one result of this, the salaries of professors and lecturers in Galway lagged behind those of their counterparts in Dublin, Cork and Belfast. Thus, in 1922–3 the total emolument of no Galway chair reached £600 (and seven of the 19 fell below £400), whereas only three of the 20 UCC chairs and seven of the 33 UCD chairs fell below that figure, and all 18 of the Belfast chairs fell in the range £900–1,100.[1]

To address this situation, the governing body on 6 March 1913 appointed one of its members 'to negotiate with and organise the county councils with a view to obtaining for the college financial assistance from the counties' and also to put in place a uniform scheme for the scholarships to be awarded by the councils. The member was given a grant of £50 for one year for the purpose, together with expenses, including those for the organisation of a meeting of county council delegates for the purpose.[2] The person appointed was the Revd John Hynes, BD, who rose meteorically thereafter in the college ranks and became probably the key figure in the evolution of the college over the period in question. A Sligo native, he was seconded to the Galway diocese and became acting dean of residence for 1911–12, during the absence of the dean, and then dean of residence in 1912. In February 1913 he was elected by Galway County Council as its representative on the governing body. In 1914 he was also appointed secretary and in 1916 also part-time lecturer in Celtic archaeology; he was also appointed registrar in that year. In 1924 he was appointed professor of Celtic archaeology on resigning the lectureship. In 1934, on the retirement of Professor Alexander Anderson, he was appointed president,[3] shortly afterwards vacating the offices of registrar, secretary and dean of residence. Commonly knows as 'Pa' Hynes, he was a popular choice with the students, who chaired him shoulder-high from the train station to the college in a torchlight parade on the night of his appointment as president.[4]

Critical to persuading the county councils to come to the college's aid was the promise by Lloyd George that, if the councils were to contribute at least £1,500 per annum for the general purposes of the college, the exchequer would provide an additional, non-statutory grant of £2,000 per annum to the college. Clearly some considerable preparatory work had already taken place, because just one week later, on 13 March 1913, a Galway University College conference was held in the Town Hall, Claremorris of delegates of the Connacht county councils and of their representatives on the governing body. A statement was unanimously agreed, to be sent to the secretary of each of the Connacht Councils, recommending the granting of the aid sought. The rationale presented was *inter alia* that the college was a Connacht, rather than a Galway, college, in drawing almost all of its 160 students from the West of Ireland, and that 'the views, political and religious, of more than three-quarters of the members of the governing body were in harmony with the great majority of Connachtmen'. It also complained at the Chancellor's unwillingness to grant the total amount of £3,500 and of his making the exchequer grant of £2,000 contingent on the Councils' £1,500.

The recommendation was that each council, in proportion to its valuation, agree to an annual contribution equivalent to a farthing on the rate, subject to the following conditions:

* The £1,500 to go to educational purposes beneficial to the people of Connacht, the details to be communicated to each Council as soon as possible.
* Unless those purposes were approved of by the Councils individually, or by a Conference similar to the present one, the Councils would cease to contribute.
* Should any Council decline to give its pro rata share, the contributions of all the other Councils would be refunded.

The councils duly contributed the amounts agreed, which were then devoted to the establishment of four new chairs (education, history with special reference to Irish history, philosophy, and commerce and accountancy) and increasing the salaries of the existing chairs. Galway was the only college which received such direct grants from county councils – and that from the poorest of the provinces; that bond with its community was to come to the fore again, as we shall see, when its future and funding were being debated under a native government.

All was not sweetness and light, however, in that relationship. In February

1916, Galway County Council and Galway Urban District Council, on foot of a petition from 146 student graduates and undergraduates claiming that an attempt was being made to oust Professor Joseph Pye from his position as registrar, threatened to discontinue their grants to the College and to cease sending their representatives to the governing body if he were to be removed from office. The councils referred to Professor Pye (himself a former member of the county council) as 'a staunch and unsupported upholder of Catholic claims at Queen's College during the period of years when such a course was neither fashionable nor profitable' and claimed that he 'would, many years ago, have been President of the College but for the fact that he was then, as he now is, an Irish Nationalist Home Ruler'.

The issue concerning Professor Pye, and also for certain other post holders, was whether his tenure of the office would, under the act, charter and statutes, legally expire on 31 October 1916; counsel had advised the governing body that it would expire on that date. What is of relevance here, however, is the effect which the councils' interventions on his behalf had in raising, in the college's eyes, the question of academic freedom.

Interestingly, later that month, when Sligo County Council was sent the Galway County Council resolution and also the students' petition, it took a very different stance. It conveyed its opinion that the governing body should, in the interests of education, have complete academic and administrative control of the college and that any attempt by an outside body to interfere with that control was almost certain to be detrimental to the interests of the college. It went on to state that, while public bodies had a right to know the purposes for which a grant of public money in aid of higher education was applied, any such grant to a university college carried with it implicitly the recognition of the right of the governing body to control and administer the college; and that it expressed its confidence in the governing body, which was now largely an elected body and composed of representatives and eminent men whose abilities or motives they should be sorry to question. It added that the students were under a misapprehension in the matter and that, given that several of them were being supported by scholarships, they should rather attend to their studies. One might speculate that this helpful balancing resolution may have owed something to Fr Thomas O'Kelly (professor of education and himself a Sligoman), who drafted most of the governing body's own response, and of course to Fr Hynes.

The governing body also had before it a letter from the eight professors whose salaries would have been directly affected by the withdrawal of the council grants. In a ringing defence of college autonomy, they declared their

> conviction that the College ought rather to suffer the loss of these grants than admit for one moment the right of any of the county councils to interfere by threats with the internal administration of the college. If once we lost our academic liberty, our right to manage our own affairs in accordance with our charter and statutes, our status as a constituent college of the National University would be endangered. How can we be trusted to teach and examine if we are open to intimidation?

They concluded, 'We are prepared to face the loss of salary if the County Councils withdraw their grants, but we are not prepared to sacrifice the honour of the College'.

In its response of 17 March 1916 to the two councils, the governing body stated that while it

> would regard the withdrawal of the County Council Grants as a very grave matter, inasmuch as it would result in the immediate inefficiency and probably in the early dissolution of the College, it is of opinion that it is far preferable that the College should face financial ruin and die with honour than live at the cost of its prestige, which must stand or fall with its academic freedom.

After detailing the widespread impact on its services to students which any withdrawal would have and complaining that the council had not first enquired into the issue through its representative (ironically, Fr Hynes in one case) or otherwise, it emphasised that it proposed to act in accordance with the act, charter and statutes and in no hostile spirit towards Professor Pye.

The response had the desired effect, as nothing further is reported in the matter and the grants continued. In the event, when the vacancy occurred later that year, the governing body, on a vote, decided against reappointing Pye from year to year. Hynes was appointed registrar in his stead (though Pye was allowed to retain his residence in the quadrangle).

The parlous financial situation continued to be the subject of representations and deputations from the college over the following years. In a letter of 12 May 1917, for example, President Anderson reminded the chief secretary that the Dublin Commissioners (whose task was the drafting of the original statutes of the NUI and its constituent colleges) in their final report had stated, in reference to Galway, that 'we continue to regard with no little apprehension its dangerous pecuniary condition' and that, despite the special income from the Connacht Councils, it was unsatisfactory 'that one of the Constituent Colleges of National University, situated in the poorest province of Ireland, is dependent on the contributions of the County Councils, while the other two, situated in wealthy surroundings, are adequately endowed'. In a letter of 5 June 1919, following a report from a commission, the college was notified that it was being given a special additional grant of £3,000 'to tide over the present emergency', pending the establishment of the University Grants Committee (UGC) to address the issue of university funding for the UK generally.

Pressure was stepped up with a submission to the Minister of Education, an tOllamh Eoin Mac Néill, on 2 February 1923, emphasising the 'lowness' of the professors' salaries, the comparisons (cited earlier) with Belfast, Cork and Dublin, and the recurrent deficit of almost £2,000. A deputation was appointed to meet the Minister for Finance, Earnán de Blaghd, and the need for an additional endowment was also mentioned in an official Dileagra (*as Gaeilge*) presented to President W. T. Cosgrave on the occasion of his visit to Galway in July. In this Dileagra, reference was made to the opportunities which the College saw for itself – subject to funding – in relation to agricultural education, the study of Gaeilge and teacher training. In spite of all that, by October of that year the non-statutory grant due since April had not yet been paid by the Government. In February 1924 a meeting was held with the Connacht and Clare members of Dáil Éireann, and a deputation subsequently met the Minister of Education.

In July 1924, in the course of a Dáil debate on a government scheme for the transfer of the College of Science and the Albert Agricultural College to UCD and the establishment of a faculty of general agriculture in UCD and a faculty of dairy science in UCC, the Minister of Education, Eoin Mac Néill, said that UCG was for him 'a very difficult problem'.[5] While it was not his intention that Galway 'should be let down in the matter of educational work', he went on:

> I leave Galway outside my proposals either one way or the other. I do not
> propose to destroy. I do not propose to construct. I hold myself, and I put it

15. Bertram Windle was President of Queen's College Cork and later University College Cork, 1904–19. He was also Vice-Chancellor and Pro-Vice-Chancellor of the NUI.

16. Alfred O'Rahilly was President of University College Cork, 1943–54 and also Vice-Chancellor and Pro-Vice-Chancellor of the NUI.

QUEEN'S COLLEGE, CORK
Procession of Her Majesty Queen Victoria, August 3rd 1849

17. Visit of Queen Victoria to Cork, August 1849.

18. Daniel Corkery, Professor of English, UCC, 1931–47.

19. The Quadrangle, University College Cork in the 1920s.

20. The Quadrangle, University College Cork. This photograph was taken in 2004.

21. Dr Michael Murphy has been
President of University College Cork
since 2007 and became Vice-Chancellor
of the NUI in 2008.

22. The Glucksman Gallery, University
College Cork.

above 23. **Monsignor Pádraig de Brún, President, University College Galway, 1945–59 and Vice-Chancellor and Pro-Vice-Chancellor of the NUI, pictured with Eamon de Valera, Chancellor of NUI.**

below l. 24. **Monsignor John Hynes was President, University College Galway, 1934–45 and Vice-Chancellor and Pro-Vice-Chancellor of the NUI.**

below r. 25. **Professor James Browne became President of NUI Galway and Pro-Vice-Chancellor of the NUI in March 2008.**

26. University College Galway in the 1890s.

27. J.E. Cairnes Graduate School of Business and Public Policy, NUI Galway.

28. Opening of Belfield campus in September 1962: the 'Turning the Sod' ceremony. *left to right* J. P. MacHale, UCD Secretary and Bursar; Frank Aiken, TD, Minister for External Affairs; unidentified man; Archbishop John Charles McQuaid; Michael Tierney, President of UCD; Eamon de Valera, kneeling, President of Ireland; Patrick Hillery, TD, Minister for Education.

29. Dean of the Medical School, Dr Denis Coffey was President of UCD (1908–40) and Vice-Chancellor and Pro-Vice-Chancellor of the NUI.

30. Dr Michael Tierney, President of UCD, 1947–64 (centre), pictured with Mr J. P. MacHale, Secretary and Bursar of UCD, 1954–87 (left) and Dr Jeremiah Hogan (right) who succeeded Tierney as President from 1964 to 1972.

31. Dr Hugh Brady is President of UCD and has been Pro-Vice-Chancellor of the NUI since 2004.

32. The Michael Tierney Building at UCD.

33. Cardinal Daniel Mannix, President of St Patrick's College, 1903–12.

34. The Junior House, St Patrick's College, Maynooth.

35. Dr Séamus Smyth, President of NUI Maynooth (1994–2004) with Niamh Bhreathnach (Minister for Education) pictured at NUI Maynooth at the Commencement Order of the Universities Act on 13 June 1997.

36. Professor John Hughes has been President of NUI Maynooth since 2004 and Pro-Vice Chancellor of the NUI. He also acted as Vice-Chancellor of the NUI from 2006 to 2007.

37. The modern campus at NUI Maynooth.

38. The NUI Maynooth flag.

to a representative body from the Galway College that I met not very long ago, that it was to my mind very questionable whether the efforts to carry on a university college in its present form and scope in Galway was the best way in which an institution of higher education could be carried on for Galway and for all that look up to Galway.

In line with his idea of a network of specialised institutions serving national needs at various locations, instead of the existing provincial institutions, he threw out the idea that Galway should specialise as a centre for the fishing industry.

In response to protests from some Connacht and Clare teachtaí dála that Galway's needs were meanwhile being ignored, the Minister for Industry and Commerce, Patrick McGilligan, denied that there was any intention to take away its present funds from Galway, as suggested by 'those who came here and interviewed me on this subject, and then retreated to Connaught and started a campaign'.[6] The Minister for Education (himself a UCD professor), referring to the 'beggarly' provision made by the 1908 Act for all colleges of the NUI, confirmed that Galway's provision would be suitably increased, but not at that point. Referring to the special claims advanced for it by them for consideration from the point of view of the Irish language, given that Galway City was 40 per cent Irish-speaking and the surrounding region 80 per cent so, he said:

> I agree, but I ask are those special claims going to be met – I am putting the question very plainly – by stereotyping the kind of university institution which is at present established in Galway? . . . I am glad that the West has wakened up to the question which was a problem to me and that is: what is the best thing to be done with regard to University College Galway? I am prepared to meet those at present interested in the college, the people of the counties which are contributory to that college, and in common with them, others representing the wide national view, and to consider with them what is the best thing to be done with regard to University College Galway, but I am quite satisfied the best thing to do is not to build on the foundations of Sir Robert Peel . . . as more or less altered under the regime of Mr Augustine Birrell. I should like the whole question to be looked into as freely and as openly as possible, and I hope to be able to provide an opportunity for doing that.[7]

He promised to take the matter forward in the autumn.

On 10 October 1924 the governing body was informed of the resolutions adopted by the local bodies in the matter and of an eight-page brochure, 'An Appeal and a Plea', written by President Anderson and circulated to the members of Dáil and Seanad Éireann, the county councils and the newspapers. It asked the president to seek an early meeting with President Cosgrave and the ministers for education and finance for a deputation comprised mainly of senior external church and political figures. It also agreed to try to get a strong expression of opinion in favour of the college from Clare County Council. The document 'An Appeal and a Plea' built the case on the basis again of its low professorial salaries – adding that student fees, rather than being paid to the professors to supplement their low salaries, should, as in Cork and Dublin, be used to improve the library and laboratories and for paying off the debt – and on the role Galway could play in the revival of Irish, including teaching Irish to trained teachers. Most of the document, which expressed the hope that 'none of its faculties would be lopped off or rendered incomplete', was, however, devoted to a defence of the medical school against the threat of closure and emphasised particularly the imminent completion of the new central hospital. It also highlighted the success of the engineering school and the newly established school of commerce. It is noteworthy, in the light of what was to happen next, that the proposed role regarding Irish related merely to the teaching of the language rather than teaching through the medium of Irish.

A letter of 7 November 1924 from the Ministry of Education noted that at the meeting with members of the executive council the college deputation had been told that its application for more funding

> could not be considered unless accompanied by evidence that the College was doing, or was preparing to undertake, work of national importance of some special kind. It was suggested that the special class of work for which Galway College appeared to be best suited was the conducting of University teaching and work through the medium of the Irish Language – the function of an Irish speaking University College.

The letter said that the minister

> desires to know if this suggestion has been considered by the authorities of the College. If it has been considered favourably by them, the Minister suggests that they should select three representatives to attend a conference with

representatives nominated by the Department of Education to consider how the organisation and working of the College might be reorganised to enable it to carry out the proposal.

The academic council expressed itself as 'favourable to making this College a College in which Irish will be the general medium of instruction as soon as the general body of the students of the college will be able to profit by such instruction', while drawing attention to practical difficulties ranging from the lack of textbooks and lack of Irish among students ('the great majority follow lectures in Irish on Irish itself only with difficulty') to the impact of reduced numbers on professors' fee income. If this last difficulty were resolved, it would recommend that all students be required to attend lectures and pass an examination in Irish before admission to second year. It also pointed to the national work already being done in the medical school, in seaweed research and in relation to Irish and called for a faculty of agriculture.

The governing body on 20 November 1924 accepted the proposal for a conference and largely adopted the Academic Council report as guiding instructions for its representatives – the president, registrar and Professors Thomas Walsh and Liam Ó Briain. When it had heard nothing further by June 1925, it reminded the minister and submitted its own set of proposals 'for the gradual conversion of the College into a Gaelic University College'. The conference eventually met on 10 November 1925 with the following terms of reference:

> To determine how University College Galway can best engage in some special work of National importance, e.g. the fulfilling of the functions of an Irish-speaking University College through the conducting of University teaching of general subjects through the medium of Irish.[8]

At that meeting doubts were expressed as to the scope of the enquiry to be made. On the following day the minister for education was in attendance and gave a detailed description of his intentions as to its work and said that he saw the college ultimately as 'not shorn of any of its faculties, but, perhaps, even added to, and in which the whole work of instruction would be in Irish'. A Subcommittee was then appointed to prepare a scheme for that purpose and an implementation plan. It met five times and its report essentially was adopted by the conference as a majority report, dated 16 April 1926; there were minority reports from two members.

In summary, the report presented the philosophical raison d'être for a Gaelic University in the context of the new state's constitutional and cultural objectives, laying particular emphasis on the literary aspect, before sketching the ultimate ideal and setting out the current possibilities. For the gradual provision of an arts and commerce degree programme it proposed four lectureships, in mathematics, history, commerce and education, to supplement the six professors already competent to lecture through Irish. Further recommendations related to a professorship of modern Irish, studentships, reduction of fees for courses through Irish, salaries to be independent of fees, and possible establishment of a faculty of agriculture and of a marine biological station.

The governing body on 4 May 1926 approved the majority report in substance, with questions of detail to be decided by the Ministry of Education and itself: it asked the government to give effect to it, as well as clearing its debt and raising salaries, and sought a meeting with President Cosgrave and the two ministers for the purpose.

The government response to the Report was much cooler. Coincidentally, heads of a bill to give effect to the transfer of the College of Science and establish faculties of agriculture and dairy science in UCD and UCC, respectively – as debated in July 1924 – were circulated to the NUI Senate for its views on 3 May 1926, and immediately raised concerns in Galway as to its own position, given that significant additional recurrent funding was also being provided thereunder for those colleges, including clearing of accumulated debt; ironically, a quarter of the increase proposed for UCC was for teaching through the medium of Irish. Steps were taken to impress on the Connacht, Clare and University teachtaí dála the college's claims, and those were also to be pressed in the meeting with the government. It was, however, Minister de Blaghd's remarks in the Dáil debate of 9 June 1926 which brought matters to the boiling point. Challenged as to the omission of Galway from the bill, he said that no progress had been made in time for those estimates and that all he could promise was that its current income would be maintained:

It is a matter for the college to think out proposals and to put them up. There was a Commission, composed mainly of representatives of Galway College, set up. That Commission presented a report, but I think anybody who read it could not fail to see that it was a disappointing document. It did not, to my mind, indicate that the authorities of the college were really in earnest about the question. They are quite in earnest about the question of getting money, but I do not know that they are at all in earnest about the question of doing special work which would entitle them to money. If they would, perhaps, take that remark to heart we might get somewhere.

If Galway is not going to do special work, then frankly as far as I am concerned I do not think it would be a wise course – it might be politically the only possible course to maintain it – to maintain it as a sort of toy college unless it does special work. On the other hand, if it does special work, and if the people concerned will give their minds to devising a scheme and the best method for doing this special work that the college can do, I do not think they will find the Government so difficult to deal with ... Cork as a matter of fact, even on the question of Irish, got ahead of Galway. They actually put proposals up to us before Galway put them up. Generally, it seemed to me to be rather more alert and rather more in earnest about the business ... I am not satisfied that it really cares a great lot about the Irish language at all. I am not sure, taking the whole body of the authorities of Galway, that they realise that if there is to be a future before that college it must make itself a distinctive and a special institution, and it ought to do work that cannot be done in the same way, or that cannot be done so effectively, elsewhere.

Those impolitic remarks elicited a strong response in the Dáil and in a letter from the President to the newspapers, pointing out that the college had put forward proposals several times with no result, that the conference in fact comprised four Galway nominees and seven others appointed by the minister for education, and that its report had been signed by that department's own general inspector and others well known for their zeal for Irish. Particular offence was taken by President Anderson at de Blaghd's 'two gibes at the College': the phrase 'toy college', given its distinguished history and graduates, and the suggestion that eminent and underpaid professors were only in earnest about money.

More significantly, however, the Galway Chamber of Commerce on 19 June 1926 called an urgent public meeting for the Town Hall on 25 June 1926 'in the hope that the people of Connacht will realise that we have arrived at a serious crisis in our affairs' and saying that 'the principle at stake is sufficiently important to justify us ... in asking every Connacht man and woman to add their voices to the just demand that, in our national development, the Western province should have and retain the place to which, as a definite and large entity in the Saorstát, it is rightfully entitled'. The chamber submitted a set of resolutions to the meeting demanding that the threats to close the college cease, that it be given an adequate endowment, that the findings of the conference regarding the gaelicisation of the college be immediately implemented, and that a centre of agricultural education utilising the Athenry Farm and the college be established. The demand for agricultural facilities sensitive to the special problems of the West, including training of instructors for Gaeltacht areas, was made in the context of de Blaghd's rejection in that Dáil debate of an agricultural faculty for Galway, on the grounds of avoiding duplication and of the decision not to provide a full agricultural faculty in Dublin or Cork either.

The meeting, described as 'monster' and 'magnificent' and during which all shops were closed, was attended by the cathaoirleach of every Connacht council, three bishops (with messages of support from others) and public figures from all the counties. The Minister for Lands and Agriculture, P. J. Hogan, emphasised, to a stormy reception, that there was no intention of closing the College and that all that was at issue was the exact amount of funding it should get. Fr Hynes insisted that, not only had threats of closure been made in the de Blaghd Dáil comments, but that the closing of the Medical and Engineering faculties had been suggested to a College deputation at a meeting within the previous month with President Cosgrave and the ministers for finance, education (now Professor J. M. O'Sullivan), and industry – indeed that the minister for finance 'spent an hour trying to convince us that we should abolish the Faculty of Medicine'. Directing his fire at de Blaghd, he queried why funding for Galway was, unlike Cork and Dublin, dependent on doing special new work and why he did not indicate that the conference recommendations were disappointing or say what he himself wanted. He also rebutted Mr Hogan's claim that the College had never sent him any detailed scheme of agricultural education. The atmosphere at the meeting is evident from the *Connacht Tribune* headlines in its account of 26 June 1926: 'The Crime against Connacht', 'Western Province's bid for equal rights', 'Government's neglect', 'Bishop of Galway's clarion call' and 'An all-Ireland question'.

A special meeting of the governing body on the following day kept up the pressure, 'protesting strongly against the derisive and insulting language used by the Minister for Finance about Galway College' and authorising the registrar to interview the editors of the local Connacht and Clare papers in the matter.

The controversy presumably hastened action on the government's part – the year before a general election – as a formal agreement was reached on 15 October 1926 between government and college in the following terms:

1   That because of its peculiar situation and opportunities, Galway College could render most useful service to the country by undertaking special work in connection with the Irish Language including the giving of University instruction through the medium of Irish and that the Governing Body should henceforth endeavour to have an increasing proportion of the work of the College done through Irish.

2   That the annual Government grant to the College should be increased from £20,800 to £28,000.

3   That the Government should give a special grant of £1,500 for the repayment of debt due by the College.

4   That the College should appoint three lecturers to lecture through the medium of Irish on Mathematics, History and Commerce, and that the people first appointed should be approved of by the Department of Education.

5   That the College will reduce its fees to approximately pre-War level as an inducement to students from the Irish-speaking districts, which are generally speaking poor districts, to prefer Galway College.

6   That the College, after consultation with the Department of Education, will establish a special scholarship for native Irish-speaking students from districts in any part of Ireland in which Irish is traditionally spoken; the cost of such scheme to be £1,000 per annum. The object of the scheme will be to increase the proportion of good Irish speakers amongst the students of the College.

7   The fees which at present go to professors will henceforth be used for the general purposes of the College.

8   That the salaries of the staff will be increased as follows . . .

9   In the case of future vacancies the Governing Body will make every effort to have them filled by appointment of professors and lecturers able to impart instruction through the medium of Irish.

10 The Governing Body will make no application for additional assistance from the State for a period of five years.

The appointment of the three lecturers was then set in train. While it had been agreed that the required approval of the Department of Education of appointees be limited to their capacity to lecture in Irish, and candidates were examined by a joint board for the purpose, the department requested readvertising of two of the posts to attract better qualified candidates. That was done, and, following further correspondence as to how the department's involvement could most appropriately be reconciled with the standard appointment procedures, the department eventually agreed not to object to the appointment of any of a list of named candidates who, in the college's judgement, possessed the necessary qualifications. The first appointments, made on 15 November 1927, were to the lectureship in history and to the lectureship in economics, commerce and accountancy; the lectureship in mathematics was filled on 6 October 1928.

The agreement was implemented on a non-statutory basis for some two years, at which stage a draft of the necessary bill was sent to the college for comment. The governing body on 26 March 1929 directed the secretary to inform the minister for finance 'that it is pleased with the Bill, and that it is prepared to fulfil the obligations imposed on it in the Bill'. When the bill came to be debated in Dáil Éireann in October 1929, the only real issue of controversy was the statutory formulation in Section 3, as follows, of the agreement regarding future recruitment:

It shall be the duty of the Senate of the National University of Ireland, the Governing Body of the College, or the President of the College (as the case may be), when making an appointment to any office or situation in the College, to appoint to such office or situation a person who is competent to discharge the duties thereof through the medium of the Irish language: provided a person so competent and also suitable in all other respects is to be found amongst the persons who are candidates or otherwise available for such appointment.

Fianna Fáil teachtaí dála, including Eamon de Valera (who happened, of course, to have been Chancellor of the NUI since 1921), pressed for the deletion of the latter proviso, on the grounds that, whereas it was most un-likely in practice that professionally unqualified candidates would be ap-pointed, there was every danger that the proviso would offer a loophole for disregarding the claims of Irish in the appointment. Minister de Blaghd, while accepting that point, referred to the new spirit in the college and ex-pressed confidence that the governing body, even those members who had no interest in Irish but who would realise that the interests of the college in terms of funding demanded it, would do the best it could for Irish. Curi-ously, in introducing that section, he also said:

> There are no penalties attached to any breach of that clause and it is recognised that it is in the nature of a headline for the College; it is something put there to enable anybody in the Governing Body or anybody interested in the College to argue that the right thing ought to be done by the appointment of Irish speakers.[9]

While this is not the place for a debate on its merits, the Section was to prove a source of controversy from time to time afterwards, with pressure on various occasions since the 1960s to repeal it, on the grounds of its per-ceived deterrent effect on candidatures and its occasional upsetting of the order of merit among candidates deemed suitable in all other respects for appointment; on that latter point, it might, however, be noted that a survey of academic appointments made over the period of 1977–99 shows that the proportion of appointments thus determined by it, contrary to the recom-mendations of the boards of assessors, was just under nine per cent. The real difficulty from the 1960s onwards was perhaps the increasing disjuncture between that blanket recruitment criterion and the operational programme offerings and requirements of the institution, reflecting a drop in student demand, in line with the decline of Irish generally in the school system. Nevertheless, the question remains whether, in the absence of that legislative requirement, Irish would, in practice, have featured at all in the college's general recruitment since the 1960s.

A notable consensus-building exercise was led by the then President, Dr Iognáid Ó Muircheartaigh, in recent years, towards resolving those difficulties while retaining the institution's strong strategic commitment to providing university education through Irish, in part through outreach centres in the

Gaeltacht (Ionaid Ghaeltachta) under an integrated Acadamh na hOllsco-laíochta Gaeilge structure. That process culminated in a unanimous request from Údarás na hOllscoile to the government in 2005 for an amendment of Section 3 of the 1929 Act, in the context of a comprehensive developmental strategy for the role of Irish. While the formulation of the amendment was not that ultimately accepted, the section was replaced in February 2006 by the following, under the University College Galway (Amendment) Act 2006:

> 3 (1) The governing authority of the College shall ensure that one of the principal aims for the operation and development of the College set out in each strategic development plan prepared after the commencement of this section is the provision of education at the College through the medium of the Irish language.
>
> (2) The governing authority and the President of the College shall each perform their respective functions and exercise their respective powers in respect of the College to ensure that the aim referred to in subsection (1) is implemented.

Returning to that 1929 Dáil debate, the more favourable government attitude to Galway evinced in the minister's comments was reflected in a new Section in the Bill, providing for a possible increase of up to £2,000 in the grant for new work to be undertaken through Irish or relating to Irish. The college's subsequent request, on foot of that, to spend that sum on filling seven new assistantships and other items was not exactly what de Blaghd had in mind, as he explained in a letter of 7 March 1930:

> If the Governing Body desires to create a post for any person of conspicuous merit whom they feel it would be undesirable to lose, or whose appointment will strengthen the College from the Irish point of view and tend to enhance its prestige, we shall be glad to receive proposals and to consider them no less favourably than the Cork proposal (*viz. enabling UCC to recruit an tOllamh T. F. Ó Raithile*) ... The Government is acutely aware of the excellent work that is being done in Galway. It is realised that the speedy Gaelicisation of Galway College is of the greatest importance. The College can therefore rely on any claims it may make for assistance necessary to develop its work being sympathetically considered ...

Following further correspondence on how such appointments, whose funding was contingent on advance government approval of the appointee, could fit with the standard freedom of choice of the appointing bodies, the government agreed that, if a better candidate than the intended appointee ultimately emerged, it would be reasonable in dealing with the situation. On that basis, it agreed in February 1931 to the college's proposal that lectureship appointments be offered to three further named persons (two in ancient classics and one in education); the statute establishing those posts was then made, the posts were advertised and the appointments made from 1 November 1931. When one of the ancient classics lectureships fell vacant in 1934, the government agreed to a proposal that it be not filled and that the funding be devoted instead to two new assistantships (physics and chemistry) for teaching through Irish.

At that point the college's future could be said to have been secured. Enrolment had already grown from 131 in 1908–9 to 260 in 1923–4, and the impact of the new Irish language development in 1926–7 was already clear, when 201 students were taking courses through Irish in six subjects other than Gaeilge, and in 1930–1, when the numbers attending lectures through Irish in mathematics, geography, commerce, accountancy, history, education, economics and mathematical physics came to 158, in addition to 340 in Gaeilge itself. In comparative terms, over the period 1921–32 the numbers presenting for NUI examinations grew from 236 to 697, compared with growth from 728 to 748 in UCC and from 1,455 to 2,203 in UCD; likewise, in terms of degrees awarded, UCG increased from 39 to 114 between 1922 and 1932, compared with an increase from 288 to 340 in UCD and a slight drop from 115 to 108 in UCC.[10]

That success – which, crucially, did not involve any diminution in the college's range of activities or faculties – had been achieved over the period through an innovative and energetic process of engagement with the region, insistent political pressure at the highest level as the new State found its feet, and the college's own remarkable capacity, under strong strategic leadership, for adapting itself to a new mission.

Relationship with the National University of Ireland

Given its own fragile situation in the early years, it is hardly surprising that the college had no time for the UCC proposal in 1918 and 1919 for the establishment of a University of Munster, a proposal which was pushed by President Bertram Windle of UCC, as Professor John A. Murphy recounts in chapter 4.

The proposal, which reached the draft bill stage in 1919 but was later dropped in the face of opposition, was regarded by the governing body of UCG on 6 May 1919 as not in the best interests of higher education, given that the NUI, with its complicated federal machinery, was only in its infancy, for example in that no university-funded posts had yet been founded, and that the multiplication of universities would result in the lowering of standards in all, as shown by the lower standards now required for their degrees by Queen's University, Belfast and the NUI than those of the Royal University (the example quoted being that Medicine and Engineering candidates were no longer required to have passed First Arts). Claiming that in any case, in terms of academic performance, UCG was no less worthy of university status than UCC, it went on:

> Each of its three Colleges was given a large measure of autonomy, so that each developing along its own lines, could supplement the work done by the other two, and that thus the three working together might form a strong teaching University fully abreast of the times in all departments of study. This was a sound policy, and it seems to us to be the duty of the Colleges to use every effort to carry it out . . . We feel strongly that the continual changing of the system of University education has an unsettling and hurtful effect, that the present time in the history of the country is not the time when such a change should be proposed, and that, in any case, a thorough enquiry into all the circumstances, and the educational interests involved, would be necessary.

Likewise, on 28 May 1925 it took no action on another UCC resolution:

> That we request the Government to institute an enquiry into the status, functions and interrelations of the three University Colleges, and the workings of the federal National University.

It would thus seem fair to say that Galway felt comfortable from the beginning with the NUI structure, particularly for the protection afforded it as the smallest member of the federation. The official Irish name of the college, adopted by the governing body on 29 November 1934 on the proposal of an tOllamh T. Ó Máille – 'An Coláiste Gaillimheach den Iolsgoil

Náisiúnta' – perhaps reflects that. The fact that the college's main battles were fought, as we have seen, directly with the government and without NUI involvement, even where the UCC and UCD situations were cited as evidence for the perceived invidious treatment of the college, presumably helped the operational cohesion of the NUI as a whole. Certainly there were various instances where, in the making of senior appointments (including the Presidency), the Senate went against the college's recommendations, even over the latter half of the period, but that would also have happened in the case of the other colleges from time to time and, furthermore, in a number of the Galway cases the governing body's recommendations ran counter to the views of its own academic council.

A rare intervention by the NUI into the internal affairs of the college occurred in 1960 in response to a proposal to limit the powers of the President. The particular context was the hostility which had arisen between the former President, Mgr Pádraig de Brún, and the then governing body in the final years of his presidency. In the wake of his retirement the governing body introduced a draft statute which would have significantly restricted the powers of the President in certain respects. On being sent a copy, the governing body was informed on 18 February 1960 that the Senate had passed a resolution, on a vote of 25 to 0: 'That the Senate ask the Governing Body of University College Galway to reconsider Draft-Statute XLVII in view of its non-conformity with the Statutes concerning the Presidents of the other Colleges'. As it happened, the academic council was also unhappy with the Draft-Statute and recommended significant amendments, and the governing body eventually agreed to amend it.

Apart from this incident, there do not seem to have been any real tensions in the college–university relationship. No doubt also such practical steps as the establishment of appointments bureaux, subsidised by the NUI, in each college to help graduates find employment, and the grant made by the Senate to each college in 1936, through the foundation of a National University Union in the interests of students and graduates, helped. Galway's share of that was £8,200, which was expended on amenities such as a club premises, the boat club, sports fields and pavilion, tennis courts and ladies' clubrooms.

In more recent decades the NUI structure has also been able to accommodate various fruitful relationships with other third-level institutions.

The first of those linkages involving Galway was the grant of recognised college status in 1978 to St Angela's College, Sligo. Originally a home economics teacher-training institution, it has undergone major development, far beyond its original remit and involving a wide range of programmes in education, nursing, food, adult education and other areas. Galway had helped that development by offering part-time BA programmes there and, since 1998, a full-time BA (Economic and Social Studies) programme, the first two years of which are taken in the college. In 2000, the college approached NUI Galway with a view to developing a more strategic linkage to assist its long-term development, while ensuring an appropriate degree of autonomy for it and preserving its independent legal status and its traditional ethos. In 2001 a draft agreement, whereby St Angela's College would become a college of NUI Galway, was prepared following consultation with the Department of Education and Science. Following prolonged discussion with the NUI, including legal advice to the effect that the proposal was consistent with the Universities Act, the agreement eventually took effect on 1 January 2006, whereupon St Angela's ceased to be a recognised college of the NUI. This is the first occasion on which an independent educational institution has become a college of a constituent university of the NUI.

Three other institutional linkages were subsequently established within the NUI structure. In 1979, a Bachelor of Technology programme in manufacturing technology was introduced in association with Galway Regional Technical College (now Galway–Mayo Institute of Technology); that arrangement was discontinued with effect from 1986.

In 1991, following an approach by Shannon College of Hotel Management, a Bachelor of Commerce programme was commenced for that college's students; the first two years were delivered at Shannon under NUI Galway supervision and the third year was taken in Galway. With Galway's encouragement, Shannon College applied for recognised college status to the NUI in 2000 and became a recognised college in 2001. More recently, in the context of the dissolution of Aer Rianta, an application by the College, which is now owned by the Dublin Airport Authority, for incorporation into NUI Galway under Section 8 of the Universities Act is now under consideration by the HEA. The third linkage, developed following an approach by that college in 2000, is with Burren College of Art. It involves the joint offering of a two-year postgraduate programme leading to the award by NUI Galway of a Master of Fine Arts degree; a PhD programme is also now being introduced.

Towards University Status

The attitude of the college towards the NUI structure was thus still positive in the early 1960s. The college's submission to the Commission on Higher Education in March 1962 said that 'We feel that the best interests of the College would be served by keeping the federal link, suitably modified where experience has shown that it restricts initiative or impedes progress.' The reasons cited were the desirability of closer co-operation between the colleges in the interests of efficiency and equality of standards, the prestige and professional recognition abroad of the NUI and its degrees, the removal of suspicion of local pressure by having academic appointments made by a federal senate, and the greater prospect of endowment from industry for a national institution.

With the publication, however, of the commission's report in 1967, the ice began to shift. The recommendation for full university status for Galway, adopted by the minister for education in 1968, meant that the framework thenceforward for discourse and internal planning was the prospect of separate university status. Shortly thereafter, the Higher Education Authority (HEA) was set up on an ad hoc basis and assigned an advisory role in relation to preparation of the necessary legislation. In response to its request in 1968, the College submitted its views on the main legislative issues in June 1969. Thereafter its main concerns were the practical ones of provision of the physical accommodation for the major enrolment increase already being experienced.

Against that background of expectation and decision, the 1974 government decision announced by the Minister for Education (Richard Burke), that UCD be given university status and that UCG and UCC be, in effect, relegated to the status of a rump NUI, consequently met with predictable outrage. In the words of the College's immediate press release, 'having tidied to his satisfaction the Dublin Room of the academic house, he has swept what he seems to regard as the academic dust of the Provincial Room under a carpet woven to the design and fashion of 70 years ago'. UCG and UCC agreed to work together against the proposal. In a subsequent trenchant dissection of the proposal, the College argued that 'freed from a federal structure which is cumbrous by nature, UCG would be in a position to assume the institutional maturity and responsibility denied it within a structure where the ultimate power of decision rests elsewhere'. When challenged as to its 1962 support for the federal structure, it pointed out that the federal structure now proposed was quite different, with the removal of UCD therefrom, and that it itself had grown enormously since then as an institution.

In the face of the concerted opposition, the government's position began to soften. On 23 July 1975, a college deputation met the minister and his officials for a full discussion of the detailed response submitted by the college. The standing committee of the college was told on 30 July 1975 that the deputation was

> given the impression that, whereas the Minister for Education made it clear that his views were not necessarily those of the government, he was much more receptive to the case for independent status for Galway than had previously been the case. He was much preoccupied with the status of Limerick NIHE and with how the university colleges could help to solve the NIHE problem.

Standing committee agreed to send to the Director of NIHE, Limerick a copy of the College's submission to the minister, together with a covering letter suggesting that it might be useful to have a discussion on matters of common interest. In response to the problem of conferral of degrees on the students who were due to complete their studies in 1976, NIHE Limerick duly, if unwillingly, became a recognised college of the NUI, under UCC supervision. When it was agreed in July 1976 that responsibility for NUI business relating to NIHE be transferred to UCG for classes subsequent to 1975–6 (UCC now looking after Mary Immaculate Training College), the president was able to report that a cordial meeting had already been held between senior officers of the two institutions. That formal and cordial relationship lasted until the transfer to the NCEA of degree-awarding powers in respect of NIHE Limerick in December 1977.

The government on 31 July 1976 finally announced that it had decided to give university status also to UCC, UCG and St Patrick's College, Maynooth, and it set up an advisory committee to assist the minister in drafting legislation. The college forwarded its views in October 1976 on the desired form of legislation and governance structures for the University of Galway. A number of fora and co-operation mechanisms, which were to prove increasingly influential, were now arriving on the scene, such as the Conference of Heads of Irish Universities (CHIU) – now the Irish Universities Association – and the Central Applications Office. One of those, with a less rosy future, was the ad hoc Conference of Irish Universities in 1974, consequent on the HEA report on university reorganisation. Understandably, perhaps, with the prospect of imminent emergence from the confines of the NUI structure, the college's attitude to such a conference was somewhat cautious. Its view in 1973 was that

> cooperation between independent institutions should not be approached through the imposition on the Universities of an apparatus with extensive powers. Rather cooperation should be considered from the standpoint of functions which independent institutions would choose to delegate to a Conference representative of themselves. The Conference should be a creation of the Universities, not imposed on them.

Again in 1975, in considering the proposed memorandum and articles of association of the conference, it reaffirmed 'that it can serve its purpose best as an autonomous University cooperating with other Universities and third-level institutions on a voluntary basis' and that the conference was merely 'one of the means by which cooperation might be enhanced'. While in 1975 the ad hoc conference had weighed in usefully in favour of university status for UCC and UCG, again in 1979, when the question of establishing the conference on a permanent basis was raised, the college's attitude remained lukewarm in regard to what the conference could usefully contribute, other than as a discussion forum; this reflected a wish to ensure that it retained the right to shape its own future as an autonomous university.

The ultimate introduction of the long-promised legislation to provide for university status for the college was initiated through the issuing by the Minister for Education, Niamh Bhreathnach, of a confidential position paper on 17 July 1995 to the presidents and provost in their personal capacity. The immediate reaction of the President, Dr Colm Ó hEocha, was one of 'dismay', terming the extent of the proposed involvement of the minister in the internal affairs of the new universities as 'profoundly disturbing'.[11]

That set the tone for the college's subsequent responses at various stages to the quite inadequate amendments proposed by the minister. The college, while welcoming such provisions as the grant of University status and the expansion in the representativeness of membership of the governing body and academic council, drew a pointed contrast between the proposed Bill, in its animating ethos of control, and the statement of the then Minister for Education, Dr Patrick J. Hillery, in his inaugural address to the Commission on Higher Education in 1960, referring to the 'ancient right to autonomy' of the universities, that 'it is right and proper that they should continue to retain it, for a large freedom is of the essence of the university'. Of all the university institutions, Galway remained the most consistently opposed to the bill, notwithstanding pressures from the newer universities and elsewhere for passage of the legislation in the then favourable Seanad voting situation: for example, the President, Dr Patrick Fottrell, reflecting the views of the governing body, refused to participate in a CHIU statement of support in December 1996 for the bill, as proposed at that stage to be amended.

In the immediate aftermath of the passing of the act, the college debated the possibilities for extension of its title in the manner allowed by Section 10 (3). It favoured 'The University of Galway/Ollscoil na Gaillimhe' as a working title, with the official name at the foot of the page. When it emerged, however, that there might be legal difficulties with that, it decided (30 January 1998) to adhere to the legal title as the operational title. A later suggestion that an extension of title similar to that obtained by UCC and UCD be sought was not pursued.

As to the impact of the Act on the relationship between the NUI and the constituent universities, a number of jurisdictional and operational issues are currently being explored by an NUI Senate subcommittee, with the aid of legal advice. It would appear that the predominant disposition of the Senate, in respect to academic matters, is to facilitate the wishes of the individual constituent university. How it can best continue to do that, while yet generating a broader debate and consensus within the NUI on substantial issues of academic principle (such as matriculation), through appropriate consultation with academic councils as in the past, represents a major challenge.

CHAPTER 6 *University College Dublin* DONAL MCCARTNEY

T HE IRISH UNIVERSITIES BILL of 1908 was, in the words of Tim Healy,
'nobody's ideal'.[1] The aim of its promoters, however, was to present a
scheme which would be acceptable to the majority while avoiding the out-
right and bitter opposition that all previous proposals over more than half
a century had aroused. After widespread consultation and negotiation,
Chief Secretary Augustine Birrell skilfully steered his bill through Parliament. By pursuing the line of least resistance he won the necessary acquiescence – however reluctantly offered and whatever the misgivings of his
supporters. Birrell, indeed, was the first to acknowledge that his measure
was not ideal but the one most readily achievable or least likely to give rise
to fatal opposition. It was on these grounds that he ruled out the scheme for
a national university of five federal colleges – Trinity, the Queen's colleges of
Belfast, Cork, Galway, and a new one in Dublin incorporating what remained
of the Catholic University. On the same grounds he also ruled out a federation of four colleges (with Trinity remaining separate and independent).
This logic left him with his scheme for a federal university of three colleges.
The Irish Universities Act (1908), therefore, excluded entirely from the scheme
Dublin University with its single component, Trinity College; and created
two new universities – Queen's College Belfast was raised to the status of a
university, while Cork, Galway and Dublin were incorporated as the three
constituent colleges of the National University of Ireland.

The Dublin college had inherited the largest medical school in the country,
along with the successful Jesuit-managed University College on St Stephen's
Green, and had the potential to become within a short period Ireland's largest
university institution. Why then was UCD not established as a separate and
independent university? After all, it had become the trend to establish independent civic universities in the great cities of England, or where federation
existed to de-federalise. Manchester, Liverpool and Leeds formerly constitu-
ents of Victoria University had recently achieved independent university

status. And Cork had been campaigning for some years for its own 'University of Munster'. But as one of the campaigners, William O'Brien MP for Cork city, said during the debate on the Universities Bill:

> It was one of the little ironies of the government of Ireland that Belfast should get a university it did not seek, while the university which Cork most earnestly asked [for] had been refused.[2]

Birrell readily acknowledged that there were weaknesses in the federal system. But the explanation he gave for his proposed federal university in Ireland was:

> Some federation is unfortunately necessary. Cork college I hope has a great future before it. I do not believe she is at the present time strong enough nor are the classes sufficiently well attended to establish Cork with a university of her own. Galway . . . is in a weaker position than Cork. Therefore some federation of these outlying colleges is absolutely necessary.[3]

This could sound as if Dublin's role in the federation was to bolster up a weak Cork and Galway. And later in the debate the Chief Secretary would repeat his explanation for associating Cork and Galway in a federal arrangement:

> I wish to heaven Cork and Galway were strong enough to support universities of their own. If they had been it would have made my task . . . much easier.[4]

The implication was that he expected the federal NUI to be no more than a temporary arrangement. And William O'Brien spoke for President Windle and others in Cork when he said in parliament that he accepted the 1908 Bill as a 'provisional arrangement' which in time would lead to an independent university as had happened in the case of constituent colleges in the north of England.[5]

Curiously, no serious discussion or deliberation was given in parliament to the question of whether UCD merited independent university status. Nor indeed can it be said that there was any significant campaign in Dublin itself for such a solution to the university question. It had long become clear that government funding or recognition would not be forthcoming for a denominational Catholic university. And following the University Education (Ireland) Act of 1879, which allowed for the establishment of the Royal University, what remained of the Catholic University had been linked with the Queen's colleges in a loose association for the purposes of curriculum, examinations and degree awards. To be able to take up the benefits of the Royal University, the bishops modified the constitution of the Catholic University to establish its own federation of Catholic colleges. The idea of federation, therefore, was nothing new for University College Dublin. Indeed every solution brought forward in the decades between 1879 and 1908 had involved University College in a federation of one kind or another – whether in an extended Dublin University scheme or of the Royal University.

Although UCD was linked with Cork and Galway in a sisterhood of constituent colleges there were many indications that Dublin was to be considered the senior sister. Professor Butcher (MP for Cambridge University) had served on the two government commissions dealing with university education in Ireland. Giving his strong and influential support to the 1908 bill, he acknowledged that a federal university was 'a delicate piece of mechanism', and to work harmoniously the representation on the governing body would have to be a fair one, in particular a just balance should be maintained between the claims of Dublin and Cork, while at the same time there must be the largest measure of college autonomy that was consistent with federation. Then he added:

> The college in Dublin would, of course, be the metropolitan college of the University, and it ought to be national and not provincial, large, well endowed and on a scale sufficient to strike the imagination.[6]

This distinction between a 'national' Dublin and a 'provincial' Cork and Galway was reflected in the governing bodies incorporated in the charters. The Senate of the university would include six persons elected by the academic council of UCD and four each elected by the academic councils of Cork and Galway; and while the individual county councils in Munster and Connacht elected one member each to the governing bodies of Cork and Galway, the local authority representatives on UCD's governing body were to be elected from a national panel – the General Council of County Councils.

The federal connection with the provincial colleges, rather than inhibiting Dublin's style, actually nourished its opinion of itself as a national institution. The colleges were only in their first year of operating under the NUI when President Windle of Cork complained to NUI's registrar: 'Can you not do something privately with newspapers to stop them calling the Dublin University College "the National University" …?'[7] However, 'National' as a synonym for UCD survived, at least down to the early 1950s, and not only in the sports pages of the newspapers. (In April 1951 an irritated President O'Rahilly of UCC wrote to President Tierney of UCD insisting that UCC and UCG 'are equally part of the National University of Ireland with University College Dublin in spite of the current misnomer for University College Dublin, namely the "National"'.).[8] So while UCC, especially under Windle down to 1919, remained uneasy in the federation, UCD under President Denis Coffey (1908–40) seemed to thrive and glory in the relationship. That was because history, as it was then unfolding, was on the side of UCD.

When the NUI experiment began, the University College and the Catholic University Medical School (which became the medical faculty in UCD) had been in their origins and ethos unashamedly Catholic. The former Queen's colleges by contrast were legally undenominational; and between 1845 and 1908 they had been frowned upon by the bishops. By the same token, the Dublin College was also much more 'nationalist' in both its political and cultural outlook. Presidential and professorial appointments in Cork and Galway down to 1908 had been in the gift of the British government with the result that a number of academics were British and/or unionist. In the early years of the NUI, therefore, and as the country was entering a more extremely nationalist and revolutionary period, differences, especially in political emphasis, provided plenty of potential for friction. And evidence of this friction flared up immediately in a row over the question of 'essential Irish' in the University.

'We take it for granted that from the outset Irish would be a compulsory subject at the Matriculation Examination.'[9] So wrote P. H. Pearse editor of *An Claidheamh Soluis* (official organ of the Gaelic League), as soon as it had been announced that the government intended to introduce legislation to extend and improve university education in Ireland. And for months before the Senate of the new university held its first meeting (17 December 1908), the Gaelic League, then at the height of its power, was organising a campaign throughout the country in favour of compulsory Irish in the National University. Spearheading that agitation were Douglas Hyde and Eoin MacNeill (president and vice-president respectively of the Gaelic League). Both were senators of the NUI as well as professors in UCD. Their colleagues in UCD and fellow senators – President Coffey and Mary Hayden – were also members of the Gaelic League and advocates of 'essential Irish'. UCD's Academic Council recommended to the Senate the adoption of Hyde's proposal for compulsory Irish. Cork's Academic Council voted overwhelmingly in favour of an open matriculation without any compulsory subjects.[10] By a vote of 21 to 12 the Senate accepted compulsory Irish. A 'nationalist' UCD had imposed its will on the NUI in the face of some bitter opposition from Cork and Galway. If Cork needed confirmation or warning of the constraints placed upon it through federation with Dublin, surely it was to be found in this co-ordinated campaign led by the UCD senators.

Cork's President Windle had reluctantly accepted the 1908 arrangement in the hope that it would not prevent his College from evolving into the University of Munster. The NUI had hardly commenced its work, however, when he began expressing severe disheartenment. 'At times I am disposed to despair of ever making the institution work', he wrote as early as 19 January 1910. Down to his retirement in 1919, Windle's correspondence with Joseph McGrath, the Registrar of the NUI, might be described as one long jeremiad lamenting federation with Dublin. He remained constantly anxious 'to dispel the idea that the University is a Dublin institution and nothing else', 'a mere trifling appendage' to UCD.[11] But he came to regard the battle as hopeless; and expressed his utter frustration with what he perceived to be UCD's absolute dominance on the Senate. 'To collar everything that can be collared and reduce us to the position of privates' was the policy of that 'terrible Dublin majority'. 'To be yoked unequally in universities as in wedlock is a terrible thing', he said, and asserted that if the dominant Dublin majority decreed it, then they would have to meet 'in the sewage station in Ringsend'. He regularly referred to their position in Cork as unfortunate '*uitlanders*'. Dublin's behaviour, he said, had alienated the southerners from the NUI; bred bitterness not easily to be allayed; and 'it certainly and finally destroys the "national" university. Poor babe – it was a weakling from birth!' It was that 'accursed institution whose speedy destruction forms the object of my sincerest prayers'. 'I wish I could shake Cork free from the whole thing.'[12]

The contrast in attitude to the NUI between Windle and President Coffey of UCD could hardly have been more striking. The more Windle whined and showed his desire to kick over the traces of federalism, the more did Coffey seem determined to make the most of the advantages that had been conferred on UCD by the 1908 settlement. And if Windle was even only half right about Dublin's dominance in the Senate, UCD was hardly likely to deplore the situation. Coffey's relationship with the NUI, therefore, was much more relaxed and amiable. He was the National University's devoted and loyal servant, dedicated to making it work. For him UCD's success coincided with the success of the NUI. On the occasion of Coffey's retirement in 1940 after 32 years on the Senate, the Chancellor, Eamon de Valera, recalled that whenever some difficulty relating to the NUI arose he generally told the Registrar to phone Dr Coffey and get his opinion, and he found that Coffey with his vast experience would almost immediately advise on what would get over the difficulty.[13] 'I love every stone of the buildings we have made' was Coffey's response to the Chancellor's address.[14] It was no more than a sincere declaration of pride in the role he had played in the early guidance of the NUI.

Not surprisingly, therefore, when in 1918–19 Windle launched a final, desperate effort to cut Cork free, he found that apart from virulent internal hostility led by Alfred O'Rahilly, Coffey and UCD were among his most resolute opponents. He was told that Coffey was 'bitterly – savagely opposed' to the plan.[15] A draft Irish Universities Bill (1919) giving Cork independence of the NUI was forwarded from Dublin Castle to the Senate on 27 February 1919. What was perceived as an attempt to have it precipitately approved was frustrated by successful delaying tactics. UCD Professor John McClelland proposed that a committee be established with powers to obtain the opinions of the colleges and Convocation and that in the meantime the registrar write to the government expressing the hope that nothing further be done until the Senate had time to consider the matter.[16] Independence for Cork, as President Anderson of Galway pointed out, would completely alter the organisation of the NUI. McClelland's line of approach therefore had the support of Galway as well as UCD senators.

In May this committee reported that the Senate should inform the Government that since the Draft Bill raised the whole question of university education in Ireland it required the most serious consideration on the part of the University and that a reply could not be made until the fullest consideration had been given to the subject.[17] Later in May when the committee's report was before the Senate, Agnes O'Farrelly (UCD) proposed, Professor Pye (UCG) seconded and the Senate unanimously passed the following resolution:

> That the Senate of the National University of Ireland deprecates the hasty introduction of legislation that will destroy the constitution of a university

the foundation of which was accepted a few years ago as a settlement of the university question, and it claims that sufficient time be given to set forth its reasoned opinion on the subject.[18]

Opposition to the plan intensified. Supporters of Sinn Féin, flushed with victory in the recent general election and the establishment of Dáil Éireann, voiced strong opposition to the idea that Dublin Castle and the British parliament should be asked to legislate on Irish university matters. An item on the agenda for the June 1919 meeting of UCD's governing body appeared under the heading 'The proposed University for Cork'. The minutes of that meeting read:

> The following resolution was proposed by Mr Ennis, seconded by Miss O'Farrelly, and passed unanimously:[19]
>
> The Governing Body are unanimously opposed to the break up of the National University of Ireland as involved in the proposals contained in the Draft Bill submitted to the Senate, and, if necessary will forward a reasoned statement for their opposition.'[20]

UCD's governing body could hardly be said to be under the control of Sinn Féin. For among the 20 persons reported as being present when the resolution was passed 'unanimously' were John Dillon who recently had lost his seat in parliament to the Sinn Féin President de Valera, and Arthur Conway, registrar of UCD, who as an Irish Party candidate had been defeated by Sinn Féin's Eoin MacNeill. Coffey, who chaired the meeting, was a well-known supporter of the Irish Party, as were the two bishops O'Donnell of Raphoe and Foley of Kildare and Leighlin who were also present. The 'reasoned statement for their opposition' was not required because earlier that same month Windle had been informed that the Draft Bill was being withdrawn on account of the opposition it had encountered.

Coffey's successor, Arthur Conway (1940–7), who had served as registrar of UCD throughout Coffey's presidency, had no reason, especially during the war years and his own short term in the presidency, to change from Coffey's policy of dedication to the NUI. It was a case of steady as she goes. But things were to change dramatically under Conway's successor – the more aggressively motivated Michael Tierney (1947–64). Even before he became president, Tierney had written about 'the unsatisfactory nature of the whole National

University system'. In its present form, he said, it would 'never have been created by any authority responsible only to the Irish people'. UCD in particular 'may fairly be said to have now outgrown, even on grounds of mere size', the federal system.[21] The irony is that Tierney, who had ended up a very poor third at the Governing Body stage of the UCD presidential election process, owed his eventual victory to the Senate, a body which ever afterwards he wanted to abolish. And no one was to put the case for an autonomous UCD more persistently or more forcibly than Tierney.

Within a few years of taking up office, Tierney was largely responsible for establishing a committee consisting of the presidents of the NUI colleges and representatives of the bishops for the purposes of discussing matters of mutual concern. At the first meeting of this liaison committee on 17 January 1951, Tierney submitted a memorandum on the university question in which he proposed the break-up of the NUI whose colleges were to become independent and 'frankly Catholic' universities.[22] Alfred O'Rahilly, President of UCC, rejected the idea on the grounds that the 1908 settlement was a much more favourable scheme than could be obtained from the current Irish government. He held that if the 1908 charters were abandoned and the Dáil given the chance to present an amending Act 'anti-clericals, friends of Trinity College, so-called liberals etc.' would become vociferous, and an attempt would be made to impose 'neutrality' in matters religious on the colleges.[23] Bishops and academics should hold firmly to 1908 as a final settlement of Catholic claims, and make the NUI Catholic by utilising the powers given under the 1908 Act and charters to extend to all its colleges such areas as philosophy, sociology, apologetics and theology.

Tierney acknowledged that the prospects of getting much further with his proposal did not seem good; so he concentrated his efforts instead on making the case for UCD's independence.[24] 'Status of UCD should be raised' was the caption over a newspaper report of remarks he had made at a public meeting in the College. He was reported as saying that 'he wondered whether the time had come for their College to take its full status as a university, whether the system they were given by the Act of 1908 had not within the past forty years outgrown its purposes'.[25] This newspaper report gave rise to a temporary but bitter private row in correspondence between the presidents of Cork and Dublin when O'Rahilly accused Tierney of having launched a public campaign to obtain independence for UCD.

[94]

In a second memorandum to the bishops' liaison committee, Tierney argued that what might seem a comfortable position from Cork took on a very different aspect from Dublin. UCD, he said, had grown enormously: it was larger than most British universities, and had at least one thousand students more than Trinity. The salient feature for UCD was the increasing competition with Trinity. Whereas Trinity was governed entirely by its own academic body which could meet frequently and act with decision, UCD was hampered by its federal nature and the rigidity of its charter. He summed up the differences by claiming that Trinity was a college masquerading as a university, UCD was a university masquerading as a college.

In 1954 Tierney organised impressive celebrations to mark the centenary of the opening of the Catholic University from which, he proudly asserted, 'University College derives by an unbroken line', with Newman as 'our first rector and founder'.[26] And he stressed that the origins of UCD were very different and quite distinct from the origins of the Queen's colleges established by Sir Robert Peel, thus distancing UCD from its NUI sisters.

An article in the *University Review* by two Cork historians, Denis Gwynn and James Hogan, was highly critical of Tierney's claims and policies. The projected move to Belfield, they wrote, could have very harmful implications for Cork and Galway; and UCD raised to the status of an independent university with all the 'advantages of metropolitan position and prestige, could hardly fail to result in a proportionate decline and impoverishment for the provincial universities'. They declared their strong opposition to any dissolution of the NUI, which they noted Tierney had described as 'eventually inevitable', and which they said was warning enough of Tierney's intentions. They added that 'the dissolution of the National University as a federal body carries a real danger to the well-being, even the existence, of the provincial university colleges'.[27]

Tierney was hurt by the realisation that two former allies and friends were seen to have joined the anti-Belfield camp, then gathering strength both within and without UCD. The *University Review*, in which the Cork historians had published their criticism, was the official organ of the recently founded Graduates' Association of the NUI, the first objective of which was 'to foster a corporate spirit among the graduates of the University'. This could be viewed as a defence against Tierney's advocacy of the break-up of the NUI. And here, in only the second issue of the journal, was the Gwynn–Hogan broadside. It was Tierney's conviction that if the Graduates' Association was not founded directly to oppose his policies, it had been hijacked from the start by his arch-critics within UCD, and used to involve elements in UCC and UCG as a weapon against him. The controversy was further inflamed when a lecture by Gwynn on Sunday 28 November 1954 was reported in the *Irish Independent* under the heading 'UCD Building Plans Opposed'.

In his lecture, Gwynn repeated, if anything in more direct language, Cork's apprehension at UCD's 'vast building programme', involving a demand for financial outlay 'which must reduce the amount available for the other colleges'. This led to a spate of letters in the *Irish Independent* and *Irish Times* over the first fortnight of December 1954, giving the impression of a bitter wrangle between academics and between the colleges and which was joined by other members of the public. It was the start of a prolonged and intense campaign that the authorities in UCD did not need, especially since the government had yet to give its approval to the Belfield project.

More immediate for Dr Tierney than the transformation of the NUI colleges into formal Catholic universities was independent university status for his own college. And more pressing than independent university status for UCD was the need to find a solution for the College's critical accommodation problem. Belfield was his absolute priority. And he regarded the Graduates' Association as propelling the opposition to his plan. Adding insult to his sense of injury was the fact that the Graduates' Association was in receipt of a grant from the NUI. So, at the meeting of the Senate in December 1954, Tierney proposed and Jeremiah Hogan, the registrar of UCD, seconded the motion 'that an annual grant to the Graduates' Association of the NUI be discontinued'. James Hogan, joint author of the offending article, speaking against the motion 'made a couple of quite disgusting speeches, feminine and malicious and shot through with an inferiority' – 'making the original offence worse by its defence', according to another senator, James Meenan.[28] Tierney 'made quite a number of speeches and interrupted very often and got increasingly implacable as time went on'.[29] The presidents of UCC and UCG unsuccessfully proposed a compromise, as did two leading members of the Graduates' Association, E. J. Conway and Roger McHugh. Tierney's motion was carried by twelve votes to eleven with apparently five abstentions. When the standing committee of the Senate met in January 1955 it sponsored a compromise: the Graduates' Association would receive a grant of £500 and nothing for the future. This was accepted by the Senate. But the issue had given rise to one of the bitterest rows ever experienced in the Senate. It destroyed such harmony as had previously existed; resulted in serious tension within the University and between the colleges; and confirmed Tierney in his view that the NUI had become much more of a hindrance than a help to UCD's development.

Not surprisingly, therefore, the evidence which Tierney submitted to the Commission on Higher Education (1960–7) reflected the annoyance he had felt that the Graduates' Association, Convocation and the Senate itself had been used in a strenuous attempt to frustrate the building plans at Belfield. He argued forcibly that UCD, with numbers equal to Trinity, UCC and UCG together, should have its involvement with the NUI discontinued; that the cumbersome constitution, the duplication of administrative work, and the complicated system of appointments only made for friction between the colleges. The case he presented had considerable influence on the Commission, for its report rejected the argument presented by UCC, UCG and the Academic Staff Association of UCD for the retention of federation, and recommended instead that the NUI be dissolved and its three constituent colleges be established as separate universities.

However, before the colleges had time to consider the report, the Minister for Education, Donogh O'Malley, announced that the Government had decided that there would be one university in Dublin with two colleges, UCD and Trinity – a solution rejected by the Commission partly on the grounds that federation had not worked for UCD. The Government's decision initiated a seven-year wrangle about the 'merger' resulting in numerous proposals, plans, meetings, negotiations and endless argument, over the location of faculties and departments. At a particularly gloomy moment for UCD when it appeared that medicine, law, veterinary medicine, pharmacy and physiotherapy were to be allocated to Trinity, Jeremiah Hogan, who had succeeded Tierney as president of UCD in 1964, turned to the Senate of the NUI for assistance. Remarkably, the NUI itself which would be affected by the 'merger' had not been consulted at all up to this point. The Senate decided that 'it should have the right to have its views fully considered by the Government', and requested a meeting between its representatives and the Government.[30] The President of UCD expressed his full appreciation for 'the extremely loyal help' that had been given by the presidents and professors of UCC and

UCG on this deputation.[31] This was one of those occasions when the link with the NUI was seen to be of significant advantage to UCD. It was followed up by what was called the NUI–Trinity agreement (1970) which in essence proposed four independent universities – Cork, Galway and two in Dublin, all cooperating with each other.

After seven years of hectic consideration, the merger proposals fizzled out with the NUI still intact and precious little rationalisation between the two Dublin colleges. The whole experience had left academics strongly suspicious of any government interference with the university colleges and strengthened the hand of those who wanted to retain the NUI. Nothing came of government plans in 1974 and 1976 to revert to the idea of making UCD one of three or four universities, although preparations for such an eventuality, with as little legislative change to the 1908 Act and Charter as possible, were discussed in the college.

 The argument between federalists and independents continued intermittently in UCD over the next twenty years. While the Irish Federation of University Teachers (IFUT) urged the dissolution of the NUI and the establishment of four university institutions (the three constituent colleges and Maynooth), the governing bodies and academic councils of the constituent colleges voted in favour of the retention of the NUI. In the 1980s it appeared as if the federalists dominated UCD's governing body and academic council; and the affable Tom Murphy, president of UCD (1972–85), had an easy relationship with colleagues in Cork and Galway. However, when Dublin City University was created in 1989, the pendulum swung again in favour of the 'independents', since the largest university institution in the city was a mere college and DCU and Trinity were full-blown universities. A working party of the governing body concluded that the best option for UCD was to request the government to extend independent university status to UCD, Cork, Galway and Maynooth within a confederate National University of Ireland.[32] Patrick Masterson, President of UCD (1986–93), raised the question of the future status of UCD at the Senate. Discussion documents, drawn up with experienced adroitness by Chancellor T. K. Whitaker, were submitted to the Senate and the relevant bodies in the colleges, and eventually became the basis of the 1997 Irish Universities Act.

This legislative measure provided a scheme for the NUI that was essentially a compromise between the federalists and the advocates of independent university status for the colleges. Major powers and functions vested in the Senate under the 1908 settlement were transferred to the governing authorities in the new universities. In summary, the 1997 act conferred on UCD virtually as much independence as Michael Tierney had so consistently demanded, while at the same time retaining the federal link with 'National' that the first president, Denis Coffey, had so staunchly defended.

CHAPTER 7 *National University of Ireland, Maynooth*

SÉAMUS SMYTH

> I can assure you though I cannot make you believe it, that nothing can be considered as satisfactory by me which does not work for the good of the National University as a whole, of which Maynooth I hope always be *magna pars*.
>
> Augustine Birrell to President of Maynooth[1]

NOWHERE IN THE WORDING of the Irish Universities Act of 1908, in the charter of the National University nor in its supplemental and amending charter is there explicit mention of Maynooth. Yet no other institution, place or issue generated as much controversy in the associated parliamentary debates as that of the Catholic seminary located in a small landlord village some twenty miles to the west of Dublin. Opponents and supporters of the legislation, both within Parliament and beyond it, were acutely aware, however, that the legislative provisions for Maynooth had the capacity to make or break the educational experiment that was embodied by the legislation. Through his construction of the framework of the Irish Universities Act of 1908 the Chief Secretary for Ireland, Augustine Birrell, sought to bring closure to the divisive and politico-religious charged complexity that had stifled developments in university education for more than half a century. The Irish university question had never been a purely educational matter. National identity, religion, and power, both ecclesiastical and secular in nature, all infused it.[2] He succeeded by establishing an undenominational university in which religious tests for professors were prohibited and while the teaching of theology was permitted it was excluded from degree awards. University degrees would be conferred, however, on seminarians residing and taught in their own private college by staff who were appointed not by the university but by episcopal trustees. It was an Irish solution to an Irish problem and the Westminster Parliament endorsed it overwhelmingly. For almost a century it endured without alteration.

The mechanism that facilitated the insertion of Maynooth into the new undenominational university was that of affiliated or recognised college. By means of this device the Catholic seminary of St Patrick's College, Maynooth and the Presbyterian training college of Magee in Derry would be entitled to take their place within the National University of Ireland and The Queen's University, Belfast respectively. Magee College opted not to avail itself of the facility, but Maynooth did and there was born a relationship that was to endure until the passage of the 1997 Universities Act. In the intervening decades, and especially from the 1960s, Ireland experienced a radical alteration in the relationship of Church and State, in the nature and demands of higher education and, more latterly, in the perceived role of universities in national economic development. Not unexpectedly, the fitness for purpose of the original codified institutional relationship linking the National University of Ireland and Maynooth became demonstrably deficient and change became a necessity, no longer simply a preferred option.

When Birrell decided to champion the cause of university legislation he faced few challenges to his proposals for the existing institutions in Belfast, Cork, Dublin and Galway. It was assumed that Belfast would emerge naturally as a Presbyterian institution, thereby complementing the largely Anglican ethos of Trinity College. Regional demographic realities would likewise be conducive to the emergence of predominantly Catholic colleges in Cork, Galway and Dublin, and in the mind of the Nonconformist Birrell these desired and predictable outcomes could be achieved best, and a parliamentary majority assured, if the new institutions were undenominational in law but supported by a governance structure capable of responding to local and regional identities. The risk in such an approach lay in the balancing of the demands of the bishops for a Catholic ethos in university education and their wish for the inclusion of Maynooth, with the reality that any preferential treatment of the episcopal view would inevitably result in defeat in parliament. In the context of the time Maynooth was an institution of major importance and its significance resonated throughout the emerging sense of a new Irish identity. Established in 1795 by an act of the Irish Parliament as a college for the education of Catholic priests, the Maynooth seminary had long been the focus of political controversy. Parliamentary debates at Westminster occasioned by the annual vote on recurrent funding had long served as opportunities for anti-Catholic outcry and only when Peel in 1845 placed the funding on an automatic budget line did the Maynooth question become less of a regular controversy. The College remained in political and popular minds as the intellectual and administrative hearth of Catholic power that transcended matters of a purely theological nature and delved deeply into the secular realm. Ultimately, any debate over affiliation of the College would be a debate over the nature and exercise of power in a rapidly changing and increasingly nationalist Ireland wherein Maynooth was a state of mind as well as an educational institution of some international repute. By the mid-nineteenth century it had emerged as the largest Catholic seminary in the world, a position it was to retain for the next one hundred years and in 1897, in recognition of its reputation and coincident with the celebration of its centenary, it was granted the status of a Pontifical University with degree awarding powers in theology, canon law and philosophy. Its Arts students were tutored for external degrees of the Royal University. As an educational institution and as a place dedicated to the formation of priests Maynooth was impressive in the calibre of its staff, the size of its student body and in the scale and architectural significance of its campus. It towered over the smaller Queen's Colleges and in 1908, for example, the number of students in Maynooth was greater than the student populations of Cork and Galway combined.[3] To cater for such a large and exclusively Catholic institution within a new undenominational university would indeed be a challenge. The Westminster debate on the University Bill, however, proved to be much less contentious than had been expected, given previous responses to the Robertson Commission's Report of 1903 or that of the Fry Commission in 1907.[4] The Act was passed with a comfortable majority and cross-party support. Much of the debate centred on the special circumstances of Maynooth and its role as an affiliated college within the emerging university.

Affiliation of Maynooth was seen by many critics as a potential threat to the undenominational character of the new university and a back-door means of allowing the Catholic Church to attain power over the new institution. In this context the provision for four members of Senate to be elected by the graduates of the University was viewed with some suspicion. It was asserted that Maynooth graduates, because of the relative size of the College, would eventually dominate the elections of Convocation and, with the assistance of churchmen already seated on Senate from other constituencies, the Catholic Church could eventually control business.[5] Even Birrell himself expressed this view privately to the president of Maynooth, although he refrained from voicing it publicly.[6] In the view of some parliamentarians there lurked the danger that the special provisions for the College might well lead to a 'shifting of the academic centre of gravity from Dublin to Maynooth'.[7]

The prominence of Maynooth warranted the design of special conditions for affiliation and Birrell's concept of recognition was masterly indeed. John Redmond, thoroughly briefed by the Jesuit president of University College Dublin,[8] pointed out that the concept of a recognised college was not something new. After all, similar provisions existed in the Charters of Liverpool, Sheffield, Manchester and Birmingham universities whose governing bodies had the right to offer recognition to colleges or institutions deemed suitably qualified.[9] It was a convincing and pivotal argument, yet in some minds the belief remained that Ireland was not Lancashire, and that Maynooth did not conform as closely to the English model as was being suggested. Other parliamentarians suggested a contrary path:

> Within twelve miles of Cambridge University there was Ely Theological College, which was devoted, he understood, to the manufacture of High Church curates. Suppose that the University of Cambridge were by some resolution to grant that a student of the Ely College who had never quitted the precincts of that college for educational purposes should come in for the examination at Cambridge, and take a degree, would the right hon. Gentleman, a distinguished Cambridge man himself, describe that student as a Cambridge man? He thought he would utterly repudiate the idea.[10]

If Maynooth students were to be considered eligible for the award of the University's degrees, it was argued, then they should be obliged to reside for some time on the campus of the Dublin college. However, funding for residential accommodation was not provided for in the bill and John Redmond's plea for the creation of a residential university on a par with the collegiate lifestyle of Trinity College Dublin, Oxford and Cambridge met with no positive response.[11] Student accommodation would be the preserve of privately built hostels or the vagaries of the rental market and there would be no ready made campus accommodation to which the Maynooth students might transfer. Nevertheless, Birrell was accused of having

> kicked the lay external students, male and female, down the front steps of the new University, and put up the notice 'This is a teaching University' at

the same time that he took measures to admit the clerical external students by a side door marked 'Recognition'. That being so the University as it stood was neither a teaching University nor an undenominational University. The position of the Maynooth student after affiliation would be this: he would have precisely the same teachers as now, he would be in the same college as now, he would come up and be examined as now.[12]

In support of the argument that Maynooth students should spend some, or all, of their undergraduate years on the campus of a constitutent college, parliamentarians quoted the views expressed to the Robertson Committee by Professor Hogan (later President of Maynooth): 'Speaking for myself, and my colleagues in the Arts Department, we are strongly of opinion that at least from the scholastic point of view these studies could be carried on far more satisfactorily and successfully in Dublin than in Maynooth.'[13] Other senior staff in Maynooth, including Daniel Mannix, the president, had subscribed to the view.[14] However, and not just for reasons of the financial cost of building a hostel in Dublin, the Trustees of Maynooth vetoed the idea.[15] Birrell, himself, retained the hope that Maynooth students would move to such a hostel but, unwilling to pick a fight with the Catholic bishops on the matter, he counselled prudence though he retained the belief that the Maynooth students would transfer eventually to Dublin.[16]

The Irish Universities Act became law on 1 August 1908 and the National University of Ireland was incorporated by charter on 21 October of the same year. Some months later, in June 1909, the trustees of Maynooth authorised Mannix, the president, to apply to the Senate of the university for recognition of certain Maynooth courses. The printed request was laid before Senate at its meeting in July 1909,[17] the meeting being chaired by Archbishop Walsh of Dublin, himself a former president of Maynooth, who had been unanimously elected Chancellor at the inaugural meeting of Senate on 17 December 1908. The submission reflected well Mannix's pride in the scholarly reputation of the institution of which he was president[18] and in it he asserted

The College Course covers a period of ten years. The last seven are devoted to Theological or other professional studies; the first three years to University work leading up to a degree in Arts. The number of students in the College roll for the year 1908–1909 was 570 and the average for the past five years was 571.[19]

All student entrants, he pointed out, had met the matriculation standards of the Royal University. In conformity with the requirement of Senate he submitted a list of the professors and lecturers, including those in the faculties of theology and canon law, who would of course have no role to play in the arts faculty of the recognised college. The college property was valued at £200,000, considerably more than the property of the Royal University that was valued at £48,644 in a document submitted by the Chancellor of the National University in 1911.[20]

The application was referred to University College Dublin for its consideration, and following receipt of a favourable report Senate granted recognition on 25 February 1910, backdated to 1 November 1909 to facilitate the existing cohort of first-year students.[21] Recognition was given for an initial period of four years in the expectation that the Maynooth students would move to a hostel in Dublin by the expiry of that period. Recognition was restricted to the faculties of arts, philosophy and Celtic studies but in 1913 recognition was granted also to the Faculty of Science and the renewal for all faculties was without term, it now being evident that the Maynooth students would not be transferring to Dublin. Three recognised teachers were allocated positions on the General Board of Studies but the president was not allocated an *ex-officio* position on that body until 1914.[22] Following the retirement of Mannix from the presidency of Maynooth in 1913 his successor, John F. Hogan, was appointed by royal warrant to the outgoing Senate and subsequently co-opted by the incoming body.[23] Thereafter all Maynooth presidents were co-opted to Senate where they were also elected to the office of pro-vice-chancellor, a tradition of courtesy that continued up until the 1997 Universities Act when a seat on Senate and appointment to the posts of pro-vice-chancellor and (for the first time) vice-chancellor became automatic entitlements.

A note of discordance with the operation of the regulations governing recognised status arose early in the relationship and it stemmed from dissatisfaction with the role of the university examiner in Maynooth examinations. The charter of the university required examinations in recognised colleges to be conducted by a university professor, in the case of Maynooth a professor from University College Dublin: he would be assisted by the Maynooth professor and the external examiner. After the conduct of the 1910 examinations Mannix expressed his surprise at this requirement and upon his prompting Senate sought clarification from the University's legal advisers.[24] The advice confirmed the legal validity of the requirement. Five months later Mannix returned to the July Senate armed with a letter of support from the Episcopal Conference and on the proposal of the Vice-Chancellor and Mannix it was resolved that

> The Senate seek such a change in the Charter of the University as to enable the Senate to authorise the Professors and lecturers of the Recognised College of Maynooth, who are Recognised Teachers of The National University, to conduct Examinations for Degrees in Maynooth in conjunction with the External Examiner only.[25]

It is difficult to comprehend Mannix's apparent failure to understand this pivotal clause in the Charter for he, together with the bishops, had been consulted in the negotiations preceding legislation. Senate included the Maynooth request in a petition for an amendment of the Charter. Birrell was not sympathetic. He believed that the role of the University Examiner was the key element in the operation of the system of recognition and wrote in trenchant fashion to the Registrar of the University stating

> When I had to consider the important question of examinations for University degrees in outside, but recognised colleges, I was most anxious to secure the rights and establish the authority for all time of the University to and over her own degrees. For by that way alone can any real difference, from a purely degree point of view, between a recognised and a constituent college be observed.[26]

He expressed his unwillingness to support the petition unless an amendment was introduced into the Charter requiring two external examiners to be appointed for a recognised college, and furthermore requiring a 'new Statute of the University be made defining the status and qualifications of extern examiners'. The Senate withdrew its request in the face of this opposition but the new President of Maynooth, Hogan, continued to pursue the matter. In a handwritten communication, Birrell bluntly informed the President that in order to garner support for the Universities Bill he had

> relied upon these very provisions for the conduct of examinations at Recognised Colleges [and] [i]f now at this early stage in the history of the university, this alteration is made and strangest of all, made at the insistence of the Senate and the single University Representative eliminated from the Examination

and Maynooth men can get one of the University degrees at the hands of her own professors and Teachers and one solitary Extern Examiner – there cannot fail to be a tremendous row and you can guess without my telling you, the moral that would be drawn.[27]

Almost a year later Birrell again wrote in response to Hogan and asserted that in respect of the Universities Bill 'Altogether I feel I not only did all that I could for Maynooth but more than most men in my place would have thought it right to do.'[28]

The matter was laid to rest and the relationship between Maynooth and the University as mediated by University College Dublin proved to be quite harmonious. Respect for clerical authority, the undoubted political power wielded by the hierarchy in an Ireland where traditional values still predominated, and the historical significance of Maynooth were all conducive to the smooth functioning of inter-institutional relations. In addition, the reputation for fine scholarship among the priest professors, and the fact that very many of the best students leaving secondary school were enrolled in the national seminary provided academic ballast for the arrangement. Professional and personal relations cultivated over years of interaction between the cognate professors in the two colleges were likewise conducive to harmony. Nonetheless the dynamics of development and institutional missions of Maynooth and University College Dublin were markedly different; inevitably the collegiate relations of earlier decades drifted apart. Maynooth, focused on clerical formation, was introspective in its educational outlook, whereas the constituent colleges of the National University were increasingly drawn into a much more complex relationship with the social and economic demands of a modernising Ireland. The range of subjects taught in the Recognised College remained virtually unaltered during the first half century after 1910, and given the paucity of staffing resources there were few opportunities for educational experimentation. Prior to the mid-1960s there was little by way of organic academic development in Maynooth where the routine of collegiate life provided a level of contentment. Financial difficulties in the College were solved, at least temporarily, by a national church collection held in 1949, the intake of seminarians was never greater than it was in the 1950s and there was little impetus for altering the smoothly functioning relationship with the National University.

Evidence of the drift of Maynooth into comparative academic isolation emerged in the College's response to the Commission on Higher Education established in September 1960. The submission of the Maynooth President, Mgr Gerard Mitchell, to the commission has been described as 'unambitious and pessimistic',[29] emphasising retention of the status quo rather than projecting enthusiasm for an attainable future. It was a far cry from the power-broking days of 1908 and earlier. The commission recommended that the constituent colleges at Cork, Dublin and Galway, should become independent universities and that two new institutions be established in Limerick and Dublin respectively. It was accepted that Maynooth could legitimately aspire to independence status or it could seek association with whatever independent entity emerged out of University College Dublin. The details of the proposed reform of the higher education sector were not given effect by the government at that time and it was to be a further 30 years before the structure and governance of Maynooth would be altered by legislation. However, as they awaited the report of the commission the trustees of Maynooth had appraised their own situation and in 1966 they instigated fundamental institutional reform, the effects of which were far reaching and mostly unanticipated by the College authorities.

By virtue of the 1966 initiative Maynooth opened its doors to students other than those who were enrolled as candidates for the diocesan priesthood. Men as well as women were encouraged to enter the college: lay as well as members of religious orders. The issue of the teaching of theology was revisited and in January the Senate of the National University considered a Maynooth request to recognise its Faculty of Theology. The matter was considered by a committee of presidents and registrars but, conscious of the restrictions on theology imposed by the 1908 act and charter and cognisant of the recommendations of the soon to be published report of the Commission on Higher Education, no action was recommended to Senate.[30] The opening up of enrolment in Maynooth was accompanied by an ambitious expansion of the spatial geography of the College. A new President, Jeremiah Newman, was the driving force behind much of the development. North of the Dublin-Galway road and at several hundred metres remove from the Georgian and Victorian buildings of the seminary, a new campus was designed and partly built. In very many ways that campus development plan may be read as a metaphor for the institutional change that underpinned it. It was not lacking in ambition. Forty acres of farmland were set aside for the anticipated needs of the expanding College.[31] An Arts building, directly funded by the state, was built and sections of the campus were allocated on leases ranging from 500 years to 999 years to congregations of nuns and priests, each of which constructed novitiate hostels according to prescribed campus design principles. Strikingly, while hostels were linked to the campus spine road, no pathways were constructed to facilitate linkage between them: the twin aspirations of participation in university academic life and the preserved and isolating protection of centres of formation mirrored the original campus of the College where seminary life was expected to remain unchanged despite the intake of lay staff and students.

The trustees did not feel it necessary to adapt the College statutes to take account of the new collegiate reality. The decision to open Maynooth to a wider enrolment of students had been prompted by the realisation that a residential college of about 500 male students could no longer hope to support the scale and diversity of academic teaching required of the humanities and sciences in the second half of the twentieth century. Either private or episcopal endowments on a massive scale, or an increase in the number of fee-paying students, would be required to ensure solvency, maintenance of standards, and improvement of facilities. The views of the president and possibly those of individual bishops notwithstanding, the trustees' decision to open up Maynooth was in reality a conservative defence and retention of a collegiate mission and identity that had flourished on campus for more than 150 years. Necessity dominated strategy and there was a hope that the limited number of non-seminarians and lay staff would have but an ephemeral impact on the core purpose of the institution. The future was to demonstrate that change, once initiated, would be difficult to contain.

The decade after 1966 was one of immense challenge for Maynooth. In the world of Catholicism the Second Vatican Council had unleashed a series of reforms and generated unrealistic beliefs in the imminence of liberal change. Some priests on the teaching staff sought laicisation and resigned: two were dismissed and the College statutes and mode of governance were subsequently tried before the High Court and the Supreme Court. The legal finding was that Maynooth was in law a seminary, validly governed by its trustees and their instruments of authority.[32] The legal position was very much at variance with the reality of life on the campus where, by the late 1970s, the majority of staff and students were lay people and the decline of numbers within the seminary was already marked and continuous. It was increasingly clear that fundamental legislative reform of Maynooth was required, within or beyond the context of its relationship with the National University, but proposals of university legislation were to prove abortive on a number of occasions and in the ensuing vacuum Maynooth sought to improve the efficiency of management and academic development by a series of limited ad hoc internal reforms.[33]

In December 1974 the Minister for Education, Dick Burke, published proposals for university reform – Trinity College Dublin and University College Dublin were to be independent universities, Cork and Galway were to remain as the National University, the National Institutes for Higher Education (NIHEs) in Limerick and Dublin were to become recognised colleges. Maynooth was to become a constituent college in the university of its choice. In the uncertain political milieu of the time the minister's proposals came to naught. Four years later a new Minister of Education, John Wilson, proposed *inter alia* the erection of Maynooth into an independent university but again legislation was not forthcoming. Alteration of the statutory bases of Irish higher education was not a priority on the government's agenda and within many of the established institutions there was an aversion to inviting reform that might weaken inherited freedoms and precedents.

Frustrated with the lack of progress, the academic bodies and the staff association within Maynooth proposed that constituent college status be sought for its recognised faculties. The trustees agreed and on their behalf the President, Michael Olden, submitted a formal request to Senate on 19 June 1984. The grounds upon which the submission was based included the argument that

> While the status of Recognised College was entirely appropriate when Maynooth was a small College with students who were exclusively candidates for the priesthood, and an academic staff exclusively clerical, we feel that the rapid expansion of the college in recent years has so changed it as to justify its seeking the status of Constituent College. [34]

The desire of the academic staff of the recognised college to 'be accorded the status of Professors and Lecturers of the National University of Ireland' was advanced as a secondary justification. No specific proposals to amend the composition of the governing body, the system of appointments, or define the relationship of the pontifical university with the constituent college were advanced but it was promised that 'We will make every effort to ensure that all such matters are expeditiously resolved to our mutual satisfaction.' It was a sparse document that left much unsaid and the core arguments that had underpinned the 1908 Act were not engaged with at this time. In his acknowledgement of receipt of the submission the Chancellor, Dr T. K. Whitaker remarked that 'a favourable decision by the University will require legislative sanction to be effective'.[35]

The Senate sought legal opinion on the submission and it was confirmed that the University itself could not grant constituent status and that it would have to progress the matter by means of a private act in the Oireachtas.[36] Encouragement for a successful progression was provided by University College Dublin whose academic council and governing body both confirmed that they would 'welcome the admission of St Patrick's College, Maynooth, as a fourth constituent college'.[37] The presidents and registrars of the constituent colleges together with representatives of Maynooth met on 30 January 1985 to discuss the Maynooth application and a subcommittee of the Senate's standing committee was established to progress the matter further. The level of activity characteristic of the six-month period that followed receipt of the Maynooth application waned as that subcommittee began to appreciate some of the complexities involved and three years later matters had progressed little.[38] The context of the discussion was altered radically when it became obvious that the government in 1989 intended introducing legislation that would award independent university status to the NIHEs in Limerick and Dublin. The National University expressed the view that its colleges too should have the title of university. Maynooth was included in the proposal for four independent universities under the umbrella of the National University. The President, Micheál Ledwith, briefed the Maynooth trustees, arguing that the enhanced status of independence might better facilitate the retention of collegiate unity generated by the tripartite assemblage of recognised college, pontifical university and seminary than would the more restrictive and previously sought constituent college status which would surely have required a division of the college.[39] In furtherance of the new goal of independent status within the National University, Ledwith made a lengthy proposal to a special Senate meeting convened for 10 December 1990.[40] The submission also included a request to remove the prohibition on the examining of theology for degrees of the National University. On 5 March 1991 the Senate forwarded to the Minister for Education its considered views on the future structure of the National University, including the request that 'St Patrick's College, Maynooth, in its faculties of arts, Celtic studies, philosophy and science, should become a constituent university of the National University of Ireland'.[41] Details of the legislative changes required to give effect to the request were spelt out in the following year by Senate which adopted, specific to Maynooth, a policy desideratum that stated:

> It is most desirable, for administrative and other practical reasons, that the offices of President of the National University, Maynooth, and President of the Pontifical University of Maynooth be held by the same person (who may in the future be a lay person, male or female). To this end, while the governing body of each of these universities must retain discretion to appoint its own President, the selection process should be such as to lead (e.g. by a degree of common representation on assessment boards) to the choice by both universities of the same candidate.[42]

It was the inclusion of this clause that gave comfort to the President of Maynooth who hoped to retain thereby the historic unity of the College.[43] In Ledwith's view two parallel governing authorities – one relating to the National University Maynooth, and the other (the trustees) relating to the Pontifical University – could separately govern the two university entities on a shared campus, while still maintaining an overall sense of unity expressed through joint appointments of the president, registrar, bursar and librarian. It was an ambitious and untried schema but it did have a certain appeal for the trustees who co-operated with the spirit of the Senate's application to the minister by accepting that the National University Maynooth should have a governing body similar in composition to those of the other three constituent universities, with the not unreasonable qualification that three places be reserved for the trustees.[44]

The Green Paper on Education, published in June 1992, endorsed the request of Senate for legislative change but among many university leaders there was a growing fear that the government would consider the Senate's request only in the context of a more root and branch approach to university legislation, undermining many traditional institutional rights in the process. In the case of Maynooth, however, tradition had created a situation whereby the *de facto* and *de jure* realities of the institution were diverging rapidly. During the second half of 1992 and throughout 1993 there was growing fear in Maynooth that the prospects of legislation would evaporate once more, as had been the case so often in the recent past. Notwithstanding the fact that in its teaching and research the recognised college was performing exceptionally well, there was a palpable sense that the legal device conceived by Birrell in 1908 in deference to the possible overwhelming strength of Maynooth was now, almost nine decades later, being perceived as a badge of inferiority. The uniqueness of the Maynooth position within the National University had, in the eyes of many, been eroded further by the admission of other recognised colleges in the period since 1975 and it was strongly felt that only legislative change could relieve the growing sense of frustration. There was no doubting the calibre of Maynooth staff. During the early 1990s five Maynooth academics had been appointed to professorships in the constituent colleges; a similar number of senior staff from the constituent colleges had been appointed to professorships in Maynooth. The college's professors were frequently nominated as external examiners in other Irish universities as well as in the British university system, but under the terms of the 1908 Act they could not act as principal examiners in their own institution. Furthermore, an increasingly competitive university environment notwithstanding, any strategic developments in the Maynooth curriculum had first to be approved by the Academic Council in Dublin prior to their being submitted to the General Board of Studies. It was not a satisfactory arrangement for what many described as 'the new Maynooth'.[45] In 1992 the Maynooth Registrar, Peter Carr, was elected to Senate by the graduates in Convocation and, although this did facilitate transaction of Maynooth business, there remained the anomaly that the Maynooth registrar did not have any *ex-officio* status on the most senior academic body in the University.

In preparation for the celebration of its bicentenary Maynooth focused its attention not only upon the celebration of a distinguished history stretching back to its foundation at the time of the French Revolution, but engaged also in strategic planning for its future in a rapidly changing Ireland.[46] Those of a historical mindset within the College were conscious that the first centenary had been marked by the granting of pontifical university status with the power to award degrees in theology, canon law and philosophy, and it was believed that the second centenary should be commemorated by the granting of university status for the faculties of the Recognised College. Optimists within the college believed that 1995, also the year of the sesquicentenary of the former Queen's colleges in Cork and Galway, might generate acknowledgement in the form of legislation. Unfortunately as the bicentenary approached that Government went out of office and the record of unrealised university legislation seemed set to continue. It was also appreciated that senior figures in the Department of Education, though keen to sponsor university legislation, were not convinced that the moment was right, given the perilous balance of power in the Dáil and (for the first time in the history of the state) the lack of a government majority in Seanad Éireann. It was in such circumstances that the Maynooth president approached the Minister, Niamh Bhreathnach, with a proposal to emulate the gesture that had marked the first centenary of the college, and to simplify passage through the Oireachtas by concentrating solely upon Maynooth at this time. The minister agreed but her personal agenda was subsequently broadened by the recommendation of officials to include legislative reform of the whole university sector. Thus were born the protracted negotiations that finally resulted in the Universities Act of 1997, enacted only a few weeks before the government fell from office.[47]

The 1997 Universities Act provided Maynooth with constituent university status for its faculties of Arts, Celtic Studies, Philosophy and Science with a governing authority not unlike that proposed to Senate in 1992 by the college. The most striking effect of the legislation was the fracturing of the unity of Maynooth. St Patrick's College would continue in existence as a seminary and pontifical university, with a student complement of about 70 seminarians and a cohort of about 200 lay students. Such an institutional division had been anticipated in June 1994 when, upon the resignation of the president, the trustees had taken the opportunity to amend the college statutes and appoint two executive heads. Management of the recognised college would henceforth be the responsibility of the master, and the executive powers of the President would be confined to managing the seminary and pontifical university. The decision of the trustees was a brave one and it was a clear signal that they supported radical change.[48]

The Senate of the National University responded positively to the 1994 division of the headship responsibilities and the master was co-opted on to Senate and elected pro-vice-chancellor in accordance with the long established courtesy that had been extended to the president of Maynooth. Subsequently the Senate agreed to a proposal on the role of university examiners brought forward by the master with the support of the president of University College Dublin. The import of the proposal was that the requirement for the presence of University examiners in Maynooth would, pending legislation, be fulfilled by the attendance at the Maynooth Board of Examiners of two professors selected by the faculties of Arts and Science in University College Dublin. It was a resolution that was warmly welcomed in Maynooth and generously endorsed by the overwhelming majority of the cognate professors in Dublin.[49]

In recognition of the second centenary of Maynooth the Senate agreed to the convening of a conferring ceremony for the award of honorary doctorates in the college, the first such ceremony to be held on that campus and similar ceremonies were authorised for 1996 and 1997. The commencement order for the Universities Act was fittingly signed in Maynooth by outgoing Minister, Niamh Bhreathnach, on Friday 13 June 1997. Under the terms of that act a commission was appointed to oversee the composition and creation of the first governing authority of National University of Ireland, Maynooth. That commission consisted of the president and registrar of the new constituent university[50] together with a representative of the Chancellor of the university and a representative of the chairman of the Higher Education Authority.[51] The new Governing Authority met for the first time on 23 October 1997 and among its distinguished members there were a future minister of Education and a future cardinal, an appropriate reflection of the evolutionary path that had led to the establishment of the institution.[52]

Over the course of the years 1997–9, National University of Ireland, Maynooth designed a logo, developed its corporate identity and successfully separated the staff of the previous single employer, St Patrick's College, into those who would be employees of the new institution and those who would remain with the private college. Almost 500 employees and an actuarially divided pension fund were transferred with few attendant personnel problems. A more contentious issue arose in terms of the acquisition of capital resources by the new institution. It soon became clear that National University of Ireland, Maynooth had been born with few birthrights and, though it was responsible for several hundred staff and some 5,000 students, it had no legal title to property on the campus, notwithstanding significant state investment in the Arts Building, the Callan Science Building and the Library. No capital funding had been provided for in the Act. Archbishop Walsh of Dublin, the first Chancellor of the National University of Ireland, had no doubt faced a comparable dilemma in 1908 but he was able to effect the transfer of title of the College of Science and the property of the Royal University without any corresponding movement of funds. Property attitudes and property prices were different in 1997. The Department of Education eventually funded the purchase of the 40-acre campus originally designed in the 1970s together with an expansion zone of an adjacent 14 acres. Adjoining land for student residences and five religious hostels on that campus were purchased by monies raised from philanthropic sources and the university formalised its use of buildings on the nineteenth-century campus by means of a leasing arrangement that provided for five year rent reviews. Between 1998 and 2004 a second science building, dedicated premises for software and electronic engineering, student recreational and residential facilities, staff offices and a new headline auditoria building were provided from an admixture of state funding and philanthropic assistance, thereby increasing the stock of buildings by more than 400 per cent in the process. When the auditoria complex was formally opened in early 2004 it was named in honour of the Nobel Laureate, John Hume, a humanities graduate of the former recognised college, and as such it embodied an organic link between the legacy of the past and the new horizons of the future. Some months after the opening of this building a new president, appointed in strict conformity with the requirements of the 1997 act, took up office. The educational land-scape crafted so carefully by Birrell in 1908 had been changed utterly.

" WHAT HAPPENED?"
" I JUST SAID THAT THE NATIONAL UNIVERSITY HAD PRODUCED NEARLY ALL OUR PROMINENT PUBLIC MEN, AND HE SAID HE WOULDN'T STAND BY AND LISTEN TO ANYONE RUNNING DOWN THE NATIONAL UNIVERSITY."

Figure 2 **A cartoon that appeared in *Dublin Opinion*, November 1927.**

1908   1918   1928   1938   1948   1958

1968   1978   1988   1998   **2008**

The Chancellors

CHAPTER 8 *William J. Walsh, 1908–21* DÁIRE KEOGH

F ROM THE EVE OF THE FIRST Home Rule crisis to the final months of
  the War of Independence, William Walsh's episcopacy spanned a critical
period in the evolution of modern Ireland (1885–1921). Throughout those
decades, the archbishop played a key role in the life of Ireland and the birth
of the new nation, to the extent that, while the Anglo-Irish war raged on, his
coffin was draped in the tricolour of the republic. Yet of all his endeavours,
the *Irish Independent* identified the establishment of the National University
as the 'crown of his life's work'.[1]

I

Walsh's patriotic credentials were impeccable: Frank Cruise O'Brien described
him not merely as a 'statesman-Bishop', but as a 'patriot Bishop too'.[2] His
father, a Dublin watchmaker, enrolled him in the Repeal Association as an
infant, and his earliest recollection was of being patted on the head by the
'Liberator' at the age of five.[3] As a youth he joined in the martial drills of the
boys' Young Ireland Club, marching like soldiers to the walls of Dublin Castle
and, as a student, his first literary efforts were in the pages of the *Nation*.[4]

   He excelled as a student, first at St Lawrence O'Toole's Seminary, on
Harcourt Street, and subsequently at the Catholic University, which was
then under the direction of Cardinal Newman. From there he went to
Maynooth, where he remained after his ordination in 1866, serving first
as professor of dogmatic and moral theology, and subsequently as vice-
president and president of the college. Walsh was a polymath, an original
all-rounder. He was, in Michael Davitt's phrase, 'an authority on almost
everything' and 'the … embodiment of all the sciences'.[5] Moreover, whatever
he lacked in natural ability was ably compensated for by his discipline and
ambition. Myles Ronan recalled his dogged determination in overcoming

a poor penmanship by starting again, 'like a schoolboy', to write in copybook hand, to the joy of researchers who trawl his extensive archive. In a display of similar resolve, he practised mind games and other techniques to extend his already tenacious memory.[6] Number sequencing was a particular talent: during the special commission called to investigate links between Parnellism and crime (1887), he assisted the nationalist party by cracking the codes used in communications between the solicitor for *The Times* and their agents.[7]

Having cut his teeth in the *Nation*, Walsh became a prolific contributor to the press, writing at length on the great issues of his day: the land, Home Rule and education. In the words of his biographer, 'the press was his pulpit, the pen was his medium'.[8] Throughout his career he was an ardent advocate of the rights of tenant farmers. As President of St Patrick's College, he added practical assistance to the national campaign by persuading the bishops to reject the notorious 'Leinster lease', demanded by the Duke of Leinster on their holdings at Maynooth, which would have contracted them out of the benefits of the 1870 Land Act.[9] A decade later he was described as 'the decisive witness' at the Bessborough Commission (1880), and he is usually credited with influencing the shape of Gladstone's subsequent Land Act (1881).[10] However, his involvement with Archbishop Croke in the Plan of Campaign proved too much for the authorities; if British intrigue had failed to block his appointment as archbishop in 1885, his support for the 'Plan' earned him a rebuke from Rome and cost him a cardinal's hat.[11]

On the national question he was a staunch supporter of Parnell's constitutional nationalism, but in the bitter divide surrounding the O'Shea divorce, Walsh was numbered amongst the 'priests and the priests' pawns [who] broke Parnell's heart and hounded him into his grave'.[12] Recent scholarship has produced a more nuanced reading of the crisis, which highlights the Archbishop's secret negotiations with Parnell in a desperate attempt to reach a compromise. Nevertheless, in the popular memory, Joyce's 'Billy the Lip' is still 'frequently depicted as the evil genius who plotted Parnell's downfall'.[13] In time he assisted in the reconciliation of the rival factions, but in later life he became frustrated with 'our once independent Irish Party', which he abandoned in favour of Sinn Féin in 1917.[14]

The education question was perhaps the closest to his heart; 'after Church matters', Ronan believed, 'the greatest work in the archbishop's life was in the cause of education'.[15] Walsh established his reputation as a distinguished scholar and teacher, but the weight of his various appointments added to his influence upon educational issues. As vice-president of Maynooth he established the Catholic Headmasters' Association, while in 1892 he was appointed to the Intermediate Education Board, a position he held for 17 years. As archbishop of Dublin, he built 70 new schools and secured state funding for the Catholic teacher training colleges at Drumcondra and Carysfort, while as a commissioner for national education (1895–1901) he contributed greatly to the development of the modern Irish education system.[16]

The greatest campaign of his career – his 'long and arduous fight' – was to secure a university which would satisfy the demands of Irish Catholic interests.[17] The *Manchester Guardian* described his as 'one of the first voices raised to denounce the shortcomings of Irish University education', but Walsh's contribution was not in raising the issue, but in bringing it to a resolution.[18] Walsh's hopes for a Catholic university were ambitious and through politics and publications he fought for justice 'in a broad and liberal spirit' for almost 50 years.[19] He rejected any tinkering with the old 'Royal University', which was merely an examining board, in favour of radical university reform, including the creation of an endowed Catholic College, alongside Trinity, within Dublin University.[20]

The eventual solution to the question was contained in the wide-ranging Irish Universities Act (1908), which the Chief Secretary, Augustine Birrell, drafted and progressed through parliament in consultation with the archbishop. Towards the end of the tortuous parliamentary process, Birrell, a religious nonconformist, joked with Walsh that while his great patron, Augustine, 'was a saint and doctor ... the honours of *martyrdom*' had been reserved for him.[21] The bill did not offer all that Walsh expected: in Tim Healy's expression, the proposed university was 'nobody's ideal', but it contained important potential which the MP emphasised to the archbishop:

> As the Tories have given Ireland nearly everything Toryism can surrender in other directions, it follows that whenever a new Tory ministry is seeking sops for Ireland, it must find an outlet for its concessions *via* education. Hence the vital necessity of getting a start made somehow.[22]

Walsh appreciated this fact, and also the scale of Birrell's achievement which has been described as 'a monument to the diplomatic qualities of the

Chief Secretary'.[23] For these reasons the archbishop threw not only his reputation and the dignity of his offices but also his energy behind the new university in a determined effort to make it succeed.

II

The task of realising the aspirations of Birrell's legislation fell principally to three individuals: William Walsh, Christopher Palles and Joseph McGrath. They shaped the university whose centenary this volume celebrates. Under the terms of the Irish Universities Act (1908) two bodies of commissioners were charged with drafting the statutes and appointing the staff of the two universities and colleges. A Dublin Commission was made up of ten members, named in the Act, while its counterpart in Belfast consisted of seven. These in turn appointed members to a joint commission, which had responsibility for the division of the property of the old Royal University and other common concerns.[24] Archbishop Walsh was invited to join the Dublin Commission, under the chairmanship of Judge Christopher Palles (1831–1920).

Palles had a long involvement with the university question and was ideally suited for the task. A Catholic and a Clongowes boy, he had excelled in mathematics at Trinity College. Yet although he inclined towards an academic career, restrictions excluding Catholics from fellowships at Trinity decided him upon the legal profession.[25] He was appointed Chief Baron, one of the senior judicial positions in Ireland, at the age of 42 (1874). According to tradition, the appointment was made by Gladstone, on the platform at Paddington Station, minutes before he left for Windsor Castle to tender his resignation to Queen Victoria.[26] At the end of his long and distinguished judicial career, Prime Minister Asquith wrote 'that the judgements of Palles C. B. [were] held in as high esteem by English and American as by Irish lawyers'.[27] Walsh also had a fine legal mind, as his evidence in the celebrated libel case of Fr O'Keeffe of Callan had demonstrated (1875). On that occasion, Judge Baron Dowse praised the testimony of Dr Walsh, describing it as the clearest and most distinct he had ever heard in a court of justice.[28]

The archbishop and the chief baron were a formidable team; they worked well together, and their friendship and effective collaboration are reflected in the voluminous correspondence between the two. Significantly, one of Walsh's last public engagements was to visit UCD in 1921 to inspect the

Palles library, which he had purchased for £1,000, on the chief baron's death and presented to the college.[29] The two were the principal architects of the university statutes and they oversaw the complex transfer of the valuable property of the 'Royal' to the National University and its colleges.[30] Walsh revelled in the task and devoted several days each week to the workings of the commission until its business was concluded in July 1911.[31] His examination of the documentation was meticulous and he was especially careful to protect the process from any future legal challenge.[32] His archive, for example, contains an apology from the senior partner in a Dublin legal firm for 'clerical errors' which the archbishop had identified in papers relating to the Blayney Endowment.[33]

The statutes which the Dublin Commission drafted for the new university were particularly progressive, reflecting the democratisation which had transformed late nineteenth-century Ireland.[34] For women the creation of the new university was particularly significant, since the Bill (1908) conferred on them equality with men in university education. Yet while the legislation has been described as a bill of rights for women, certain anomalies remained.[35] These included restricting the franchise in UCD Governing Body elections to matriculated students of the old colleges on St Stephen's Green and Cecilia Street. The effect of this was to disenfranchise many of the women graduates of the Royal University, or so Mary Hayden (1862-1942), historian and campaigner for women's rights, informed the archbishop.[36] Characteristically, Walsh replied by return inviting her to submit the draft of an appropriate clause which would correct what she had described as 'an injustice to the Dublin women students'.[37]

Other approaches to the archbishop were less altruistic. These often sought Walsh's patronage for their candidacy for places or university positions.[38] William A. Magennis, professor of metaphysics and later member of Dáil Éireann, sought a recommendation of his candidacy for the presidency of UCD to Chief Secretary Birrell; George Ashlin appealed on behalf of the Royal Institute of Architects for the creation of a chair of architecture within the university, while Sir Hugh Lane subsequently recommended Richard Orpen, 'the most imaginative and talented architect in Ireland' for the position.[39] There were numerous appeals from students, in spite of Walsh's stern reputation, including one from 12 scholarship students urging to him to plead with Fr William Delany to advance their stipends.[40]

There were individuals, however, who questioned the archbishop's wisdom in devoting so much of his attention to the university. In October 1908, a correspondent from Larne took him to task for attending the opening meeting of the Law Students' Debating Society. In an ominous allusion to the Gospel parable of the rich man and the beggar, he reminded Walsh that 'the Church has invariably in the past dined with Dives'. The rising tide of socialism, he warned, would not be stemmed by 'merely bestowing a blessing on Lazarus and counselling him to be patient'.[41] This charge was disingenuous in Walsh's case; throughout his career he had sought 'justice for Ireland', while later in that month he met with James Larkin in an unsuccessful attempt to find a mediated solution to the carters' strike.[42]

III

In a departure from usual practice, the Chancellor of the National University was to be elected. Given his continuing efforts on the Dublin Commission, coupled with his lifelong campaign for university reform, it was perhaps not surprising that Archbishop Walsh was elected Chancellor of the National University at the first meeting of its Senate in December 1908. While the Annual Register saw his election as confirmation of the worst fears of Northern Protestants, it is significant that the choice was unanimous and supported by its unionist members.[43] In any event, if chancellorships were usually ceremonial offices, Walsh, who was particularly proud of his election, broke the mould by continuing to direct the development of the new university.[44] In this he was ably assisted by the third of the founding triumvirate, Joseph McGrath, who was registrar of the NUI until his death in 1923.

McGrath was an extremely efficient administrator; he had served as secretary to the Royal University and in other honorary positions, including the vice-presidency of the Royal Dublin Society and the Society for the Prevention of Cruelty to Children. It was an acknowledgement of his ability that as registrar he enjoyed a annual salary of £1,000 (the equivalent of over €500,000 today based on average earnings), but the university charter noted that his successors would be paid half that sum.[45] As a further recognition, he was knighted in 1911 for his service to university education. Like the chief baron, he was educated at Clongowes Wood and enjoyed a longstanding personal friendship with Walsh, which had survived the archbishop's differences with the Royal University. They shared a common interest in music and the very modern hobbies of photography and cycling. Amongst their correspondence are letters from the archbishop extolling the virtues of 'the freewheel' and seeking advice on 'an important point about the purchase of a new bicycle'.[46] McGrath was a regular social visitor to the 'Brick Palace' at Drumcondra, where the archbishop had established his *curia*, and the extent of their friendship is reflected in the familial issues discussed in their correspondence, including Walsh's response to the news that the registrar's son was about to join the Jesuits.[47]

Although the archbishop complained of the gruelling demands involved in administering 'a big machine' like the Dublin diocese, he was constantly available to 'Sir Joseph' and the work of the NUI.[48] It was not unusual for them to exchange three or four letters in one day, and on occasion the archbishop's diary was so full that he could not begin NUI business until after eleven o'clock at night.[49] Even during his annual continental cycling holiday, which was usually centred on some opera festival, Walsh had his university papers dispatched to him twice each week from Archbishop's House.[50] The registrar valued the advice which the Chancellor was never slow to offer, from the choice of the NUI motto, *Veritati fir fer* (truth, strength, courage), to micromanaging the business of the university.[51] He took pains to examine, amend and correct minutes, notices, invitations and routine items of business. His comments from one sample letter are indicative of his meticulous style: 'The draft letter seems to me a magnificent statement of our case. I have taken the liberty of suggesting a few verbal changes which I think make the statement a little more powerful.'[52]

In financial matters, too, he assumed direct responsibility, whether it was pressing Augustine Birrell and the Treasury to ring-fence capital funding, in order to protect it from possible effects of Home Rule legislation (1914), or choosing between estimates for minor repair work at the NUI offices on Merrion Square. In the latter deliberations the Chancellor displayed his skills as a bursar which he had acquired as vice-president of Maynooth: 'The difference of price is very wide. Possibly the lower ones ... are willing to lose something on this small job for the sake of getting in touch with a body that is supposed to have £150,000 to spend building a new university.'[53]

Once again, when planning meetings of the University Senate or Convocation, his attention to detail was scrupulous. Whether it was satisfying statutory requirements, ordering the precedence in processions, or seating strategically key allies and advisers, no item was left to chance. In his preparations for the fraught convocation of 1910, Walsh, writing from Bologna, expressed particular concern about the possibility of an invasion by 'crotchety' graduates of the Royal University who had claimed rights to attend.[54] In this and in other instances, Sir Joseph addressed the anxieties of the Chancellor with good humour, often offering his suggestions 'with fear and trembling'.[55]

There were, of course, fundamental issues for the Chancellor to negotiate. At the outset, the implications of the 'non-denominational' status of the university appeared paramount. Bishop O'Dwyer of Limerick had dismissed the chief secretary's proposal as a 'Birrelligious university', while the Archbishop of Armagh, Cardinal Logue, described it as 'a pagan bantling [child]', but hoped that in time it could be baptised and made Christian.[56] Certainly the appointment of William Walsh as Chancellor suggested that this would be so. At one level, in a very conspicuous way at the 'Red Mass' which opened the 1909 academic year, he lamented the absence 'of provision or maintenance of any church or chapel' in the university.[57] Yet, curiously, the archbishop made no overt manoeuvre as Chancellor to *Catholicise* the NUI. His archive reflects his interest in the religious welfare of students, the appointment of deans and the like, but there is little to suggest a concerted effort on his part to 'baptise' the University. Indeed, he left such matters to the 'representatives of the episcopal interest' on the various governing bodies and avoided infringing upon their responsibilities.[58] Furthermore, he tirelessly defended the integrity of the Universities Act (1908), flawed as it was, and expressed 'trouble and unease' when Peter Finlay SJ was appointed to the professorship of Catholic theology at UCD, an extra-mural chair funded by the bishops.[59]

That the 'godless' university became Catholic owed very little to the efforts of its first Chancellor. There were other forces at work across the University, especially in Cork where the influence of Bertram Windle was particularly potent. Writing to the archbishop to announce the generous Honan bequest, the president of the university, who had recently been made a Knight of St Gregory, declared:

> since I became a Catholic . . . I have always wished and tried to do what little lay in my power for the Church. I look upon this university as one of the greatest – I think the greatest – opportunity that I have ever had and hope to

build up a college here in Cork which will be a centre of Catholic influence for the south of Ireland.[60]

In the last analysis, Donal McCartney's observation in relation to UCD was true of the entire university: 'the Catholic atmosphere of the college was guaranteed at the start through its government, its academic staff, and its body of students'.[61]

And what of the 'national' character of the new university? Great hopes had been pinned on the university to act as an intellectual centre for the emerging nation.[62] These sentiments of Dillon, Hyde and Pearse were also those of Archbishop Walsh who had been an enthusiast for the Irish language since his days at Maynooth. A warm supporter of the Gaelic League, he had prompted Fr Eugene O'Growney to write his 'Simple Lessons' in Irish and devised for him an effective phonetic plan.[63] From the outset, the Gaelic League campaigned for the establishment of an Irish studies faculty in the new university, which in Eoin MacNeill's view would give it 'a distinct standing before the world' and lift it out of 'the common category of English provincial universities'.[64]

Such ambitions were admirable, but the extension of the League's plan to include Irish as a compulsory subject for matriculation polarised the 35 members of the University Senate.[65] The bishops opposed the measure; amongst other things they feared a flight towards Trinity or Queen's, but many younger priests were conspicuous in supporting the cause of the language. The college presidents were largely negative, and Windle, in his correspondence with the Chancellor, was characteristically vocal in his condemnation of the 'miserable machinations' of the Gaelic League and their willingness to wreck 'the whole higher Education of Catholics' in pursuit of 'narrow and selfish ends'.[66] He was equally scathing in his criticism of the 'blindness of the priests' who had supported compulsion, believing that their desire was more 'to give the hierarchy a blow than anything else'.[67]

In public the Chancellor remained neutral bravely resisting attempts by both sides to be drawn. Privately, however, he opposed the move, believing that the best way to encourage 'an Irish atmosphere about the University [was] to leave Irish optional but to treat it with marked favour in the way of marks, prizes chairs etc.'[68] Significantly, too, he identified ulterior motives in the League's campaign. The real agenda, he informed Joseph McGrath, was not for Irish to be essential for university entry. What they really wanted was to have Irish made, 'through the university, an obligatory subject in the intermediate schools in the country'.[69] Yet what had been a particularly divisive issue was effectively decided by the influence of the popularly elected county councils, who offered funding and scholarships to the colleges on condition of support.[70] In the face of such carrots, many succumbed, including Windle, whose dramatic turnabout won him the 'withering contempt' of the Archbishop of Tuam.[71] When the measure eventually came before the Senate of the University in June 1910, it was accepted by a majority.

There were other vital academic issues for the Chancellor to consider. Throughout the debates on Birrell's education proposals, Walsh's great concern had been to secure equality with Trinity College and '*status* in the world of learning'.[72] In his actions as Chancellor, he sought to establish the reputation for the NUI and to prevent it from appearing in any way inferior to TCD. The context of the bicentenary celebrations of the Trinity Medical School (1912) presented him with a very serious dilemma, not least because he had been scathing in his public criticism of the school some years earlier (1905). In his correspondence with Sir Joseph he teased out the various options to mark the occasion:

> I feel that we ought to do everything possible to show civility on such an occasion. I am, as you know, altogether opposed to giving their men *ad eundem* degrees because, as is obvious, they would insult us if any of our men applied for an *ad eundem* to them . . . We are not yet two hundred years old and I have very little doubt that long before we reach that venerable age, they will be only looking for an opportunity to show civility to us.[73]

Ultimately a formal address was decided upon, and an ad hoc meeting of the Senate was called to give its approval. Yet even then the Chancellor left nothing to chance, not least an improper Latin translation which might have exposed the new university to ridicule: 'But what about "*Medicinale Collegium*"?' he asked McGrath: ' . . . *Medicinale* is not a classical word, and so far as it is a Latin word at all it means (*me pudice*) medicinal in the sense in which we speak of medicinal herbs, i.e. health giving.'[74]

A similar fixation with the academic reputation of the university was reflected in the practice of discussing student matriculation marks at the Senate, a tradition which the president of UCC described as an absurdity worthy of Gilbert and Sullivan.[75] Yet Walsh's anxieties were not unfounded, and there was a risk that standards were being eroded by the regularity with which courtesy degrees were conferred on graduates of the old Catholic University.[76] Similarly, the frequency with which Senate members proposed honorary degrees had become a cause of alarm. In January 1915, the archbishop recommended that honorary degrees be kept 'within reasonable bounds', in an attempt to correct an atmosphere in which, as the president of UCC protested, certain Senators imagined 'that you give a man an honorary degree in the same way as you stand him a drink in the nearest bar'.[77]

IV

The honesty of such communication reflects the candour of expression which is one of the most striking features of the Chancellor and Registrar's correspondence. In the first instance, the Senate was greatly divided and its membership reflected the full spectrum of the Irish political divide in what was an intensely politicised period. Moreover, from the outset, the principal partners of the National University had little enthusiasm for the project and made no attempt to hide their frustration. In this context, Archbishop Walsh was the perfect Chancellor. Neither was he satisfied by Birrell's legislation, but he had accepted it in good faith, conscious of the opportunities which it afforded. Added to this, he brought to the chair a reputation as an honest broker and a champion of arbitration; in 1890, for instance, he was awarded the freedom of the City of Cork for his role in resolving a protracted strike on the Great Southern and Western Railway.[78]

From the outset, the forces pulling the NUI apart were often more apparent than those that united it. The dynamics of the university were curious and cannot be explained by simple regional rivalries. In a palpable way, UCD felt that it was *the* National University; Cork was an unhappy partner in the enterprise, while neither college believed that UCG was worthy of their company. Such realities made Walsh's tenure as Chancellor especially challenging since even the routine exercises of a university required protracted negotiations. The selection of external examiners for the 'National' was a case in point, as the process became a battleground in which the Cork faction rejected the appointment of 'third or fourth rate . . . Dublin physicians and surgeons'.[79] After 1914, too, political divisions within the Senate became more pronounced, following elections which saw its composition transformed by the arrival of younger, more nationalist members. Within that context, Walsh was determined to prevent 'hostile or … unfriendly relations' between the various parties.[80] Yet even the calendar provoked discord, with the Chancellor warning the registrar 'to look out for squalls in this apparently simple business'.[81] On one occasion the president of UCC noted that Walsh and the Senate assumed duties which in any other university would have been handled by the registrar.[82] That this was so reflected a desire on Walsh's part to preserve a consensus across the university.

If relatively minor affairs proved contentious the larger issues were insurmountable, particularly the discussion on where to locate the new headquarters for the NUI. In this, too, regional rivalries were to the fore, and Windle was vehemently opposed to suggestions that the university buildings would be located on Earlsfort Terrace, Dublin. Such a location, he argued, would reduce the university to a 'mere trifling appendage to UCD'.[83] There were, however, more fundamental issues to consider, including the disenchantment of the south with the whole NUI structure. As early as January 1910, the president of UCC alerted the Chancellor to the likelihood of a break up of Birrell's university:

> The cynic would urge that if the NUI goes on the rocks, Cork will the sooner come by its own. This is not my view. I do not want to see the NUI fail, though I do want to get quit of it myself. It is rather a dashing of one's spirits, however, when one hears prominent persons (as I did in Dublin last week), saying that it would be better for the Dublin College not to waste money over building since they would be amalgamated with TCD before five years were out . . . I would like to leave Dublin flourishing and with good will on both sides and set up for ourselves in Cork.[84]

Within months, Windle's *Annual Report* for 1909–10 contained the first in a series of public appeals for an independent university, which culminated in the abortive University of Munster campaign of 1918.[85] Similarly his correspondence with McGrath spared no punches in his repeated descriptions of his colleagues' contempt of the 'miserable university', which 'like the god-father of fiction never did anything for us'.[86]

The Chancellor was under no illusion about the enormity of the crisis facing his university. In private correspondence with McGrath he acknowledged

39. Archbishop William J. Walsh was elected as First Chancellor of the National University of Ireland on 17 December 1908. He remained in office until his death in 1921.

40. Archbishop Walsh made a futile effort to save the life of Kevin Barry, a medical student at UCD, who was executed on 1 November 1920 for his part in the killing of three British soldiers.

41. The Rt Hon Baron Christopher Palles, Chairman of the Dublin Commissioners, who drew up the first statutes for the National University and made the first appointments (1908). Portrait by Henry von Herkomer (1903).

42. Eamon de Valera pictured outside the entrance to UCD, Earlsfort Terrace, with a group of students (including Cumann na mBan members) following the reception on 20 November 1921 to mark his appointment as Chancellor of the National University.

43. Honorary conferring of Joseph P. Kennedy, father of US President John F. Kennedy by Chancellor Eamon de Valera in 1938.

44. Honorary conferring of US President John F. Kennedy by Chancellor Eamon de Valera on 23 June 1963.

45. A letter from US President John F. Kennedy to Dr Michael Tierney, Vice-Chancellor of the National University, following his honorary conferring the previous month.

THE WHITE HOUSE

WASHINGTON

July 11, 1963

Dear Mr. President:

One of the proudest moments in a very memorable trip was the occasion on which you awarded me the honorary degree of the National University. This honor, which has deep associations with past and present Irish scholars, reinforced my deep feelings of kinship with Ireland and its people. It was thoughtful of you to bestow this honor on me and I am most grateful.

Sincerely,

Dr. Michael Tierney,
Vice Chancellor,
National University of Ireland,
President of University College,
Ireland.

46. Chancellor T. K. Whitaker with Gemma Hussey (Minister for Education, 1982–6) at the Commemoration of the 75th Anniversary of the NUI in 1983.

47. Honorary conferring of President of Ireland, Mary Robinson by Chancellor T. K. Whitaker (1991).

48. Inauguration of Chancellor Dr Garret FitzGerald with outgoing Chancellor Dr T. K. Whitaker (November 1997).

49. Honorary conferring of Bertie Ahern, former Taoiseach (2006).
left to right Professor Paul Giller (Registrar and Vice President for Academic Affairs, UCC), Dr Hugh Brady (President, UCD), Dr Iognáid Ó Muircheartaigh (President, NUIG), Bertie Ahern, Dr Garret FitzGerald (Chancellor, NUI), Dr Attracta Halpin (Registrar, NUI), Professor John Hughes (President, NUIM).

50. Honorary conferring of John Bruton (Taoiseach 1994–7) by Chancellor Garret FitzGerald in 2005.

51. Chancellor Garret
FitzGerald presenting
Professor William J. Smyth
with the Irish Historical
Research Prize at the NUI
Awards ceremony at Croke
Park on 15 November 2007.

52. Portrait of Chancellor
Garret FitzGerald by Carey
Clarke, commissioned
for the NUI Centenary.
Dr FitzGerald was elected
as Chancellor of the NUI
in 1997 succeeding Dr T. K.
Whitaker.

that 'it becomes more and more manifest that the *University* is not to be what was contemplated . . . as a possibility in the Charter'.[87] He questioned the wisdom of investing £40,000 of public money on university buildings, but he remained sanguine about events. Indeed, one wonders if he was overly concerned at the prospect of a collapse of the NUI. Its constituent colleges were, after all, thriving regional universities which would, as Windle suggested, survive the demise of the federal structure. That they had this status was due in no small way to Walsh's own efforts as Chancellor.

In spite of failing health, Walsh continued to direct the university through the trials of the Great War and the Irish Revolution (1916–21). The Chancellor was at pains to preserve the independence of the university in the face of pressure from the castle during the war, including representations from Birrell with regard to 'the *extra-professional* utterances' of Eoin MacNeill, 'a learned *Early Irish Historian* who holds a Chair (Value £600 per annum)'.[88] In 1915, when Baron Wimborne was appointed lord lieutenant, the NUI drafted a fawning address which was clearly intended to secure Treasury funding for university accommodation. The address referred to the students who were active in the 'momentous struggle in which the Empire is at present engaged' and expressed confidence that in years to come the University would look back with pride on these 'bright and inspiring examples of service'. In a marginal comment, Walsh wryly remarked 'very doubtful about this suggestion'.[89] During the 1916 Rising he failed to condemn the insurgents. In the War of Independence, his sympathies were on the republican side, as was reflected in his conspicuous celebration of the requiem mass for Terence MacSwiney, a graduate of UCC and Lord Mayor of Cork who had died on hunger strike in Brixton Prison. Just months before his death, the archbishop made a futile effort to save the life of Kevin Barry, a student at UCD condemned for his part in the killing of three British soldiers. Walsh's biography contains a poignant account of the aged bishop being carried up flights of stairs at Dublin Castle in this desperate attempt.[90] There may indeed have been some truth in Sir Shane Leslie's assertion that had Walsh survived he might have averted the Civil War, given his influence upon Eamon de Valera, who compared his relationship to the archbishop with 'the intimate personal affection of a son for a father'.[91]

Walsh's sudden death on 9 April 1921 occurred at the height of the War of Independence. The obituaries in the Irish and British newspapers echoed the sentiments of the editorial of the *Freeman's Journal* which described the archbishop as 'a great Irishman and a great churchman . . . a scholar, a theologian, a born administrator [and] a citizen of statesmanlike quality'. Only the *Telegraph* departed from this spirit. In an embittered appraisal, written by T. P. O'Connor MP, who was still reeling from Walsh's rejection of the Irish Party, he described a career which 'ought to have been uniformly great [but] became tortuous, then unnoticed, finally almost forgotten'.[92] Such sentiments, however, did not reflect the sense of the people of Dublin who lined the streets to pay their respects to the archbishop. Nor were they shared by the gravediggers at Glasnevin Cemetery who abandoned their strike to make preparations for Walsh's funeral.[93] In university circles, too, Walsh was universally mourned and successive memorials praised his devotion to the cause of education for over half a century. The NUI Senate described his passing as 'a national bereavement'. That address attributed not only the foundation of the university to his efforts, but also its survival and success, in so far as his 'wise guidance' had led it through the great difficulties of its early years.[94] The Governing Body of UCD, for its part, mourned the death of the Chancellor as 'a kind friend, a wise counsellor, and a great Irishman'.[95] No epitaph would have satisfied William Walsh more.

CHAPTER 9 *Eamon de Valera, 1921–75* JOHN WALSH

EAMON DE VALERA SERVED as Chancellor of the NUI for over half a century – his term began before Ireland became an independent state and ended not long after Irish accession to the European Communities. He remained Chancellor throughout a remarkable public career as a revolutionary leader, prisoner of state, successful politician, head of government and President of Ireland. His commitment to the National University was evident: he served for a longer period as Chancellor than in any of the more powerful and prominent positions, which he held during his public life.

The election of Eamon de Valera as Chancellor of the National University of Ireland was essentially a political act. He was a graduate of the university and also held a degree from its predecessor, the Royal University, but he was not nominated on the basis of his academic qualifications. He was well known and respected by several senior academics on the Convocation of the NUI, but this was not their primary motivation when they supported his nomination. De Valera was the sole surviving commandant of the 1916 Rising. He was also the President of the Irish Republic and head of the revolutionary government established by the First Dáil in 1919. De Valera owed his nomination as Chancellor to his pivotal role in the nationalist struggle for independence: in selecting de Valera, the Convocation of the NUI was not simply electing a new Chancellor, but affirming its commitment to the cause of nationalist Ireland.

The struggle for national independence between 1916 and 1921 greatly influenced the National University, its Convocation being dominated from 1919 by fervent nationalists, including Eoin MacNeill, Patrick McGilligan and Michael Hayes. Senior academics within the NUI, such as Dr Michael Cox, the chairman of Convocation and Fr Timothy Corcoran SJ, Professor of Education in UCD, were also firmly supportive of the nationalist cause.[1] The leading nationalist members of this body engineered de Valera's selection as Chancellor in 1921. Following the death of Dr William Walsh in April 1921, de Valera was approached to allow his name to go forward by a group of leading graduates, including Michael Cox and Fr Corcoran, his former teacher in UCD. The President expressed some misgivings to other members of the government about the possibility of defeat in the election, but agreed to accept nomination as a candidate on the basis that 'actual election at the time might be of public value and of help to our Cause'.[2] It is unlikely that de Valera feared defeat, but he was concerned that he should be the sole candidate to safeguard his political standing. He was promptly nominated by his supporters and was elected unopposed as Chancellor on 20 July 1921.[3] De Valera immediately issued a telegram to Dr Cox accepting the office of Chancellor, asserting that 'the conferring of this honour on the head of state indicates the path Ireland desires to tread'.[4] De Valera was well aware of the reasons for his nomination and hoped to secure some advantage for the nationalist cause from such a public endorsement by the NUI graduates.

The new Chancellor soon emphasised his concern that the National University should play its part in the development of the Irish nation. Nationalist rhetoric featured strongly when the authorities of the NUI held an official reception for their new Chancellor in Earlsfort Terrace on 19 November 1921. De Valera was praised as a great political and military leader by Michael Hayes TD and Dr Michael Tierney.[5] De Valera himself made speeches in Irish both to the NUI graduates and later to the students, in which he discussed the proper place of the university within the national struggle for independence. He told the students that the National University should reflect the spirit of the nation and contribute to the achievement of the nation's highest ambitions.[6] At the same time, the new Chancellor emphasised that he saw the university as a centre of Irish culture and higher learning, not simply a convenient instrument for fulfilling social or economic demands.

De Valera had not even been formally installed as Chancellor when his government – and Irish society – was bitterly divided by the conflict over the Anglo-Irish Treaty. He received a copy of the treaty signed by the delegates in London on 6 December in the Mansion House, while he was about to chair a symposium hosted by the NUI.[7] De Valera's opposition to the Treaty divided him from many of his former admirers, not least within the NUI: several of his leading supporters in the election for Chancellor, such as Michael Hayes and Patrick McGilligan, soon became lifelong political opponents. Moreover the political turmoil which followed the split over the Treaty meant that de

Valera had little opportunity to act as Chancellor of the NUI in the short term. He was formally inaugurated as Chancellor and chaired his first meeting of the University Senate on 19 December 1921, on the same day that the Dáil was continuing its divisive public debate on the Treaty.[8] The Chancellor then proved unable to attend any further meetings of the Senate for almost three years, as the split within Irish nationalism became irrevocable and led rapidly to civil war. De Valera's absence was to some extent beyond his control, as he was for a time a prisoner of the new Free State government in 1923; he was also preoccupied with rebuilding the strength of the defeated anti-Treaty party following the end of the Civil War. However, he was never completely detached from the affairs of the NUI even during this turbulent period. He engaged in correspondence with the registrar of the NUI, Joseph McGrath, in 1922, authorising him to hold meetings of the Senate and other university committees throughout this period.[9] But it was not until the end of 1924 that de Valera was able to give considerable attention to the office of Chancellor: he chaired his first regular meeting of the Senate on 5 December 1924.[10] He would remain a constant presence at the apex of the NUI for almost five decades.

While de Valera was to be deeply engaged in the activities of the NUI throughout his long term as Chancellor, he did not attempt to intervene actively in routine business or decision making, unlike his predecessor. He delegated authority extensively to successive registrars and relied on them to conduct the normal business of the National University. He was consulted on matters such as the organisation of meetings of the Senate, the conferral of degrees and the awarding of honorary doctorates: in general he approved as a matter of course the recommendations made by the Registrar. The registrar or vice-chancellor of the day also referred important financial decisions affecting the NUI to de Valera, but usually his agreement was obtained without difficulty. The Chancellor, who himself lacked the time to examine closely the finances of the National University, normally trusted the judgement of the NUI's senior staff and gave his assent to the financial decisions which they proposed.[11] He regarded the position of Chancellor as a formal and ceremonial office: he presided over the activity of the National University, but rarely intervened directly to influence its decisions or to shape its academic policies.

The second Chancellor's vision of the office was illustrated by his tribute in April 1940 to Dr Denis J. Coffey, on his retirement as President of University

College Dublin and Vice-Chancellor of the NUI. Acknowledging his reliance on Coffey's expertise as an experienced academic and university administrator, de Valera commented:

> I would like to say that, as Chancellor, when I came to preside at meetings I thought it my duty to read the Statutes of the University and to a certain extent make myself familiar with the regulations, but I found after one or two meetings that there was no need for it at all. I am afraid Doctor Coffey taught me to be lazy, for after the experience of the first two or three meetings I felt I could rely on Dr Coffey to keep me right on all occasions.[12]

The Chancellor generally accepted the advice offered by senior academics within the University Senate or by the administrators of the National University. He was not an assertive or dynamic chair of the Senate, nor was he expected to be by its members. McCartney rightly comments that 'he was quite content to play the role of Chairman of the Board, rather than Managing Director'.[13] Certainly de Valera had no wish to treat the office of Chancellor as an executive position; he had more than enough executive responsibilities in his public life without attempting to become chief executive of the National University.

The Chancellor did, however, exercise fully the relatively limited formal powers of the office. While his predecessor, Dr Walsh, had not voted in the Senate, de Valera frequently did so: he attended Senate meetings to vote in the election of Professor Arthur Conway as president of UCD and of Pádraig de Brún as president of UCG, for example.[14] Indeed he occasionally exerted a pivotal influence on important academic appointments, notably in 1954 when the Senate made the final decision in a contest for the post of Associate Professor of Surgery in UCD. The Senate voted twice in a closely contested election between the two leading candidates for the position and was evenly divided in each ballot: de Valera then decided the contest by giving his casting vote to Dr Patrick A. FitzGerald, who was immediately declared elected to the vacant post.[15] De Valera's willingness to exercise his legitimate powers in this instance was fully consistent with his vision of the office as mainly an honorary, ceremonial position.

This vision of the office as primarily ceremonial did not mean any lack of interest or disengagement from the affairs of the NUI. He gave considerable attention to his formal responsibilities and maintained an impressive record of attendance at meetings of the Senate of the NUI despite his extensive commitments as a TD, party leader and head of government after 1932. There were some unavoidable absences by the Chancellor. The Senate noted at its meeting on 10 March 1932 that a letter of regret for his inability to attend had been received from 'Eamon de Valera . . . President, Executive Council of Saorstát Éireann, Chancellor of the University'.[16] This was perhaps not surprising, as de Valera had been elected President of the Executive Council for the first time on the previous day. He immediately assured the Senate of his intention to 'remain associated with the work of the University, as far as his new duties will permit'. The Senate in turn unanimously passed a resolution welcoming de Valera's willingness to remain as Chancellor and conveying its best wishes for the success of his term as President of the Executive Council.[17] De Valera remained a constant presence at meetings of the Senate throughout the 1930s, despite the demands of leading a government, producing a new constitution in 1937 and pursuing an active foreign policy which involved a gradual transformation of the relationship between Britain and Ireland. He attended all meetings of the Senate in 1935; he was also present at a meeting on 19 May 1938, when 'congratulations were extended unanimously to An Taoiseach (the Chancellor) on the success of his recent negotiations in London'.[18] The strength of de Valera's engagement with the NUI was underlined by his attendance at this Senate meeting not long after the successful negotiation of the Anglo-Irish agreements in April 1938, and shortly before a general election in which he regained an overall majority in the Dáil. De Valera remained closely engaged with the activity of the NUI and deeply interested in the progress of its constituent colleges throughout his various terms as taoiseach between 1932 and 1959.

While de Valera hardly ever involved himself in the internal policy-making of the National University, he was willing to intervene to clarify the formal relationship between the NUI and the Irish state. He responded decisively in 1938 to a query from Alex McCarthy, the newly appointed registrar of the NUI, concerning the traditional position of the king as visitor of the University. The right to appoint the visitor was recognised in the original statutes of the NUI as part of the prerogative powers of the king, but this role was now an awkward anomaly following the adoption of de Valera's constitution in 1937, which removed all powers of the King except for the purpose of external association with the Commonwealth. McCarthy raised the matter personally with de Valera in July 1938, seeking clarification on the position of the visitor within the new constitutional framework. De Valera's response left no room for doubt: the king no longer had any function at all in relation to the National University. Maurice Moynihan, the secretary to the government, issued a detailed reply to the Registrar's query on 28 July, which had clearly been dictated by de Valera.[19] Moynihan asserted that the new constitution allowed the government to exercise all powers previously held by the king, unless other provisions were specifically made by the constitution. Moynihan made the taoiseach's views plain: 'It is therefore regarded as being quite incompatible with Article 49 of the Constitution that any function of a Visitor should continue to be exercised by the King.'[20] The taoiseach informed McCarthy that all powers previously exercised by the king in relation to the NUI had been fully transferred to the government. De Valera also advised the registrar that he saw no difficulty in the way of amending the statutes of the NUI and its colleges to reflect the new constitutional position.[21] The Chancellor's view prevailed and nothing more was heard about the formal powers of the king in relation to the NUI. The correspondence about the future of the visitor was not of great importance in itself, but it highlighted de Valera's concern to establish the National University firmly within the constitutional framework of the independent Irish state and to remove all formal remnants of British rule affecting the university. It also marked a rare decisive intervention by de Valera in the affairs of the NUI and under-lined his concern to define the university's formal relationship with the Irish state. His intervention in this instance was exceptional and is explained not only by his concern for the development of the university as a national institution, but also by his political and constitutional preoccupations as Taoiseach in the 1930s.

The colleges of the NUI did not benefit greatly in financial terms from de Valera's pivotal position within Irish politics up to the late 1950s: this was due mainly to the poverty and economic weakness of the new state, although the low priority given to education generally by most politicians in the first generation after independence also contributed to the underdevelopment of higher education. De Valera himself was concerned to provide greater state funding for university education, although his efforts in this regard were seriously restricted by financial constraints and the adverse consequences of some of his own economic policies, notably the failure of protectionism to develop the Irish economy. The Chancellor's most significant intervention to assist the colleges of the NUI came towards the end of his tenure as head of government.

De Valera began his final term as taoiseach in 1957 at a time when the university sector was struggling with a severe accommodation crisis. The number of students in the NUI approximately doubled from 2,684 in 1930–1 to 5,980 in 1957–8.[22] While this represented a very limited expansion in the proportion of the population involved in university education, the increase had occurred over three decades in which there had been minimal capital development in the university sector. The colleges were therefore badly overcrowded, unable to cope with any further expansion and facing arrears of building work, which they lacked the funding to undertake.[23] The college authorities appealed for assistance to de Valera, as the long-serving Chancellor of the NUI, shortly after his return to power. The Taoiseach responded positively, securing the cabinet's agreement in August 1957 to establish a commission to consider the accommodation needs of the NUI.[24] The recommendations of the commission proved significant in securing additional state funding for all three university colleges within the NUI, but de Valera's initiative was particularly important for the future of UCD.

The authorities in UCD sought the endorsement of the government for the transfer of the college from Earlsfort Terrace to a new site at Belfield.[25] This was vigorously promoted by the president of UCD, Michael Tierney, and had been supported by the governing body of the college since 1951.[26] De Valera himself initially raised the idea that Leinster House might be used to meet some of UCD's most pressing accommodation needs, on the basis that the location of the Oireachtas there was originally intended to be a temporary measure. The Chancellor discussed his long-term aspiration that the area between Earlsfort Terrace and Pearse Street might become the cultural centre of the city, in his address at the Golden Jubilee celebrations for the NUI in December 1958.[27] But he also commented that his favoured solution 'had become an impossible dream' due to financial and other difficulties.[28] He considered that any attempt to revive such a project would merely delay further the action necessary to meet the urgent accommodation needs of UCD and the other colleges. De Valera's address on this occasion gave a broad hint that he was willing to support the transfer of UCD to Belfield.

The majority of the commission established at de Valera's instigation concluded that the accommodation available to UCD in Earlsfort Terrace was completely inadequate and recommended the transfer of the entire college to the new site on the Stillorgan Road, at an estimated cost to the state of £6,700,000.[29] The Commission's proposed solution enjoyed the crucial support of the taoiseach. Indeed Michael Tierney appealed to de Valera in April 1959 to secure a decision on the future of UCD before his retirement as taoiseach.[30] De Valera was sympathetic to the concerns of the UCD authorities and he ensured that the cabinet acted decisively on the recommendations of the commission. While the Department of Education took the lead in proposing that the government should approve the transfer of the college, de Valera played the crucial part in securing the cabinet's support for the initiative, directing Maurice Moynihan to send a favourable response to the Department of Education's proposal on 29 April.[31] Despite some opposition within the government to the proposed transfer, de Valera's view prevailed. The cabinet approved in principle the transfer of UCD to Belfield on 26 May 1959.[32] The UCD authorities were in no doubt about the importance of de Valera's role in securing official approval for the move to Belfield. Dr Tierney recorded his gratitude to the taoiseach on 4 June 1959: 'It is indeed a matter of great satisfaction to everyone in University College Dublin that you have been able to do the college this memorable service, which we hope will cause you to be numbered for the future among its chief benefactors.'[33] The government's decision certainly did not receive universal support among the staff of UCD, nor did it end the controversy over the move to Belfield. But Tierney was correct in drawing attention to the crucial part played by de Valera, on the eve of his retirement from active politics, in securing the state's commitment to the development of the Belfield site. De Valera played a low-key but very influential role in deciding the future of the largest constituent college of the NUI in his final term as Taoiseach. It was his single most important intervention in shaping the future development of the National University.

De Valera's retirement from active politics in 1959 brought no change in his long-standing relationship with the NUI, despite some public speculation to the contrary. When he announced his intention to run for president in January 1959, speculative reports appeared in some newspapers suggesting that he was about to retire as Chancellor as well as head of government. The most spectacularly ill-informed report appeared in a British newspaper, the

Sunday Dispatch, on 18 January 1959. This article suggested that de Valera would resign as Chancellor before the campaign for the presidency began; it was also reported that Dr John Charles McQuaid, the Catholic Archbishop of Dublin, would be elected unopposed to succeed de Valera, on the day after his resignation.[34] The report went on to quote an anonymous member of the convocation of the NUI, who asserted that 'Dr McQuaid's candidature is supported by the great majority of members. He would make an ideal Chancellor'.[35] The report proved entirely unfounded. While some members of the Convocation certainly did favour the election of McQuaid as de Valera's eventual successor, the archbishop was a controversial figure whose selection would have drawn criticism both within and outside the NUI. More importantly, however, de Valera had no intention of resigning as Chancellor. The *Irish Press* almost immediately made clear de Valera's true position, recording on 21 January the taoiseach's comment that there was 'no foundation' for the report.[36] In fact de Valera remained as Chancellor for a further 16 years and outlived his potential successor, Dr McQuaid.

Following de Valera's election as President of Ireland in June 1959, the Senate unanimously expressed its appreciation that 'after nearly forty years of invaluable service as Chancellor, he should be pleased to continue to serve the University in this capacity'.[37] The presidents of all three university colleges warmly welcomed his decision to continue as Chancellor; de Valera in turn assured the Senate that it would be 'a great pleasure' for him to remain in this position.[38] The widespread support within the NUI for this may have been due in part to reservations about his potential successors: allowing the office of Chancellor to revert to the Catholic Archbishop of Dublin did not command universal support among members of the Convocation, while the rumour that Myles na gCopaleen might be nominated to contest an election was even less welcome to most members.[39] But the former taoiseach's personal prestige, his stature as a national and international leader and his good relations with prominent figures in Trinity College, Dublin were also considerable advantages for the National University. Moreover, de Valera's impartiality in chairing the Senate was widely acknowledged by its members and his independence between the four different institutions within the NUI was also fully recognised.[40] De Valera as Chancellor was in many respects a unifying figure within a diverse institution.

The election of the Chancellor as president did not cause any fundamental

change in the way that de Valera engaged with the NUI. He remained assiduous in his attention to formal business – indeed his record of attendance
at the University Senate was as impressive as ever. But the volume of his
correspondence as Chancellor gradually declined in the 1960s, reflecting
his increasing age and ill health. He showed considerable interest in the
deliberations of the Commission on Higher Education, which was established by the government in 1960. De Valera issued a circular to members
of the Senate in July 1961, encouraging them to make representations to the
commission on issues affecting the NUI. He suggested that members of the
Senate should prepare memoranda on subjects of their own choosing for
submission to the commission.[41] But de Valera did not initiate any further
correspondence as Chancellor after 1961, nor did he make any comments
of his own on letters or documentation, which he received through the NUI
office. He was even more willing than previously to allow the business of
the University to be conducted by the Registrar and administrative staff of
the NUI: he had a high regard for the staff of the NUI and relied on them
completely. De Valera paid a warm tribute to the then Registrar, Seamus
Wilmot and the staff of the NUI office in December 1971, at a function to
celebrate the 50th anniversary of his election as Chancellor. He commented
that they were the best of all the staff who worked for him – which was no
mean compliment – and that their work-rate was 'a model to the whole
country'.[42] The office of Chancellor, which had always been regarded by
de Valera as primarily honorary and ceremonial in character, became an
exclusively ceremonial position during his final decade in office.

Nevertheless de Valera showed a striking commitment to the office and
a continuing interest in the NUI until the end of his life. Following his
retirement as President in 1973, he continued to act as Chancellor, attending
his final meeting on 17 July 1975 at the age of 92.[43] He had by then outlived not
only most of the colleagues who had originally served with him on the Senate,
but also several potential successors. De Valera died on 28 August 1975,
having served as Chancellor of the NUI for 54 years. The Senate passed a
resolution on 18 September, which paid tribute to de Valera's 'wise guidance,
calm influence and impartial Chairmanship'.[44] They recorded their gratitude for his part in the development of the NUI, which had ensured that 'the
whole structure of Irish society is indebted to the graduates of his beloved
National University'.[45] The warmth of the tribute paid by the Senate reflected

in part his stature as the dominant political figure in the Irish state since independence; but it also underlined a genuine appreciation among senior NUI staff and graduates of his consistent engagement in the activity of the National University for more than half a century.

De Valera placed a very high value on the office of Chancellor: he regarded it as a mark of honour from his fellow graduates and appreciated particularly the formal connection with the NUI, which the office represented. He greatly valued his continuing engagement with the National University, in part due to his own academic background but also because he appreciated the NUI's strong association with Irish nationalism. De Valera maintained a considerable interest in higher education throughout his public career, although his sympathy for higher learning frequently did not translate into greater state support for university education in general or the NUI in particular. The crucial role he played in guaranteeing the essential support of the state for the transfer of UCD to Belfield marked a rare political intervention on his part to assist a college of the NUI.

De Valera fulfilled the formal responsibilities of the office with exceptional diligence over five decades. He had neither the inclination nor the opportunity to seek a more assertive leadership role within the National University. He offered firm guidance to the officials of the NUI on the relationship between the National University and the Irish state, but did not generally attempt to intervene in the academic or administrative business of the institution. His vision of the office as a ceremonial position was arguably well suited to his time: his low-key approach made the Chancellor a unifying figure in a relatively new and diverse institution, where the different colleges were seeking to develop their own distinctive identity. It was ironic that de Valera, who was the most dominant and controversial public figure of his time, made the office of Chancellor a symbol of unity and impartiality for the different institutions of the National University.

CHAPTER 10 *T. K. Whitaker, 1976–96* RONAN FANNING

I N 1999 A CANDIDATE taking the BA examination in history in University College Dublin wrote:

> The person choosing to read a long survey of Irish history, for example from 1600 to the present day, is letting him or herself in for a long tale of misery and hardship. Cromwell, the Famine, emigration, independence but seemingly little improvement in the country. Then, suddenly, towards the end of our hypothetical book, our reader comes across a chapter with a title such as 'New Beginnings' or 'Turning the Tide'. . . The Messiah, in the shape of T. K. Whittaker [*sic*] has arrived . . .

That passage, forged under examination pressure, explains more succinctly than any words I can readily find why it was that the National University of Ireland chose Thomas Kenneth Whitaker to succeed Eamon de Valera as their third Chancellor. Its sentiments had been uncannily anticipated nearly forty years earlier in the address delivered by James Meenan on the occasion of the NUI conferring Ken Whitaker with an honorary doctorate in 1962. Reflecting on the extraordinary influence of *Economic Development*, the seminal analysis of the Irish economy published under Whitaker's name in 1958, Meenan observed that

> this study pleased all the economists; it pleased all the politicians so much that our economic affairs have been conducted ever since, with increasing success, on the basis of a White Paper which bore a greater resemblance to Mr. Whitaker's recommendations than is usual in this imperfect world. To please the economists and the politicians, and at the same time to excite the imagination of the public, has been given to few.[1]

Thomas Kenneth Whitaker, a native of Rostrevor, County Down, was born on 8 December 1916, the son of the assistant manager of a local linen mill and the district nurse who was his second wife. The family moved to

Drogheda during the Civil War and he was educated at the Christian Brothers' school where, in 1934, he sat the leaving certificate and took first place in the clerical officers' examination. 'Once in a blue moon the open competitive examination for the civil service brings to light a man of ... exceptional type who no power on earth can prevent from sprinting like a flash to the top of the ladder':[2] so it was with Ken Whitaker. He was again placed first in ensuing civil service examinations and, at the age of 20, became private secretary to the Minister for Education, Tomas Ó Deirg; in 1938 he became an administrative officer in the Department of Finance where his subsequent rise through the ranks was meteoric. He also obtained external degrees – a BSc (Econ) and MSc (Econ) – from the University of London by private study.[3] In 1956, at the tender age of 39, he was appointed secretary of the Department of Finance – in effect, the head of the Irish civil service – at a time of deep and seemingly inescapable economic depression. He arranged the terms of Ireland's entry to the IMF and World Bank in 1957 and negotiated initial funding from the Ford Foundation for the economic research institute that became the ESRI. *Economic Development* provided the basis for Ireland's First Programme for Economic Expansion and, in 1961–2 (having toured the capitals of the EEC6 in 1960), working closely with the Taoiseach, Seán Lemass, he chaired the inter-departmental committee that paved the way for the Europeanisation of Irish foreign policy and, a decade later, for Ireland's entry into the EEC. In 1965, Whitaker initiated and attended Lemass's no less historic meeting with Northern Ireland's Prime Minister, Terence O'Neill, in Stormont. On his retirement from the Department of Finance, he became Governor of the Central Bank (1969–76) from which unlikely eminence he played a decisive, although then anonymous, role in sustaining the next Taoiseach, Jack Lynch, at the height of the Northern Ireland crisis.

The chancellors of the National University of Ireland had hitherto been notable for a low profile in their conduct of that office. Although the first Chancellor, Archbishop William Walsh, had been pro-active in his first years in office, ill health meant that he attended only one meeting of the Senate in 1914–21. Civil war and subsequent imprisonment meant that his successor, Eamon de Valera, was also an absentee Chancellor for his first three years in office. 'During these nine critical years in which Vice-Chancellors had presided ... the Senate developed a momentum of its own'. When de Valera did take up the reins of office, 'he was quite content to play the role of Chairman of the Board rather than Managing Director', relying heavily upon the registrar and vice-chancellors, in particular upon Denis Coffey, the long-serving president of UCD.[4] Although assiduous in taking the chair at meetings of the Senate, the habit thus established of leaving the direction of policy to others was reinforced by the demands upon de Valera of political office.

On 19 May 1976, at his installation as Chancellor, Whitaker told the Senate that

> he was grateful to the many graduates who voted for him. He felt a responsibility to use all this goodwill for the benefit of Irish University education. He appreciated the support all the more because he was not a scholar or an academic person. He was an external graduate of the London University, who was 'nationalised' in 1962 when he received an honorary doctorate in Economic Science from the National University ... His experience was as an administrator concerned with policy issues. A figurehead Chancellor would be no use to anyone. He wanted to understand all the issues in third-level education in order to participate more effectively in Senate discussions on matters of policy ... He was very conscious of the responsibility of succeeding Dr Eamon de Valera who had discharged the office with such dignity for 54 years. The Senate of the National University of Ireland was well placed to exercise leadership in relation to the development of higher education in Ireland.[5]

Those words carried enduring conviction: thirty years later Ken Whitaker still spoke with an air of modesty and faint surprise that he had been entrusted with the chancellorship of the NUI despite his lack of a formal university education. He also spoke of the sense of culture shock he had experienced at his first meeting of the Senate. The style of chairmanship of the long blind and latterly deaf de Valera had been relaxed, to say the least. Nothing in Ken Whitaker's vast administrative experience had prepared him for a meeting – 'the most chaotic and largest I'd ever had to preside over' – where the thirty or so participants continuously chatted and gossiped, interrupted only by the sporadic interjection 'The Senate has decided?' from the Registrar of the NUI, John Bourke, as he wended his way through the agenda; sometimes meetings, which began in mid-morning, were so discursive that they adjourned for lunch. But the new Chancellor soon set his stamp upon things and it became the turn of disconcerted members of the Senate to experience culture shock when one meeting ended in half an hour; the norm was that meetings thereafter ran from 11 to 1.[6]

If Ken Whitaker is the personification of change in the history of twentieth-century Ireland, Eamon de Valera is, for many historians, the embodiment of stagnation. While that contrast can be exaggerated and is in many respects often over-simplified, it is indisputably true for historians of the NUI. The grotesquely long tenure of de Valera as Chancellor – from a year before Ireland became independent until two years after Ireland joined the EEC – was a massive obstacle to change either in the structure of the NUI or in the relationship between government and the universities. Ministers for Education in de Valera's governments were unlikely even to glance in the direction of a structure at whose apex 'the Chief' was enthroned like a colossus; intermittent and short-lived inter-party governments were similarly albeit less reverentially inhibited. Whether the Presidents of UCD, UCC and UCG who invited Ken Whitaker to become a candidate for the chancellorship of the NUI saw him as a catalyst for change is a moot point. Yet the winds of changes that had swept through secondary education in the 1960s were bound to begin gusting at the doors of the universities and it may be of significance that the initial overture came from the politically astute Tom Murphy, the President of UCD.[7] No one was better qualified than Whitaker to manage change and, in particular, to mediate between the NUI and government. How he exercised that role is the subject of this essay.

The portents for change soon appeared when, on 30 July 1976, the Minister for Education, Dick Burke, announced that the constituent colleges of the NUI and St Patrick's College, Maynooth were to become independent universities. When the Senate considered the implications of this announcement, at an extraordinary meeting on 26 November 1976, the apocalyptic items proposed by the Chancellor for consideration included: the effect of dissolution on the full-time posts of registrar and 14 staff; the future of the premises (including Seal, portrait, gowns and records); a host of financial issues; the 'Appointed Day for dissolution'; and the 'preservation of existing rights of Professors and statutory officers'. Yet the mood of the meeting, which seemed to accept the ministerial declaration as a *fait accompli*, was remarkably quiescent: it merely decided to inform the Department of Education 'that new legislation should provide for the formal appointment to the new Universities of all statutory appointees in the NUI and that their full rights be incorporated in the legislation'. Even more remarkable was the response when the Chancellor 'asked if the Senate wished to express a view on the Government's decision. It was confirmed that the Senate had no negative view on the decision'.[8] That muted response, Ken Whitaker surmised thirty years later, may have been an early intimation of the wish of the constituent colleges for a loosening of the ties that bound them to the NUI.[9] In the event, the coalition government of 1973–7 was nearing the end of its days and Dick Burke's proposal came to nothing.

The mid-seventies have been 'characterised as a period of drift or confusion concerning the future structure of higher education'[10] and the best part of a decade elapsed before Gemma Hussey, the Minister for Education in another coalition government, this time led by Garret FitzGerald (a long-standing member of the NUI Senate who was to succeed Whitaker as Chancellor in 1996), told the Dáil in May 1984 of her 'intention to reactivate the question of providing legislation in regard to the structure of our Irish universities'[11] – an announcement that prompted the formal application by St Patrick's College, Maynooth for the status of a Constituent College within the NUI.[12] Gemma Hussey was among the many admirers of Ken Whitaker – 'an extremely nice person, interesting and polished and witty too' she recorded in her diary after the 'rather posh' dinner in the Berkeley Court Hotel to celebrate the 75th anniversary of the NUI[13] – but although her intentions were embodied in a White Paper,[14] they suffered the same fate as Dick Burke's.

The summer of 1984 also witnessed the imbroglio between the NUI and the government over the award of an honorary degree to the American President Ronald Reagan on the occasion of his Irish visit. Reagan was unpopular in Ireland and the award sparked protests, not least from among the members of the Senate of the NUI. When the dust had settled, the Chancellor made clear the strength of his personal feelings on the issue of the principle involved in awarding honorary degrees to visiting statesmen. He traced the origin of the practice to requests from government that had begun 30 years earlier, when Eamon de Valera was at once Chancellor and Taoiseach, because the state had no honours system of its own. Visiting foreign statesmen who had received such honorary doctorates at the instance of the government included Pandit Nehru (1956), President Kennedy (1963), President Kaunda of Zambia (1964) and the Indian Presidents Radahkrishnan

(1964) and Reddy (1982). Where there had been no request from the government – as in the case of the recently retired French President de Gaulle's
visit in 1969 – the NUI had taken no initiative, thus reinforcing the presumption that 'the University is in this area acting merely as a proxy for the Government'. In the Reagan case Whitaker had taken the view

> that the question of an honorary degree should be considered only at the
> express request of the Government. When the request was made he had
> advised the Senate that, in the light of precedent, 'the principal relevant
> considerations were (a) the request of the Government in relation to their
> invitee to Ireland and (b) the status of the proposed recipient as the Head of
> an important state (and government) with which Ireland maintained friendly
> relations' and that these should 'take precedence over any views which, as
> individual members of the Senate, we might have on U. S. policies, domestic
> or international. This general approach was, I believe, reflected in the voting,
> which yielded more than the two-thirds majority required for an affirmative
> decision. It would be unwise, however, to discount the risk of an embarrassing
> outcome to such votes in the future.
>
> Of its nature, any convention that presumes a particular outcome to the
> exercise by the University of its own prerogative is unsatisfactory. Misgivings
> are reinforced when serious differences arise, within the University and the
> community, as to the policies of a proposed recipient of a University honour
> whose main or only claim to recognition is on the political plane. The Uni-
> versity, far from having anything to gain in such cases, can only lose through
> the misunderstanding and division its decision produces.
>
> I am not referring merely to the recent controversial case of President
> Reagan. My remarks are of general application. The Government's next dis-
> tinguished guest might conceivably be the President of the USSR. Indeed it
> is hard to identify any foreign Head of State (the Pope apart) who would today
> be hailed unanimously in the Republic as the deserving recipient of a formal
> honour: the country is now full of Skibbereen Eagles!

Whitaker concluded by suggesting that it was time that the convention
regarding visiting statesmen be revisited and that the NUI should 'reclaim
unqualified discretion . . . in the matter of the award of honorary degrees and
that the Government should be so advised'.[15] He had already taken the pre-
caution of sending the then Taoiseach, Garret FitzGerald, a rough draft of

his letter *before* the Reagan conferring ceremony in Galway, explaining that he had wanted him 'to see it as Taoiseach before anyone else on the Senate of NUI because relations with the Government are involved. I would be glad if you could indicate your acquiescence in the course proposed.'[16] The taoiseach's response was all that the Chancellor could have hoped for or expected. Responding in kind, in a personal 'Dear Ken' letter, he also authorised him to indicate his own 'feelings on this matter' to the Senate of which he himself had been long a member:

> Whatever merit there may have been in the past about an informal arrangement between the Government and the National University of Ireland in connection with the award of honorary degrees to visiting Heads of State which aroused no controversy, it seems to me that now the matter has become one of public debate it would be better for all concerned and particularly for the University, if the practice of an honorary degree being awarded at the request of the Government came to an end . . .
>
> I propose therefore to inform the Department of Foreign Affairs, as well as my own Department [of the Taoiseach], that no further initiatives should be taken on behalf of the Government in respect of honorary degrees for visiting Heads of State and that in the future it should be a matter entirely for the University itself to decide on its own initiative and responsibility whether it may wish to propose the award of an honorary degree to such personages . . .
>
> Should the Senate wish to be kept informed on an informal basis of pending visits of Heads of State so that they might give consideration to the award of honorary degrees in certain cases, this could of course be arranged – but only if this were the wish of the Senate and entirely on its own initiative.[17]

The episode serves as a classic example of the discreet determination with which Ken Whitaker strove, both in the Senate and in the corridors of power, to uphold the dignity and reputation of the NUI throughout his chancellorship.

Yet there was no gainsaying the asymmetrical relationship between the government and the University. The NUI's impotence was again exposed by its inability even to ensure the survival of its recognised colleges in the face of the government's arbitrary decision to close Carysfort College of Education; the Senate at its meeting on 13 March 1986, could do no more than communicate their regret at the lack of consultation to the Department of

Education and ask that 'the facilities and potential of Carysfort should continue to be effectively used for the benefit of Third Level education'.[18]

Whitaker was also concerned about the future of another recognised college, Maynooth, and in November 1989 he intervened personally in an attempt to smooth the way for its becoming the fourth constituent university of the NUI suggesting that the composition of its Governing Body should be brought into line, *mutatis mutandis*, with the other governing bodies.[19] He returned to the theme early in 1990 when he identified its

> major 'peculiarities': Maynooth has no provision for appointments by the NUI Senate to its Governing Body. While the staff of Maynooth, both academic and administrative, and the students, are well represented, there is no place for public representatives, whether from Government or Local authorities. The Bishops have four representatives, a situation unique to Maynooth.[20]

Another cause of contention between the NUI and the government was the matriculation examination offering an additional route to the Department of Education's leaving certificate examination for would-be entrants to the NUI. Trinity College had suspended its matriculation examination in 1979 and there was mounting public pressure for UCD to follow suit, spearheaded by the education correspondents of the *Irish Times* (Christina Murphy) and *Irish Independent* (John Walshe) and by Kieran Mulvey, the general secretary of ASTI (Association of Secondary Teachers, Ireland). A report from the NUI's Committee of Registrars recommending the retention of a reformed matriculation examination laid bare deep fissures in the Senate. The Standing Committee, dominated by the university presidents and registrars, disagreed and recommended suspension. But the Senate in turn disagreed, although their decision, on 28 January 1988, to seek 'informal discussions with the Department of Education on the feasibility of initiating reforms in the current structure of examinations at the end of Second Level', in effect opened the door to change.[21] Although Whitaker was regarded as an impeccably impartial chairman who 'never made the mistake of getting involved in discussion',[22] he felt the prolongation of the debate was damaging the NUI by exposing it to public criticism and he tried to push the matter to a conclusion at the Senate in April 1989. He argued:

That the NUI had acknowledged the equivalence in all subjects of Leaving Certificate (Pass) and Matriculation for almost fifty years and there was no suggestion that this acceptance should now cease. Other third-level colleges, moreover, relied almost exclusively on the Leaving Certificate.

That the examination was both time consuming and 'a very costly affair' (1988 – £599,408).

That the distinction sometimes drawn between the Leaving Certificate as a 'scrúdú fágála' and the matriculation as a 'scrúdú inontrála' was 'facile' and unpersuasive.

While acknowledging that 'it might be very difficult in practice, once it was suspended, to reinstate the Matriculation in its present wide form', if concerns arose about a particular subject notwithstanding the safeguards under negotiation with the Department of Education, 'recourse could be had, if all else failed, to holding a separate Matriculation Examination in that subject'.[23]

The issue became entangled in the ramifications of the government's decision, announced by the Minister for Education, Mary O'Rourke in January 1989, to confer university status on the two National Institutes for Higher Education (NIHEs), in Limerick and Glasnevin, which prompted the Senate decision that 'consideration to be given, in the context of the existing National University system, to Constituent Colleges being re-named as Constituent Universities, and to the working of the federal system being made smoother and more efficient'.[24] It was in this context that the four presidents sought to defer a decision on the fate of the matriculation examination pending consideration of the future structure of the NUI, and in April 1989 the Senate decided by 'a pronounced majority' to continue holding the examination at least until 1991.[25]

Whitaker now took care to keep lines of communication open to the Department of Education. 'I want to "fill you in" on the recent NUI Senate decision', he advised Declan Brennan, the Secretary of the Department of Education; Brennan had been one of Whitaker's private secretaries when he was Secretary of the Department of Finance and he wrote to him on first name terms suggesting they meet for 'a short talk, preferably over lunch in Elm Park [Golf Club]'. By this stage the Chancellor's main concern was to keep the department informed of 'the process which is now actively under way to consider which of the two possibilities – complete and separate independence or continued association with a federal NUI with changes in their titles, status and functions' would provide the most appropriate future structure for the NUI's four colleges; he told Brennan that he and the four college presidents 'will be ready at any time to come to the Department to discuss this matter with you or the Minister and yourself, if so desired'.[26] But when a meeting with Mary O'Rourke was duly arranged – in Leinster House on 25 May 1989 (the same day that the legislation conferring university status on the two NIHEs came before the Dáil) – it was at her request because her own view on the NUI matriculation examination 'was being misrepresented in such a way as to cause some division between the NUI and her Department'. She was particularly exercised by the phrase 'megaphone diplomacy' in a newspaper article after the NUI Senate's discussion in April, so much so that she returned to the point three times in the course of a short meeting. The Chancellor told the minister of the concerns of the NUI colleges that their status 'would be diminished by not being designated as Universities. At the same time, they would consider, as an alternative to being completely separate institutions, an arrangement under which they would have a large degree of autonomy, while still retaining the federal dimension.' While the minister was willing to discuss such issues 'in due course', her immediate concern was the matriculation examination which, she believed, 'had "outlived its usefulness"'.[27]

Sensitive to the rising political temperature, Whitaker did not want the NUI to get involved in a struggle he thought they were bound to lose[28] and, to one as well versed in the ways of governments, for a minister to offer such an opinion underscored his anxieties about the dangers of procrastination as the prospect of legislation on 'the future of the University in the context of the recent Government decision to create two new universities' loomed. That was the subject of a special meeting of the Senate on 13 July 1989. The options considered by the presidents, reported the Vice-Chancellor, Michael Mortell, the president of UCC, were

1   That no change be introduced – and that the NUI federal system be strengthened.
2   That maximum autonomy be devolved to the Colleges within the NUI system.

3 That the Colleges would abandon the federal system and seek new legislation.

The presidents agreed 'that new structures should evolve to provide autonomy by amending the 1908 Act rather than by recourse to new legislation. It was hoped that legal opinion would show how this could be done'. In summing up what he described as 'an extremely constructive discussion', the Chancellor emphasised the following points.

1 The common objective seemed to be the achievement of the Title and the status of a university for the three constituent colleges and St Patrick's College, Maynooth, with some caution regarding titles, (i.e. NUI at Dublin, or NUI. Dublin), but in a manner which would preserve the federal dimension.

2 ...The degree of autonomy that would be sought by the institutions and the need for achieving a balance between autonomy and the retention of essential functions in relation to (a) appointments, (b) courses of study and (c) matriculation entry standards.

3 ...The range and scope of the autonomy envisaged for the colleges and the areas to be reserved for the central federal authority.

4 It would be important to ensure that NUI spoke with one voice.[29]

The Chancellor, again, perhaps, because of his long experience of government, was less sanguine than the presidents about the prospect of confining legislation to a mere amendment of the 1908 Act. But although he thought it self-evident that 'the objective of affording virtual autonomy, with university title and status' to the colleges would require legislation, he argued that 'requisite revisions should be identified and kept as few and straightforward as possible' with the objective 'of minimising our exposure to Government and Parliamentary revision of our proposals'.[30]

In October 1989 the Chancellor again questioned the Senate's decision – 'an interim one at best'– to continue holding a separate matriculation examination at least until 1991, saying that the NUI 'would be unwise to lock itself into an academic fortress for the next three years, impervious to the opinion of Government, of teachers' organisations and of a large section of parents and the general public'. He asked that the matter be put back on the agenda for the Senate meeting in November 1989, with his 'strong personal recommendation . . . in favour of ceasing to hold a separate Matriculation Examination as soon as may be fair and practicable'.[31] What had now become the standard arguments were yet again rehearsed and the upshot was a decision that the Senate, 'with the minimum of further debate', should vote on a specific motion at its next meeting in January 1990.[32]

'It is understood the Senate deferred a decision until their next meeting . . . despite angry opposition to the exam from teachers and parents', reported one newspaper the next day. 'The Minister for Education, Mrs Mary O'Rourke, also wants the Matric abolished.'[33] By the end of November, this kind of publicity was compounded by press reports on the prospect of a legal battle to break up the NUI and of a potential conflict between the governing bodies of the constituent colleges and the Senate of the NUI.[34] But the Chancellor's efforts were finally crowned with success when the motion was carried by the narrowest of margins: 17 votes for and 15 against.[35]

The debate on the future structure of the NUI now gathered momentum and a special meeting of the Senate on 10 December 1990 considered conflicting reports from the four colleges. The President of UCD, Patrick Masterson, reported that six faculties had voted for autonomy: three in favour of heavily devolved powers entailing legislation, and one for minimal changes that 'might be feasible within the existing terms of the Act and Charter'. UCC wanted 'substantial devolution by means of minimal legislation'; their President, Michael Mortell, 'favoured short, sharp legislation'. This was endorsed by Colm Ó hEocha, the President of UCG, where 'a distrust of new legislation' had featured prominently in the discussions; he 'emphasised that four NUI institutions, working together, would have greater strength than if they were separated' and suggested the University of California as a model. The preferred model for Micheál Ledwith, the President of Maynooth, was the University of Toronto.[36] It fell to the Chancellor to create unity from this diversity. His first step was a draft document for the consideration of the Senate that set out a 'general approach': 'despite differences as to the extent and degree of change desired, it is the common preference of the four colleges that, while continuing to participate in an NUI system, they should each have the status and title of a university and have greater autonomy'.[37] That formula was affirmed at another special meeting of the Senate in February 1991 which considered a 'Revised Draft Submission for Approval' and when, to the surprise of many, the four presidents signed up to a common approach on the sensitive issue of title – 'The National University of Ireland, Dublin', 'The National University of Ireland, Cork', etc. – although they might extend those titles to indicate that they were successors to a specified constituent university e.g. UCD. It was also agreed that a final submission, having been sent for consideration to the presidents, should then be sent to the Minister for Education without again being referred back to the Senate.[38]

The speed with which this united front had been created – within two months – was remarkable and it was arguably Ken Whitaker's greatest achievement as Chancellor. The key to his success was that he had 'a greater notion of the role of the NUI than some of the Presidents'.[39] That said, the respect he commanded among the presidents was palpable: 'you could sense it, you could touch it'; even Tom Murphy, not the most pious of men, spoke of him in a 'reverential way'.[40]

On 5 March 1991, the Chancellor duly wrote to the Minister for Education outlining the NUI's proposals and hoping for early legislation to put those proposals into effect. But it was not until 19 June that the Minister met an NUI delegation composed of the Chancellor, the registrar and the four presidents. Although the minister initially described the proposals as 'an admirable example of pragmatism', she also identified what she regarded as the main disadvantage of 'still tinkering with the 1908 Act' and 'suggested that the terminology of the 1908 Act' might be inappropriate in the Ireland of the 1990s. Why would the NUI not go the extra mile? Why were they 'satisfied to amend the 1908 Act rather than contemplate a new Act'? The Chancellor replied that

> the 1908 Act established the status of the NUI and its Colleges. Preserving historical continuity was a vital element in providing all graduates with access to Degrees of international status. The NUI regarded it as important to preserve its identity as an institution established in 1908 rather than one newly-arrived in 1992 or later. He considered that the 1908 Act was basically satisfactory and could be updated without great difficulty.

Mary O'Rourke's own instincts were minimalist in regard to university legislation – she said that 'her mind "would go that way too, if only to see it done"', adding that a major Act 'would require "huge work"' – but she again queried 'whether it might not be preferable now to take a more bold approach, instead of adopting a timid and pragmatic position'. Ken Whitaker had never had qualms about contradicting ministers and he retorted 'that "bold" could also prove to be "foolish", stressing that the NUI proposals were courageous and innovative in seeking to balance the preservation of the NUI system, with significant functions, with the conferring of a higher status and autonomy on the Colleges'. Although Mary O'Rourke's approach was non-confrontational and she clearly wanted the meeting to end on a positive note, her concluding remarks were portentous: first, that the meeting should be regarded as exploratory; and, second, that, 'while it was her duty to bring the matter to the attention of Cabinet, she could not rule out the possibility that someone in Cabinet could bring forward other proposals, such as the bringing in of a general University Act'; in which case, the Chancellor suggested, the NUI proposals could become part 1 of such an Act.[41]

Six years had elapsed and Ken Whitaker's Chancellorship had ended before the enactment of the University Act of 1997, but the essence of the NUI strategy fashioned under his leadership in 1991 remained unchanged. Although Séamus Brennan had replaced Mary O'Rourke as Minister for Education when Albert Reynolds became Taoiseach in February 1992, the basis of what she had agreed with the NUI was embodied in the Green Paper, *Education in a Changing World*, published in June 1992 which provided for 'legislation to amend the 1908 Act, on the basis of the proposals put forward by the Senate of the NUI, in order to create four constituent universities within a federal NUI structure'. The NUI welcomed the new government's commitment 'to protect the independence and traditional democratic decision-making structures of the universities' and to preserve their diversity. But it took yet another change of government and the advent of a Labour Minister for Education, Niamh Bhreathnach, before the White Paper *Charting Our Education Future* was published in April 1995. Chapter 5 of the White Paper signalled the abandonment of the minimalism that had characterised the attitude towards legislating on the universities of Fianna Fáil ministers for education. It included commitments to broadening the composition of the universities' governing bodies and to statutory representation for students as well as for academic and non-academic staff. It also spoke of 'more comprehensive legislation' underpinning such principles as 'appropriate public accountability' and 'changes to reflect the role of universities in modern society' – in particular, 'the enhancement of the[ir] developmental role'. But it also seemed to offer reassurance to the NUI in the shape of an unequivocal commitment 'to proceed this year with the amendment of the National University of Ireland legislation, on the basis of proposals put forward by the Senate of the National University of Ireland'. [42]

That reassurance evaporated in the bombshell that burst over Merrion Square in July 1995 when the publication of the Department of Education's 'Position paper on university legislation' was accompanied by a letter from the Minister to the Chancellor challenging the need for the retention of a restructured NUI with very limited functions. The Chancellor responded swiftly to what was, in effect, nothing short of a threat to dissolve the NUI. He expressed astonishment that the ministerial commitment in the White Paper to introduce legislation 'on the basis of proposals put forward by the Senate of the NUI should now be abruptly discarded in favour of quite different proposals emanating from the Department'. Where the NUI proposals had envisaged combining 'a high degree of autonomy and status for the Colleges with the preservation of the federal fabric under the NUI Charter, appropriately amended' the Department's position paper envisaged 'the dissolution of the NUI, the scrapping of its historical Charter and the conversion of the Colleges into standardised separate elements of the new university system'. He also questioned whether the abolition of the NUI would lead to large savings as their central services 'would still have to be provided by the individual Colleges without the benefit of economies of scale' and stressed its quality control functions and the reputation of its degrees 'built up nationally and internationally over the past 87 years. Individual universities would be starting from scratch and could take a considerable time to achieve equivalent recognition. National as well as international loss could be involved'.

It was a measure of Whitaker's stature that the speed and forcefulness of his response triggered an immediate ministerial retreat: in a letter of 20 July Niamh Bhreathnach conceded that she did not regard the retention or dissolution of the NUI as 'an issue of fundamental principle'; she also undertook to consider the Chancellor's views before framing her legislative proposals. The university presidents endorsed the Chancellor's views at a meeting in the NUI on 24 July and a united response to the Department of Education reiterated those views: it took issue, in particular, with the suggestion in the Position Paper that 'it is not certain that all four colleges are in agreement with the form of legislation proposed by the NUI Senate', pointing out that the Senate's proposals of November 1992 had already been approved by the governing bodies in the NUI colleges. These exchanges were discussed at a meeting between NUI officers and the Secretary of the Department of Education on 1 September 1995 when the NUI's worst fears were assuaged by the Departmental statement that 'it would not be going the route of dissolution'.[43] That assurance was duly incorporated in the Universities Bill eventually published on 30 July 1996 which established the constituent colleges – as well as St Patrick's College, Maynooth – 'as universities in their own right, while maintaining the umbrella of the NUI'.[44]

A special meeting of the NUI Senate to consider the Bill took place on 3 October 1996. Introducing the discussion, the Chancellor 's 'main criticism' of the Bill was 'its invasion of the legitimate management freedom of a university, particularly in sections 22 and 33, which provided for the ultimate control by the HEA of the numbers and grades of university staff and of the distribution of the overall budget between different activities, as well as ultimate Ministerial control of fees'.[45] These points found cogent expression in the formal 'Response of the NUI Senate to the Universities Bill, 1996' forwarded to the Minister for Education. The detailed and meticulous notes in his own hand on the initial draft of this document[46] reveal the Chancellor's hands-on role in the preparation of the response, a role he invariably played in the NUI's direct dealings with government throughout the 20 years of his Chancellorship. He was also 'personally unhappy' about the section of the Bill (32) dealing with equality policy. While 'strongly in favour of equality of opportunity' and of 'equal access to higher education for all who have the necessary educational standards and of generous help for the disadvantaged to attain this standard', he was unpersuaded that the 'orientation' of this section was 'fair or valid'. He then sounded a note all too rarely heard from more pusillanimous university leaders obsessed with genuflecting to the idols of political correctness:

> so long as the demand for university places exceeds the supply, the allotment of places is rightly determined by reference to educational attainments and there should be no obligation, express or implied, on a university to give preferential access to any category on any other ground. Educational deficiencies associated with inequalities of a social, economic or other nature should be addressed and rectified, as far as possible, at the pre-university level.

If there is to be any positive discrimination, it should be prescribed by Act of the Oireachtas. A governing body would, I think, need such cover if it were to grant preferential access to scarce university places. Conceivably, such discrimination might fail a test of constitutionality.

Equally, in the context of this section, gender balance should be subjected to academic merit.[47]

It was 30 October 1996 before Niamh Bhreathnach finally introduced her Universities Bill in the Dáil and the story of the events leading to its enactment in a much amended form falls outside this account of the Whitaker Chancellorship. He had given 12 months' notice of his intention to resign as Chancellor and, when he chaired his last meeting of the Senate on 7 November 1996, he spoke of his sense of privilege at his role in the evolution of the universities – 'particularly in the reconstruction of the NUI, now being given legislative form' – over the previous 20 years. The essence of the wide-ranging tributes were epitomised in the praise of the Vice-Chancellor, Art Cosgrove, the President of UCD, for 'his wise counsel and wisdom, gained from his wide-ranging and distinguished experience as a public servant'. He had 'sustained the University at a time of unprecedented change', declared the Master of Maynooth, W. J. Smyth; 'for many people, Dr. Whitaker would enter the history books as a hero, and also as a sculptor of modern Ireland'.[48] That larger role will doubtless be the stuff of history for generations to come but what is already beyond doubt is that, in 1990–6, Ken Whitaker was the sculptor of the reconstituted National University of Ireland that ultimately emerged in the Universities Act of 1997.

CHAPTER 11 *Garret FitzGerald, 1997–* MAURICE MANNING

G ARRET FITZGERALD WAS ELECTED Chancellor of the National University of Ireland in 1997. The huge expansion in the number of eligible electors resulted in a decision being taken that all those who wished to vote were obliged to apply in writing for a ballot paper – a factor which resulted in a much smaller than usual turnout of voters. In a poll of 2,630 votes FitzGerald was elected with 70 per cent of votes cast.

FitzGerald was ironically the first Chancellor to have been an active academic in his previous life, even if his academic career was shared with a range of other occupations during a lifetime of public service – careers in air transport, economic consultancy, journalism, politics and business. He was also a leading member of the European Movement.

Garret FitzGerald was born in Dublin on 9 February 1926, the youngest of four sons of Desmond FitzGerald and Mabel McConville. His parents, both advanced nationalists, were from different religious backgrounds – his father a Roman Catholic while his mother was an Ulster Protestant. One of FitzGerald's earliest childhood memories was a lesson in religious tolerance, as he tells in his autobiography 'I was four or perhaps just five, playing on the study floor, my mother seated near me. I made a derogatory remark about the Protestant religion of the then Vice President (of the Irish Free State) Ernest Blythe. He was a close family friend of almost twenty years standing. My mother eyed me sternly and responded quietly, "you do know that I am a Protestant too, dear, don't you?"'[1]

Both parents were involved in the 1916 Rising, each of them serving in the GPO, and they continued as active members of Sinn Féin throughout the War of Independence. The Civil War saw them take opposite sides, Desmond FitzGerald becoming Minister for External Affairs and later Minister for Defence in the Free State governments between 1922 and 1932 while his mother was an ardent and committed Republican. One consequence of this was that the young Garret FitzGerald had and maintained friends on both sides of the political divide – something very unusual in those days and it was these friendships which tempered any inclination on his part to the type of political partisanship that was the norm through much of the early twentieth century. He was particularly close to the MacEntee and Ryan families and was later to develop a good relationship with Eamon de Valera during the latter's last years as Chancellor of the National University of Ireland. He studied at Coláiste na Rinne and at Belvedere College (where he was classmate of the future Cardinal, Archbishop Desmond Connell), and then at University College Dublin, at that stage located at Earlsfort Terrace. He graduated from UCD in 1946 with a degree in history and modern languages and shortly afterwards was called to the Irish Bar.

His first career was with the national airline, Aer Lingus, which had been founded in 1937 but had had little opportunity to develop during the years of the Second Word War. FitzGerald was among a small number of young graduates appointed in 1947 when the airline entered its first real phase of expansion. He found himself, at the age of 26 responsible for Aer Lingus's economic planning, rates and fares. He also exhibited an extraordinary grasp of the detail of airline scheduling, which, along with an interest in railway schedules, became a life-long obsession. Indeed he has recounted an incident in later life when his ability to deconstruct schedules enabled him to estimate with remarkable accuracy the size of the Aeroflot fleet, which was regarded at the time as a state secret.[2] He left Aer Lingus in 1958, retaining a great affection for the airline though this did not prevent him as taoiseach in 1986 from ending Aer Lingus's monopoly and allowing Ryanair to compete directly.

From his earliest days he was convinced that Ireland's best interest lay in membership of the developing European Economic Community and after leaving Aer Lingus worked to prepare the highly protected Irish industrial sector for the free trade era which he felt was inevitable. He later became economic consultant to the Federation of Irish Industry and played a part in securing agreement between the federation, the government and the Irish Congress of Trade Unions to the establishment of a Committee on Industrial Organisation of which he was an active member. Between 1961 and 1965 this committee surveyed the whole industrial sector and initiated a rationalisation of industry in preparation for membership of the European Economic Community.

Also at this time he established, in conjunction with the Economist Intelligence Unit of London, an Irish economic consultancy firm which served the needs of both the private and public sectors until the early 1970s. It was also at this time that he began his involvement with journalism, becoming a columnist with the *Irish Times* – a position he resumed when leaving politics – and at different times during the 1960s and early 1970s he was the Irish correspondent for the BBC, the *Financial Times* and the *Economist*.

It says something for the extraordinary energy and output of FitzGerald at this time that in addition to the above activities he was appointed a lecturer in economics in UCD in 1959. His academic interests had now moved largely, though not exclusively, to economics and in 1969 he was awarded a PhD for his thesis on Irish economic planning. During this period he published *State Sponsored Bodies* (1961 and 1963) and *Planning in Ireland* (1969), and also became actively involved in the politics of University College Dublin. He was elected to the governing body of that college by the graduates in 1965 and quickly became an outspoken critic of many aspects of what he saw as an authoritarian and closed style of governance. He was an active participant in the movement for university reform which led to the so-called 'Gentle Revolution' of 1969 and at this time was also involved in the street protests around the Wood Quay issue and the demolition of Georgian buildings on Hume Street in Dublin.

In 1973 he was elected to the Senate of the National University of Ireland, again from the graduate panel. He had considerable admiration for the Chancellor, Eamon de Valera and has written warmly of his conversations with de Valera at that time and also of his admiration for the way in which de Valera presided fairly over the Senate. As a Senate member he was not a particularly strong supporter of the establishment of the day, sitting at the 'awkward squad' table with colleagues such as Professor Enda McDonagh and Professor John A. Murphy.

In 1965 he entered politics. There was no inevitability about his joining his father's old political party. He was approached by Seán Lemass for whom he had great admiration, about running for Fianna Fáil. He supported many of Lemass's modernising policies and thought hard about the offer before declining. He probably felt most at home in the Labour Party and in fact declined to run for Fine Gael in the 1965 general election because he felt the party's economic and social policies were not sufficiently developed; he informed the leader James Dillon privately of this decision. However, after the change of leadership in 1965 and the renewed commitment of the party to the *Just Society* policies, he ran for Fine Gael and was elected in that year to Seanad Éireann. He made an immediate impact, concentrating in particular on issues such as education, finance, Europe and later in an intense way on the problems arising from the Northern Ireland conflict. He was elected to Dáil Éireann in 1969 and held his seat until his retirement in 1992.

In 1973 he became Minister for Foreign Affairs just weeks after Ireland acceded to the European Community. His emphasis as minister was on formulating for Ireland an integrationalist EU policy and in 1975 he ran Ireland's first presidency of the EEC. During this presidency he led the EC delegation in the final negotiations for the first Lomé Convention between the EC and 46 African, Asian, Indian Ocean and Pacific countries and signed this convention on behalf of the EC. During the presidency he also initiated the first contacts on behalf of the EC Council of Ministers with the revolutionary Portuguese government. Later in 1976 he negotiated an agreement with the European Commission that accorded Ireland the unique right to expand its fish catch at a time when other countries were required to cut back.

As Minister for Foreign Affairs FitzGerald also pursued a policy of reconciliation with the unionist leaders and community in Northern Ireland, backing the firmly anti IRA stance of Taoiseach Liam Cosgrave; in domestic politics he actively supported social democratic policies. Unusually for a sitting politician he continued to publish. *Towards a New Ireland*, a radical reappraisal of traditional attitudes to Northern Ireland appeared in 1972, and in 1979 his book *Equal Partners* was published by the United Nations. In 1984, when he was taoiseach, the Royal Irish Academy published his paper on the decline of the Irish language in 320 baronies between 1770 and 1870; in 2004 the Royal Irish Academy published a further paper of his on the state of the Irish language in the 2,450 out of the 3,850 electoral divisions where it still survived in the years immediately before the Famine.

In 1977 he was elected leader of Fine Gael. Although his election was unanimous it was not universally welcomed within the party. His liberal policies, especially on issues such as divorce and contraception, alienated some of the more traditional members of the party, and his policy of reconciliation in Northern Ireland was not always fully welcomed by some of the more nationalist elements. In spite of this he was undoubtedly the most successful leader in that party's history. He served twice as taoiseach (1981–2 and 1982–7). It is not within the scope of this essay to assess the performance of these governments which he led, save to mention the negotiation of the Anglo-Irish Agreement in 1985, which paved the way for the subsequent agreements culminating in the Good Friday or Belfast Agreement.

Garret FitzGerald resigned as leader of Fine Gael in 1987 and left politics in 1992. In a sense, he then began again where he had left off before entering politics, with economic consultancy but now on a global scale, membership of the Trilateral Commission, membership of the Council of State and of the Royal Irish Academy as well as a range of *pro-bono* activities. He also resumed his journalism especially for the *Irish Times* and continued to publish extensively. His autobiography *All in a Life* was published in 1991; *Reflections on the Irish State* followed in 2002, and *Further Reflections – Ireland and the World* in 2005. He also has written extensively in academic journals.

As NUI Chancellor, Garret FitzGerald followed in the tradition of T. K. Whitaker as an activist, policy-driven and innovative Chancellor. He was also, however, an embattled Chancellor, fighting against a variety of factors to secure a meaningful role for the NUI following the changes brought about by the Universities Act, and by radical and extensive changes in Irish society generally, including a changing perception of what the role of higher education should be in this new environment.

Garret FitzGerald's tenure as Chancellor was to a great extent shaped by the Universities Act – the elements of which are discussed elsewhere in this book. As far as the new Chancellor was concerned, that debate was now over, and it fell to him to handle and, in so far as he could, shape the new realities. He had to accept the reality of a new and restricted range of functions for the NUI, but with no clarity or certainty, with no agreement as to how these functions could be defined, and with the ever-present threat that in the process of redefinition the new functions could come to lack any real meaning. He had to adjust to the loosening of the federal ties and in particular to the devolving of power to the four autonomous universities, all of which continued to award degrees of the NUI.

All of this was taking place in an external environment which was putting a high emphasis on radical restructuring of third- and fourth-level education. The impetus for change was, by and large, positive, driven by the needs of a society enjoying unprecedented economic growth and which saw investment in higher education as a major driving force in this growth. But with this investment came a demand for restructuring, greater accountability, the elimination of unnecessary duplication, specialisation and a capacity to compete to the highest international standards.

Pressure for change also came from the new university presidents. By the 1990s they found themselves in a position where they were obliged to compete more and more with each other for state funding and increasingly for external funding; at the same time they had to work with each other to present a coherent university strategy to an increasingly demanding government. This new situation made for tensions and added new and at times edgy competitiveness to the relations between them, at a time when all of them found themselves engaged in major and usually controversial restructuring processes within their own universities.

Not immediately, but certainly after 2002, the NUI which in the past was regarded at least by some universities as a benign, if somewhat arcane presence, was increasingly seen as lacking relevance and indeed as somewhat of an unnecessary and intrusive hindrance to their activities. This view of the NUI was not shared by all presidents but increasingly as FitzGerald's tenure moved on it showed itself in the frequent absences of presidents from Senate meetings, through decisions unilaterally taken, generally on relatively unimportant issues and from the individual universities' point of view within their sphere of competence, but done in such a way and without consultation as to lead to confusion and confrontation.

The attitude of FitzGerald to the changing mood was that of a realist. His political career had been based in great part, whether in his early attitude to the EEC, to the emerging problem in Northern Ireland or to the economic crisis of the 1980s, on the ability to face change and seek to control rather than be driven by events. This was the approach he now adopted, seeking to use the period following the passing of the 1997 act as a time for considered reflection on the role, activities and nature of the NUI as a federal university in the new circumstances. He sought in particular to concentrate on policy matters relevant to the university as a whole and to higher education in general.

It was a realistic and focused approach but it served in part to highlight the weakness of the NUI's position, finding itself in a no-man's-land, trying to speak for its own constituent universities who were at best reluctant participants and unable to speak for the other universities – TCD, Dublin City University and University of Limerick – who were outside the federal structure and who along with the constituent universities were represented, first within the Conference of Heads of Irish Universities, later the Irish Universities Association.

The first area of reform was the matriculation, which has already been discussed in previous chapters. A number of changes were introduced which in general broadened the matriculation base and extended access to students who would previously have experienced difficulties in matriculating – specifically disadvantaged students, students with a learning disability and students entering art and design studies and nursing studies, both new disciplines within the NUI. The position of Irish within the matriculation was not changed.

Other initiatives included the monitoring of the standard of compatibility of NUI degrees, improving and expanding the external examiner systems, introducing a new NUI qualification framework, increasing the value of NUI awards, and the establishment of new postdoctoral fellowships. In addition the NUI offices at 49 Merrion Square were extensively refurbished, while number 48 was rented as a means of generating more income.

All of these developments were reported in a document later published,[3] prepared in 2002 for the Senate by a committee chaired by Professor Tom Dunne, whose brief was to document the changes since the passing of the Universities Act, to articulate the role of the Senate and to propose a developmental agenda for the incoming Senate and for the NUI as a federal university. In a real sense the relatively minor nature of the changes made and the aspirational nature of most of the recommendations, which largely involved a co-ordinating and facilitating role for the NUI, merely served to underline the weakness of the NUI's position. In a situation where the main power players – the university presidents – were at best polite but unenthusiastic and the government indifferent, the report made no real impact nor did it attract any media coverage or lead, as its authors had hoped, to a debate in the constituent universities.

It certainly did not change the minds of the presidents of University College Dublin or University College Cork. It was clear that neither President Wrixon nor President Brady saw any real role for the NUI. Neither had served on the Senate prior to their election or had any experience of the NUI and clearly had very little regard or affection for it. Each president saw himself with a major reform package to implement and saw the NUI as having little to offer towards the realisation of their ambitions. More than that they claimed they simply did not know what it meant to be 'a constituent university of a university – it is a unique legislative provision with no known precedence or parallel'.[4] They rejected the view that the NUI had any ongoing role in regulating the affairs of constituent universities. From their perspective there was no room for compromise and neither saw compromise as being in the best interest of the institution they led.

But perhaps the most telling indicator of their attitude to the NUI connection can be found in section 5.1 of the NUI report. Dealing with future developments it noted that the Universities Act expected that the titles given to the newly constituted constituent universities, and as previously agreed by them, would be *National University of Ireland* followed by the location in each case, i.e. *National University of Ireland, Dublin, Cork, Galway, Maynooth.* In the event Galway and Maynooth enthusiastically embraced this name change. Dublin and Cork flatly refused to do so. Their governing authorities, with the consent of the Senate were given permission by the Minister for Education and Science to retain University College Dublin and University College Cork as the main element in their name. Symbolically this incident summed up, better than any debate, the true feelings of all four universities to their future with the NUI.

Clearly Garret FitzGerald had a very different perspective from that of the Dublin and Cork presidents. As Chancellor he was charged with the protection and continuation of the National University of Ireland. He passionately believed that the National University of Ireland had a positive national role to play, especially in formulating policy, maintaining the quality of degrees, giving leadership and fostering collegiality. He did not believe the NUI was intrusive or that its presence affected the smooth running of the constituent universities. He was prepared to examine any such issues if brought to his attention and to seek to have them resolved. Curiously, few such issues were ever raised in any specific way and in all cases he indicated a willingness to enter dialogue, a willingness which was not reciprocated.

The issue of the future role of the NUI and its relationship with the constituent universities continued to dominate the life of the 2002–5 Senate and invested many of the meetings with a tension that had rarely before characterised the proceedings of that body. The matter spilled into public view with the decision of UCD to confer honorary degrees at the KClub on the occasion of the Ryder Cup in September 2006. This incident led to further attempts to resolve the issue, but without success. Eventually, after much recrimination, the Senate sought its own legal advice which it received in May 2007. It was, in the words of the NUI's own sub-committee on the future role of the NUI, expressed 'with clarity and elegance of expression'.

That, however, was the only comfort. The essence of the legal opinion was quoted in paragraph 13:

> It is apparent that the act has hollowed out the practical and functional jurisdiction of the NUI vis-à-vis the constituent universities while leaving it in place as an institution. The NUI may continue to provide a valuable forum for discussion and cooperation between the constituent universities but the limits of the legal power of the NUI to assert any jurisdiction in respect of the constituent universities are in my view contained in the restrictive provisions of Section 47.[5]

The opinion also confirmed that the Senate had no power to make statutes to regulate the affairs of the constituent universities and that any power given to the Senate in section 33 of the Universities Act 1997 should be seen as merely facilitative. It also stated that the NUI had no power to ensure the comparability of NUI degrees in the constituent universities. There was much more in a similar vein. Like it or not, the position of the presidents was vindicated.

The Senate had no alternative but to adopt the opinion which it did at a special meeting in the Royal Hospital at Kilmainham just before it went out of office in September 2007. It proposed 'a new relationship between the Senate and the constituent universities based on mutual respect'. But there were few specifics, nor was there any sense of enthusiasm from the presidents.

Garret FitzGerald had fought long and hard for a different outcome. He fought with courtesy, patience and tenacity, but he was hampered from the outset by the weakness of the NUI's position in the Universities Act, by the fact that a federal system which did not include three of the country's seven universities was seriously flawed in seeking to speak for the university sector, and by the fact that the leadership of the two biggest NUI universities saw little value in the NUI as a means of developing the potential of their own universities. Carving a new role and developing the remaining potential of the NUI after the Universities Act was always going to be difficult. Without the support of the two biggest universities it was almost certainly a doomed enterprise.

Garret FitzGerald's last task as Chancellor may well be to see if this 'new relationship' (hardly a Kilmainham manifesto) can have any real meaning, or whether after a hundred years of service to the Irish nation and Irish education the National University of Ireland finally folds its tent and quietly slips away. Could the matter have been handled differently? The answer is yes, certainly with more civility and more sensitivity, but the outcome would not have been very different. The brutal clarity of the legal opinion left no room for further debate on the central issue.

Figure 3 A tree-planting ceremony to commemorate the centenary of the NUI was held on 3 July 2008, when Chancellor Garret FitzGerald planted a tree in the grounds of NUI. Pictured *left to right* Dr Michael Murphy (President, UCC), Dr James Browne (President, NUI Galway), Dr Attracta Halpin (Registrar, NUI), Chancellor Garret FitzGerald and Dr Hugh Brady (President, UCD).

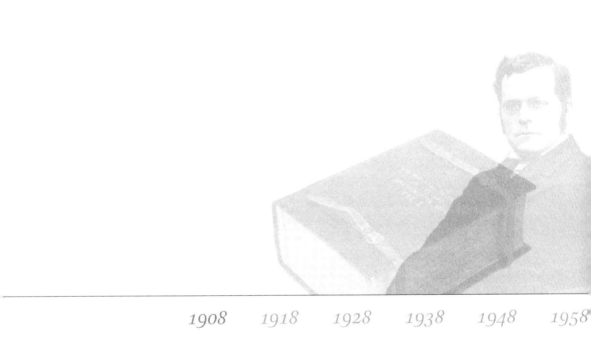

1908 1918 1928 1938 1948 1958

1968   1978   1988   1998   2008

The Functioning of the NUI

CHAPTER 12 *The Senate and the Changing Role of the Registrar*

ATTRACTA HALPIN

T HE IRISH UNIVERSITIES ACT 1908 which passed into law on 1 August 1908 sets out in its First Schedule the composition of the Governing Body of the 'new university having its seat in Dublin'.[1] The NUI Charter granted on 2 December of that year provides at chapter x (1) that the Governing Body 'shall be styled the Senate', naming in x (2) the members of the first Senate. Chapter XII of the Charter provides that 'there shall be a Registrar and other proper officers of the University. The first Registrar is Joseph McGrath LLD'. At the first meeting of the Senate on Thursday, 17 December 1908, Joseph McGrath briefly took the chair, vacating it almost immediately afterwards on the election of Archbishop William Walsh as Chancellor.[2] Since then the Registrar has played a central role in relation to the NUI Senate and to the university as a whole. This essay considers the nature of that role and of the Senate itself as these have evolved since the foundation of the university. It discusses the changing environment for Irish higher education, particularly since the Universities Act 1997, and considers the changes effected by that legislation, starting with a brief chronology of appointments to the post of Registrar since 1908, drawing on minutes of the Senate and correspondence in NUI archives for some of the details. The essay considers the changing dynamic in the relationship between NUI and its member institutions, particularly in recent times. It focuses on some key periods and events and draws a number of conclusions concerning the Registrar, the Senate and ultimately the hundred-year-old university.

NUI Registrars 1908–2008

While there have been just four chancellors in the hundred years' history of the National University of Ireland, there have been eight registrars. Four of these died in office, two worked till the age of 70, the seventh retired in 2004 and the eighth is the author of this essay. Sir Joseph McGrath, the first registrar had previously been one of the two co-secretaries of the Royal University of Ireland. At the Senate's first meeting, Joseph McGrath reported that he 'had been advised that the duty devolved upon him of convening this first meeting, and that, in preparation therefore, he had had to provide Minute Books, Attendance Books, Stationery'. Reflecting an apparently seamless transition from Royal to National, Joseph McGrath went on to remark that he had 'had to call upon the services of certain members of the staff of the Royal University of Ireland'.[3] These included Frederick Wiber and Alexander McCarthy who in their turn also became NUI registrars.

Knighted in 1911 prior to the visit of King George V in that year, Sir Joseph McGrath reported to Senate in July 1911 that 'with the assent of the Chancellor and Vice-Chancellor, he had had the University buildings decorated on Coronation Day, and during the King's visit'.[4] As registrar, he was to play a very significant part in the development of the National University of Ireland. He was influential in putting structures in place for the implementation of the Irish Universities Act 1908 and the Charter of the University, the management and development of its academic life, the approval of programmes of study, the organisation of examinations and the awarding of degrees. From the beginning, he enjoyed high status within the University. This is reflected in Senate decisions such as that of 17 December 1908 which places the registrar fifth in order of precedence within the Senate, directly after the NUI Chancellor and the presidents of the constituent colleges,[5] and, rather charmingly, that of February 1910 'that the Registrar's residence be connected with the Telephone Exchange',[6] or of 1914 that he be provided with a residence 'adjoining the University Building'.[7] The Registrar similarly accorded high status to the staff of the NUI office: in a letter to Chief Baron Palles – a member of the Senate – he expresses the assumption 'that the position of the members of the National University Staff will be comparable in dignity and emolument with those of the Staffs of more important Public Offices in Dublin'.[8] Sir Joseph McGrath was registrar during the transition to national independence which, apart from a few masterly examples of understatement, passed relatively unremarked in the minutes of the University. (In May 1916, for example, they refer to 'the recent dislocation of postal facilities, etc.' and 'the recent disturbances in Dublin'.[9])

Sir Joseph McGrath's capacity as an administrator, his rigorous approach to the development of academic structures and the setting and maintenance of academic standards clearly contributed to consolidating both the organisational structure and the academic credibility of the new university and ensuring its success as a national institution. He fell into ill health towards the end of his career and was absent from Senate meetings from June 1921. Following his death in March 1923, Frederick Wiber, who was chief clerk and had taken over the running of NUI during the illness of the registrar, was 'elected to the position' of registrar in February 1924.[10] In the interval between the two appointments, the post of registrar appears to have experienced a significant diminution in status when the Senate decided to reduce the salary from the £1,000 agreed in 1913 to '£800 per annum rising by yearly increments of £25 to £900 per annum'.[11] The decision may have been based on purely economic grounds, reflecting new austerities in the new state, or else on a view that the nature of the post had changed, given that the groundbreaking work of establishing the university had been completed. It was not until 1928 that the salary for the post again reached £1,000.[12]

On the death of Frederick Wiber on 11 July 1936 (two days after a meeting of Senate which he attended),[13] his colleague from the Royal University of Ireland, Alexander McCarthy, who had succeeded him as chief clerk, was appointed acting registrar. Once again it took a further year for the post of registrar to be filled. This time the delay was due to the intervention of two members of Senate, Professor Tomás Ó Máille and Liam Ó Buachalla, who in December 1936, entered a motion seeking to make a 'good knowledge of Irish, such as will enable him to carry on the work of the University in Irish' a requirement of the Registrar post.[14] Consideration of the motion occupied the Senate over several meetings till an amended version of the motion was unanimously carried.[15] Ultimately legal advice was obtained to the effect that if the Senate wished to make Irish a requirement for the post of registrar, it would have to introduce a new statute. The Senate duly passed Statute LII in April 1937 and took steps to fill the post by open competition. A further consideration then for the Senate was whether the proposed new statute 'should apply to the current vacancy'. On the casting vote of the Chancellor, it was decided that it should. In October 1937, Alexander McCarthy was appointed registrar, the interviewing board reporting that 'considering the character of the ordinary work of the registrar's job, Mr McCarthy has qualifications to carry through that work in Irish'.[16] There is nothing to indicate

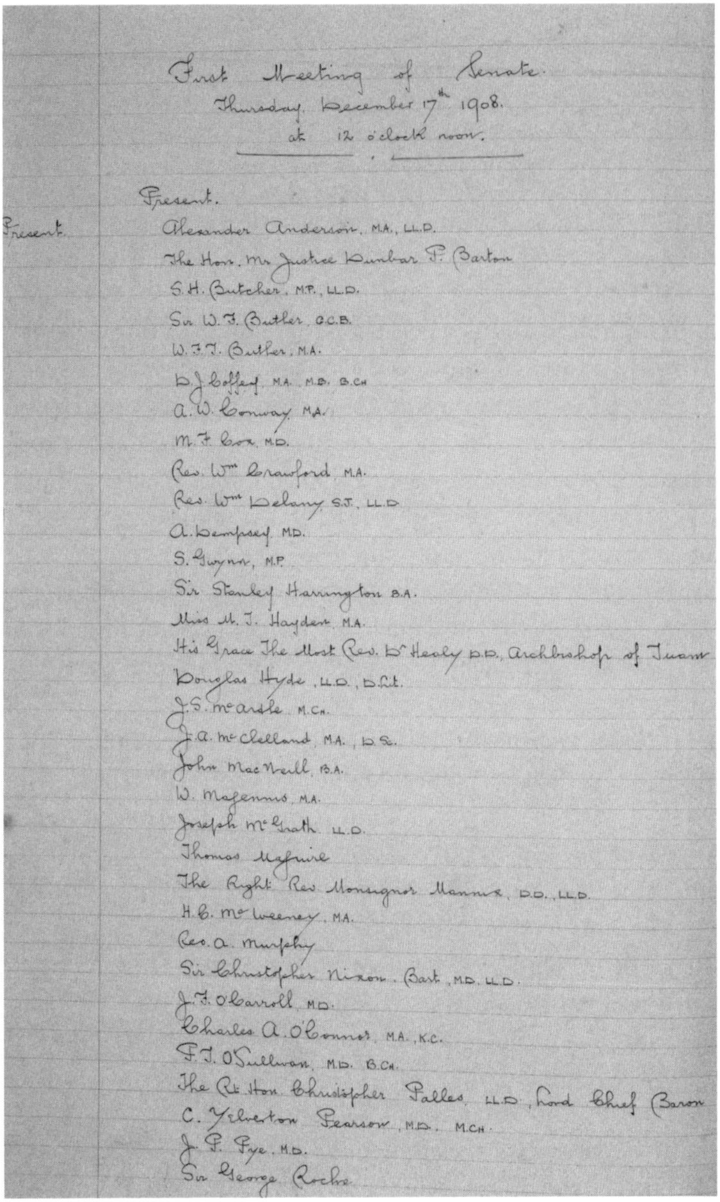

First Meeting of Senate.
Thursday December 17th 1908.
at 12 o'clock noon.

Present.

Present. Alexander Anderson, M.A., LL.D.
The Hon. Mr Justice Dunbar P. Barton
S.H. Butcher, M.P., LL.D.
Sir W.F. Butler, G.C.B.
W.F.T. Butler, M.A.
D.J. Coffey, M.A. M.B. B.Ch
A.W. Conway, M.A.
M.F. Cox, M.D.
Rev. Wm Crawford, M.A.
Rev. Wm Delany, S.J., LL.D.
A. Dempsey, M.D.
S. Gwynn, M.P.
Sir Stanley Harrington, B.A.
Miss M.T. Hayden, M.A.
His Grace The Most Rev. Dr Healy, D.D., Archbishop of Tuam
Douglas Hyde, LL.D., D.Lit.
J.S. McArdle, M.Ch.
J.A. McClelland, M.A., D.Sc.
John MacNeill, B.A.
W. Magennis, M.A.
Joseph McGrath, LL.D.
Thomas Maguire
The Right Rev. Monsignor Mannix, D.D., LL.D.
H.C. McWeeney, M.A.
Rev. A. Murphy
Sir Christopher Nixon, Bart, M.D., LL.D.
J.F. O'Carroll, M.D.
Charles A. O'Connor, M.A., K.C.
F.J. O'Sullivan, M.D., B.Ch.
The Rt. Hon. Christopher Palles, LL.D., Lord Chief Baron
C. Yelverton Pearson, M.D., M.Ch.
J.P. Pye, M.D.
Sir George Roche

Figures 4 & 5 **Minutes of the first meeting of the NUI Senate, 17 December 1908, where Archbishop William Walsh was elected as the first Chancellor.**

P. Semple, M.A.

A. Senier, Ph.D., D.Sc.

G. Sigerson, M.D.

L. A. Waldron, M.P.

His Grace The Most Rev. Dr Walsh, D.D.
        Archbishop of Dublin

@ C. A. Windle, M.A., M.D., D.Sc., F.R.S.

Chairman of Meeting 1. On the motion of Mr Sergeant O'Connor, K.C., seconded by Sir Christopher Nixon, it was unanimously resolved that the Registrar (Joseph McGrath LL.D) take the chair.

Election of Chancellor 2. The Registrar having taken the chair, the Lord Chief Baron moved, and Dr Windle seconded, the following resolution:—

    That His Grace The Most Rev. Dr Walsh, Archbishop of Dublin, be, and hereby is, elected Chancellor of the University.

    The resolution was passed unanimously

    The Registrar accordingly vacated the chair, which was then taken by His Grace The Most Rev. Dr Walsh, Archbishop of Dublin, Chancellor of the University.

    The Chancellor returned thanks to the Senate for his election.

Legal Assessor. 3. Mr Sergeant O'Connor, K.C. was requested by the Chancellor to act as his Legal Assessor, and expressed his willingness to do so.

whether he took advantage of the year's interval since the post had become vacant to enhance his proficiency in Irish. In deciding to appoint the internal candidate over a number of external candidates, the Senate noted that 'the office of the registrarship needs a special and intimate acquaintance with its work, and needs it in practice from hour to hour'.

On the death of Alexander McCarthy in August 1952, Séamus Wilmot was appointed registrar,[17] the first NUI graduate to hold the post. A playwright (*Baintiarna an Ghorta* was produced by the Abbey Theatre in 1938) and novelist (*The Splendid Pretence*, 1947; *Mise Méara*, Cork University Press, 1947) in Irish and English, he was the longest-serving registrar, holding the post for 20 years until his retirement at the age of 70 in 1972. His time in office may be seen as one of considerable stability for NUI and for Irish higher education as a whole, the era of great expansion and change not beginning until the first beneficiaries of Donagh O'Malley's free second-level education scheme started to leave school in 1971. Séamus Wilmot was succeeded by John Bourke who had also been chief clerk.[18] John Bourke was registrar during a fairly eventful if slightly schizophrenic period for NUI: in the period 1975 to 1978 the university expanded significantly as six institutions became recognised colleges following government policy decisions in May 1976 aimed at restricting degree-awarding powers to the universities.[19] Dr T. K. Whitaker was installed as Chancellor; but by November of that year, the Senate was faced with the prospect of the dissolution of the University following the announcement of further changes in Government policy for higher education.[20]

John Bourke retired, also aged 70, in 1979. In deciding to fill the vacancy, the Senate, in the light of the impending changes announced by the government, pondered 'what changes in staff should be considered bearing in mind the possible short life of the University'.[21] A further minute later that year refers to 'the uncertain future of the university'.[22] In this climate of uncertainty, Michael Gilheany was appointed registrar in 1979 and held the post until his unexpected death in 1987.

The appointment in 1987 of Michael Gilheany's successor John Nolan marked a break with tradition in that he was the first registrar to be appointed without the advantage of 'special and intimate acquaintance . . . from hour to hour' with the specifics of the work.[23] However, he had skills that were clearly recognised as transferable: he had previously been registrar of

Carysfort College which had been a recognised college of NUI until the implementation of a government decision of 1985 that it should close. John Nolan was registrar during a major turning point for the university: with the passing of the Universities Act 1997, the nature of the federal university was altered fundamentally, its main member institutions became autonomous universities and their relationship with the centre became less clearly defined.

The registrarship of NUI, typical of the upper echelons of administration both in higher education and elsewhere, was until recently, a very male domain. Notwithstanding the provision in the NUI Charter that 'women shall be eligible equally with men to be Members of the University, or of any Authority of the University, and to hold any office or enjoy any advantages of the University' the first seven registrars were all men.[24] In 2004, I became the first woman to hold the office of registrar, having been assistant registrar since 1997.[25]

The Role of Registrar

Within what has been termed 'the academic civil service'[26] the role of registrar is a senior one. The NUI Registrar has a full chapter in NUI Statutes. Chapter xxxv of Statute LXXXVI sets out the qualifications for the post ('a graduate of the University . . . a knowledge of the Irish language . . . Such administrative experience as the Senate may deem satisfactory') and the range of functions and responsibilities associated with it. The first responsibility relates to the title of the post 'The Registrar shall keep the register of graduates, and the other registers of the University'. Other responsibilities mentioned include the preservation and safe custody of documents, the preparation of testimoniums, the keeping of accounts, the supervision of the Matriculation Examination (discontinued in 1992), the summoning of meetings of the Senate and other committees, the conduct of the correspondence of the University and the care of its buildings.[27]

Secretary to the Senate

Acting as secretary to the NUI Senate has been at the core of the role of successive registrars since 1908. The first Senate which took office in that year had 35 members. Viewed one hundred years on, it can be seen as a most distinguished and interesting body, including several members whose names are still known today. In addition to the first Chancellor, Archbishop William Walsh, whose importance in Irish public life is recounted in chapter 8, it included the future first President of Ireland, Dr Douglas Hyde; the Irish nationalist MP Stephen Gwynn, author, journalist and survivor of the Great War; The Revd William Delany SJ, who is mentioned in *Ulysses*, and the subject of a monograph in connection with his involvement in the campaign for a national university;[28] Monsignor Daniel Mannix, later long-serving and controversial Cardinal Archbishop of Melbourne;[29] Dr George Sigerson, noted surgeon and writer, founder of the the Feis Cheoil and Sigerson Cup. Nine of the members had medical qualifications.

The current Senate has 38 members, the extra three members accounted for by the elevation of Maynooth as a full constituent university. The composition of the Senate is set out in of the Universities Act 1997.[30] Chaired by the Chancellor, and with the four constituent university presidents and the NUI Registrar as *ex-officio* members, the Senate includes four members elected by the governing authorities of each of the constituent universities; eight members elected by the general body of the university, including the graduates, known as Convocation; eight appointed by the government; and up to four co-opted members. The heads of the NUI Recognised Colleges, not already co-opted as members, attend meetings of the Senate as observers.

Meetings and procedure of the Senate are held in accordance with chapter XII of Statute LXXXVI. This specifies that 'twenty-one days notice of every meeting of the Senate . . . shall be sent by the Registrar to each Member of Senate', requires members of Senate to give the Registrar at least 14 days' notice of any business they wish to raise and provides, quaintly in the age of the twenty-four seven mindset, that no ordinary meeting of Senate 'shall be held during the months of July, August or September'. Meetings of the Senate are now held four times a year.

As secretary to this large committee, the registrar is responsible for advising the Senate about requirements that must be complied with in legislation and in the NUI Charter and Statutes. The registrar's role involves preparing the agenda and documentation for meetings, circulating these to members, organising and participating in the meetings, preparing the minutes and communicating the decisions. While over the hundred years of the life of the Senate changes in the language of the minutes of its meetings may be discerned, in format and presentation they are a model of consistency. In general, they record the decisions taken, but they also frequently seek to contextualise the decisions by conveying the discussion surrounding the issues and the arguments pro and con. In presenting the record of such discussions, registrars over the years clearly worked hard to achieve a cool mandarin style: the argumentation is refined, emotional expression is avoided, ideas are expressed cogently and lucidly. The unbroken set of minutes of the meetings of the Senate from 1908 provides a broad perspective of doings of the university, its deliberative processes and its academic culture. While its record in relation to the making of academic appointments may be criticised for valuing democratic over meritocratic processes of decision making, the Senate that emerges from a reading of the minutes is a high-minded, high-principled and dignified body, driven by a concern for the promotion of learning and scholarship across the range of disciplines studied in the university, with a particular enthusiasm for the language and culture of Ireland, committed to high academic standards, fair in its dealings with students, international in outlook and notably eager – particularly in the early days – to cultivate relationships with universities outside Ireland.

In fulfilling the role of secretary to the Senate, the Registrar works closely with the Chancellor who chairs the meetings of the Senate. Writing on university governance, Michael Shattock expresses the view that 'good governance is in part the product of good working relationships between the chair of a committee and its secretary when both are intent on forwarding the interests of the body they serve'.[31] Over the century, the university has benefited from positive relationships between the chancellors and the registrars who worked with them. The National University of Ireland has been extraordinarily well served in its four chancellors, each of whom has been a major figure in the life of Ireland. Successive NUI registrars can surely count the experience of working with such exceptional individuals as a very positive aspect of the job.

If the procedures governing its meetings are relatively unchanged, the business of Senate has changed radically. Notwithstanding the tremors caused by changing government policy or the tensions that came to the surface from time to time, the Senate remained an extremely powerful body from its foundation until 1997. Constituted under the 1908 Act as the governing body of the university, and empowered under its Charter 'to exercise all the powers and discretions of the University' and 'regulate all matters concerning the University', the Senate was at the head of a single university, comprising three constituent colleges and a number of recognised colleges.[32] The Senate appointed the presidents of the constituent colleges and the professors and lecturers in those institutions. NUI was the validating and awards body for the whole university. The NUI Registrar accordingly exercised considerable power.

The Universities Act 1997 saw the constituent colleges and the recognised college at Maynooth become constituent universities, with the Senate retaining a restricted range of functions, notably the determination of matriculation requirements and the appointment of extern examiners.[33] The 1997 Act effectively loosened the ties of the federal university, leaving NUI intact at the centre as an awarding body, specifically in respect of recognised colleges, but devolving power from the centre to the institutions and creating four autonomous constituent universities which continue to award degrees of the National University of Ireland.

In discussing the changing university, Rowland warns that 'it is important not to allow the politics of nostalgia to lead us to suppose that the past was more stable than the present'.[34] However, the changes introduced by the Act, coinciding with the other major changes in higher education, and changes in the leadership of the constituent universities, unsettled the federal structure, created an identity crisis for the Senate and brought new challenges for the registrar. While the Senate is still clearly in terms of its Charter and Statutes the 'Governing Body of the University', it has become less clear what now constitutes the university, what is the nature of its relationship with the constituent universities, each with its own governing authority, and how best these should be managed. Shattock has expressed the view that 'university governance remains a contested subject and one which is evolving to fit a changing environment'.[35] The changes the Universities Act 1997 introduced for the National University of Ireland are still being worked through, ten years after it was passed.

The difficulties being experienced by the Senate are not unique to the National University of Ireland. In an age that Barnett has described as 'supercomplex' for universities,[36] university senates or governing bodies elsewhere are under siege, their size and cumbersome workings seen as out of sympathy with a *Zeitgeist* which, influenced by structures of corporate governance, promotes the greyhound qualities of leanness in structure, speed and flexibility in movement as desirable characteristics of university governance. This is reflected, for example, in the conclusion of the 2004 OECD examiners' report which considers that governing bodies in Ireland are too large to play the important strategic role they should now be exercising and its recommendation 'that university governing bodies be reduced in size to a maximum of 20, including student members, to improve their effectiveness and that lay members be required to constitute a substantial majority'.[37] As Shattock points out, 'the difficulty has been to engage senate effectively with the wider strategic issues that affect their universities in a world where external pressures, changes in funding policies and new Government . . . initiatives are cumulative in effect, interrelated and demand detailed background knowledge to be understood'.[38] The difficulty of engagement is particularly acute for the NUI Senate because of the federal, or – as it is now coming to be understood – confederal structure of the university, with the power shared between the members of the confederation rather than, as previously, coming from the top. The structure creates greater distance between the Senate and the constituent universities making it seem remote and its role poorly understood.

The Senate which held office in the period immediately following the Act sought to address these issues, circulating a document *The NUI Federal University in an Era of Transition* (2002).[39] The document set out a vision of the role to be played by the Senate. This generated little response from the constituent universities. The challenge for the registrar, now, as secretary to the Senate, is to play an active part in the definition of a viable role for the Senate so that it can be seen not just as 'part of the "dignified" apparatus of governance'[40] and to generate a meaningful agenda which will engage the continuing interest and support of the constituent universities, without crossing the lines of their autonomy. Linked with this creative challenge is the further challenge of mediating the relationship between the Senate and the constituent universities, towards greater mutual understanding. Characterising the cumulative challenge for universities as one of 'institutional adaptation to changing environments', Gumport and Sporn conclude from the literature on the subject that 'university administrators are increasingly called upon to orchestrate that adaptation'.[41] A recent European University Association report calls on higher education institutions 'rather than seeing themselves "set in stone" . . . to apply their institutional creativity to a constantly changing environment'.[42]

If its role is contested, the Senate has, nonetheless, promoted a number of useful initiatives since 1997. While allowing that extern examiners now represent just one element in quality assurance, the Senate has reinvigorated the extern examiner system,[43] introducing more comprehensive reporting and devoting more attention to general academic issues arising from the reports of extern examiners. Among the issues that have been addressed are the awarding of honours degrees and the proportions of degrees awarded in the various classifications. In response to consistent comments from extern examiners over a number of years that the proportions of 'good honours' degrees awarded by the NUI universities were significantly lower than those awarded by comparable universities in and outside Ireland, a Senate sub-committee chaired by the Chancellor undertook, in collaboration with the constituent universities, a systematic statistical analysis of degree examination results. This supported the view that too few NUI graduates were awarded first class honours and second class honours grade one degrees. Related to this, proposals were presented by the Senate to the academic councils of the constituent universities for a revision of the bands of marks common throughout the NUI institutions and the introduction of grade descriptors in respect of each degree classification. These proposals were accepted. The cumulative effect of these initiatives has been an increase in the number of 'good honours' degrees awarded to NUI graduates. NUI continues to analyse annually the statistical data on examination results provided by the constituent universities.

NUI awards constitute a further area of activity expanded and revitalised by the Senate.[44] Since the foundation of the university, the Senate has sought to allocate funds to support academic excellence. The NUI travelling studentships were introduced in 1910. The Irish Historical Research Prize, originally awarded in connection with the travelling studentships, was set up as a separate award in 1921. Over the years, various bequests have been received enabling the funding of other awards. In 1998, following the restructuring of the university's investments, additional annual income was generated for awards enabling, for example, the establishment of in a postdoctoral research fund which currently supports two postdoctoral fellowships, one in the humanities and one in the sciences, each currently valued at €80,000 and offered bi-annually. The total value of NUI awards now exceeds €1 million annually.

Committees of the Senate

Much of the work of the Senate is organised through committees. The registrar acts as secretary to the two major committees of Senate, the Finance and Standing committees and also to the newly established Committee for Honorary Degrees. The registrar chairs the Committee of Registrars, a useful forum for the registrars of the constituent universities and to which major academic issues are usually referred by the Senate for advice. The registrar also chairs the Steering Committees for recognised colleges and the Publications Committee which makes recommendations to the Senate on the awarding of grants towards publications. A new committee, comprising the registrars and two further representatives from each constituent university, one in the humanities and one in the sciences, supports the process of examining NUI higher degrees on published work, which have grown in importance with the renewed focus on research.

The NUI Office

If the role of the Senate is problematic, the work of the NUI office continues to expand. The Registrar manages a small staff, currently of 15, who provide a range of services to the constituent universities and recognised colleges, to graduates of the university, to potential students, to schools, as well as providing an information service to the general public. In addition to the registrar's office, there are four divisions within NUI: conferrings and awards; finance and administration; records; and systems.

The registrar's office provides the secretariat to the Senate and its committees and organises events and ceremonies, such as the NUI honorary conferring ceremony held annually and the annual awards ceremony. The office also administers the extern examiner system, liaising with the constituent universities and recognised colleges and communicating with the 850 or so extern examiners appointed by the Senate for taught programmes, and with as many again in respect of research degrees. Services in relation to NUI matriculation, such as the provision of information to schools and students, and the processing of applications for exemptions and communications with the Central Applications Office are handled in the registrar's office.

The finance and administration division manages the NUI's finances

and is responsible for payments and payroll and for the upkeep and maintenance of the NUI offices which are listed Georgian buildings.

An important service provided by NUI to the constituent universities and
recognised colleges is the production of testimonia. In this, the staff in the NUI
Conferrings Division liaise with colleagues in the examinations and conferrings divisions in each of the NUI institutions. Data are transferred electron-
ically and testimonia are printed, sealed and despatched in time for conferrings
and presentation ceremonies in Ireland and increasingly overseas. Over 25,000
testimonia are now issued annually for conferrings and presentations. With
the focus on lifelong learning, the national policy objective of expanding
access to and widening participation in higher education and the establishment of the national framework of qualifications, the range of NUI qualifications has expanded and new qualifications have been introduced. In addition
to providing degree parchments for conferrings, NUI supplies increasing
numbers of certificates and diplomas which are presented at ceremonies
throughout the year. NUI also provides a follow-up service to graduates, issuing replacement parchments, translations and certifications. The organisation of competitions for post-doctoral fellowships, travelling studentships,
scholarships and other NUI awards, in collaboration with colleagues in the
constituent universities and recognised colleges and with extern examiners,
is a further major area of activity within the conferrings and awards division.

A major responsibility of the Registrar is the maintenance of the registers
of graduates. There are two main registers, the Seanad Éireann register of
graduates eligible to vote in the election of three members of Seanad Éireann
for the NUI constituency and the Convocation register used for elections to
the NUI Senate.[45] The maintenance and updating of these registers is an
ongoing activity in the Records Division, reaching peak period in election
years. One such was 2007 which saw both a Seanad Éireann election in July
and a Convocation election in October. In the first, Joe O'Toole, Feargal
Quinn and Ronan Mullen were returned as members of Seanad Éireann,[46]
while at the second, in accordance with the gender-balancing provision of
the 1997 Act, 'four men and four women' were elected as members of the
NUI Senate. There are some 100,000 graduates on the current registers. The
vice-chancellor is returning officer in the NUI Seanad Éireann constituency
while the registrar is registration officer.[47]

Conclusions

David Holmes, registrar of Oxford University until 2006, describing the nature of that post, defines three areas of responsibility: the secretarial, the advisory and the managerial, which neatly categorises much of the work of the registrar of the National University of Ireland.[48] Over the hundred-year history of the university, the registrar has been at the centre of NUI and each of the registrars has contributed to the making of this great national institution. In the beginning the role was ground-breaking, involving the creation of new structures for the organisation of the university and the conduct of its academic life in the period of transition to nationhood. Over a half-century of relative stability followed. However, the expansion in higher education from the late sixties, the exponential growth in student numbers, the increased scale and complexity of the NUI institutions, and the pressure for modernisation in structures of governance and increased accountability, all combined to create the context for the Universities Act 1997 which altered the power balance within NUI. Since then, raised expectations on the part of government of the potential of the universities to act as drivers of the economy, a new focus on the development of fourth-level education for an increasingly knowledge-based society, with strong emphasis on research and funding allocated on a competitive basis; a general 'warming' in the climate for higher education, together with changes in the leadership of the NUI universities are creating pressures for further change. In this radically changing climate, the NUI Registrar faces new challenges in seeking to contribute, in collaboration with the Senate and the member institutions, towards the redefinition of the National University of Ireland, and the reinvigoration of its structures and activities.

CHAPTER 13 *The Recognised Colleges* JOHN NOLAN

I N NUMERICAL AND chronological terms, the story of the NUI Recognised Colleges during the period 1908–2008 is easily told. During those hundred years the NUI Senate granted recognised college status to 12 colleges and institutions. The first college to become a recognised college was St Patrick's College, Maynooth, in 1910. It was not until the mid-1970s, when major developments were taking place in third-level education in Ireland, that seven further colleges applied to the Senate for recognised college status. During the period 1996–2005 the Senate approved applications for recognition from four other colleges or institutes.

Arising from various developments in government policies relating to certain third-level institutions during the late 1970s and 1980s, and developments associated with the introduction of the Universities Act in 1997, seven colleges ceased to be recognised colleges so that, by the final year of the university's centenary, the NUI had a total of five recognised colleges.

The main purposes of this essay are:

1   To identify the NUI's statutory basis for granting recognised college status.
2   To highlight the historical context and significant aspects of the various applications for NUI recognised college status made by the 12 institutions during the past hundred years.
3   To examine how the administrative relationship between the NUI and the recognised colleges functioned.
4   To assess the overall impact of recognised college status on the 12 institutions and on the NUI.

While the main focus of attention within the NUI federal university system during most of the past hundred years was centred on the three Constituent Colleges of UCD, UCC and UCG, and the Recognised College of St Patrick's College, Maynooth, the story of the twelve recognised colleges, particularly from the mid-1970s, is an important dimension of NUI's history when, in keeping with its 'national' role, the NUI facilitated and accommodated a range of diverse colleges and institutions by granting them recognised college status and conferring NUI degrees on their graduates.

Statutory Provisions Governing Recognised Colleges of the NUI

The key statutory provision governing NUI Recognised Colleges is subsection (4) of section 2 of the 1908 Act, which makes it possible for matriculated students of the university, who are pursuing 'a course of study of a university type' approved by the Senate, in any college 'recognised' by the NUI, to be entitled to the same privileges as matriculated students of the University, including ' the right of obtaining a degree'.

These privileges cannot be granted to the students of a college in Munster (excluding the County of Clare) without the consent of the Governing Body of University College Cork, or to the students of a college in Connaught or in the County of Clare without the consent of the Governing Body of University College Galway, or to a college elsewhere in Ireland without the consent of the Governing Body of University College Dublin.

The terms and conditions a college or institution must meet in order to obtain recognised college status from the NUI, which are set out in Clause XXI ('Extension of Privileges to Certain Matriculated Students') of the NUI Charter, include requirements that the university must be satisfied as to the general character and financial position of the college as a whole, the adequacy in numbers and qualification of its teaching staff, the university standard of the teaching, and the adequate provision of resources. Moreover, as part of the recognition process, it is the prerogative of the Senate to determine which members of staff in the college seeking recognition should be approved as recognised teachers of the NUI.

The NUI Charter also makes provision governing the university examinations in the recognised colleges, including the appointment of intern examiners from the relevant constituent college, as well as the extern examiners.

Up to 1997, regulations relating to degrees and examinations could not be made without report to the Senate from the General Board of Studies (GBS), and in framing such report the GBS had to consider the representations of the academic council of each constituent college, based on the relevant faculty reports. From 1909 until the introduction of the Universities Act 1997, which revoked the provisions in the NUI Charter relating to the GBS, the board normally held meetings in February and November of each year, its chief business being the consideration and approval of courses of study and the appointment of extern examiners of the university, for every examination leading towards a degree.

The Supplemental and Amending Charter of 1914 extended the composition of the GBS by including, inter alia, the president of any recognised college as an *ex-officio* member of the Board.

The powers of the Dublin Commissioners, who had made Statute A containing 55 chapters, were exercised until July 1911, after which the NUI Senate and the governing bodies of the constituent colleges made their own statutes. By 1951, 85 statutes had been made by the NUI Senate, at which time it decided to introduce a consolidated statute, to be known as Statute LXXXVI.

From 1951 until 1997, when the Senate ceased to make statutes affecting the constituent colleges, Statute LXXXVI, containing 70 chapters, which 'regulated all matters concerning the University', became the key statute reference point for the making of all subsequent statutes by the Senate. The detailed provisions governing recognised colleges and recognised teachers, which are set out, respectively, in chapters 59 and 60 of Statute 86, specify the conditions to be fulfilled by a college before the Senate may grant recognition.

Recognised colleges are also governed by the provisions of other chapters in Statute LXXXVI and subsequent statutes which, in various ways, extended NUI's relationship with them, such as the Convocation elections of the Chancellor and eight members of Senate; matriculation regulations; conduct of examinations; ceremonial of conferring degrees.

The Earliest Applications for Recognised College Status: 1909–10
1909: The first NUI Recognised College – St Patrick's College, Maynooth

In July 1909, the Right Revd Monsignor Mannix, DD LLD, President of St Patrick's College, Maynooth, who was included in the list of 39 persons nominated 'as the first Senate' applied to the Senate 'to grant St Patrick's College Maynooth, and to the Professors and Lecturers named in the appended statement, all the privileges that may be granted under the provisions of Statute "A" of the University, Chapters XLVI and XLVIII'.

The Senate, in February 1910, adopted the report of the General Board of Studies recommending that 'St Patrick's College Maynooth be admitted to be a Recognised College of the University in the subjects in the Faculties of Arts, Philosophy, and Celtic Studies'. (For the remainder of this section of the essay, the name 'Maynooth' will be used to represent the Recognised College of St Patrick's College, Maynooth). The Senate also decided that:

1 Recognition would be for a period of four years from 1 November 1909.
2 Those members of the teaching staff specified in the application would be appointed as recognised teachers for the same four-year period.
3 The Governing Body of Maynooth would be entitled to select three representatives from among the recognised teachers of the university in the Faculties of Arts, Philosophy and Celtic Studies to represent the college on the General Board of Studies, and
4 The Revd Dr McGinley would be appointed as Supervisor of Examinations in St Patrick's College, Maynooth, for the examinations of the year 1910.

In May 1912, the Senate appointed a list of professors (from UCD) to assist in conducting the first university examinations in St Patrick's College, Maynooth.

When Mgr Mannix was appointed as Coadjutor Archbishop of Melbourne in February 1913, the under-secretary appointed the Very Revd John F. Canon Hogan as a member of Senate. It is interesting to note that while Mgr Mannix and his successor, Canon Hogan, were elected to be members of the Senate's Standing Committee, they were not elected as members of the Senate's Finance Committee.

At the Senate meeting in December 1913 the following resolution was adopted on the motion of the Very Rev. Canon Hogan, seconded by the Vice-Chancellor: 'that the recognition of St Patrick's College Maynooth be renewed in the Faculties of Arts, Philosophy, and Celtic Studies, and that recognition in the Faculty of Science be added thereto'.

The first full meeting of the new Senate, constituted in accordance with the First Schedule of the 1908 Act, which was held on 10 December 1914, co-opted four members and, at the conclusion of the first vote, Hogan, the President of Maynooth, now the Rt Revd Mgr Hogan, was unanimously elected, and declared co-opted. At that same meeting, a resolution 'that the President of

St Patrick's College Maynooth be appointed as Pro-Vice-Chancellor for such period as the said College shall be a Recognised College of the University', was declared carried unanimously.

The Senate, in May 1915, approved Draft Statute v concerning the filling of vacancies on the General Board of Studies, in accordance with the Supplemental and Amending Charter and, consequently, the President of Maynooth became an *ex-officio* member of the General Board of Studies.

Being the first institution to be granted NUI Recognised College status, it was not surprising that the formal procedures and administrative processes governing the relationship between the NUI and Maynooth, as they evolved over the next five decades, would have a significant influence on the arrangements that would be put in place for subsequent colleges or institutes applying for recognised college status, many of which occurred in the mid-1970s.

Those procedures included the processing of proposals for new courses, together with the associated marks and standards for the university examinations to be forwarded to the UCD Registrar, who referred them to the relevant UCD faculties, and to the UCD Academic Council, following which they were submitted for consideration at the meetings of the GBS in November and February. The report of the General Board of Studies was then considered by the Senate at its next meeting, following which Maynooth was informed as to the Senate's decisions on its proposals.

Maynooth differed significantly from all the other recognised colleges in that its president, who was also a pro-vice-chancellor of the NUI, could confer degrees in the Recognised College at Maynooth, an arrangement which continued up 1997 when the Recognised College of Maynooth became a constituent university of the NUI.

At the co-option meeting of Senate in 1924, the president of Maynooth was co-opted unanimously. From that time onwards, it became 'custom and practice' that the president of Maynooth would be co-opted unanimously and elected as pro-vice-chancellor of the university, and a member of the Standing Committee. It was not until 1940, however, that the President of Maynooth was appointed as a member of both the Standing and Finance committees of the Senate.

The above arrangements and protocols effectively established Maynooth, the first recognised college of the NUI, as being close in status to that of the constituent colleges – perhaps 'a half of a constituent college'. This is reflect-

53. Dr Attracta Halpin has been Registrar of the NUI since 2004.

54. Dr John Nolan, NUI Registrar, 1987–2004.

55. Eamon de Valera's first visit to NUI as President of Ireland.
left to right Monsignor de Brún (President, UCG), Eamon de Valera, Henry St J. Atkins (President, UCC), Michael Tierney (President, UCD), Seamus Wilmot (Registrar, NUI).

above 56. **National College of Art and Design (NCAD), a Recognised College of the NUI since 1996.**

below 57. **Royal College of Surgeons in Ireland (RCSI), a Recognised College of the NUI since 1977.**

above 58. Shannon College of Hotel Management, a Recognised College of the NUI since 2000.

below 59. Milltown Institute of Theology and Philosophy, a Recognised College of the NUI since 2005.

60. Institute of Public Administration (IPA), a Recognised College of the NUI since 2001.

61. Chancellor Garret FitzGerald pictured with *left to right* Mr Joe Higgins, former TD and the current Chair of Convocation, Mrs Linda O'Shea Farren.

62. Michael Francis Cox, MD LLD, was the first Chairman of Convocation. He remained in office from 1909 until 1924.

63. Eamon de Valera, Chancellor of the NUI with members of the Committee of Convocation, 19 November 1921.
Seated from left Mary Kate Ryan, Assistant in French; Rev. Timothy Corcoran SJ, Professor of Education (UCD); The Chancellor, Eamon de Valera; Dr Michael Cox, Chairman of Convocation; Arthur E. Clery, Professor of the Law of Property and Contracts (UCD).
Standing from left James Creed Meredith, K.C., Judge of Dáil Éireann High Court; Patrick McGilligan, Assistant in Latin; Louise Gavan Duffy, Assistant in Education; Ian Bloomer, Demonstrator in Engineering; William J. Williams, Lecturer in Education, Royal College of Science; Mary Macken, Professor of German (UCD); Michael Hayes, Assistant in French; Michael Rynne, President of the Students' Representative Council.

64. A copy of the University Education (Ireland) Act 1879 was recorded in the RUI Roll of Senate and Graduates, Vol.1.

65. A copy of the Royal Charter, issued on 13 April 1880, was recorded in the RUI Roll of Senate and Graduates, Vol.1.

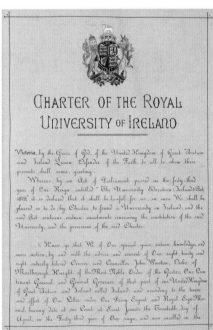

66. The Royal Charter issued to the Royal University of Ireland in 1880 with the seal below.

67. The leather-bound box containing the Royal Charter and seal of the Royal University of Ireland.

68. The Royal University of Ireland Roll of Senate and Graduates, Vol. 1.

ed, to some extent, in the relative payments provided by the NUI for the NUI supervisors of examinations in the three constituent colleges and Maynooth in 1940. The payments were as follows: UCD £331 (+ £224 for clerical assistance); UCC £331 (+ £55 for clerical assistance); UCG £279 (+£55 for clerical assistance); Maynooth £173.

In the early part of the 1980s, Maynooth, having established a successful record of achievement as a recognised college, expressed a desire for a greater degree of independence within the NUI federal system which, in effect, meant a significant reduction in the hands-on role played by the UCD intern examiners, appointed by the NUI Senate for monitoring the University's examinations at Maynooth.

In June 1984 the trustees of Maynooth submitted an application to the NUI Senate for constituent college status, emphasising that, while the status of recognised college was entirely appropriate when Maynooth was a small college with students who were exclusively candidates for the priesthood, and an academic staff exclusively clerical, the rapid expansion of the college in recent years had so changed it as to justify its seeking the status of constituent college. Following its consideration of Maynooth's application, the NUI decided to seek a legal opinion on what would be the minimum legal changes necessary to have Maynooth included as a constituent college. It was the view of the university solicitor that this would entail the university having to promote a private act in the Oireachtas. The Senate, at its meeting in January 1985 decided to invite Maynooth to prepare a written submission setting out the structures and form of legislation envisaged for Maynooth as a constituent college of the NUI.

While progress on this matter was rather slow, the Maynooth situation received more focused attention in the early 1990s, as discussions on new university legislation were under way within the constituent colleges and the Senate during that period. In 1994, the trustees of St Patrick's College, Maynooth appointed Dr William J. Smyth as master of the recognised college at Maynooth, who was co-opted as a member of Senate on 27 July 1994, elected as a pro-vice-chancellor of the university, and appointed to the Finance and Standing committees of the Senate.

The Senate in November 1994 decided that a sub-committee would review the arrangements and procedures governing the existing NUI–UCD–Maynooth arrangement. In January 1995, the Senate, having considered the report of the sub-committee, recommended that, in view of the impending change in the status of Maynooth, a new arrangement would be introduced whereby the Dean of the UCD Faculty of Arts and the Dean of the UCD Faculty of Science, whose term of appointment would be for a period of three years or until new legislation would be implemented, would represent NUI in Maynooth. By July 1995, the Senate noted that the new arrangement was 'working well'.

Following the introduction of the Universities Act 1997, Dr Smyth was appointed, on 16 June 1997, as president of National University of Ireland, Maynooth, a constituent university of the National University of Ireland. The Senate at its meeting in November 1998, elected Dr Smyth to the position of vice-chancellor of the NUI and noted his appointment as having special significance in the history of NUI in being the first occasion when a president of NUI Maynooth was elected to the office of vice-chancellor.

Applications from other colleges and institutions in the early part of the twentieth century

In addition to Maynooth's application in 1909, the Senate considered applications from several other colleges and institutions seeking recognised college status in the early part of the twentieth century, including St Mary's University College (1909), the Sacred Heart Convent, Mount Anville, Dundrum (1909), Loreto College, St Stephen's Green (1910), and the Apothecaries Hall (1910). Following considerable deliberation on those applications, most of which were referred in the normal manner to the UCD Governing Body, the Senate decided in October 1912, on the basis of legal advice, that the applications 'for the recognition of these respective Colleges could not be complied with'.

An application was submitted by the Principal of the Crawford Municipal Technical Institute, Cork in 1916, which was supported by UCC. In April 1918, the Senate approved a draft petition for a Second Supplemental and Amending Charter to make provision for the acceptance of particular courses of study in special subjects taken outside the university or the constituent colleges, such as courses at the Crawford Municipal Technical Institute, Cork, in mechanical engineering, electrical engineering, engineering chemistry, workshop practice, design and drawing, courses in hospitals and similar courses within the terms of Clause xx, 4 (b) of the Charter. As this provision seemed to satisfy the requirements of both the Crawford Institute and UCC, the Senate decided that the application from Crawford 'should not be complied with'.

An application for recognised college status from the De La Salle Training College, Waterford, in December 1921, was referred to the UCC Governing Body. However, consideration of this matter became entangled with the whole debate within the NUI on the provision of a degree course for primary teachers in the early part of the 1920s.

The Mid-1970s: NUI Grants Recognised College Status to Seven Institutions

Although the NUI degree of Bachelor of Education (BEd) for primary teachers was not introduced until the mid-1970s, the question of a university degree for primary teachers had seriously engaged the deliberations of various bodies, including the NUI Senate, in the early part of the twentieth century.

Access for primary teachers to university degrees was first raised in the NUI in October 1911 when the Senate decided that the question of whether it was desirable 'to bring students of Training Colleges into connection with the University for the purpose of enabling teachers to secure Degrees or Diplomas, and by what means this may be effected' be referred to the Standing Committee. In its response at the following Senate meeting, the Standing Committee stated that it did not see how students of training colleges could be admitted to the degrees of the university 'without going through the Ordinary Course'.

This issue surfaced again in 1921 when the Convocation of NUI raised the matter with the NUI Senate, and the secretary of the Cork branch of the Irish National Teachers Organisation (INTO) wrote to the NUI enclosing a resolution passed by that body urging the NUI Senate 'to give National Teachers every possible facility to qualify themselves by University training', and suggesting that a conference be convened to consider this matter.

During the period 1921–5 the NUI gave considerable time and attention to this issue. A conference organised by the INTO was attended by a Senate delegation. The academic councils of UCD, UCC and UCG discussed the report prepared on this matter by a special Senate committee and submitted comprehensive responses to the NUI. Various approaches to providing a university degree for national teachers were put forward. For example, UCC recommended the institution of a special professional degree of BAE (Bachelor of Educational Art) or BEd (Bachelor of Education), of three years' duration, with a corresponding Master's degree, MAE or MEd, 'thus doing for the teaching profession what was already done in the case of medicine and engineering'. In contrast, UCG supported the scheme advocated by the Senate Committee's Report, i.e. teachers obtaining a degree (BA or BSc, with Education as a sub-title) on a four years' course: the first half of this period to be spent in the training college and the second half in the university college. There were also differing views on whether 'a professional degree should be a necessary qualification for first recognition of National Teacher'.

At the Senate meeting in April 1924, Dr Coffey, Pro-Vice-Chancellor, who had led an NUI delegation to the Ministry of Education, reported that the result of its interview with the minister on 21 March 1924, in reference to the extension of university privileges to national teachers and teachers in training, was to confirm all that was contained in letters of March 1924 from the secretary of the Ministry of Education, that is that the minister's acceptance of the university scheme as now proposed was subject to the university's acceptance of the existing college programme (final year) without additional subjects. This referred to the Senate's decision in the previous year that 'teachers who have already completed their course of training be permitted to enter for the First University (Common) Examination'. In April 1924, the Senate decided that 'the courses for the Training Colleges were adequate for the First University (Common) Examination, and that students be allowed to present themselves in five subjects instead of six'.

The Senate considered the outcome of the meeting with the Minister of Education as being 'most satisfactory', as it would allow the examination to be conducted in accordance with the university statutes. That meant that an examination by university examiners would be held in connection with the Final Year's Training College Examination, on which the candidate's answering, if satisfying the university examiners, would give the successful students exemption from the course of the first university year and first university examination. From the NUI's standpoint, that seemed to resolve the whole issue of 'bringing students of training colleges into connection with the university for the purpose of enabling teachers to secure degrees'.

The Senate's treatment of this matter, which had serious national, regional and local dimensions, exemplified some of the key advantages and limitations of the NUI federal university system, whereby the issues were examined and ventilated in a democratic and thorough manner in the academic councils and governing bodies of the three constituent colleges. Moreover, regional and local considerations, especially in relation to Cork and Galway, which sometimes differed considerably from the Dublin situation, had to be taken into account – all of which combined to make it extremely difficult at times to forge a clear consensus on a Senate policy position. It was also an example of 'big wheels grinding slowly', a situation which some outside the NUI system often found difficult to understand. Reconciling shades of differing opinions often resulted in prolonged consideration, postponement, considerable delay and, occasionally, no action at all being taken. Despite all the effort and concern which had characterised the debate within the NUI, the constituent colleges, the INTO and the Department of Education, a degree course, designed specifically for National Teachers, was not provided.

In 1925, 42 training college students, 15 from St Patrick's Drumcondra, Dublin, 13 from De La Salle College, Waterford, nine from Carysfort College, Blackrock, County Dublin, and five from Mary Immaculate College, Limerick, passed the First University (Common) Examination. From the time of its implementation in the mid-1920s until the mid-1970s, the First University (Common) Examination was the sole route for qualified national teachers to proceed to university studies leading to the BA degree. The NUI examination records show that, in the years preceding the introduction of the BEd degree, the numbers of students presenting for the First University (Common) Examination were, as follows: 1971: 35; 1972: 12; 1973: 21 .

The Mid-1970s: a University Degree for National Teachers – Phase 2: NUI Grants Recognised Status to Three Colleges of Education

There was a sense of *déjà vu* about the arrangements governing the provision of a degree for national teachers in the mid-1970s. As had happened almost half a century earlier, the main players were again the training colleges, the INTO, the Department of Education, the NUI and its constituent colleges. During the intervening fifty years, national teachers had continued to seek a university degree. Reports such as the Commission on Higher Education in 1967 and a report on teacher training published by the Higher Education

Authority (HEA) in 1970 had both urged that a university degree be provided for national teachers.

Meetings between the INTO and representatives of the Dublin training colleges were held during the early part of the 1970s. In May 1973 the secretary of the Department of Education requested UCC to participate with the authorities of Mary Immaculate Training College, Limerick and officers of the department in drafting a three-year course leading to a university degree for students of the college, involving the acceptance of education as an examination subject for the award of the degree.

A key initiative in this consultative process was the request from the Minister for Education, Richard (Dick) Burke, to the NUI to provide a university degree for national teachers. From the NUI's perspective the most appropriate procedure by which such provision could be effected was on the basis of the Senate's consideration of formal applications from the three main training colleges to become recognised colleges, in accordance with the NUI Statutes.

In July 1974, formal letters of application for the recognition of their colleges (now known as Colleges of Education) as recognised colleges of the NUI were submitted to the Senate by the Revd Dr D. F. Cregan, President of St Patrick's College of Education, Drumcondra, Dublin, Sr M Regina Durkan, President of Our Lady of Mercy College of Education, Carysfort, Blackrock, County Dublin and Sr M. Loreto Ni Chonchubhair, President of Mary Immaculate College of Education, Limerick.

In accordance with the NUI Statutes, the applications from the two Dublin colleges of education were referred to the UCD Governing Body, and the application from the Limerick College of Education was referred to the UCC Governing Body. By February 1975, UCD and UCC had completed their reports on the applications, which were then submitted to the General Board of Studies meeting in February 1975. The Board recommended that the Senate should declare by resolution the three colleges of education to be recognised colleges of the university, provided that all the conditions set out by UCD and UCC would be fulfilled by the colleges. The board also recommended that the degree to be awarded in all three colleges should be Bachelor of Education (BEd). The Senate at its meeting in April 1975 adopted the recommendations of the General Board of Studies, and granted recognised college status to the three colleges of education, with effect from the start of the academic year 1974–5.

More than fifty years after the question of a degree for primary teachers had first been raised, the important milestone was finally reached. The Senate's decision was welcomed enthusiastically by the three colleges of education and the INTO. It was also welcomed by Richard (Dick) Burke now the former Minister for Education, when he addressed the first cohort of BEd graduates in Our Lady of Mercy College of Education in 1977.

The conditions stipulated by UCD and UCC in their reports to the General Board of Studies included such requirements as:

* extending certain teaching resources and library facilities
* appointing additional academic staff
* setting up a method of appointment for new posts as recognised teachers which should involve an assessment board of five members, three to be appointed by the recognised college and two from the constituent college; the recognised college to make the appointment, with the condition that it should take effect only if the NUI Senate agreed to grant recognition to the candidate appointed
* putting in place procedures for approval of courses and examinations
* establishing a protocol for the Examinations Board, consisting of the president of the constituent college (or his nominee), chairman, the university examiners in the subjects involved, and the Registrar (Examinations Officer) and heads of the relevant departments in the recognised colleges

While the Senate's decision of July 1975 marked the launch of a university degree for national teachers, it is unfortunate that it did not take appropriate steps to ensure the harmonisation of the structure of the BEd degree courses in the three colleges of education. In retrospect, it might have been more appropriate for the NUI Senate to have agreed to the provision of a three-year degree course for national teachers, and to have appointed a Senate committee, comprising representatives from both UCD and UCC, to design the structure and content of that course, and to settle important related matters, such as the award of honours and access to postgraduate studies.

In the absence of such a co-ordinated approach, it is not surprising that different course structures emerged, that emphasis was given to certain course elements in some colleges and not in others, and that the question of an honours award and arrangements for access to the BA degree and the postgraduate courses of MEd and MA were not settled for some considerable time.

The key differences between UCD and UCC in relation to the structure of the BEd degree course seems to have been attributable to the concept and orientation of the new degree for primary teachers, as envisaged by the two constituent colleges. It is clear from the reports of the two constituent colleges that the 'BA-structured' BEd degree UCC had in mind for the Limerick College of Education differed significantly from the BEd degree envisaged by UCD for the two Dublin colleges of education.

In line with its own BA degree, structured on a 4–2–2 type of three-year course, UCC informed 'the College of Education representatives that the structures for the proposed Degree (i.e. BEdSc) should conform to those of a BA Degree (General) in UCC, with Education being a subject in each of the three years'. While UCD also intended that the BEd Degree course would be structured on a 3–2–2 type three-year course, in line with the format of its own BA Degree course, it stated in its key recommendations that 'the courses offered in the Colleges proposed for recognition should constitute a professional training of university standard', and that 'a balanced course of professional and academic studies should satisfy professional as well as academic requirements', and that as in the case with other professional degrees, 'the title should indicate the nature of the professional qualification' and, accordingly recommended that the title should be Bachelor of Education (BEd).

The key difference between the 'Cork' and 'Dublin' BEd degree structures concerned the relative 'weightings' given to the subject of 'Education' and to 'the Academic subject'. UCC recommended that BEd graduates of the Limerick College be granted exemption from the First Arts examination, and in the 'academic' subject at the BA (General) Degree Examination. UCD recommended that BEd graduates in the Dublin Colleges be exempt from the First Arts course and examination and from the First Arts course and examination in the 'academic' subject and admitted to the Second Year Honours course in that subject at the discretion of the faculty. Thus a more favourable exemption in the BA degree at UCC was granted in the 'Academic Subject' for BEd graduates from the Limerick College, and accordingly, earlier access to postgraduate studies in that subject.

After a long discussion at the meeting in December 1976 the Senate voted by 14 votes to 11 in favour of making honours available at the BEd degree examination,

Three Colleges of Education Cease to be Recognised Colleges of the NUI
Our Lady of Mercy College of Education, Blackrock, Co Dublin

In 1985, against a background of the government's decision to introduce stringent financial cutbacks in state funding and a lower actual level of primary-teacher retirement than that projected in the government's white paper of 1980, and its consequences for the levels of teacher supply during the following decade, the government decided that one of the colleges of education should be closed. The Minister for Education announced that Carysfort College would no longer be accepting applications from school leavers and in 1988 the President of Our Lady of Mercy College informed the NUI that the college would cease to be an NUI recognised college. The Chancellor, Dr T. K. Whitaker, conferred the BEd degree on the last cohort of student teachers at Carysfort College in July 1988.

Mary Immaculate College of Education, Limerick

In December 1991 Mary Immaculate College informed the University that, in January 1990 when the college was ready to submit a proposal to the NUI to introduce a BA degree, the then secretary of the Department of Education advised the Limerick college not to proceed with the proposed BA Degree course, and to open discussions with the University of Limerick as another possible option.

Arising from discussions with the Trustees of Mary Immaculate College and the authorities of the University of Limerick, the secretary of the Department of Education drafted a memorandum of understanding on a linkage between the two institutions, which they accepted in October 1991, and which was announced by the Minister for Education in November 1991. The college acknowledged that, since 1974, it had had a very happy relationship with the NUI, but that it had no option but to agree to a linkage with the University of Limerick. The college wished to make arrangements with the NUI so that its departure from the NUI would be harmonious and would accommodate the students qualifying with BEd degrees of the NUI during the period 1992–4.

St Patrick's College of Education, Drumcondra, Dublin

In July 1990 the Senate approved the recommendation of the UCD Academic Council of the proposed BA degree at St Patrick's College. Although the Senate received no formal communication from the Department of Education concerning the changes the department had in mind for the colleges of education in Dublin and Limerick, it was understood that, as in the case of Mary Immaculate College, Limerick, the Department of Education was making similar arrangements for St Patrick's College of Education whereby that college would become an associated college of Dublin City University.

In its consideration of the status of the recognised college of St Patrick's College, Drumcondra, in November 1992 and the proposed linkage between that college and Dublin City University, the Senate noted correspondence from the manager and president of St Patrick's College, Drumcondra, expressing their gratitude for the great benefit of the BEd Degree since its inception, as well as the Chancellor's reply that the university, for its part, was always glad to have St Patrick's College, Drumcondra, as one of its recognised colleges and regretted that the friendly and fruitful association was now ending.

Two further Recognised Colleges in Limerick

In addition to the Recognised College of Mary Immaculate College of Education, the Senate granted recognised college status to two other institutions in Limerick in the mid-1970s, both of which were to have a shorter association with the NUI than any other recognised college.

The National Institute of Higher Education, Limerick (NIHEL)

In a letter dated 22 August 1975, the director of the National Institute of Higher Education, Limerick (NIHEL), Dr Edward M. Walsh, applied to have the institute recognised by the NUI. In accordance with the NUI Statutes, the NUI Senate referred the application to UCC in October 1975. In March 1976 the Vice-Chancellor summoned an extraordinary meeting of the General Board of Studies to consider the UCC Governing Body's report, which gave its consent to the granting of recognition to NIHEL. The institute had applied for recognition of degree programmes in five areas of study: (i) Administrative systems; (ii) Business Studies; (iii) Electronics; (iv) European Studies; (v) Materials and Industrial Engineering.

The UCC Governing Body recommended the award of the degree of Bachelor of Technology (BTech) in respect of (iii) and (v) above, which was viewed as 'involving a widening of the range of degrees in the University so as to cater for this type of training in an Institute with a technological orientation'. The degree of Bachelor of Commercial Studies (BCS) was recommended in respect of courses (i), (ii) and (iv).

The UCC Governing Body stipulated a number of conditions to be satisfied which related to (*a*) the method of appointment of recognised teachers (*b*) the restructuring of syllabuses and course content (*c*) the procedure for the approval of courses (*d*) the formal arrangements for meetings of examiners, and (*e*) the review of courses after a period of three years.

After a long discussion the General Board of Studies recommended that the report be adopted and the National Institute of Higher Education, Limerick, be accepted as a recognised college of the NUI in accordance with the report of the UCC Governing Body. This was approved at an extraordinary meeting of Senate on 11 March 1976. The coming together of the two institutions was not without some 'marital difficulties'. On the one hand, NIHEL might have felt that the NUI, as a long established academic institution, was not sufficiently flexible to accommodate the 'more modern' course structures in an institute with a technological orientation. On the other hand, in processing the application for NUI recognised college status from NIHEL before reporting to the NUI Senate, the Committee appointed by UCC was augmented by staff from other institutions to deal with study areas in which the UCC staff may have lacked adequate expertise.

In October 1976 the Senate approved the proposal in the letter of 16 July 1976 from the president of UCC, recommending that he and the president of UCG had agreed that UCG would, on behalf of the NUI, be responsible for NIHEL and would deal with all student matters in the institute except fourth-year students in the session 1975–6 for whom UCC would be responsible. At the conferring ceremony held in July 1977, the Chancellor of the NUI, Dr T. K. Whitaker, conferred degrees on NIHEL graduates.

Recognised College Status granted to Thomond College of Education, Limerick

In July 1976 the Senate, having considered a letter dated 12 April 1976 from the Director of Thomond College of Education, Limerick, Dr James Christian, applying for acceptance as a recognised college, decided to refer the application to the UCC Governing Body. The report of the UCC Governing Body was submitted to the meeting of the General Board of Studies in November 1976. It noted that Thomond College had applied for recognition of a degree programme of integrated academic and professional studies pursued concurrently over four years to produce specialist teachers of physical education who were, in addition, able to teach competently in another area of the school curriculum.

The UCC Governing Body recommended that the relevant degree for this programme should be Bachelor of Education (BEd) and that honours as well as pass awards would be appropriate on the basis of approved common courses. It also recommended that all of the existing full-time permanent teachers and two part-time teachers be accorded the status of Recognised Teacher in the appropriate subjects. The Senate, at its meeting in December 1976, having considered the report of the General Board of Studies of November 1976, decided that Thomond College of Education Limerick be accepted as a recognised college of the university in the subjects set out in the report of the UCC Governing Body.

NIHEL and Thomond cease to be NUI Recognised Colleges

Following a change in government in 1977 it was decided to revert to the binary system. One of the consequences of that decision was that National Institute for Higher Education, Limerick and Thomond College, Limerick were directed by the Department of Education to terminate their affiliation with the NUI and to re-engage with the National Council for Education Awards (NCEA), whose degree-awarding powers were restored.

In December 1977, the Senate noted (i) the letter of 21 November 1977 from the private secretary to the Minister for Education enclosing a copy of a press release issued on 18 November 1977 regarding the government's decision to restore degree-awarding powers to the National Council for Education Awards (NCEA) and that that body would be the Degree-awarding authority for NIHEL and Thomond College, and (ii) the letter from the Director of NIHEL enclosing a copy of a letter he had written to the NCEA stating that the governing body of NIHEL had decided on 1 December 1977 to apply to NCEA for the accreditation of degree-level programmes and the award of degrees to eligible students.

At that same meeting, the Senate, having considered a letter from the president of UCG stating that, 'in view of the Minister's statement, UCG understands that its function in relation to the Recognised College of NIHEL will cease following the meeting of Senate', adopted unanimously the motion that 'recognised college status be withdrawn from NIHE, Limerick as from 15 December 1977'. A proposal from the president of UCC 'that recognised college status be withdrawn from Thomond College of Education as from 15 December 1977' was also adopted unanimously.

1977: The Royal College of Surgeons in Ireland becomes a Recognised College

The Royal College of Surgeons in Ireland (RCSI) was founded in 1784, by Royal Charter from King George III, to educate surgeons who at that time were trained separately from physicians. After 1886, the training of physicians and surgeons merged, and the college began to train doctors in its medical school. Under its charter the RCSI was entitled to award licentiates to students who successfully completed the medical programme and passed the required examinations of the medical school.

Following discussions with University College Dublin, a formal application for recognised college status was submitted to the NUI by Dr H. O'Flanagan, president of RCSI, in February 1977. In its report to the General Board of Studies, the UCD Governing Body, stated that it welcomed the application of the RCSI, particularly because of the historic links between them and noted that, before the foundation of the Royal University, almost all of the students of the Catholic School of Medicine qualified through the college; thereafter, until the foundation of the NUI, the great majority of the students continued to do so.

At its meeting on 14 July 1977, the Senate approved the recommendation of the General Board of Studies that the report of the UCD Governing Body be adopted and that RCSI be accepted as a recognised college of the university.

In the words of a former UCD president 'the wheel had now turned full circle, giving the University an opportunity to repay a debt of honour'.

In accordance with the statutory arrangements applying to the other recognised colleges, the arrangements between the NUI and RCSI, with particular reference to the role of the UCD intern examiners acting on NUI's behalf, soon settled down and functioned effectively. However, given the proximity of the two institutions in the city centre, the qualifications of the respective academic staffs in UCD and RCSI, the particular orientation of the RCSI as a private institution, and its predominantly international focus, it was not surprising that, from time to time, tensions arose between the RCSI and representatives of the UCD Faculty of Medicine who represented the NUI in RCSI.

In the early 1990s, following suggestions in the *Medical Times* and some of the national newspapers that RCSI was contemplating either becoming an independent institution or forming a new relationship with another university, a meeting, chaired by the NUI Chancellor, was arranged between NUI, UCD and RCSI to provide RCSI an opportunity to clarify the situation. Arising from the discussions at that meeting it was agreed that the NUI would set up a Joint NUI/UCD/RCSI working party to address key issues of concern to the RCSI.

It is important to note that, during this period, RCSI invited UCD to become involved, as a partner, in a new joint venture in Penang, Malaysia, with the intention in the first instance of establishing an undergraduate degree programme in medicine, leading to the award of the NUI degrees of MB, BCh, BAO. Under this unique arrangement, students from Malaysia would come to Dublin, to be admitted to RCSI or UCD, for their pre-clinical studies, following which they would return to Penang (where a local consortium planned to provide a suitable building for the programme, i.e. Penang Medical College) to complete their clinical studies. UCD agreed to participate in this new programme. The project was also endorsed and supported by the Minister for Education in Penang, on the understanding that students who successfully completed the medical programme and passed the required university examinations would be conferred with the degrees of MB, BCh, BAO of the National University of Ireland.

In November 1994, the Senate recommended that, in view of the more positive and co-operative spirit governing the UCD/RCSI proposal on the Penang Medical College project, a working group, comprising the NUI Registrar, the Dean of the UCD Medical Faculty, and the RCSI Registrar, would

review the existing NUI/UCD/RCSI relationship and submit recommendations on appropriate formal procedures and arrangements for the future
between NUI and RCSI, which would also encompass the proposed developments in Penang. The Senate also agreed in principle to the joint UCD/RCSI
written proposal on the Penang undergraduate medical programme.

In light of those developments, the NUI agreed to a revised arrangement
for transacting the academic business of RCSI within NUI, which took the
form of a Joint NUI–UCD–RCSI Steering Committee, comprising the NUI
Registrar (chair), the UCD Registrar, the RCSI Registrar, the UCD Dean of
the Faculty of Medicine, and the RCSI Dean of the Faculty of Medicine. As
RCSI expanded in the 1980s and 1990s, providing a more diverse range of
courses in medicine and health sciences and, confident that the quality of
its academic staff was on a par with any other medical institution in Ireland,
the college felt that there were good grounds for UCD's involvement in its
activities to be discharged with a 'lighter touch'.

The UCD 'competitive' dimension became more obvious when RCSI
began to develop a new degree programme in physiotherapy, a discipline
where UCD was also in competition for the recruitment of new undergraduate
students. As in the case of the Recognised College of St Patrick's College,
Maynooth in the mid-1990s, RCSI felt that on the basis of (i) its successful
record as a recognised college for almost 30 years, (ii) its entry standards
which were as high as those for entry to the other medical faculties in the
NUI, (iii) the range and standard of its courses, (iv) the growth in student
numbers and academic staff, and (v) its involvement in funded research
programmes, a strong case could be made for seeking a revision of its existing
arrangement with the NUI.

Such an arrangement, while not equivalent to a constituent university
position which was not legally possible under the Universities Act 1997, could,
in RCSI's view, be less constrained than the existing recognised college
arrangement which enabled the medical faculty of one of the NUI constituent
universities (i.e. UCD), with which it might be in competition from time to
time, in terms of new developments in the wider sphere of medical education,
to be privy to RCSI's proposed developments.

In a document submitted to the Senate in October 2005, the RCSI proposed that the NUI would set up a special senate committee which would
be responsible for processing the academic business between the NUI and

RCSI, while routine administrative matters (e.g. financial, ceremonial) between the NUI and the RCSI would be dealt with directly between the NUI Registrar and the RCSI Registrar. It was suggested that the proposed special senate committee would be comprised of the NUI Registrar (chair), two members of Senate nominated by the Chancellor, the Registrar of RCSI, and an appropriate number of extern examiners, to be determined by the committee, who would have the necessary expertise in the courses being proposed, from time to time, by the RCSI.

1978: St Angela's College of Education, Lough Gill, County Sligo

In 1976 the Senate, having considered a letter from An tSr Bríd Ní Áinle on behalf of St Angela's College of Education, Sligo, for acceptance as a recognised college of the university, decided to refer the application to the governing body of University College Galway. A working party was appointed by UCG to examine the application. Visits to St Angela's College took place in January and September of 1977, and the working party also met with the authorities of St Angela's on a number of occasions in UCG.

The UCG report noted that St Angela's College, owned by the Ursuline Community, was founded in 1952 as a training college for the education and training of teachers of home economics, and since that date has been recognised and funded by the Department of Education, and by student fees. The Senate at its meeting in April 1978, having considered the report of the General Board of Studies on the UCG Governing Body's report on St Angela's application, declared the college to be a recognised college of the NUI.

At the beginning of the new century St Angela's College sought a new relationship with NUI Galway as a means of 'enhancing the College's capacity to develop and progress'. NUI Galway was sympathetic and wished to facilitate this aspiration. It established a Coisde liaison with St Angela's aimed at exploring developmental opportunities in the north-west region, and in relation to cross-border initiatives. A draft proposal entitled 'Agreement for Institutional Linkage' was drawn up setting out the terms under which the two institutions would 'enter into an arrangement comprising collaboration and liaison whilst preserving and reserving their respective independent legal identities'.

Following its consultation with the Department of Education and Science on the matter, NUI Galway requested the NUI to examine the legal feasibility of accommodating the proposed 'Agreement' within the NUI Charter, or by a possible amendment thereto. When this matter was considered by the Senate in June 2001, it was acknowledged that the legal position of such a change in status of St Angela's and its proposed relationship with NUI Galway and with the NUI was unclear. The Senate decided that it would be important to seek legal advice to ensure that the proposed new arrangement between NUI Galway and St Angela's would be permitted by the Charter and be legally correct.

After a lengthy period of deliberation on key legal aspects of the proposed linkage between the two institutions, the matter was finally resolved in 2006 when St Angela's College ceased to be a recognised college of the NUI and became a college of NUI Galway. At the Senate meeting in November 2005 the President of St Angela's College, Dr Anne Taheny, reported that the necessary arrangements would be fully in place by the end of the year to enable the college to become a college of NUI Galway, and to receive its funding through the HEA instead of through the Department of Education and Science. She thanked the Senate for having facilitated St Angela's College in this transition. In January 2006, the Senate noted the letter of December 2005 from the President of St Angela's College indicating that the agreement with NUI Galway would come into effect on 1 January 2006. The Senate decided, accordingly, that St Angela's College would no longer be a recognised college with effect from that date, and wished St Angela's College well in its new status as a college of NUI Galway.

Relationships Between the NUI and the Recognised Colleges During the Mid-1970s

Renationships between the NUI and the recognised colleges manifested themselves at a formal, statutory level, as well as at administrative and operational levels. Presidents of the recognised colleges were entitled to be *ex-officio* members of the General Board of Studies. This membership provided them with the considerable documentation submitted for consideration by that board, including proposals submitted by their own colleges to the relevant constituent colleges and the General Board of Studies' response to those proposals. It also ensured that they soon become familiar with the NUI's procedures for processing academic developments within the federal university system. Attendance at GBS meetings provided opportunities for the presidents to meet with a wide cross-section of administrators and academics from the constituent colleges, the other recognised colleges and the NUI central office. Presidents hosted the NUI conferring ceremonies held in the recognised colleges, at which the BEd graduates were normally conferred by the Vice-Chancellor or Pro-Vice-Chancellor, assisted by the Registrar of the NUI. It was customary for the Chancellor to confer the first degrees in a recognised college. In relation to the day-to-day administrative relationship between the NUI and the recognised colleges the NUI made it clear from the outset that the key transactions would be discharged between the NUI registrar and the registrar of the recognised college.

The importance of this 'administrative linchpin was firmly established when, in 1977, the NUI Registrar, Dr John Bourke, invited the registrars of the newly approved recognised colleges to a meeting in the NUI office to develop a uniform administrative approach to ensure an efficient and effective processing of all university business between the NUI and its recognised colleges. The agenda for that meeting, which encapsulated the full range of regulations and procedures governing all administrative matters relating to the courses, examinations and conferrings in the recognised colleges, became the template for all future administrative business between the NUI and its recognised colleges.

The registrars of the recognised colleges at that time, who were also appointed by the Senate as NUI supervisors of examinations in their colleges, were: Stiofán B. Ó hAnnracháin (St Patrick's College, Drumcondra), Seán A. Ó Broiméil (Mary Immaculate College, Limerick), John Nolan (Carysfort College, Blackrock), Professor W. A. McGowan and Joseph Grace (Royal College of Surgeons in Ireland); Leo Colgan (NIHEL), Liam Dugdale (Thomond College).

Another vital component in the overall functioning of the NUI–recognised colleges process was the important contribution made by the intern examiners from the constituent colleges, appointed annually by the NUI Senate to monitor courses and examinations in the recognised colleges. Those intern examiners worked closely with their counterparts in the recognised college, who were the heads of departments in the various subject areas of the BEd Degree. Meetings between the two parties were arranged at mutually agreed key times in the cycle of the academic year (i) to review course developments and new course proposals; (ii) to settle the marks and standards for the university examinations governing the courses offered; (iii) to arrange the monitoring of teaching practice by the constituent college personnel, and (iv) to arrange for the sampling of examination scripts and oral tests, and to monitor the standards achieved by the students, with particular reference to honours awards. The university intern examiners also attended the formal examination board meetings, chaired by the president of the constituent college or his nominee, which determined the overall examination results.

Representation of Recognised Colleges on the NUI Senate

Under the 1908 Act, the President of Maynooth was included in the list of members nominated by the Dublin commissioners to the first Senate. After the Senate came into full 'working order' in 1912, the only legal avenue to Senate membership for a representative from a recognised college, when a new Senate was coming into office for a five-year period, was either by inclusion amongst the four members nominated by the government or through the co-option procedure whereby, the combined 31 members who had already been either elected or nominated met to co-opt four additional members of Senate.

Apart from the President of Maynooth, no other president of a recognised college was co-opted as a member of Senate until November 1997 when the President of the RCSI (or his nominee), on being proposed by the President of UCD and seconded by the UCD Registrar, was co-opted. This new development arose from a meeting in January 1993 when the Standing Committee of Senate accepted in principle the desirability of representation of recognised colleges, under the existing statutory provision governing 'persons co-opted', and recommended that the NUI Registrar would prepare a memorandum on how this might be implemented, including consideration of 'presence' at Senate meetings. At its July meeting, following its consideration of the registrar's memorandum, the Senate agreed that the representation of the recognised colleges on the Senate should be facilitated under the co-option statutory provisions as, and when, it arose.

At a meeting in October 1997, shortly before the Senate to hold office for the period 1997–2002 was formed, the Standing Committee noted the Registrar's memorandum on co-option of members of Senate, and the Chancellor drew particular attention to the Senate's July 1993 position in relation to representatives of recognised colleges on the Senate. Arising from the constitution of the Senate membership, as modified by the Universities Act 1997, UCD accepted that each of the four constituent universities had adequate membership on the NUI Senate and, accordingly, it would now be appropriate to allocate the four co-option memberships to the recognised colleges. Despite this, the other three constituent universities decided not to change their traditional position of putting forward one of their own representatives for co-option.

At the next meeting of Senate in January 1998, on the Chancellor's proposal, the Senate agreed that the presidents of recognised colleges, if not already co-opted, should be invited to attend Senate meetings. As a result of this decision, the heads of the following recognised colleges attended meetings of the Senate: St Angela's College of Education; the National College of Art and Design (NCAD); Shannon College of Hotel Management; the Institute of Public Administration.

It should be noted that, prior to the Senate's first consideration in 1996 of recognised college representation on the Senate, there were two representatives on the Senate who, while included in the four persons nominated by the government as members of Senate, held senior administrative positions in recognised colleges. These were: Seán A Ó Broiméil, Registrar of Mary Immaculate College of Education, Limerick, nominated by the government in 1982, and Dr Edward M. Walsh, Director of the National Institute of Higher Education Limerick, nominated by the government in 1977. In January 1999 the Senate decided to recommend to the next Senate (coming into office in 2002) that the co-option provision be used to secure full representation for the recognised colleges on the Senate.

Financial Arrangements Between the NUI and the Recognised Colleges

Up to 1987 the main source of NUI's funding was a grant-in-aid from the state, through the Higher Education Authority. This annual subvention, together with the income NUI received from Matriculation and other fees, covered all of NUI's expenditure on the administrative services it provided for the federal university system, including the provision of an extern examining system. The constituent colleges were not required to make any payments to the NUI. It was probably for historical reasons that St Patrick's College, Maynooth, although a recognised college, was treated like the three constituent colleges, and not required to make any financial payment to the NUI.

When seven colleges became recognised colleges of the NUI in the mid-1970s the NUI decided that it would be a matter for those colleges to make their own arrangements in relation to the payment of examiners involved in the examinations leading to the award of NUI degrees. The NUI set the level of examination fee to be paid by examination candidates, which was forwarded by the recognised colleges to the NUI. Following the conferment of degrees in the autumn, the NUI deducted basic charges 'for university services', arising mainly from the provision of testimonia for conferring ceremonies and related administrative matters, and returned the balance of the overall examination fee income to the recognised colleges, who used this money to pay their academic staff for invigilating at examinations and correcting examination scripts.

This situation changed significantly in 1987 when, at a time of stringent cutbacks in government expenditure, the HEA informed the NUI that, apart from a grant of £10,000 under the provisions of Section 7 of the Irish Universities Act of 1908, its annual grant-in-aid was being discontinued. In response to this unexpected and severe financial blow, the Senate was forced to carry out a range of economic measures aimed at offsetting an immediate and significant deficit. Included in those measures was a decision to introduce a charge to recognised colleges for university services, based on the level of student numbers then enrolled in the main colleges of education, and to be increased annually in accordance with the rate of inflation.

A further financial arrangement between the NUI and both the constituent colleges and recognised colleges was introduced following the Senate's decision in 1992 to cease holding a separate matriculation examination. Prior to that date the NUI received a certain level of income from fees paid by students who either (a) applied for matriculation on the basis of their Leaving Certificate results, often referred to as 'buying the Matric', or (b) applied for and paid an examination fee to sit the matriculation examination held at various centres throughout the country. Those fees were paid directly to the NUI.

In anticipation of the situation that would arise following its decision to cease holding the matriculation examination, the Senate decided that, after

1993, a new matriculation fee (a composite fee based on the matriculation registration fee and the matriculation examination fee), to be introduced on a phased basis, would be paid in three instalments by new entrant undergraduate students, second-year students, third-year students, and postgraduate students. This new matriculation fee would be paid directly by students at the time of their registration in the constituent and recognised colleges, following which the fees would be forwarded to the NUI. From 1996, this new arrangement became the main source of NUI's annual income. Accordingly, all colleges which became recognised colleges of the NUI after that date were required to make payments annually to the NUI comprising (i) a charge for university services and (ii) a matriculation fee in respect of each student registering for a course of studies leading to the award of an NUI degree.

The Universities Act, 1997 and the NUI Recognised Colleges

The most significant change governing recognised colleges arising from the Universities Act 1997 was the change in status of the Recognised College of St Patrick's College, Maynooth which, along with the three constituent colleges of the NUI, was constituted as a constituent university of the National University of Ireland. Apart from this change, the new act did not concern itself with the other recognised colleges, now reduced to three – the Royal College of Surgeons in Ireland, St Angela's College of Education, County Sligo and the National College of Art & Design.

The amendment to clause XIX of the NUI Charter by deleting 'The General Board of Studies' – which was necessary to avoid any conflict with the functions of the new NUI constituent universities, as set out in Section 13 of the 1997 Act, which included the functions of providing courses and conducting examinations, and the role of academic councils in Section 27 of the Act, 'to control the academic affairs of the constituent university' – also had the unintended effect of removing the NUI's formal administrative structure for processing the key academic business matters of the recognised colleges in relation to the award of NUI degrees and other qualifications.

In July 1998, the Senate noted the NUI Registrar's report that, in the absence of the General Board of Studies, it was appropriate to review procedures for processing the academic business of recognised colleges in relation to NUI degrees and other qualifications. Following discussion, the Senate decided to adopt, as a general model for recognised colleges, the proposed formal arrangement suggested by the NUI Registrar of a steering committee along the lines of the recently established Joint NUI–UCD–RCSI Steering Committee, which would comprise: the NUI Registrar (Chairperson); the registrar of the relevant constituent university, together with the dean(s) of the relevant faculty(ies), and the director/registrar of the recognised college concerned, together with another relevant representative. The steering committee would evaluate proposals from the recognised college and forward recommendations to the dean/faculty/academic council in the constituent university, which in turn, would report to the NUI Standing Committee and Senate.

In July 1999, the Senate endorsed the steering committee arrangement which seemed to be working well in assisting developments in the recognised colleges, and in ensuring that their academic business would be processed efficiently and expeditiously between meetings of the Senate. It was also acknowledged that the format of presentation of Steering Committee reports was helpful in providing the Senate with an appreciation of the developments taking place in the NUI recognised colleges.

Steering Committee meetings were accordingly arranged on the basis of at least one meeting during the autumn, spring and summer terms, and on dates set well in advance of the relevant faculty and academic council meetings, as well as allowing adequate time for reporting to the next NUI Senate meeting. The agenda for such Steering Committee meetings included the following key items of business: the introduction of new degree and diploma courses; proposals for changes in courses and in marks and standards for examinations; the introduction of new degree and diploma titles (and programmes); appointment of extern examiners; procedures for postgraduate degrees (PhD, MSc, MD, MAO); financial matters.

1996–2006: Four Colleges/Institutes Granted Recognised College Status

In the context of the general debate in the 1990s on new university legislation and the question of degree-awarding status, it was understood at the time that certain Regional Technical Colleges (RTCs) had begun informal exploratory discussions with some of the NUI constituent colleges on the possibility of degree-validation arrangements. There was also an awareness that the Department of Education would be positively disposed to such an arrangement.

Against that backdrop the Senate, in November 1996, gave preliminary consideration to the question of extending recognised college status to the RTCs. Acknowledging that it would be both timely and appropriate for the NUI to formulate a policy on this matter, it was agreed that the UCD Registrar, in consultation with the other registrars, would prepare a position paper on the matter for consideration by Senate. However, as the main focus of attention in 1996 was on the forthcoming university legislation and its implications for the four NUI constituent universities, no further progress was made on the matter of RTCs becoming recognised colleges of the NUI.

Five colleges ceased to be recognised colleges of the NUI, two in the latter part of the 1970s, one towards the end of the 1980s and two more in the mid-1990s. Following the introduction of the Universities Act in 1997, the Recognised College of St Patrick's College, Maynooth became a constituent university of the NUI. However, during the period 1996 to 2005, there was further expansion in the number of recognised colleges.

1996: The National College of Art and Design

The National College of Art and Design was founded in 1746 as a 'little academy for drawing and painting', which was supported by the Royal Dublin Society. In 1924 the college came under the control of the Department of Education. From 1936 it was styled 'The National College of Art', awarding its own diplomas. In 1971 the college was reconstituted by an act of the Oireachtas, when many of its functions were placed under a board appointed by the Minister for Education. The college moved to premises in Thomas Street, Dublin in 1980.

In July 1996, the year when the college celebrated its 250th anniversary, the NUI Senate, having considered a report from the UCD Governing Body, decided to approve NCAD's application, which had been submitted by its Director, Professor Noel Sheridan, and granted recognised college status to the National College of Art and Design. In July 1998, a new School of Design and Industry was opened on the Thomas Street campus, which brought all the college activities to one location. The college provides degree and postgraduate programmes in art and design education, fine art and a range of design disciplines.

The first intake of students registering for courses of study leading to the award of degrees of the NUI took place in November 1999. In January 2000, a ceremony to mark the NCAD becoming a recognised college of the NUI was hosted by the director of the NCAD. The platform party included the NUI Chancellor, the President of UCD and Vice-Chancellor, and the Taoiseach, Bertie Ahern.

As arranged for the other recognised colleges, the NUI set up a steering committee as the formal mechanism for dealing with all aspects of recognised college status and for processing the academic and administrative business between the two institutions. The NCAD was represented on the steering committee by its Director, Professor Colm O'Briain, who succeeded Professor N. Sheridan in 2002 and Mr Ken Langan, Registrar.

In June 2002, the first NUI degrees were conferred on NCAD graduates by Dr Art Cosgrove, President of UCD–NUI Dublin and Pro-Vice-Chancellor of the University. In the early years of its new status as a recognised college, considerable progress was made on the formulation and implementation of regulations and procedures governing degree courses, and a range of titles of Master's degree titles was approved for introduction in 2006.

2000: Shannon College of Hotel Management (SCHM)

Founded in 1951 by Dr Brendan O'Regan to train managers for the Irish hotel industry, Shannon College of Hotel Management has become Ireland's leading hotel college and has established an international reputation for excellence. The college believes that industry experience at operational, supervisory and trainee management levels is a central part of management training. Equally important are the development of product knowledge, business skills and foreign language fluency, formed the basis of its diploma course in international hotel management.

Prior to its becoming a recognised college of the NUI, Shannon College had established a relationship with UCG (NUI Galway after 1997), whereby graduates of the college's diploma course who obtained the required grades were allowed to enter the final year of the BComm degree at NUI Galway. In November 2000, the NUI Senate, having considered a report from the NUI Galway Governing Body, decided to approve the application submitted by the Director of Shannon College of Hotel Management, Phillip Smyth, and to declare Shannon College to be a recognised college of the NUI.

The NUI set up a steering committee to oversee all aspects of the new relationship between the two institutions, to assist academic and professional developments, and to ensure that business between the two institutions was processed efficiently and expeditiously. It was also agreed that, in addition to the steering committee, there could be a mechanism at senior management level between SCHM and NUI Galway aimed at exploring, in the region, collaborative strategic developments of mutual benefit of both institutions.

Two modes of entry at degree level were established: a new three-year Bachelor of Business Studies (BBS) and the BComm degree, whereby the students in the third semester of Year 3 could complete the prerequisite modules for the BComm Degree at NUI Galway. On the commencement of year 4, the BBS students continue their studies at SCHM, while the BComm students complete their studies at NUI Galway, at the conclusion of which they also received an NUI Diploma in International Hotel Management.

The first NUI conferring ceremony at Shannon College of Hotel Management, at which the Chancellor of the NUI, Dr Garret FitzGerald presided, was held in November 2005.

2001: The Institute of Public Administration (IPA)

The genesis of the Institute of Public Administration arose from the deliberations of a group of senior public servants who saw the need for a modern professional education for members of the Irish public sector and for the informed analysis and evaluation of Irish public policy making. The founders of the IPA were distinguished public servants. One of the signatories of the IPA's Articles and Memorandum of Association, Dr Garret FitzGerald, now Chancellor of the NUI, was to become Taoiseach. Arising from these deliberations, a formal organisation, the Institute of Public Administration, was founded in 1957. It became a company limited by guarantee in 1963 and is a non-profit-making voluntary body.

The IPA is the only organisation in Ireland offering a comprehensive range of services in public administration – in research, education, training and publications. From the outset, the IPA was anxious to pursue best practice. Senior staff visited the École nationale d'administration in Paris to study its methods and the reasons for its far-reaching influence on the higher echelons of the French civil service, and throughout French public life. In order to create a similar influence on the Irish public sector a School of Public Administration was established within the IPA, and this latter evolved into its education division. A particular feature of the IPA's education provision is the availability of all its education programmes through distance education in order to service the needs of a geographically dispersed public service. External accreditation for the IPA's undergraduate degree programme was first granted in 1982 and for its programmes at postgraduate level in 1994.

In January 2001, the NUI Senate, having considered a report from the UCD Governing Body, declared the IPA to be a recognised college, with effect from September 2001. Its application for recognised status had been submitted in July 1999 by the then Director, John Gallagher, assisted by Pat Hall. A ceremony to mark the IPA's recognised status, which was held in November 2002, was opened by the NUI Chancellor, Dr Garret FitzGerald, and attended by Noel Ahern, minister of state at the Department of the Environment, Heritage and Local Government.

The NUI established a Steering Committee to oversee academic and administrative business between the NUI and the IPA, which was represented by the Director, John Cullen, and Assistant Director, Dr Michael Mulreaney. As part of the new relationship between the NUI and the IPA, the NUI nominated Professor F. Roche, UCD Faculty of Commerce, as a member of the IPA board. The NUI Steering Committee made considerable progress in restructuring the IPA's suite of part-time undergraduate and postgraduate degree programmes, focusing on the disciplines germane to the understanding and practice of public management. In December 2003, the NUI Chancellor, Dr Garret FitzGerald, conferred the first NUI degrees on IPA graduates.

2005: The Milltown Institute of Theology and Philosophy

The Milltown Institute is 'a specialist college that is open to everyone, young and old, believers and non-affiliated'. It offers civil and ecclesiastical awards up to doctoral level in theology, philosophy and spirituality. The institute's suite of academic programmes comprises two strands: one, leading to pontifical awards, and the other leading to civil awards, the latter being the courses for which NUI recognition was sought in its application of June 2002, to become a recognised college.

In January 2004, having considered a report from the UCD Governing Body, the Senate approved in principle the application from the Milltown Institute of Theology and Philosophy seeking recognised college status, subject to a number of conditions relating to such matters as governance and management structures to be put in place at the institute, the need for additional academic staff appointments, quality assurance procedures, and the level of the Institute's funding base to support the courses to support the courses it planned to submit for recognition.

To examine and report progress on the above conditions NUI established an interim steering committee, on which the institute was represented by its President, Brian Grogan. During the following year progress was made on a number of issues. It was agreed to set up quality assurance procedures whereby NUI extern examiners and UCD intern examiners would monitor academic standards and quality. The institute confirmed that its funding base had been secured at a level sufficient to support the academic quality of its courses and its plans for strategic development. Progress was also achieved on arrangements for appropriate governance and management structures in relation to the recognised college dimension of the institute. It was clarified that the General Council of the Pontifical Athenaeum and the governing body of the recognised college would be two distinct groups of representatives, but with the president/chief executive officer, senior management team, registrar and bursar common to both structures, and that the accounts for the recognised college would be 'ring-fenced'.

As the approval of the institute's courses by the Higher Education and Training Awards Council (HETAC) would expire with the 2004–5 student intake, it became an urgent matter for the institute that the commencement of its NUI recognised college position would be settled as a matter of urgency. Responding to this situation, the interim steering committee decided that, in light of the progress made on the conditions stipulated by the Senate in January 2004, the institute should submit an amended document for consideration by a UCD working party and the UCD Governing Body, with a view to reporting to the Senate in January 2005.

Further meetings were held between the relevant parties during the period December 2004–March 2005, and at its meeting in April 2005, the Senate adopted the recommendations of the UCD Governing Body and declared the institute to be a recognised college of the NUI with effect from 1 September

2005. Recognition was granted for a period of two years, on the understanding that a formal review would be completed by November 2006.

At a formal ceremony, in October 2005, to mark the institute's becoming a recognised college of the NUI, attended by the NUI Chancellor and the Minister for Education and Science, Mary Hanafin, the President of the institute said that the newly established recognised college at Milltown had been greatly encouraged by the Chancellor's remarks and looked forward to the prospect of developing joint degrees between UCD and the institute. In October 2006, NUI degrees were conferred on graduates of the recognised college at the Milltown Institute by the Chancellor of the NUI, Dr Garret FitzGerald.

Conclusion

Despite its authority under the 1908 act and NUI Charter to grant recognised college status, the NUI never formulated a specific policy on recognised colleges. It viewed its role, not as an 'aggressive acquirer', but as a 'benign facilitator' of colleges and institutions seeking recognised college status.

From the mid-1970s, in keeping with its 'national' role, the NUI facilitated and accommodated requests from a range of diverse institutions, whose ethos, academic and cultural orientations differed in various ways from NUI's traditional university system. Several requests for such NUI recognition were initiated by the Department of Education. In response to the minister's request in the early 1970s to provide a degree for primary teachers, the NUI devoted considerable time and resources to processing applications for recognised college status from the three largest teacher training colleges. Arising from the government's decision in the 1970s to abolish the binary system, the NUI granted recognised college status to Thomond College, Limerick and the National Institute for Higher Education, Limerick, for which it introduced two new university degrees. It is both surprising and regrettable to note, therefore, the inappropriate treatment of the NUI by the Department of Education in relation to its decisions concerning a number of NUI Recognised Colleges, with particular reference to the closure of Carysfort College, the re-engagement of the NIHEL and Thomond College with the NCEA and, in the 1990, the new alignment of Mary Immaculate College, Limerick and St Patrick's College, Drumcondra with, respectively, the University of Limerick and Dublin City University.

The colleges and institutions which became recognised colleges of the National University of Ireland during the past hundred years readily acknowledge the significant benefits they enjoyed from their new status within the university community in Ireland. During that time there was no instance of a breakdown in relations between the NUI and any of its recognised colleges, although the latter represented a range of diverse institutions. Apart from St Angela's College, which became a college of NUI Galway in 2006, the NUI records show that no college or institution decided to cease being a recognised college of the NUI; whenever withdrawal of a college or institution from the NUI occurred it was always at the minister's behest.

A significant consequence of the NUI's processing of applications for recognised college status, and particularly the conditions specified by the NUI before recognition would be granted, was that the various colleges and institutions were then in a stronger position to make a case to the relevant authorities for the provision of additional financial and other resources.

NUI recognised college status provided a framework which lifted all aspects of academic and professional activity in the recognised colleges. It enhanced their profile within the Irish higher education sector and boosted their self-confidence in setting new targets and taking on fresh challenges and opportunities. The most significant benefit derived from becoming recognised colleges of the NUI was the entitlement of the graduates of those colleges to degrees of the National University of Ireland, which are acknowledged as degrees of the highest quality, nationally and internationally.

NUI Maynooth's case for becoming a constituent university of NUI was greatly enhanced by the way it developed as a recognised college of the NUI, and the standard of its courses and examinations which were monitored by NUI intern and extern examiners, which enabled it to establish a 'parity of esteem' vis-à-vis the three NUI constituent colleges.

For the Royal College of Surgeons in Ireland, the recruitment of overseas students from many countries is made more attractive by the prospect of graduating with degrees from the National University of Ireland. This is underlined by the assurances sought by the Malaysian Education Authorities before the joint RCSI–UCD–Penang Medical College agreement was signed.

Other colleges, such as Shannon College of Hotel Management, the Institute of Public Administration, the National College of Art and Design and the Milltown Institute greatly value the profile which the NUI recognised college status provides in helping to promote the awareness of their programmes at home and abroad.

In the mid-1970s, the change in status to NUI recognised colleges provided a fresh stimulus and a new sense of purpose for the teacher training colleges. This major change, along with the necessary public funding made available by the Department of Education for the rapid increase in student numbers, the provision of capital projects, and the appointment of additional staff, combined to enable the colleges to design new and challenging programmes and experiences for their students. For the first time ever, graduating student teachers could be awarded an honours degree which, for the duration of their careers, they received an honours allowance from the Department of Education – in December 2006, the allowance rate for a primary degree (honours) was €4,831. Moreover, new pathways to a variety of postgraduate studies were opened to primary teachers within the university system.

As graduates of the NUI, the students graduating from recognised colleges are automatically enrolled on the NUI's register of graduates, thereby becoming members of NUI's Convocation, which entitles them to vote in the election of the NUI Chancellor, and in the election of eight members of Convocation to the NUI Senate. They are also entitled, on submitting a completed registration form to the NUI, to be entered on the Register of Electors for the NUI constituency which elects three members to Seanad Éireann, the election for which is held not later than 90 days after the dissolution of Dáil Éireann.

CHAPTER 14 *The Role of Convocation* LINDA O'SHEA FARREN

T HE NAME 'CONVOCATION' means the act of calling together or assembling and is derived from the Latin words *con-* meaning together and *vocare*, *-atum* meaning to call. Convocation of the National University of Ireland, which is the NUI's statutory graduate representative body, is one of the statutory authorities of the NUI. The others are the Chancellor, the Vice-Chancellor, the Pro-Vice-Chancellors, the NUI Senate and the faculties.

The first member of Convocation registered was the first Chancellor of the NUI, the Archbishop of Dublin, William J. Walsh. Douglas Hyde was the 24th, also as an *ex-officio* member in his capacity as a member of the first Senate appointed by the king. Today, all NUI graduates, including honorary graduates, are automatically members of Convocation. However, this was not always the case. In fact, clause XVII of the NUI Charter provides that

> The Convocation shall consist of the Chancellor, the Vice-Chancellor, the members of Senate, the Professors and Lecturers of the University, and the Registered Graduates of the University who are enrolled as Members of Convocation. Statutes shall be made determining the conditions of enrolment, including the annual fee, or a composition therefor, which shall be necessary for enrolment . . .

Fees were payable annually or on the basis of life membership. In the early years, life membership cost 15 shillings, while the fee for annual membership was 5 shillings. Eamon de Valera, BA (1904) is entered among the early members of Convocation as of 29 April 1910, the day of the first meeting, under the name Edward de Valera with an address at 33 Morehampton Terrace, Donnybrook, Dublin 4. His membership lapsed thereafter and, upon obtaining his BSc degree in 1914 he was re-registered as of 22 September 1914, by reinstatement fee pursuant to Statute I, Chapter xviii, para. (ii), this time as a life member. Seven years later, he would become Chancellor of the

69. Chancellor of the Royal University of Ireland (1903–6), Reginald Brabazon, 12th Earl of Meath (1841–1929). Lord Meath was also appointed Knight of the Order of St Patrick in 1902 and is pictured wearing its insignia, more commonly referred to as the Irish Crown Jewels, which were later stolen from Dublin Castle in 1907.

70. An eminent public figure in Irish life, Thomas (Tom) Kettle was an active MP for the Irish Parliamentary Party and a popular teacher when appointed as Professor of Economics in UCD by the NUI in 1909. A lieutenant in the Dublin Fusiliers, he died on 8 September 1916 on the Somme in the assault on the village of Ginchy.

AT A SPECIAL PUBLIC MEETING OF THE Royal University of Ireland HELD IN THE UNIVERSITY BUILDINGS AT 4·30 P.M. ON FRIDAY THE 10ᵗʰ OF APRIL 1885. DEGREES WERE CONFERRED UPON THEIR ROYAL HIGHNESSES WHOSE NAMES ARE HEREUNTO SUBSCRIBED.

IN THE FACULTY OF LAW

Doctor of Laws Honoris Causá

Albert Edward P.

IN THE FACULTY OF MUSIC

Doctor of Music Honoris Causá

Alexandra

above l. **71. The Royal Charter for the National University of Ireland was granted by King Edward VII in 1908.**

above r. **72. The Princess of Wales, later Queen Alexandra (1844–1925).**

left **73. The future King Edward VII and Queen Alexandra were conferred with an Honorary LLD and DMus respectively by the RUI in 1885. Note that the then Prince of Wales signs his name as Albert Edward.**

Edward the Seventh by the Grace of God

74. The Royal Charter issued to the National University of Ireland on 2 December 1908.

75. The NUI Senate Minute Book, Vol. 1.

76. The Coat of Arms of the National University of Ireland. NUI Senate Minutes, 14 July 1911:

The Committee on Arms and Seal has unanimously agreed to recommend the arms blazoned in the accompanying drawings:

Vert, an Irish Harp or, strung argent, surmounted by a five-pointed star, rayonné, of which four rays, in cross, are longest, of the second.

It follows logically that the National University of Ireland should assume the National Arms of Ireland, with a difference.

The tincture, vert (green), is that of the official flag of Ireland, and has been long identified with this island. [...]

The form of the Harp is not that granted by Henry VIII., but that sanctioned by the Crown and Parliament of Ireland, and recognised subsequently by the Crown and Parliament of the United Kingdom of Great Britain and Ireland. [...]

That the form of harp, showing the winged female figure [...] was supposed to be ancient Irish is shown in Moore's poem, referring to a legendary origin. In all probability however, it arose from a poetic personification of the Harp, to which life and intelligence were accredited as inscriptions show, notably that which declares – 'Ego sum Regina Cithararum.' *[...]*

The Radiant Star, surmounting the Harp, on the Shield represents the 'Reult Eoluis', or Star of Knowledge, familiar to readers of Irish Literature: its five points symbolize the five ancient chieftainries, here united in a common centre of light and learning.

The motto borne on the scroll above the Shield – 'Veritati' – explains to what purpose the University is dedicated, whilst that on the scroll beneath, in the Irish Language, indicates the means. For 'Fir Fer' – 'The trueness of man' or 'Manhood's Truth' was the ancient chivalric challenge which, of old, claimed and consecrated absolute fairness in all effort.

The lettering reproduces that of the Book of Kells.

NUI Senate Minutes, 27 February 1912:

The following Arms agreed to by the Seal and Arms Committee and by Ulster, King of Arms, were adopted:

Vert a Harp or with seven strings argent in chief on a star of five points of the second a trefil slipped of the field. And for Mottoes, Veritati in Irish character above the shield and Fir Fer in Irish characters below the shield.

It was directed that the University Seal should be made accordingly and that the Registrar should obtain a Grant of Arms from Ulster, King of Arms.

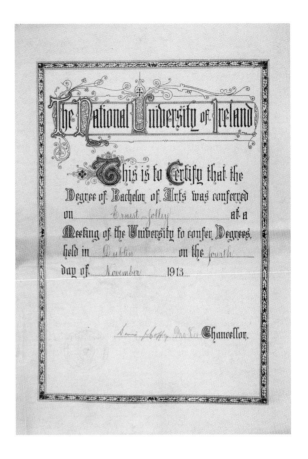

above l. **77.** **An example of a Bachelor of Arts degree testimonium conferred by the RUI on students on 27 October 1887.**

above r. **78.** **An example of a Bachelor of Arts degree testimonium conferred by the NUI on students on the 13 November 1913. Testimoniums of the RUI and the early NUI were printed in English. During the 1920s there were a number of motions put forward to the NUI Senate for testimoniums to be printed in Irish and Latin. On the 9 March 1933 the Senate adhered to a resolution of Convocation that 'when the existing stocks are exhausted, the Degree Testimoniums are to be in Latin only'.**

below l. **79.** **An example of a Bachelor of Arts degree testimonium conferred by UCD in 2008.**

above Form has been filled up in my own handwriting.

Candidate's usual Signature, *Kevin G Barry.*

Address to which communications
up to the time of the Examination are to be addressed.

8 Fleet St

Dublin

Dated 9th day of *May* 1919

80. **Kevin Barry (1902–20)** matriculated in the NUI on 9 May 1919 and entered UCD as a medical student. An active Republican, his execution by the British on 1 November 1920 (just two months before his nineteenth birthday) gained much public attention both nationally and internationally owing to his young age.

The entire of the above Form has been filled up in my own handwriting.

Candidate's usual Signature. *Edward de Valera*

Address to which communications
up to the time of the Examination are to be directed.

"University College" Blackrock

Co Dublin

Dated day of 1901.

81. **Eamon de Valera (1882–1975)** graduated from the Royal University of Ireland in 1904 and was one of the leading figures in the setting up of the Irish Free State. Inaugurated as Chancellor of the NUI in 1921, he remained at the head of the University until his death in 1975.

10. Language selected out of Group II. given above. *French*

The entire of the above Form has been filled up in my own handwriting.

Candidate's usual Signature, *Patrick S. Dinneen*

A 1. Dated 22nd day of *August* 1882.

82. **Patrick Dinneen (Pádraig Ó Duinnín) (1860–1934)** was ordained a Jesuit priest in 1894 and studied English, classics and mathematics at UCD. An avid supporter of the Gaelic League, Dinneen compiled the first Irish-English dictionary, *Foclóir Gaedhilge agus Béarla*, which was published by the Irish Texts Society in 1904.

The entire of the above Form has been filled up in my own handwriting.

Candidate's usual Signature, *Louise Gavan-Duffy*

Address to which communications
up to the time of the Examination are to be directed

C/o Mrs George Hall. Ayahae

Edge Hill Wimbledon Surrey England

Dated 28th day of *April* 1907.

83. **Daughter of Charles Gavan Duffy, Louise Gavan Duffy (1884–1969)** undertook a BA degree with the NUI in 1907. A member of the Gaelic League and Irish speaker, Gavan Duffy was influenced by the educational ideals of Pearse. In 1917, she co-founded Scoil Bhríde, the first all-Irish primary school which continues to the present day.

3. Language selected out of Group II, given above. *French*

The entire of the above Form has been filled up in my own handwriting.

RECEIVED
10 AUG 82

Candidate's usual Signature, *Mary I Hayden*

Dated 8th day of *August* 1882

84. Mary Hayden (Máire Ní Eideáin) (1862–1942) graduated from the RUI with a BA degree in 1885, and an MA degree in 1887. A leading campaigner for women's rights in the university she became a member of the Senate of the NUI and was appointed the first Professor of History in UCD in 1911.

Candidate's usual Signature,

Address to which communications up to the time of the Examination are to be directed. *29 Windsor Avenue. Fairview, Dublin.*

Dated 1st day of *May* 1899.

85. James Joyce (1882–1941) studied modern languages with the RUI graduating with a BA degree in 1902. A renowned writer of international acclaim, Joyce spent much of his adult life moving between Trieste, Zurich and Paris and never returned to Ireland after 1912. His most notable works include *Dubliners* (published 1914), *Ulysses* (published 1922) and *Finnegans Wake* (published 1939).

wish to be examined in the event of a centre being located there. *Dublin*

The entire of the above Form has been filled up in my own handwriting.

RECEIVED
MAY

Candidate's usual Signature, *Thomas Kettle*

Address to which communications up to the time of the Examination are to be directed. *Clongowes Wd. College Sallins Co. Kildare*

Dated 16 day of *May* 1897.

86. Thomas Kettle (1880–1916) graduated with a BA degree in 1902. Renowned barrister, politician and journalist, Kettle was appointed Professor of National Economics at UCD in 1909. He began the First World War as a war correspondent with the *Daily News* but was killed at the Battle of the Somme in 1916 fighting with the 9th Battalion of the Royal Dublin Fusiliers.

12. Name of Place, taken from list on opposite page, at which you wish to be examined in the event of a centre being located there. *Dublin*

The entire of the above Form has been filled up in my own handwriting.

Candidate's usual Signature, *Kathleen Y. Lynn*

Address to which communications up to the time of the Examination are to be directed. *Alexandra College Dublin*

Dated 28th day of *April* 1893.

87. Kathleen Lynn (1874–1955) was one of the first women in Ireland to be awarded a medical degree from the RUI in 1899. Political activist and feminist, pioneer of children's medicine in Ireland and co-founder of St Ultan's Hospital in 1919 (first infants' hospital in Dublin), she supported the promotion of Montessori education by establishing a Montessori ward in the hospital.

88. Thomas MacDonagh (Tomás Mac Donnchadha) (1879–1916), graduate of both
the RUI and NUI. A Poet and teacher, he became the founder of the Association of
Secondary Teachers in Ireland (ASTI). He became a lecturer in English with UCD
while also devoted to the revival of Irish. A signatory of the Proclamation of the
Republic, he was executed by firing squad for his role in the 1916 Rising.

89. Patrick Pearse (Pádraig MacPiarais) (1879–1916) graduated with a BA degree in
modern languages from the RUI and a law degree from King's Inn. A member of the
Gaelic League, he promoted Irish through education, establishing the bilingual St
Enda's School (Scoil Éanna) in 1908. A signatory of the Proclamation of the Republic,
he was executed by firing squad for his role in the 1916 Rising.

90. Alice Perry (1885–1969) attended Queen's College, Galway and graduated with a
first class honours degree in civil engineering from the RUI in 1906. Perry was the first
female engineering graduate in Ireland and Britain. She was briefly County Surveyor
in Galway and remains the only woman in Ireland to have held the position of a
County Surveyor (Engineer).

91. (Johanna) Hanna Sheehy Skeffington (1877–1946) graduated from the RUI with a
BA degree in 1899 and MA in 1902. An active agitator for women's suffrage, founding
the Irish Women's Franchise League in 1908 with her husband Francis and writer
James Cousins. Politically active throughout her life she travelled extensively to
publicise Ireland's political plight.

92. Francis Skeffington (1878–1916), a graduate of the RUI, was a controversial
journalist, pacifist and a keen proponent of women's suffrage with his wife, Hanna
Sheehy. Appointed the first lay registrar of UCD in 1902, he resigned shortly thereafter
due to lack of support for the admission of women to the college. He was arbitrarily
killed by British forces during the 1916 Rising.

university, which entitled him to membership of Convocation *ex-officio*.

Convocation's records show that there were 9,934 members of Convocation on 31 December 1936; 10,667 by 1937; 11,313 by 1938; 11,583 by 1939; 12,445 by 1940; 13,147 by 1941; 13, 946 by 1942; 14,859 by 1943; 15,175 by 1944; 18,119 by 1947. The records of the election of eight members of Convocation to the NUI Senate held on 14 October 1949 show that there were 19,160 members on the Convocation Register, to whom voting papers were sent. Interestingly, 1,133 of these voting papers were returned marked 'Gone Away' or 'Not Known' and 70 were returned marked 'Deceased'. The total poll was 2,803, but 282 of the votes cast were invalid.

Three changes brought in by the NUI Senate in the early 1950s resulted in the diminution of the role and influence of Convocation even before the 50th anniversary of the NUI. In February 1950, the NUI Senate decided to amend Statute LXXXII, chapter 1, section 4 so that the Roll of Convocation would be kept in such a manner as the Senate would determine, instead of the manner that Convocation might determine. The following year, the onus was put on each member of Convocation to apply for a voting paper for the election of eight members to the NUI Senate in consolidated Statute LXXXVI. This change resulted in a strongly worded motion proposed by Dr Annie Keelan of Merrion Square (who challenged any contention that the question of expense could justify the alteration) and seconded by Mrs Eileen McCarvill of Fitzwilliam Square:

> That Convocation disapproves of certain changes which have been enacted in the new consolidated Statute LXXXVI, which in the opinion of Convocation are ultra vires the Charter of the National University of Ireland, chapter XI, Section I, in that the status, powers or constitution of an authority, viz. Convocation, have been changed without giving such an authority an opportunity of pronouncing an opinion upon the proposed changes and that Convocation is of the opinion that by putting the onus on each member of Convocation of applying for a voting paper for the election of eight members to the Senate of the University, voters are inconvenienced and candidates nominated for the election are placed at a disadvantage; that this change in the method of election may give rise to misuse with the result that the eight members returned would not be representative and that the procedure being undemocratic may lead to undesirable and corrupt practices.

The motion was passed, along with many other related motions, at the Annual General Meeting of Convocation held on 9 November 1953.

In a further protest at the onus being placed on each member of Convocation to apply for a voting paper for the election of eight members to the NUI Senate, a motion

That Convocation representatives in the Senate of the University be asked what opinion they expressed when the matter of the alteration of Statute LXXXVI was before the Senate; also, that it be brought to the attention of the representatives that Convocation considers that at least those representatives who live in Dublin should attend its meetings in order to inform themselves of the views of Convocation and to inform it of developments in the Senate that are of interest to Convocation.

This was passed unanimously at a meeting of Convocation held on 9 November 1953.

A further decision by the NUI Senate to publish communications to Convocation by advertisements in particular newspapers, instead of by writing to Convocation members individually, was seen by many as another retrograde step. A motion was proposed at a meeting of Convocation held on 23 March 1954, and again at the Annual General Meeting held on 30 November 1954, which was presided over by Chancellor Eamon de Valera:

That the Committee of Convocation is of the opinion that the minute of the Senate of the University limiting the number of daily newspapers in which it may issue notices to graduates is undemocratic, as it prevents readers of newspapers other than those named by the Senate from learning of meetings of Convocation and of other information which they are entitled to receive.

This echoed the sentiments of active Convocation members peppered throughout the minutes of meetings in the 1950s in relation to what was perceived as interference by one authority of the university, the Senate, in the affairs of another authority of the university, Convocation, resulting in a diminution of democracy and in the role and influence of Convocation. Many matters relating to Convocation and the NUI Senate are still governed by this 1951 statute, in particular procedures in relation to the holding of elections.

* * *

Clause XVIII of the NUI Charter confers statutory powers on Convocation

* To elect a person to be Chancellor of the University in succession to the
  first or any subsequent Chancellor
* To elect its own Chairman, who shall, in the absence of the Chancellor,
  be entitled to preside at its Meetings
* To elect representatives on the Senate
* To discuss and pronounce an opinion on any matter whatsoever relating
  to the University, including any matters referred to them by the Senate

Clause XIX of the NUI Charter further provides that Convocation

> may from time to time make regulations for governing their proceedings, sub-
> ject to this Our Charter and to the Statutes and Regulations of the University.

In its almost 100 years' history, Convocation of the NUI has elected as
Chair of Convocation eight men and one woman.

Years in office	Name of Chairman of Convocation	Length of term
1910–24	Michael F. Cox	14 years
1924–32	Arthur E. Clery	8 years
1932–40	Patrick McCarvill	8 years
1940–53	Thomas O'Rourke	13 years
1953–5	Patrick F. Bulman	2 years
1955–84	Dónall Ó Móráin	29 years
1984–97	Paul Cannon	13 years
1998–2003	James Heffron	6 years
2003–	Linda O'Shea Farren	Current Chairman

Michael Francis Cox who took office as chairman of Convocation in
1910, was appointed a member of the NUI Senate by the king under clause
X of the 1908 NUI Charter. Subsequent chairmen of Convocation were not
automatically members of the NUI Senate. Indeed, no subsequent chairman
of Convocation served as a member of the NUI Senate, until the current
holder of the office. In 1895, Michael Francis Cox had been conferred with
an MD *honoris causa* by the Royal University of Ireland and, while serving as
chairman of Convocation, the NUI conferred an honorary degree of LLD on
him in 1915. For the final two years of his term as chairman of Convocation
(1922–4), which period included the Civil War years, Michael Francis Cox

was also President of the Royal College of Physicians of Ireland. He was also the author of books entitled *The Country and Kindred of Oliver Goldsmith* and *Notes on the History of the Irish Horse*.

By the time the second Chairman of Convocation took office in 1924, the Easter Rising of 1916 had taken place and the Civil War of 1922–3 had just ended. In those years around the foundation of the state, Convocation of the National University of Ireland had become increasingly political. On 20 July 1921, three years before Arthur Clery became second Chairman of Convocation, it had elected Eamon de Valera Chancellor of the NUI – only five months before Dáil Éireann approved the Anglo-Irish Treaty against de Valera's advice and he had resigned as President of the Dáil. Three years into his eight-year term as the second Chairman of Convocation, Arthur Clery was elected as a Republican TD in the fifth Dáil in 1927, but he did not take his seat.

Prior to his election as the third Chairman of Convocation in 1932, Patrick McCarvill had succeeded Sean MacEntee when he was elected a Sinn Féin (Anti-Treaty) TD for Monaghan in September 1923 and was re-elected in June 1927. He had also fought in the GPO garrison in the 1916 Rising and had won Sigerson Cup medals for UCD in 1917–18. Patrick McCarvill's election as Chairman of Convocation in 1932 saw him in office for the celebration of the 25th anniversary of the NUI in 1933. Thomas O'Rourke, BA, BComm, the fourth Chairman of Convocation, served throughout the Second World War and into the early 1950s. This proved to be a particularly bad period for reaching a quorum at meetings of Convocation with no meetings taking place for almost three years from March 1945 to January 1948 and again no meeting until October 1949, followed by meetings in November 1950 and March 1952.

After a short two-year period from 1953 to 1955 as the fifth Chairman of Convocation, Patrick F. Bulman, BComm, was succeeded in 1955 by Dónall Ó Moráin, BA, who went on to become the longest-serving Chairman of Convocation spanning three decades of immense change in Ireland from the mid-1950s right through to the mid-1980s. As founder of Gael Linn, Dónall Ó Moráin's long term as Chairman of Convocation inevitably saw a new emphasis in Convocation on revival of the Irish language.

In the mid-1930s, around the time of the 25th anniversary of the National University of Ireland, a confederation of Irish societies of the NUI, Trinity

College and Queen's University Belfast called An Comhchaidreamh was established. In 1942, the confederation started a monthly journal in Irish called *Comhar*. In 1943, the government established a new national organisation called Comhdháil Náisiúnta na Gaeilge to spearhead revival of the Irish language. However, within a few years, An Comhchaidreamh and another young organisation, Glún na mBua, had gained effective control of Comhdháil Náisiúnta na Gaeilge. Under their influence, Comhdháil Náisiúnta na Gaeilge began to lobby for a new approach to the revival of the Irish language.

In the early 1950s, in an effort to raise funds to promote the Irish language and culture, Dónall Ó Moráin (who had been involved in An Comhchaidreamh) and other university graduates and students conceived the idea of adapting the successful football pools in the UK to Gaelic games scores in Ireland. Thus the Gael Linn organisation was born in 1953, first establishing a private members' lottery and using the funds so collected to promote the language through innovative teaching, publishing, cinema and developing the economic life of the Gaeltacht. Two years later, Dónall Ó Moráin was elected Chairman of Convocation of the National University of Ireland. This brought the role of the NUI in the revival of the Irish language back to centre stage. Dónall Ó Moráin was in office for the celebration of the 50th anniversary of the NUI in 1958 and, indeed, up to its 75th anniversary in 1983.

The election of Paul Cannon, BSc (1945), MB BCh BAO (1948), MSc (1950), BA (1993), MA (1997) as the seventh Chairman in 1984 brought a medic back to the helm of Convocation. Among the first tasks undertaken by Professor Cannon was the revision of the regulations governing Convocation by way of memorandum and regulations adopted on 23 April 1986. In 1998, the election of UCC Biochemistry Professor James Heffron, BSc (1964), PhD (1969) as the eighth Chairman of Convocation meant that Convocation was run from Cork until Dublin-based practising solicitor and New York lawyer, Linda O'Shea Farren, BCL (1981) was elected the first woman Chairman in December 2003, having been elected a member of the NUI Senate by Convocation on 16 October 2002.

* * *

In its almost hundred years' history, there have been only four chancellors of the NUI. The Archbishop of Dublin, William J. Walsh, was appointed Chancellor by the king on 2 December 1908, the date of the NUI Charter. However, clause VII of the NUI Charter provided that

> The first Chancellor of the University shall be elected by the Senate at their first meeting; and if not a member of the Senate will be nominated by us as an additional member thereof.
>
> Any succeeding Chancellor shall be elected by Convocation, and if a member of the Senate is elected to be Chancellor, his election shall create a casual vacancy in the Senate.

In accordance with this procedure, Archbishop Walsh was elected Chancellor by the NUI Senate on 17 December 1908, two weeks after his appointment.

The first meeting of Convocation of the NUI was held on 29 April 1910 and was chaired by the Chancellor. The fact that the Chancellor was an archbishop and that, of the 153 members of Convocation who attended the first meeting, almost half – 70 in all – were members of the clergy give an indication of the influence of the Church on university life in those early days of the NUI. This is something of an anomaly given that clause 3(1) the Irish Universities Act, 1908, upon which the NUI was founded, prohibited any test whatsoever of religious belief on any person,

> as a condition of his becoming or continuing to be a professor, lecturer, fellow, scholar, exhibitioner, graduate or student of, or of his holding any office or emolument or exercising any privilege in ... nor ... shall any preference be given to or advantage be withheld from any person on the grounds of religious belief

Clause 10 (2) of the 1908 act also provided that the council of any county or county borough in Ireland

> may assist, by means of exhibitions, scholarships, bursaries, payment of fees or otherwise, any students ... provided that in no case shall any grant under this section be subject to or conditional upon any religious qualification or be devoted to any religious purpose.

Indeed, this affiliation between Church and university continued, with

Convocation formally conveying its congratulations to John Charles McQuaid when he was made Archbishop of Dublin in December 1940, resulting in a flattering letter of acknowledgment back from the Archbishop on 14 March 1941.

In a letter from Archbishop Walsh to the then Clerk of Convocation, J. G. Swift MacNeill, KC MP, on 22 November 1916, some eight years after his appointment as Chancellor, declining to fix an hour for Convocation meetings lest it be 'outside his sphere' as Chancellor, when the University Statutes empowered Convocation to make regulations governing its own proceedings, the Archbishop thanked the Clerk of Convocation for his inquiries about his health, adding 'But for an increasing deafness, I am fully able for my work. I fear that the deafness will incapacitate me for the chairmanship duties of the Chancellor'. Despite this, Archbishop Walsh served as Chancellor for another four and a half years until his death on 9 April 1921.

Following the death of Archbishop Walsh, an election meeting of Convocation to be held on 19 December 1921 was called, with nominations for the office of Chancellor to be received on or before 19 July 1921. As the nomination of Eamon de Valera, BA (1904), HDip in Ed (1910), BSc (1914) was the only nomination for Chancellor received, the Chairman of Convocation wrote to de Valera the following day to inform him

> that you have alone been duly nominated within the time fixed by the University Statutes, viz: on or before July 19, 1921, for the office of Chancellor of the National University of Ireland, and that accordingly under the provisions of Statute I, NUI, chapter five, section ten, you are Chancellor of the National University of Ireland on and from this date.

De Valera was formally received as Chancellor of the NUI on Saturday, 19 November 1921 in an elaborate ceremony, at which two addresses of welcome from Convocation were presented to the Chancellor – one in Irish read by Michael Hayes and one in Latin read by Michael Tierney. Indeed, it was commented upon in the media that, with the exception of the brief speech of Dr Denis Coffey, then President of University College Dublin, no word of English was spoken during the ceremonial proceedings. On Monday, 21 November 1921, the *Irish Times* reported,

> Convocation of the National University of Ireland arranged a picturesque reception for Mr de Valera at University College, Dublin on Saturday, when

he formally took his place as Chancellor of the University in succession to the late Archbishop Walsh. The staff of the College, the graduates and students, the members of Convocation Committee and the general public made a striking demonstration. A company of Irish Volunteers connected with the College stood to attention as the gates were opened to receive the Chancellor. Professors and graduates in their academic robes lent a touch of colour to the assembly. The Chairman of Convocation (Dr Cox) and the Clerk (Mr Swift MacNeill) received Mr de Valera and conducted him to the robing room, from which a procession of students, graduates, bachelors, masters and doctors representing the constituent colleges of Dublin, Cork, Maynooth and Galway led him to the Council Chamber, where he was received by the President of University College, Dublin (Dr Coffey) and other officials representing the Governing Body. The Lord Mayor, as a member of that body, was present. In addition, there was a large attendance, including many ladies.

When the Chancellor had taken his seat, Dr. Coffey welcomed the new Chancellor, saying that in the great assembly which he was about to meet, he would receive signal testimony of loyal obedience and profound respect, and of the warmest personal affection . . . 'This day will remain forever one of the most notable in the history of the University.' The Chancellor, speaking in Irish, acknowledged the demonstrations of goodwill. He continued, 'The chieftaincy of this nation's University at this time certainly presents a field for endeavour and achievement wide enough to satisfy the deedful lust of an Alexander. I am not blind to the wealth of opportunity you have entrusted to me. I promise to try to prove worthy of the trust.'

In reply to an address presented by the students assembled in the Central Hall of the College, the Chancellor said:

A nation's University should not be a machine for casting standard types and stamping them off. Nor should it be merely a venerable seat of learning – a musty old library could be that! These are only what a University may degenerate into if it stands serenely apart in artificial isolation. A nation's University, to be worthy, should throb with the full current of the nation's life, scintillate with the living fires of the nation's soul, reflecting back again upon the nation its own most energising beams, and transmitting to all mankind the glow of its warmth and its light. This is what we ambition for our University, and our University, like our nation's newborn freedom, is young. The morning is with us and we are exultant in its freshness and in our own vigour. The lavish love of the Gael for its own will soon make the starving niggardliness of the foreigner a nightmare of the past. Already we are rich in prestige and wealthy in the heritage of our mother of scholars and of saints. Standing here on the threshold of the future, then, we may well salute it, and resolve together to make our dreams for our University and our nation come, every one of them, true.

De Valera served as Chancellor of the NUI for 54 years, more than half of the life of the university to date, until his death on 29 August 1975. While serving as Chancellor he also served as Minister for External Affairs, as Taoiseach three times and as President of Ireland. At a meeting of Convocation held on 11 November 1952, more than 30 years into his chancellorship and while he was serving the second of his three terms as Taoiseach, Convocation passed a motion

> desiring to make Mr de Valera, Chancellor of the University, aware of the earnest wishes of the graduates that a speedy and permanent recovery from his temporary inability be granted to him

which was reported in the *Irish Independent* the following day. As he was to go on to serve as Chancellor for a further 23 years, clearly the earnest wishes of Convocation were granted.

De Valera was succeeded by then former secretary of the Department of Finance and author of the *Programme for Economic Expansion* (1958), T. K. Whitaker, BA, MScEcon, when he was elected by Convocation on 5 May 1976. Unlike the election of de Valera as Chancellor, Dr Whitaker had eight other candidates to compete with. However, he obtained 4,245 of the 7,766 valid votes cast and was elected with 3,156 votes more than his next nearest rival, the only woman in the race. The following year, the Fianna Fáil Taoiseach Jack Lynch nominated Dr Whitaker as a member of the 14th Seanad Éireann and in 1981 the then Fine Gael Taoiseach Garret FitzGerald (who was to go on to become Chancellor himself) nominated Dr Whitaker as a member of the 15th Seanad Éireann, where he served as an independent senator until 1982. After 20 years serving as Chancellor of the NUI, Dr Whitaker decided to resign as of 31 December 1996. Five years later, in 2001, an RTÉ programme voted Dr Whitaker the Irishman of the twentieth century.

The current Chancellor, Garret FitzGerald, who was born four years after de Valera became Chancellor of the NUI, was elected by Convocation as fourth Chancellor on 15 October 1997. Of the 2,630 valid votes cast, Dr FitzGerald polled 1,733 votes; Pierce Hugh Purcell polled 835 votes; and 62 votes were cast in favour of Patrick Anthony Jones. At that time, the NUI had over 38,000 students. Prior to his election as Chancellor of the NUI, Dr FitzGerald served as a member of Seanad Éireann, as Minister for Foreign Affairs and twice as Taoiseach.

Speaking after his election as Chancellor, Dr FitzGerald said:

> The Challenge for me as Chancellor of the National University of Ireland is to lead this great university into the next millennium. The status of NUI has been clearly defined in the Universities Act 1997. My role as Chancellor will be to draw together the constituent parts of the University, so as to enable it to harness its great federal strength for the advancement of higher education and the promotion of research. Universities today are acknowledged to be among the most important resources available to a nation in the promotion of its economic, social and cultural objectives. It is a great honour for me to have been elected to be at the head of one of Ireland's foremost national institutions.

Chancellor FitzGerald did indeed lead the NUI into this millennium and, as the NUI goes into its centenary year, he is celebrating his eleventh year as Chancellor.

*   *   *

The Irish Universities Act 1908 provided for eight members of the 35 member governing body of 'the new university having its seat in Dublin' – that is, the NUI Senate – to be elected by Convocation, and this remains the situation 100 years later. While the 1908 act did not provide that four of these must be men and four women (as section 45 (2) of the Universities Act 1997 subsequently provided), it did stipulate that at least one of the four members nominated by the king be a woman. Clause v of the NUI Charter further provided that 'women shall be eligible equally with men to be

[238]

Members of the University or of any Authority of the University, and to hold any office or enjoy any advantages of the University'.

Douglas Hyde, who went on to become President of Ireland, was one of the original members of Senate appointed by the king under the 1908 NUI Charter. After this first term of the NUI Senate expired, the first election by Convocation of eight members of the NUI Senate for a term that included the period of the 1916 Rising and expired on 31 October 1919, was held on 6 October 1914. Douglas Hyde was elected by Convocation in this first election along with Patrick Merriman who went on to become President of University College Cork in 1919 at the end of that term on the NUI Senate, and Revd Thomas A. Finlay, SJ.

Louise Gavan-Duffy, sister of George Gavan-Duffy, Minister for Foreign Affairs in the first Dáil, also ran for election to the NUI Senate on 6 October 1914 but was not elected on that occasion. Eighteen months later, she was to ask to see Padraig Pearse at the GPO on Easter Monday 1916 and, according to her own witness statements, 'I said to him that I wanted to be in the field but that I felt that the Rebellion was a frightful mistake, that it could not possibly succeed, and that it was, therefore, wrong.' Pearse suggested that she help out in the kitchens and she agreed to this since it was not active service. She stayed there throughout the week until the GPO was evacuated on the Friday. The year after the 1916 Rising, Louise Gavan-Duffy founded Scoil Bhríde in Ranelagh, Ireland's first Gaelscoil for girls, and she was elected to the NUI Senate by Convocation in the next (second) election held on 7 October 1919.

Convocation's affairs are managed by a council of up to 28 members plus the Chairman and the Clerk of Convocation. Council must meet four times per year. In the 2002 elections to the NUI Senate, half of the eight members of the NUI Senate elected by Convocation were already, or subsequently also became, members of Council of Convocation. Despite the fact that clause XVIII of the NUI Charter provides that eight members of Convocation be elected as representatives on the NUI Senate, this crossover of membership between the NUI Senate and Convocation had not always existed.

While the regulations state that the main elections to Council of Convocation shall take place at the Annual General Meeting, casual vacancies can be filled by co-option. In addition, co-option can be used by Council to ensure balance in terms of areas of discipline, geographical spread, gender, etc. Each member of Council can serve for up to three years. Because the terms of office of the various Council members are staggered, there is an ongoing element of institutional memory in relation to the issues being considered by Council at any time.

In addition to the Chairman of Convocation, who must be elected at an Annual General Meeting, the other officer of Convocation is the Clerk. In accordance with more recent regulations, the Chairman of Convocation serves for six years and the Clerk of Convocation serves for five years. After each Annual General Meeting of Convocation, the Council elects five of its members who, together with the Chairman of Convocation and the Clerk, form the Standing Committee. The NUI Senate appoints the Clerk on the recommendation of Council of Convocation. Since 1966, there have been six Clerks of Convocation – Anrai Ó Braonáin, Peadar Ó Dubhghaill, Con O'Rourke, Angela Hoey-Heffron, Dr Michael Cosgrave and the current Clerk Thérèse Madden. The Clerk receives a modest annual stipend from the NUI Senate, but all other positions on Convocation are entirely *pro bono*.

The statutory power of Convocation to discuss and pronounce an opinion on any matter whatsoever relating to the National University of Ireland, including any matters referred to them by the NUI Senate, was conferred on it by clause XVIII of the 1908 NUI Charter. As Convocation automatically includes all 250,000 or so NUI graduates, not just those registered to vote in Seanad Éireann elections, this is a significant power.

Council can consult with its members through its Annual General Meetings or indeed can call an Extraordinary General Meeting if a significant and urgent enough matter were to arise. The first meeting of Convocation was held on 29 April 1910 with 153 members attending. Half that number (77) attended the second meeting on 18 April 1911, and fewer again (57, including de Valera) attended the third meeting of Convocation on 20 October 1911. In a letter to the then Clerk of Convocation, J. G. Swift MacNeill, on 4 April 1917, Archbishop Walsh wrote:

> It is an extraordinary thing that there should be three successive failures to get a quorum together for a meeting of Convocation. I do not feel quite satisfied that I am doing right in encouraging the loose system that prevails, as I feel that I am doing something to encourage it by calling meeting after meeting. I do not think I should go on putting a number of members to the

trouble of attending at the place of meeting when the graduates of the University care so little about the work of Convocation that, out of the hundreds of them who live in or about Dublin, not even forty can be got together for a meeting. So, if we do not succeed in getting a quorum together on this occasion, Monday, April 16th, I must leave the matter in the hands of the Senate.

*　　*　　*

Despite low attendance at Convocation meetings from its very inception, including regular failure to reach a quorum throughout its history, in the early years, including the years around the foundation of the state, Convocation of the National University of Ireland was very influential in Irish society. At a meeting of Convocation held as early as 14 December 1915 (which itself had to be delayed an hour for failure to reach a quorum), an extensive report prepared by the Annual Committee of Convocation on the facilities existing in the various universities in England, Scotland and Wales for lectures delivered in the evening and leading up to university degrees was adopted by Convocation, and reported in the national newspapers:

> There will always be persons of the University type whom the rules of business or professional life will preclude from attendance at lectures delivered in the day time. There are graduates, too, members of the old University College, Dublin, who succeeded in obtaining their degrees through attendance partly or altogether at evening lectures, and the University has no reason to be ashamed of them. We earnestly desire that the influence of our University should permeate the whole country and provide leaders in all walks of life. This object would, in our judgment, be more fully attained by the adoption of a system of evening lectures.

In proposing the motion to adopt the report, Matthew Fitzpatrick from Cabra said that he thought that 'many deliberately kept away from the meetings because they did not agree with evening classes' while 'in the past under the Jesuits, with less funds, evening classes had been successfully run'. Seconding this motion, Alderman James C. McWalter remarked that 'in the future, men would be so pressed to make a living that they would not have time for University education and would have to avail of the evening courses'. Convocation kept the pressure on in relation to this issue and, eventually, evening classes leading to degrees were introduced in the NUI.

The First World War was ongoing at this time, and after the motion was carried, the Secretary of the meeting mentioned that he had 'received from the front' the notice of the meeting that he had sent to Convocation member the Revd Gwynn, SJ which 'bore the brief intimation "died from wounds"', whereupon the Chairman of Convocation moved a vote of condolence with the relatives of Fr Gwynn, SJ who he said had 'died like a man from wounds received on the battlefield'.

In the 1930s, Convocation was concerned with jobs for graduates, the following motion being unanimously carried at a meeting held on 12 December 1933:

> That Convocation notes with alarm that Irish University Graduates are not finding opportunities for training and employment in any of the new and important Industries that are being established in the Saorstát, and calls upon the Government to take such steps as may be necessary to ensure that the administrative and technical management of Irish industry will ultimately be in the hands of Irishmen; and that Convocation directs the Clerk to forward a copy of this Resolution to the Executive Council of the Government of Saorstát Éireann.

While meetings of Convocation were few and far between during the years after the Second World War, this concern of Convocation with jobs for graduates persisted, as indicated by the fact that the following two motions were passed unanimously at a meeting of Convocation held on 14 November 1950:

> That this Meeting of Convocation of Graduates of the National University of Ireland deplores the recently developed policy of the City of Dublin Vocational Educational Committee of placing Graduate Teachers in positions inferior to non-Graduates.
>
> That Convocation views with concern a departure from the practice of filling certain of the higher posts in the public service by Open Competition, a departure which operates against the best interests of graduates of the National University of Ireland.

And at a meeting of Convocation held on 11 November 1952, Convocation went so far as to approve unanimously a motion:

That, having regard to the fact that the majority of the Graduates of the National University of Ireland who remain in this country take up salaried employment, Convocation is of the opinion that the Senate of the University should, in the interest of Graduates, interest itself generally in the necessity for a thorough and immediate review of the whole Income Tax code.

A report of the full and frank debate on this motion appeared in the *Irish Independent* the following day, including the following contributions which show that 'the university men' in those days didn't pull any punches:

Senator Prof. G. O'Brien, supporting the motion said … Some people were hit far harder than others by income tax. As far as income tax was concerned the people could be divided into three classes. The first was those who had to pay every penny of the amount with which they were assessed, which was possibly just, but severe. The second class included those who, owing to the nature of their business, were not necessarily always in a position to give a full or punctual return of their income and in that way were able to evade part of the tax and elude the Inspector's net. Everybody was aware that people did that. The third class included those who did not actually evade, but who took advantage of a peculiarly favourable basis of assessment which resulted in the position where a number of people of assessable income were not assessed. Those people very properly took advantage of the peculiar mode of assessment.

Dr Roger McHugh said that big business combines had various methods of evading income tax. Farmers very rarely paid anything at all, and skilled tradesmen moved from one job to another when they knew that income tax collectors were after them.

By the mid-1940s, Convocation was querying the effectiveness of the Irish Universities Act 1908 on which the NUI was founded and a motion:

That the time is opportune for the setting up of a Commission to inquire into the working of the Irish Universities Act 1908, and to ascertain how far it meets present day requirements, so that the necessary legislation may be introduced to implement the recommendations of the Commission

was proposed at a meeting of Convocation held on 13 March 1945.

As the University was approaching its 50th anniversary, Convocation had lost much of its energy, particularly following Statute LXXXVI, which was passed by the NUI Senate in 1951. However, subsequent to this, Convocation became active again, especially in relation to revival of the Irish language under the long chairmanship of the founder of Gael Linn, Dónall Ó Móráin. The fact that the NUI has retained its Irish language requirement for entry to the University to this day is a testament to the efforts of all of those members of Senate and Convocation over the hundred-year history of the NUI who fought for its retention.

In more recent years, the activities of Convocation have focused on facilitating debate through annual conferences on major developments in the university sector such as the EU Bologna Declaration and the OECD Review of Higher Education in Ireland. Convocation also hosts an annual lecture series. The 2005 lecture was held in the Aula Maxima at University College Cork to coincide with Cork's year as EU City of Culture when Professor John A. Murphy spoke eloquently on the topic 'Town and Gown: The Changing Relationship'. The 2006 lecture was held in Milltown Institute, Dublin to mark its acceptance as a recognised college of the NUI and Joe Higgins, TD spoke convincingly on the topic 'The University of the Future: Corporate Creature or Independent Institution?' Convocation now has a website at www.nui.convocation.ie. The 2008 lecture was held in St Patrick's College, Maynooth, when Archbishop Diarmuid Martin very authoritatively addressed the topic 'The Role of Education in the New Ireland'.

* * *

In addition to the specific powers granted to Convocation under the NUI Charter, graduates of the NUI (all of whom are nowadays automatically members of Convocation), who are registered to vote in Seanad Éireann elections, elect three members of Seanad Éireann in accordance with the Seanad Electoral (University Members) Act, 1937.

In the almost 70 years since graduates of the NUI could elect three members of Seanad Éireann, they have elected the following 18 men and 2 women as Senators:

Name of Senator elected by NUI graduates	Year first elected to Seanad Éireann
Helena Concannon	1938
Henry L. Barniville	1938
Michael Tierney	1938

Michael J. Ryan	1944
George A. T. O'Brien	1948
Roger J. McHugh	1954
Patrick M. Quinlan	1957
Dónall Ó Connalláin	1961
Bryan G. Alton	1965
John S. Horgan	1969
T. Augustine Martin	1973
Gemma Hussey	1977
John A. Murphy	1977
Liam B. (Brendan) Ryan	1981
James C.I. Dooge	1982
Michael D. Higgins	1983
Joseph J. (Joe) O'Toole	1987
Feargal Quinn	1993
John Joseph (Joe) Lee	1993
Ronan Mullen	2007

Although Convocation is the NUI's statutory graduate representative body, in more recent times the alumni associations of the individual colleges under the NUI umbrella, which are now constituent universities, have essentially taken the place of Convocation. One great advantage of Convocation over the individual alumni associations of the separate constituent universities or recognised colleges of the NUI is that it encompasses graduates of all four constituent NUI universities and all recognised NUI colleges. In a sense, therefore, it can 'be above' whatever tensions may be ongoing in any of the individual universities or recognised colleges and look to what is best for the NUI as a whole.

Convocation is, however, grossly underfunded, receiving an annual stipend of approximately €6,000 from the NUI Senate, with which modest funding it has to run its entire affairs and try to communicate with its vast graduate body. For the individual alumni associations of the separate constituent universities or recognised colleges of the NUI, it is in their universities' interests to keep in touch with their alumni, so the funding follows. Accordingly, nowadays, the individual alumni associations are far better funded than Convocation and have a far higher public profile.

CHAPTER 15 *The Archives held in the National University of Ireland*
NÓIRÍN MOYNIHAN

T HE NATIONAL UNIVERSITY of Ireland holds the archives of the Royal
    University of Ireland (RUI) and the archives of the National University
of Ireland (NUI).

The archive is a significant repository of primary material relating to over
125 years of university education in Ireland. The records also reflect the cultural, social and political developments in the country and contain information and documentation relating to important figures who played a part in
the origins and the development of the state. The records have been widely
consulted in connection with the articles for this NUI centenary publication.

This brief essay includes lists of the main classes of records in the RUI
and NUI Archives in Appendix A and Appendix B respectively, below. It is
intended as an introduction to the archive rather than a comprehensive
listing of its contents.

The Royal University of Ireland (1882–1908) was established under the
terms of the University Education (Ireland) Act 1879 as an examining and
degree awarding body only, with its seat in Dublin. In 1882, the year the Act
came into effect, the RUI offices were located in 25 Merrion Street, Dublin,
and in 1883, they moved permanently to Earlsfort Terrace.

The Irish Universities Act 1908 dissolved the RUI and Queen's College
Belfast, and established two new universities, Queen's University Belfast
and the NUI as a federal university with its seat in Dublin and with three
constituent colleges, University College Dublin, University College Cork
and University College Galway. The act made provision for the transfer to
NUI of the RUI students and graduates, of University College, Queen's College Cork and Queen's College Galway, as well as the property of RUI. As
part of these arrangements, the records of the RUI were transferred to NUI
central office which remained on the old RUI premises in Earlsfort Terrace

until 1912 when the office moved to its current location at 49 Merrion Square. The Act also provided for the appointment of existing RUI officers to positions in NUI – the first NUI Registrar was Sir Joseph McGrath, formerly one of the two co-secretaries of the RUI. Three of the other four university staff members listed in the first NUI Calendar 1911, Alister McAlister, Mathew Kane, and Frederick H. Wiber, were former RUI officers. Frederick Wiber went on to become registrar of the NUI in 1924. The structure and organisation of the NUI, with its Senate and its committees, replicated that of the RUI; the role of the NUI central office as the seat of the new federal university was comparable with that of the former RUI office. It is evident from the archives that the continuation of structure, organisation and staff in key positions meant little changed in terms of administrative structures, procedures, systems and style so that the transition from RUI to NUI was very smooth.

The 1997 Universities Act which amended the Irish Universities Act 1908 granted consititunt university status to the three former constituent colleges and to St Patrick's College, Maynooth, which are now autonomous institutions within the NUI framework. Among the powers devolved to the constituent universities include the power to appoint their own presidents, professors and lecturers and to award degrees of the National University of Ireland. These changes are reflected in the archive.

APPENDIX A

The Archives of the Royal University of Ireland (1880–1908)

The University Education (Ireland) Act 1879 established the RUI and made provision for the dissolution of the Queen's University of Ireland (1850–82), to take effect from 1882.

The Royal University of Ireland was empowered to examine and confer degrees on matriculated students of the university, either male or female, who passed the prescribed examinations. The University had no teaching role and candidates were not required to be resident in a college, or attend lectures or a course of instruction except for degrees in medicine and surgery.

The records reflect the workings of the RUI as an examining and degree awarding body which drew students from colleges within and outside

Ireland as well as from students engaged in private study. It was the first university in Ireland to admit women which adds to the significance of the records. Charlotte M. Taylor was the first woman to sign the Roll of Graduates when she was conferred with the Bachelor of Music degree on 22 October 1884. She was conferred with the Bachelor of Arts degree at the same ceremony.

1 Queen's University Material in RUI Archive
I Queen's Roll of Matriculated Students (1864–82): 1 volume

The University Education (Ireland) Act 1879 made provision for the graduates and students of the Queen's University to become students and graduates of the RUI. This volume contains a printed alphabetical list of students with the year of matriculation and college. The details of those students who subsequently passed examinations of RUI were updated by hand.

The RUI Senate Minutes (Vol. 1) record that after initial reluctance to do so, the Secretary to the former Queen's University forwarded the Roll Book, Charters and Seal to the RUI Senate and requested that 'if the Senate did not require to retain them they might be returned to him, as the Senate of the Queen's University had desired that they might remain as heirlooms in his family'. The Senate decided that 'due to the nature and character of the book' they were obliged to retain it. The Charter and Seals, however, are no longer in the NUI Archives.

II Queen's University Calendars: 1859, 1861, 1866–8, 1870–7, 1879–82
III Queen's University Regulations (Vol. 1): 1861–6

2 RUI Foundation Records and Related Material
I The Charter
II The Coat of Arms
III University Statutes

3 Conferring Documents: Samples of RUI Parchments

4 Matriculation Records
I Bound volumes of completed matriculation application forms 1881–1909

These important records consist of the Matriculation application forms completed and signed by the students concerned. The forms are contained in alphabetical order within bound volumes, by year. They contain valuable biographical information, such as name, date and place of birth, father's name and occupation, home address, school attended.

The records cover a period of dynamic cultural, literary and political activity in Ireland and many of the main protagonists feature in these records: James Joyce (BA 1902); Patrick Dinneen (an tAthair P. Ó Duinnín) (BA 1885, MA 1889); Patrick Pearse (BA 1901); Eamon de Valera (BA 1904); Thomas Kettle (BA 1902); Joanna Sheehy (BA 1899, MA 1902); and Kathleen Lynn (MB BCh BAO 1899). Douglas Hyde was awarded an honorary degree of DLitt by the RUI in 1906.

These records are a valuable source of genealogical information as well as information on the socio-economic background of the students.

II Roll of Matriculated Students: 6 volumes 1881–1909

This contains summary details of each student including date and place of birth, age at time of Matriculation, date, venue and result of examination and include details of examinations passed subsequent to Matriculation.

5 *Graduate Records*

Roll of Senate and Graduates in Vellum (2 bound letter volumes) 1881–1909

These rolls were signed by the member of Senate and by the graduates at the conferring ceremonies. Volume 1 contains the text of the University Education (Ireland) Act 1879 and of the Charter written by a highly skilled calligrapher. The Royal Crest painted on the Charter with gold and silver leaf is of very high quality.

6 *Examination Records*

I Examination broadsheets 1881–1909/10 (bound volumes)

II Examination application forms c.1880–1909 (bound volumes)

III Examination attendance registers (2)

Contain signatures of candidates at commencement of university examinations, 1885–1910. Also include travelling studentship and prize examinations. See also Appendix B NUI Archives 6 (4).

The significance of the rolls and of the examination records is enhanced as they contain signatures and examination information relating to many of the dominant historical and literary figures of the period.

7 Administrative Records

These records contain samples of all printed documents, forms, standard letters, circulars, reports and other documents issued by RUI by year and reflect the administrative workings of the university. Samples include: printed copies of Senate Minutes; Abstract of Results of Examinations; Examination Admission Cards; Examination timetables; Notices to Candidates at Examinations; Certificates (e.g. Certificate of Clinical Clerkship): 10 vols 1881–1905.

8 Senate Records including Sub-Committees

1 Senate Minutes (handwritten and printed), 1880–1909

The Senate Minutes, Vol. v (1902–7), illustrate the impact that the political activity in the country during this period, in particular the Home Rule campaign, had on the University. They include a detailed 'Statement of Proceedings in reference to the Disorder on Degree Day, 27 October 1905. [To be supplied to the Government, by order of Senate, 4 May 1906]'. This event precipitated a crisis in the RUI culminating in the resignation of the Chancellor, the Earl of Meath in February 1906. The statement includes an account from the Chancellor which describes the incident and how it was interpreted by the University authorities. It tells how the platform reserved for the Chancellor and Senators and other dignitaries

> was forcibly invaded by a mob, presumably composed of undergraduates or students preparing for the University examinations, who, brandishing sticks and taking possession of the organ gallery, prevented the eminent musician . . . playing of the National Anthem . . . In order that there should be no doubt as regards the object of this outrage, individual members of the crowd which raided the platform shouted out that they were there for the purpose of preventing the National Anthem from being played. Other disloyal cries were raised . . . It is also stated that after the retirement of the Senate their seats were occupied by the triumphant mob, one of whom attempted to address his fellow students and the public from the Chancellor's seat. It is difficult to conceive a more flagrant exhibition of disloyalty defiantly and successfully carried out within University walls . . . The authority of the Senate has been slighted . . . and the honour of the University has received a severe blow from which it will take time to recover.

The statement records the four members of the 'disorderly crowd' who were identified. They were a graduate, Thomas Kettle, BA, two undergraduates, J. E. Kennedy and Sarsfield Kerrigan, and Thomas J. Madden LRCS and PI who had no connection to the university. The letter from each of them refusing to attend a meeting of the Senate Standing Committee when summoned to do so and challenging the university's disciplinary jurisdiction is printed in the minutes. The incident was widely reported nationally and internationally.

II *Standing Committee Minutes, 1880–1909*

III *Finance Committee Minutes, 1881–1908*

IV *Other Committee Records: Medical, Library, Convocation, Conversazione and Miscellaneous committees: 10 vols.*

9 *Correspondence Records*
Letter books (outgoing) 1880–1909: 49 vols.
The files of incoming correspondence have not survived.

10 *Calendars and Examination Papers 1883–1909 and 1909 Supplemental*
Calendars 1883–6 contain the RUI examination papers. Calendars Part 2 1887–1909: from 1887 the RUI Examination Papers were published separately as Part 2 of the RUI Calendar.

11 *Photographic Portraits*
HM Queen Alexandra
HM King Edward VII
The Rt Hon. Christopher T. Redington

APPENDIX B
The Archives of the National University of Ireland
The record classes in the archive reflect the structure, organisation and functions of the NUI as a federal university, and record the workings and developments of the University since its foundation in 1908. Taken as a whole, the archival records demonstrate the major contribution the University and its graduates have made to national life over the last 100 years.

1   *Foundation Records and Related Material*
I   *The Charter (3 sets held in specially designed metal boxes)*
II   *The NUI Coat of Arms*
III *1908 Act Copies*
IV   *NUI Statutes, 1911–present*
V   *Minute Book Joint Committee (Irish Universities Act 1908), (1909–11) 1 volume.*

2   *Senate Records*
These include:
I   *Minutes of Senate Minutes (printed) (1909–present)*
II   *Minutes of Senate main sub-committees*
including Standing Committee, Finance Committee, Miscellaneous Committees (1908–32) and General Board of Studies (abolished 1997), 1909 to 2000. From 2000, the minutes of the Standing and Finance Committees are incorporated into the Senate Minutes.
III *Documentation relating to other Senate sub-committees*
NUI Registrars' Committee and Recognised Colleges Steering Committee and other ad hoc committees. The reports from these committees are included in the Roneo Files (see iv below).
IV   *Roneo Files*
These are the most important files in NUI and contain all the documents relating to meetings of Senate, including the reports of its sub-committees (*c.*1909–present). (Explanatory note: the Roneo files contain documents copied internally. They are distinguished from the Senate files below which contain printed documentation.)
V   *Other Senate Files*
Comprising printed documents, e.g. Senate minutes, applications for Professorships and Lectureships (up to 1997), Annual NUI Accounts circulated to Senate (*c.*1909–present).

3   *University Registers*
Rolls of Registers including:
I   *Members of Senate, 1909–c.1960s*
II   *Members of General Board of Studies, 1909–c.1960s*
III *Members of Faculties (early years)*
IV   *Members of UCD, UCC and UCG (early years)*

v   *Matriculated Students, 1909–12*

vi *Registers of Students Transferred from RUI (2 vols)*

4   Graduate and Conferring Records

i   *Roll of Graduates, 1909–75 (2 vols)*

ii   *Register of Degrees Conferred, 1914–16*

iii *Register of Ad Eundem Degrees*

iv   *NUI Annual Lists of NUI Degrees and other Qualifications Conferred (1909–present)*

v   *NUI Graduate File Cards, 1908–91*

vi   *Honorary Degree Citations, 1940–present (incomplete)*

vii *Samples of Old NUI Parchments*

5   Matriculation Records

These include:

i   *Bound Volumes of Completed Application Forms, 1909–92 (c.320 vols)*

The Matriculation Application records consist of the completed Matriculation Examination and Matriculation Registration application forms. They record details of every applicant for Matriculation from 1909 to 1992, including date and place of birth, address and occupation of father as well as examination information. They reflect the expansion of access to third-level education following the introduction of free secondary education and local authority grants for third-level education in the 1960s. They are also an important source of genealogical data.

ii   *Matriculation Regulations Booklets, 1911–present (some missing)*

iii *Matriculation Examination Papers, 1910–92 (some missing)*

iv   *Matriculation Examination Broadsheets, 1909–92 (series completed)*

6   University Examinations Records, Undergraduate, Postgraduate and Prize Examinations

These include:

i   *Travelling Studentships and other Prize Examination Regulations/NUI Awards booklets, 1924–present*

ii   *Travelling Studentships and Bursaries Examination Papers Booklets, 1910–2001*

iii *Examination Broadsheets, 1909–76*

IV Examination Attendance Register
Contains signatures of candidates at commencement of university examinations (Autumn 1899–1910) and prize examinations (Autumn 1899–1976). This register is an example of how RUI procedures were 'converted' into the NUI administrative systems. See also Appendix A, RUI Archives, Item 6 (iii)

V University Examinations Broadsheets, 1909–86

VI Marks and Standards for University Examination, 1913–2001

VII Books of Examiners, Supervisor of Examinations and External Examiners, 1917–97

VIII Books of External Examiners, 1997–present

7 Correspondence Records

I Letter Books (Outgoing), 1909–present

II Correspondence Incoming, 1909–present

8 Papers of Sir Joseph McGrath, RUI Co-Secretary (1892–1908) and First NUI Registrar (1908–21)

I Correspondence Incoming, 1904 [1911–12] 1914
Includes correspondence from the Chancellor, Archbishop Walsh

II Office Diaries, 1892–December 1921
The entries are short and include family matters. Reference to the 1916 Rising is made in the entry for Monday 24 April 1916 as follows: 'Sinn Féin Rising today. The "Shinners" stopped trains about 12 o'c at L[ansdowne] Rd and dug trenches on the line, near the Barracks[?]'

9 NUI publications
These include:

I NUI Calendars, 1909–present

II Graduate and Sessional Lists, Results of Examinations, Honours Lists
Published periodically (completed series)

10 Convocation records
The material relating to Convocation is incomplete

I Minutes of Convocation, Vol. 1 (1911–53)
Only the first volume of the Minutes of Convocation has survived. The nationalist character of Convocation after 1918 reflected the changed political

landscape of the country at large. This are several examples of this in the minutes including the resolution (in Irish and English) of sympathy to the family of Terence MacSwiney, a graduate of the university and a member of Convocation, following his death on hunger strike and stating its confidence that 'the stainless examples of his sacrifice will be for all time, an inspiration and a model of patriotism to the members of our University' passed at its meeting in November 1920. In May 1921, Convocation passed a resolution (in Irish and English) expressing 'our deep regret with the relatives of Frank Flood, a student of this College, in their sad bereavement, with profound admiration for his sacrifice in the cause he espoused'.

The election by Convocation of Eamon de Valera as Chancellor of the NUI to succeed Archbishop Walsh was another example of the impact that the political and cultural nationalism of the period had on the University. The minutes of the Meeting of 19 November 1921 contain the plans for the reception for the newly elected Chancellor and the Academic Procession. Newspaper cuttings describing the event are pasted into the minutes.

A folder, containing photocopied material relating to the election includes a copy of the letter dated 20 July 1921 from Michael Cox, Chairman of Convocation, to de Valera informing him that, as the sole nominee for the office of Chancellor on 19 July 1921, under the terms of NUI Statute 1, he was the Chancellor of the National University of Ireland from that date. The copy of the letter was given to NUI by the Taoiseach's office 27 January 1959, with a note stating that the Taoiseach had the original.

II   *Annual Committee Minute Book, 1919–33*

III   *Other Convocation Material*

This includes miscellaneous election material, rolls and registers. Convocation documentation and correspondence are also included in the NUI Correspondence (Incoming) files.

8   *Seanad Éireann Records: NUI Constituency Records and Registers (incomplete series)*

9   *Select (i.e. Incomplete) Catalogue by Topic and Correspondent*
The following records were listed by Archives Consulting Services in 2006:

I   *Chancellors' Correspondence, 1909–2004*

II   *NUI and Dept of Education and Science Correspondence, 1921–2003*

III NUI and Commission on Higher Education Correspondence, 1960–1
IV NUI and Higher Education Authority Correspondence, 1984–2004
V Archives relating to the proposed merger of TCD and NUI, 1967–9

NUI wishes to thank the Heritage Council for the grant towards the cost of listing these records.

STORAGE AND ACCESS

The NUI records are stored on mobile shelving units in 49 Merrion Square, except for, inter alia, the bound volumes of matriculation application forms, examination broadsheets and graduate file cards (1909–1) which are currently stored off site. The RUI records are stored in a separate room in 49 Merrion Square.

The NUI office is the central administrative office of the university and the archives are not open to the public. However, the NUI is happy to facilitate bona fide researchers who wish to consult the records. Application for access should be made to the NUI Registrar, 49 Merrion Square, Dublin 2. Telephone + 353 (0) 1 439 2424 email: registrar@nui.ie

Figure 6 **Dr Pat Fottrell, President NUI, Galway (1996–2000), Dr Séamus Smyth, President NUI, Maynooth (1997–2004), Dr Art Cosgrove, President UCD (1994–2003), Ms Niamh Bhreathnach, Minister for Education, Dr Michael Mortell, President UCC (1989–99), pictured in NUI Maynooth at the Commencement Order for the Universities Act on 13 June 1997.**

1908   1918   1928   1938   1948   1958

1968   1978   1988   1998   2008

The Challenge of Change

CHAPTER 16 *The National University of Ireland and the Changing Structure of Irish Higher Education, 1967–2007*

JOHN COOLAHAN

F OR ALMOST FOUR DECADES following independence university affairs slipped from public attention in the Republic of Ireland. Lack of public interest coincided with financial neglect of university education by the state. The universities adopted a low public profile, with no significant campaign to inform public opinion on the position and role of the university. Full-time student numbers in the three constituent colleges of the National University of Ireland increased from 1,881 in 1925, to 4,880 in 1945 to reach 6,210 by 1960. But, even with the addition of Trinity College Dublin, the total in 1960 only reached 8,653,[1] which was a tiny proportion of the relevant age cohort in the population. The Investment in Education Report (1966) calculated that less than four per cent of the school leavers in 1963 went on to university.[2] While student numbers were small as a proportion of the population, students in the NUI colleges had more than trebled from 1925 to 1960. However, accommodation, resources and staffing had not kept pace with the increase in student numbers. Accordingly, there was intense overcrowding, over-stretching of staff and limited promotion of research.

Appraisal and Reform

In contrast to the earlier four decades, the decades since 1960 witnessed a great deal of analysis and appraisal of higher education, and a level of action on a range of fronts which transformed the profile of higher education. The transformation involved great expansion of existing institutions and the establishment of many new ones: the setting up of an independent planning and budgetary agency to oversee many of these institutions; the foundation of a course validation and award-giving body for the non-university sector;

and the establishment of a national clearing house for higher education applications. An impressive diversification of courses took place in response to the changing needs of individuals and society. The universities' monopoly of higher education ceased, leading to wider roles for some existing institutions and for newly established ones. The 1960s was a period of rapid socio-economic and cultural change in Ireland. Government became much more actively involved in higher education policy, which was now regarded as having social and economic significance within a fast-changing society. Government policy was not always consistent and this sometimes gave rise to uncertainty and unease in higher education circles. Nevertheless, the overall effect of government action was to lead to a paradigm shift in the place of higher education within modern Irish society.

By the late 1950s, the government had recognised that serious problems existed regarding the physical infrastructure of university education. The minister for education appointed a commission to examine the accommodation needs of the NUI colleges, chaired by Justice Cearbhaill Ó Dálaigh. The commission issued reports on individual colleges and a final report in May 1959. The final report noted that the problem of accommodation was a long-standing one that had been neglected:

> The result is that colleges have become more and more overcrowded, and arrears of building have been accumulating . . .
>
> Already breakdown point has been reached in the colleges . . . The situation is that university teachers and students have to work under very trying and, in some cases, almost impossible conditions.[3]

The only satisfactory solution to the UCD overcrowding situation was 'transfer of the entire college to a new site', and the Belfield campus was endorsed as suitable. The report was critical of the colleges for not publicising their problems sufficiently, remarking, 'We cannot but feel that the colleges might have done more to bring their needs to the knowledge of the public.'[4]

Action could no longer be postponed and, in June 1959, the government decided to transfer UCD to the Belfield site. The shift to the spacious campus with modern buildings was largely completed by the early 1970s. On a smaller scale, the 1960s also saw expansion of buildings and facilities in UCC and UCG, as the NUI colleges were all gradually equipped for a new era in Irish university education. Trinity College, colleges of education and a host of new higher education institutions also engaged in new building plans, which over the years greatly changed the physical landscape for higher education.

The government also turned its attention to qualitative aspects of higher education provision and, in 1960, the Minister for Education, Patrick Hillery, appointed a commission on higher education. Its terms of reference were very wide and in effect included the reviewing of every feature of higher education. The commission took seven years to conclude and present its report, a very long time at a period when many higher education issues were pressing for resolution. While the commission was engaged on its deliberations several other educational inquiries were set up and a number of important decisions were taken by government. The Investment in Education team was set up in 1962 to inquire, primarily, on first and second-level education, and reported in 1966. In 1963, a joint study with the OECD was undertaken in relation to scientific research and technology. Furthermore, in 1963, the minister for education announced his intention of establishing regional technical colleges and, in 1966, Minister Donogh O'Malley set up a steering committee to advise on the proposed regional technical colleges.

The report of the Commission on Higher Education was published in 1967. First, the commission set out and assessed the structure of the existing provision for higher education. This produced a rather dismal picture but one that influenced the commission greatly in its recommendations for the future. The piecemeal character of the system and the lack of planning machinery came in for criticism. The commissioners considered that increasing numbers of students, low entry standards, and inadequate staffing and accommodation, placed academic standards in jeopardy. They were not impressed by what was being achieved in the areas of postgraduate studies and research; they criticised the appointments system within the NUI, and the constitution and administrative structures of the higher education institutions. In general, they considered that the inadequacies revealed were 'so grave as to call for a concentrated effort to remove them'.[5]

The commissioners sought to maintain the existing universities for what they saw as their proper role, and as an attempt to protect standards they proposed a new type of third-level institution – the 'new college', and recommended diverting some of the professional work of the universities to other existing institutions for applied research. The 'new college' was devised essentially to help meet the growing demand for third-level places, to enrich the intellectual and cultural life of the provinces, and to provide forms of higher education that were lower in standard and with a different emphasis from that of a university. Among other significant recommendations was the dissolution of the NUI in favour of independent university status for the constituent colleges. However, the commission was strongly in favour of greater co-operation between the universities and recommended the establishment of a statutory council of Irish universities, with a right to determine policy in a number of academic areas. It also recommended the setting up of a statutory commission for higher education, with overall planning and budgetary responsibilities, which 'would be the keystone of the future structure of higher education'. New governing structures for the universities and other higher education institutions should be introduced, along with new appointment procedures. It urged the promotion of research and postgraduate studies, improvements in staff–student ratios, a student grants scheme, and improved student facilities. Reaction to the report was mixed, and the time lag since the commission had begun its deliberations meant that the debate had, in some respects, moved on. An issue that gave rise to great public debate concerned the future structure of university education. Here government thinking diverged from that of the commission. The commission had recommended the dissolution of the NUI in favour of independent status for its constituent colleges, while leaving Trinity College as it was; the Minister for Education, O'Malley, rejected this advice. On 18 April 1967 he made the dramatic announcement that it was the government's intention to establish a single multi-denominational university in Dublin, to contain two colleges based on UCD and Trinity College. O'Malley argued that his proposal made economic, educational, and social sense. It certainly caught the attention of the general public. The minister's perspective was not, however, shared by many interested parties, and very divergent views were expressed in the ensuing controversy.

On 5 July 1968 the new Minister for Education, Brian Lenihan, announced the government's detailed proposals on the reorganisation of the universities. The NUI was to be dissolved, with UCC and UCG gaining independent status. Trinity and UCD were to form a single university based on the two colleges. The statement set out a division of faculties between the colleges. Maynooth College was to become an associated college of this new university. In line with the commission's report, a conference of Irish universities was to be set up to deal with academic issues common to all universities. Also in line with the report, a permanent authority to deal with financial and organisational problems of higher education was to be established.

This latter proposal was the first to be implemented. In the following month, August 1968, the Higher Education Authority (HEA) was established on an ad hoc basis; it was given statutory recognition in 1971. Its terms of reference were wide ranging in respect of the budgetary and planning aspects of higher education. The minister informed the HEA at its first meeting on 12 September 1968 that it was 'an autonomous body' and 'in no way an executive arm of the Government or of any Department of State'. The first task deputed to the authority was to advise the minister on the nature of the legislation required to put into effect the 'decisions already taken by the Government on higher education'. Accordingly, the HEA opened discussions with university interests and sought their opinions on the proposed changes. In its report, the HEA's favoured solution was for two universities in Dublin linked by a statutory conjoint board. Certain faculties should be developed in one institution only, with special joint arrangements for medicine and engineering. It also recommended that the NUI constituent colleges of UCC and UCG be recognised as independent universities.

Subsequently, arrangements for course rationalisation took place between UCD and Trinity College. Apart from that, no structural changes took place at that time in the framework of universities' provision from what it was prior to the establishment of the commission. Accordingly, the NUI federal framework remained intact.

The government found itself in agreement with the Report of the Steering Committee it had established on the regional technical colleges, which also reported in 1967.[6] It endorsed the government's plans for these colleges, and by adopting the report's recommendation for the establishment of a National Council for Educational Awards (NCEA) for non-university qualifications the government was indicating that it favoured a binary third-level system, on the lines evolving in England in the post-Robbins Report era. As early as 1969, in its first published report, the HEA recognised that higher education was developing on a binary pattern, referring to the 'university' and the 'non-university' sectors standing 'almost wholly apart from each other'.[7]

The first five Regional Technical Colleges (RTCs) commenced operation in autumn 1970 and by 1977 they were joined by four more. The National

Council for Educational Awards was set up on an ad-hoc basis in March 1972, modelled on the CNAA in Britain. The NCEA became the validating body for courses in the RTCs and the awarding body for qualifications for most of the courses on offer. A new type of third-level institution – the National Institute of Higher Education (NIHE) was located in Limerick, and received its first students in 1972. A similar institute was established in north Dublin, with students attending from 1980. The City of Dublin Vocational Education Committee in 1978 reorganised its six colleges into a single third-level entity, the Dublin Institute of Technology (DIT).

In 1973, the Minister for Education, Richard Burke, requested the universities to investigate the possibility of awarding degrees to primary school-teachers. The discussions proved successful and a new professional degree course, the BEd, was established in 1974. The larger colleges of education, St Patrick's Drumcondra, Our Lady of Mercy College Carysfort and Mary Immaculate College, Limerick became recognised colleges of the NUI. The Church of Ireland college and those at Marino and Sion Hill became associated colleges of Trinity College for the new degree arrangements. Later St Angela's College of Home Economics, Sligo, also became a recognised college of NUI, while St Catherine's Sion Hill became associated with Trinity College. The Royal College of Surgeons became an NUI recognised college in 1977. Thus, the NUI now had six recognised colleges. Teachers in the newly established Thomond College in Limerick and in the National College of Art, Dublin, had their qualifications awarded by the NCEA.

By the early seventies, it seemed clear that Irish higher education had been given a binary model for its development. However, this presumption was rudely shattered by the publication in December 1974, by the coalition government, elected in 1973, of a radically new plan for higher education. The document indicated that the central issue in planning was 'whether to continue and to develop the existing binary system, or to initiate the establishment of a fully comprehensive system of higher education', and government opted for the comprehensive model. Among specific proposals there were to be three universities in the state – the National University of Ireland, comprising UCC and UCG; the University of Dublin (Trinity College); and a university constituted from the existing UCD. Maynooth would have the option of becoming a constituent college of any of the three universities. These proposals were, of course, directly contrary to those of the previous government. The NIHE at Limerick would become a recognised college of the National University, as would Thomond College, and the NIHE in Dublin would become a recognised college of one of the Dublin universities. The NCEA would lose its degree-awarding powers but would become a council for technological education with responsibilities for co-ordinating and awarding non-degree third-level qualifications. The range of bodies designated under the HEA would be extended, and a conference of Irish universities, which had met on an ad hoc basis since June 1974, would be made permanent. The two proposed Dublin universities would acquire a conjoint board, and a division of faculties between the two was set out.[8]

The clear aim of this policy was a concentration of higher-level institutions within a framework of three universities. Other third-level institutions would be linked to one or other of these universities for all degrees and postgraduate work. The status of the NCEA would be reduced. The overall role of the HEA would be expanded as the key overseeing body of the third-level institutions. The conference of Irish universities and the conjoint board of the two Dublin universities were intended to improve co-ordination and co-operation between the universities.

While the emphasis of the new policy was clear, this government shared the previous government's failure to set out a detailed rationale, or an overall conception of what constituted university education. The public was presented with decisions on restructuring, but without the benefit of the arguments on which they were based. Like the previous government's recommendations for higher education, the coalition proposals were highly controversial; in the same way, they were destined for the most part not to be implemented. However, degree-awarding powers were removed from the NCEA, which created some immediate problems for the non-university sector. The most awkward of these faced Thomond College and NIHE, Limerick, which were now forced to adapt their courses in line with NUI requirements.

In July 1976, the government amended its policy and announced proposals for the setting up of five universities, based on TCD, UCD, UCC, UCG, and Maynooth, with scope for associated and recognised colleges linked to them. A working party, chaired by the minister for education, took on the task of preparing the necessary legislation. The return of a Fianna Fáil government, following the general election of 1977, led to a further change of policy whereby the 'comprehensive' model was abandoned and the 'binary' model reinstated. The emphasis of legislation now shifted towards giving statutory status to the new institutions. Degree-awarding powers were restored to the NCEA under new legislation in 1979. Thomond College was given statutory status in 1980. In the same year the NIHEs in Limerick and Dublin were established as independent institutions looking to the NCEA for the validation of their courses and the awarding of their qualifications. The series of legislative enactments in 1979–80 put the seal on the binary approach and gave the new institutions the sense that their foundations were secure. However, a decade later in 1989, the NIHEs were raised to the status of independent universities – the University of Limerick and Dublin City University – the first universities to be established since the state's foundation.

The decade 1967 to 1977 can thus be regarded as very turbulent, complex and confusing with regard to national policy on the expanding higher education sector. Many of the new institutions felt buffeted by the contradictory policy directions. They did not enjoy a stable period of 'settling down' and establishing a clear sense of their own identity. The universities were uncertain for many years of what their future configuration would be. A notable feature of the government's policy initiatives, the 'merger' proposals of Minister O'Malley and the 'comprehensive' model favoured by the Coalition Government in 1974, was their surprise elements. They had not been preceded by any consultation with the major parties involved. As regards the existing universities, following all the proposals and subsequent discussion, the outcome was that no change took place in their legislative status from that which existed in 1960.

The government produced a White Paper on Educational Development in 1980. The opening paragraphs indicated that the government was determined that its own priorities would be paramount in the allocation of funding for higher education, and there were signs of impatience with the HEA's status as an independent agency between government and the higher education institutions. The announcement that a bill was to be introduced at an early date for the dissolution of the NUI and the establishment of its constituent colleges as independent universities was not carried through. The early to mid-1980s were a period of stringency in the national finances, and there was little scope for new investment in higher education. In 1984, the Minister for Education, Gemma Hussey, published a Programme for Action in Education, 1984–7. Chapter 6 of this programme was devoted to higher education. Its proposals reflected a concern to secure greater productivity and economies in higher education. To improve the 'throughput' of students, it was proposed to explore several alternatives: the possibility of a four-term academic year, cutting back four-year degree courses to three years; the introduction of a unit cost system of funding; a rationalisation of courses within and between institutions. Priority in financial support was to be given to technological studies, and links between higher education and industry were to be intensified. It was also stated that legislation would be brought forward to establish independent universities.[9] Little of this was carried out.

Expansion and Development of Higher Education Institutions

The new Regional Technical Colleges began their operations in the 1970s, against the background of a very undeveloped provision of technical and technological education of a higher education standard. Early in 1969, the Minister for Education announced that the colleges would be managed by a board of management appointed in accordance with section 21 (2) of the Vocational Education Act of 1930. It was also significant that the staff union of the colleges was to be the Teachers' Union of Ireland, which was strongly established in the second-level vocational schools. The consequences of these structural arrangements – which existed until the Regional Technical Colleges Act 1992 was put in place – were many and proved constricting to the colleges as they shaped their future predominantly as third-level institutions.

Originally, the emphasis of the colleges was very much on a teaching role, with little emphasis on, or provision for research. The RTCs were funded directly by the Department of Education by means of an earmarked grant channelled through the Vocational Education Committee. The NCEA became the validating body for courses in the RTCs and the awarding body for qualifications for most of the courses on offer. The NCEA appointed boards of studies, who, in turn, set up panels with expertise necessary to carry out the assessment of specialised areas. The course framework evolved to include: a National Certificate to be awarded after the equivalent of two years' full-time study; a National Diploma to be awarded either after a further year of specialised study, or on the completion of a third-year course; and a degree which would require the equivalent of four years' full-time study.

Students in the non-university sector benefited from funds provided by the European Social Fund (ESF) from 1975. By 1984–5 there were 12,000 students on ESF-funded courses. The number of full-time students in the RTCs grew impressively in their first ten years of operation, from 194 in 1970 to 5,965 by 1980. The RTCs had about 10,000 part-time students at that time.[10] Within a further decade the number of full-time students had almost trebled to reach 16,800 by 1990–1. Students in the RTCs benefited from much more favourable staff–student ratios than existed within the universities, but the administrative staff was more limited.

When the City of Dublin Vocational Education Committee (CDVEC) reorganised its six colleges into the Dublin Institute of Technology in 1978, many of degree courses benefited from validation arrangements by Trinity College Dublin, an arrangement which continued for about 25 years. The CDVEC did not align its awards with the NCEA. Student numbers in the DIT expanded impressively so that by 2000–1 it had 9,873 full-time and 5,443 part-time third-level students.[11]

The two NIHEs, located in Limerick (1972) and Dublin (1980), pressed for recognition as universities, claiming that such a title would be much more beneficial in enabling them to fulfil their missions. In 1986 the government appointed an international study group led by Dr Tom Hardiman, which, among other things, was asked to examine the case for the establishment of a technological university with the two NIHEs as constituent colleges. The report of the study group concluded that the two NIHEs should be self-accrediting and established as independent universities – the University of Limerick and Dublin City University. In May 1989 legislation was passed in the form of an amendment to the NIHE acts to change the titles of the institutes to universities, and those of the directors to presidents, to confer the power to award degrees, diplomas and certificates and to give the governing authorities the authority to extend the functions of the universities with the approval of the Minister for Education. Thus, these two institutions moved into the university sector, which was interpreted by some commentators as a weakening of the binary model.

While a great deal of public attention was periodically focused on the governments' legislative intentions, many of which did not come to pass, at another level an unprecedented period of growth and development was taking place regarding the academic life and facilities of the universities. Each of the universities benefited from new buildings and physical infrastructure.

In the case of UCD, it transferred from a confined city centre site to the more spacious surroundings of its current campus in Belfield, Stillorgan. The University of Limerick also benefited from a spacious, pastoral setting on the outskirts of Limerick. While not having the same space, Dublin City University has established itself as an impressive campus on the northern suburbs of Dublin. The other four institutions – Trinity College, NUI Maynooth, UCG and UCC – all greatly expanded and improved their physical plant and environment.

The campuses catered for a greatly expanding student clientele. Table 16.1 reflects growth of full-time university student numbers over recent decades.

Table *16.1* **Growth in University Full-Time Student Numbers, 1965–2005**

1965–6	1975–6	1985–6	1995–6	2004–5
16,007	23,121	32,388	56,698	78,970

Source Interim Report of the Technical Working Group (HEA) 1996, p. 24 and figures supplied for the HEA, DES.

This represented an almost five-fold increase since 1965, with university students now comprising about 60 per cent of all higher education students. The proportion of women students increased from about 30 per cent in 1964–5 to about 50 per cent in 2002–3. The number of postgraduate students rose from the very small base of about four per cent of total student numbers in 1964–5 to reach about 20 per cent in 2002–3. In 2004–5, there were also 16,166 part-time students enrolled in the universities.

Changing the Legislative Framework for Higher Education

During the 1990s it was realised that investment in education was crucial in human resource development. The remarkable levels of economic growth, which emerged gradually over the decade, provided both the resources and fostered the confidence for such investment. Arising from its own analysis and engagement with international organisations such as the OECD and the EU, Ireland was alert to the emergence of the knowledge society. Within this context, it was recognised that higher education and research would assume greater priority of attention.

The Department of Education and Science and key agencies in higher education have, over recent years, engaged in much debate, reflection and planning as they seek to chart the way forward for higher education in this challenging era. In 1992 the government published its Green Paper *Education for a Changing World*. The section on higher education opened with a strong recognition of its achievements, stating: 'Higher education has contributed greatly to the personal education of students, to cultural, economic and social development, to the promotion of the professions, and to the provision of new knowledge and scholarship.'

In setting out proposals under many headings, the document referred to the approach in Ireland as being 'fully in line with approaches in all other developed countries'. It set out proposals on such themes as course structures, research, quality assurance, funding and co-ordination, college–industry links. Taken together, these signalled many new directions for policy within the higher education sector. With regard to legislation, it noted that the NIHEs at Limerick and Dublin had been granted independent university status by legislation in 1989. It focused attention on new legislation in hand to give the DIT and the RTCs statutory status with more institutional autonomy. The Green Paper stated that new legislation would be prepared to give greater autonomy to the colleges of the federal National University of Ireland (NUI). It also promised that more comprehensive university legislation would be brought forward for all the universities 'that would be more compatible with the role, function and operation of the universities in modern society'.[12] These statements signalled the most comprehensive legislative package for higher education ever attempted in Ireland.

During the 1980s the RTCs and the DIT had expressed their dissatisfaction with their mode of governance under the vocational education committees, regarding it as an outdated and restrictive framework. Eventually, in 1991, a bill was introduced, designed to give the RTCs a greater degree of autonomy and self-governance and, following long debates in the Dáil, the bill became law as the Regional Technical Colleges Act (1992). The RTCs, however, which continued to be monitored directly by the Department of Education and Science pressed for more power and status with Waterford RTC, in particular, pressing for recognition as a university. In 1995, the HEA Steering Committee Report recommended that the title of RTCs should be altered to 'Regional Technical Institutes'. In 1997 the minister for education agreed to confer the title Institute of Technology on Waterford RTC, but, predictably, this caused concern to other RTCs which considered that they also had a claim to such

status. The minister appointed a special group to advise her on the technological sector. It recommended that all RTCs should be designated Institutes
of Technology, which was implemented in January 1998. It was also envisaged that institutes could in future apply, following the fulfilment of certain
criteria, to award their own sub-degree and degree qualifications. By 2003, two
institutes – Waterford and Cork – had the right to award their own degrees.

Contemporary with the Regional Technical Colleges Act of 1992 was a
separate act relating to the Dublin Institute of Technology, which removed
it from the authority of the City of Dublin Vocational Education Committee.
The DIT Act allowed it to confer diplomas, certificates or other awards. The
DIT was also granted other functions which could include the conferring of
degrees, postgraduate degrees and honorary degrees, which, under the act,
could be assigned to it by the minister for education. In December 1995, the
minister for education appointed an international review team to review
quality assurance procedures in the institute. In its report, published in the
following year, the group recommended that degree-awarding powers be
extended to the Institute for the awards to be granted from the year 1998–9,
which came into effect as recommended. For the debate in the Dáil on the
Universities Bill, 1996–7, the DIT lobbied strongly that it be awarded recognition as a university under Section 9 of the bill. This was not conceded, but
the minister for education agreed to set up a body to advise the government
on whether the DIT should be established as a university. This international
review group reported in 1998.[13] From a range of options the review group
recommended that, pending some developments, university status could
be granted within a three to five-year timespan. In its response to this report,
the Higher Education Authority recommended against the award of university status, and stated that it would require a further review group in later
years, if DIT was to be designated as a university.

Thus, it can be noted that the original non-university sector of higher
education had experienced a very significant alteration within the last 15
years. The two NIHEs were designated as universities; the RTCs obtained
new legislation and were renamed as institutes of technology with expanded
powers; the DIT also received new legislation, increased academic powers,
and has been seriously considered for university designation. Yet in parallel
to these developments, official policy statements and reports have continued
to emphasise the binary character of the higher education. One of the

distinguishing features of Irish educational policy formulation in the recent past has been the extensive consultative process on which the stakeholders have engaged. The Green Paper was debated widely for 15 months before the establishment of the National Education Convention in October 1993. This was a forum for multilateral dialogue by all the education partners under the control of an independent, academic secretariat. The responsible agencies in higher education made presentations and engaged in discussions. Key issues raised by the Green Paper were explored, with more detailed discussion focusing on research and quality assurance. A good degree of consensus was established between participants.

Shortly after the National Education Convention, in December 1993, the minister for education requested the Higher Education Authority to set up a steering committee to advise her on the future development of the higher education sector. A technical working group, set up to support the steering committee, issued an interim report in January 1995. The steering committee's report, *The Future Development of Higher Education*, was published in June 1995.[14] The government also published its White Paper, *Charting Our Education Future* in 1995.

Having stated at the outset that 'the State will respect the autonomy of institutions to determine ways and means through which they will fulfil roles, within the overall aims for the system and the policy framework articulated by the minister',[15] the White Paper went on to set out government policy positions on key areas of higher education. Originally, the minister for education intended to abolish the National University of Ireland and give independent status to its constituent colleges. The Senate of the NUI opposed this approach and intervened successfully in securing the retention of the NUI as an institution. The White Paper endorsed this as government policy, while stating that the constituent colleges would receive greater autonomy. More comprehensive legislation for the university sector as a whole was promised. As was to be expected, the prospect of university legislation aroused a good deal of interest and debate.

Eventually, in July 1996, the Universities Bill was published. It was a comprehensive measure that applied to all universities in the state. The bill provided for the retention of the NUI while recognising its constituent colleges as largely autonomous universities. The bill did not clarify the extent of the powers of the NUI Senate vis-à-vis the constituent universities. Legal clarification was sought by the Senate and the universities in 2007, which indicated that the academic powers of the Senate had been greatly diminished by the new legislation. More broadly, the bill set out the objects and functions of a university, the structure and role of governing bodies, staffing arrangements, composition and role of academic councils, arrangements for planning and evaluation of progress and sections relating to finance, property and reporting. With such a comprehensive approach, it was not surprising that the bill drew a great deal of reaction, with the universities expressing concern on many aspects of it, particularly those sections where great sensitivity existed on the interface between the powers of the minister for education and science, and the HEA vis-à-vis the institutions. Arising from discussions with involved parties and debates in the Dáil, a large number of amendments were made to the draft legislation, which was enacted in May 1997. The Universities Act 1997 is the most significant piece of university legislation since the state was founded. It represented a modernisation of the university system in line with contemporary thinking on the role of the university in modern society. It would appear that a reasonable balance was struck between safeguarding key aspects of institutional autonomy and providing for the needs of public policy and accountability, while updating the composition of governing authorities and modernising institutional procedures.

New accountability procedures were incorporated in the Universities Act for the mass higher education era. The governing authorities were required to see that strategic development plans were prepared for periods of not less than three years. They were also required to see that the chief officer of a university established procedures for evaluating the quality of teaching and research carried out in the university. The Higher Education Authority was given an overseeing role with regard to strategic plans and quality assurance procedures. Each university was now required to prepare an equality policy focusing on access by economically and socially disadvantaged students and on equality, including gender equality, in all activities of the university. The chief officer was also required to prepare an annual report on the operation of the university during the year. New budgetary arrangements were introduced, unit cost accounting prevailed and the HEA and the Comptroller and Auditor General were given significant powers of approval and investigation. Such measures reflect tighter accountability procedures in view of the large public investment in higher education. Overall, it can be concluded that the Universities Act 1997 was a landmark in the history of university education in Ireland.

Of great significance for the extra-university sector was the establishment of an interim National Certification Authority, TEASTAS, in September 1995. TEASTAS laid the groundwork for the Qualifications (Education and Training) Act 1999. This Act established the National Qualifications Authority of Ireland (NQAI), the Higher Education and Training Awards Council (HETAC), and the Further Education and Training Awards Council (FETAC). These latter councils absorbed the work of the NCEA, NCVA and a range of other existing award agencies. The awards of the ITs are under the general aegis of the NQAI. The universities and DIT are awarding bodies in their own right. They are required to liaise with the NQAI so that their awards fit within the NQAI's National Framework of Qualifications, which was formally launched in October 2003. The framework, based on the guiding principles of access, transfer, progression and quality, aims to provide a comprehensive pattern of awards whereby all certificated study and approved learning experience are accredited in a way which maximises the opportunities for citizens to progressively engage in education. The awards are structured on ten levels based on learning outcomes criteria.

The changed role of the Higher Education Authority, set out in the government's White Paper, *Charting Our Education Future*, also presaged new developments for the framework of higher education. The Institute of Technology Act 2006 has brought the DIT and the other ITs under the remit of the HEA. As with other areas of higher education policy, the issue of research has come under close scrutiny in a range of reports and policy documents from the early 1990s. This was against a backdrop of very inadequate funding of research allied to a serious underestimation of its significance for a developed country with aspirations for economic growth and social development. The analysis, diagnosis and prescriptions had been made and, crucially, the political, public and collegiate will were not found wanting with regard to strategic decisions in setting a new and dynamic agenda for high-level research. The Programme for Research in Third Level Institutions (PRTLI) was launched in 1998. This programme, which is managed by the HEA, has established a competitive framework for research bids by higher education institutions. It is now beginning its fourth cycle and has already expended well over €600m. This was part funded by the private sector, which is a recent trend in Irish education funding. The PRTLI focuses on building institutional capacity (physical and human capital) across a range of disciplines, and funds priority areas. The PRTLI has significantly improved the national research infrastructure and has made Ireland a more attractive location for world-class researchers. The improved research capacity has also attracted investments from other sources, such as the Framework Programmes of the EU. The PRTLI also encourages cross-institutional collaboration in research applications.

The minister for education and science set up two new research councils, which had been earlier recommended. These are the Irish Council for Science, Engineering and Technology (IRCSET) and the Irish Research Council for the Humanities and Social Sciences (IRCHSS). These councils operate a competitive research bidding process by individual researchers, or small clusters of researchers. A new agency, Science Foundation Ireland (SFI) was established to invest in basic research in economically strategic priority areas. The first two areas selected for SFI funding were biotechnology and ICT. The SFI has been very successful in attracting world-class scientists to work in Ireland, and in raising consciousness about the need for investment in science. Spending by the Health Research Board and Enterprise Ireland has also been increased. In its National Development Plan, 1996–2006, the Irish government allocated €2.5 billion to research, technology and innovation and in the National Development Plan for 2007–2013, €6.1 billion has been allocated for that purpose. Thus, over recent years, a dramatic change has occurred in research in higher education in terms of policy, funding and administration.

The era of mass higher education has brought forward a new emphasis on accountability, transparency and quality in the operation of higher education institutions. In 1995, the Conference of the Heads of Irish Universities (CHIU) took the initiative of establishing new forms of quality assurance within the universities. It developed a system whereby the work of departments and administrative units would, on a cyclical basis, be subject to self-appraisal reviews, monitored and publicly reported on by external peer reviewers. The Universities Act 1997 also had provisions for overall institutional reviews, which were conducted by the European Universities Association (EUA) on behalf of the HEA in 2004. The institutions have also set up quality promotion units, which engage in staff development activities. In 2003, the CHIU,

in association with the HEA, set up the Irish Universities Quality Board,
(IUQB) which acts as a guarantor of Irish university quality standards, and
liaises with similar international agencies. In 2005 CHIU transformed itself
into the Irish Universities Association (IUA), in which the seven universities
formulate and pursue collective policies. Quality assurance mechanisms
have tended to be well rooted in the traditions of the institutes of technolo-
gies, which had to comply with the evaluative requirements of the NCEA
and currently HETAC.

It can truly be maintained that higher education in Ireland has been
transformed during the 40 years since the Commission on Higher Education
reported in 1967. This is most strikingly evident in the expansion of student
numbers which have taken place. From very small numbers in the 1960s, full-
time students in higher education for the year 2004–5 numbered 135,360,
with a further 35,047 part-time students.[16] It is also manifested in the range of
new institutions which have emerged to accompany the then two universities
– the University of Dublin (TCD) and the federal National University of Ireland.
Massive infrastructure improvement has occurred, as well as a great diversification of courses, and new forms of teaching and learning and course
structure. A very impressive expansion of research has been linked to much
greater internationalism. A range of legislative enactments have been made
to underpin the new developments and to establish appropriate relationships between the state and the institutions. New governing structures now
operate in all institutions which involve modern accountability procedures.
Quality assurance processes are well established within the institutions. A
range of agencies with well-defined functions are in existence such as the
HEA; the NQAI with its two bodies HETAC and FETAC; the IUQB; the IUA;
the CDITs; the SFI; the IRCSET; and the IRCHSS.

Thus, when the OECD was invited to review Irish higher education in 2004,
it encountered a system which had undergone a great deal of change over a
relatively short timespan, and which was poised for further development in
the light of the government's strategic objective of 'placing its higher education system in the top ranks of the OECD'. The review team recognised the
achievement of the system in maintaining standards while engaged in an
impressive quantificatory expansion. However, it made a range of recommendations which, in its view, were needed if Ireland were to achieve its ambitious
higher education objectives in a highly competitive, global environment.

Among these was considerable further investment in higher education. The team's report also called for a more unified strategy for tertiary education which it considered would be effected by a new National Council for Tertiary Education, Research and Innovation, bringing together all relevant government departments. The report also called for further improvements in the governance and management of higher education institutions. It urged that the institutes of technology and the universities be brought together in a strategic framework, with clear differentiation of roles between the two sectors, under a new Tertiary Education Authority. The OECD team recommended increased autonomy for the institutions working under modernised management. It urged greater resourcing of research by government and industry and a unified framework for the disbursing of research funds. It sought an increase in postgraduate studies. The report made recommendations for the increase of adult and disadvantaged students within tertiary education, in the context of a declared policy of lifelong learning.[17] The recommendations of the OECD team have not been adopted as a cohesive framework, but they have affected policy in a variety of ways, and some of the recommendations seem likely to have long-term impact.

A major Irish university institution, the National University of Ireland, is celebrating its centenary in 2008. It emerged in 1908 as a federal university structure after a long and difficult policy gestation. Its birth coincided with, and was shaped by historical events which eventually led to political independence in 1922 for 26 counties of the island. It, and its constituent and recognised colleges, have played a very significant part in the shaping of modern Ireland. The National University and its colleges adapted and adjusted to the many developments and changed circumstances for higher education, over the last forty years. At the request of the NUI Senate, the Irish Universities Act of 1997 retained the federal concept of the National University but gave much greater autonomy to the four colleges under its aegis – UCD, UCC, UCG and Maynooth. The academic linkages between the National University and the colleges remained close and harmonious following the passing of the 1997 Act. However, certain tensions have been emerging more recently as legal clarification is sought on the relative authority of the NUI Senate and the four universities. It would seem that if the National University is to move into its second century that a new basis for its operation will need to be devised.

CHAPTER 17 *Coming to Terms with the 1997 Act: The National University of Ireland Senate, 1997–2007*

TOM DUNNE

T HROUGHOUT ITS FIRST hundred years the National University of Ireland has lived with threats of defection or dissolution. One of the architects of the 1908 Act, Bertram Windle, President of University College Cork, considered it as a mere stepping stone to the independent university status he had sought, and continued to seek (see chapter 4 above). He deeply resented the conflation of 'National' with 'Dublin', the ubiquity of which, on the other hand, made UCD enthusiastic supporters of the new system – until the late 1940s, when Michael Tierney became President and set out to abolish the NUI (described by Donal McCartney in chapter 6). He obtained the support of the Commission on Higher Education, which reported in 1967, and, in the wildly fluctuating proposals from a series of governments over the next 30 years, the abolition of the NUI was proposed in 1968, 1976 and in 1980. However, on the advice of the NUI Senate, supported by the presidents of the then constituent colleges and Maynooth, the NUI was retained in the 1997 Universities Act, which, at the same time, established the constituent colleges and Maynooth as independent universities. The Act was badly drafted in that it did not specify how this regime of newly independent institutions within a long-established federal system would operate.

Up to 1997 the NUI system had been held together by the exercise of significant powers by the Senate – notably of appointment to senior academic posts, including president – and by a pervasive sense of mutual interest and goodwill. The Senate elected in that year (to which I was co-opted) was acutely aware of the problems posed by the fact that, while the Act was clear about some of the powers transferred to the universities (e.g. of appointments), it had little to say about the residual powers of the NUI, and how they were to be reconciled with the independence of the universities. Under the chairmanship of the Chancellor, Dr Garret FitzGerald (elected in 1996, but a member of Senate for many years previously – see chapter 11 above), the Senate proceeded with pragmatism, caution and sensitivity. One of the powers specifically given to it by the act – 'reviewing the content and teaching of courses' – was not used; another, control of the external examiner system, is being devolved to the universities; and individual universities were facilitated in various ways over matriculation requirements. Senate focused its work on monitoring and improving the standards and compatibility of NUI degrees (as all degrees of the constituent universities were designated in the Act), on developing a new NUI qualifications framework, and on promoting scholarship through greatly enhanced studentships and fellowships, and through support for academic publishing.

The general environment in which the new universities operated also changed radically and rapidly around the same time (see chapter 16 above). The third-level sector had been expanded greatly to include seven universities, all of which were pitched into intense competition for research and capital funding, public and private, and for the best students from Ireland and abroad. Collective issues arising from this, from relations with government (which was now demanding greater accountability and radical restructuring), and with their funding agency, the Higher Education Authority, were now dealt with mainly through a new body, whose very name – the Conference of Heads of Irish Universities – reflected new realities, particularly the dominant role of university presidents. Perhaps for that reason it was renamed the Irish Universities Association in 2005. One of its initiatives, the Irish Universities Quality Board, set up to monitor and support the quality assurance schemes established by the individual universities, as required by the 1997 Act, oversaw far more elaborate procedures than the external examiner system of the NUI. University presidents, with their greatly enhanced executive powers, dominated their academic councils and governing bodies as never before. They were also greatly deferred to by Senate, but that body contained a range of independent constituencies and voices, and was not guaranteed to support them individually or collectively. Any challenge to presidential authority, however muted, was met with a response that underlined the difficulty of the Senate's position. A new type of president was emerging, chosen not solely on academic criteria, but because of links to business, or the ability to raise significant funding. Their ambition was to make their institutions 'world class', even if that was to be at the expense of other universities in the NUI family. Operating as they were under intense pressure, their instinct often appeared competitive rather than collaborative. During the decade when Senate was preoccupied with the future of the NUI, they used increasingly the language of the marketplace rather than the language of the university, emphasising the importance of 'the NUI brand', the need to demonstrate 'added value', and the role of various 'stakeholders'. Their focus was more and more elsewhere, and some of them made no secret of their impatience with the NUI and attended meetings rarely.

Similar trends and pressures were also experienced in other federal university systems at this time. An interesting comparison, as its ethos and operation have affinities with NUI, is the University of London. This year it is coming to terms with the constitution of Imperial College as an independent university, and several other of its most prestigious institutions – University College, London School of Economics and Political Science, and King's College – are set to follow Imperial's example. An argument can be made that such elaborate federal structures are unsuited to the modern university. The registrars of the NUI universities quoted Michael Shattock's *Managing Good Governance in Higher Education* (2006), that 'the difficulty has been to engage senate effectively with the wider strategy issues that affect the universities in a world where external pressures, changes in funding policies and new government initiatives are cumulative in effect, interrelated and demand detailed background knowledge to be understood'.[1] Senates may indeed be unsuited to dealing swiftly with some external strategic issues in the funding and political areas, but they are not needed, nor were they established, for that purpose. Presidents now have their 'management teams' and consultants, their business and political governors, and the IUA as a common managerial vehicle. But universities should not be all – or even primarily – about managing. Other 'strategic issues' will seem to most members of our universities to be even more important, such as the promotion of the highest quality of teaching and curriculum development, the encouragement of research and publishing, the leadership role of universities in the public sphere, and their contribution to the culture and ethos of their society. In Ireland the NUI has contributed significantly in such areas for a century, and has still much to offer, if a way can be found to harness the skills and energies of its members.

Despite the uncertainties about the reconstituted NUI, and the pressure on the universities to meet certain expectations, there was little overt conflict or disagreement during the first Senate of the new dispensation. Indeed, just as it was about to go out of office in late 2002, it gave a warm welcome to a document, 'The NUI Federal University in an Era of Transition', which made a series of recommendations to enhance the role and effectiveness of the Senate. It was produced by a sub-committee which I chaired, and which also included Professors John Coolahan and Sheelagh Drudy, with Dr John Nolan, the NUI Registrar, as convenor. We reviewed the statutory role and function of the NUI under the 1997 Act as then generally under-stood (by officers of the constituent universities as well as other members of Senate), and highlighted some of the solid, if unexciting, work done during the previous five years, during which, for example, after detailed statistical analysis, Senate had proposed to the universities reforms of the marking bands and performance indicators used in examinations, and these pro-posals were accepted, resulting in a higher proportion of high honours degrees. As Maurice Manning points out in chapter 11 above, the proposals that came from our sub-committee were mainly 'aspirational'. Among sug-gestions for enhancing the work of the NUI, we proposed the promotion of a greater sense of NUI identity among staff and students, partly by com-municating better with them. To that end, Senate decided on the publication of this report as a pamphlet, and its distribution to all academics in the constituent universities.[2]

There was little feedback, and this drew attention to a significant weak-ness of the NUI througout its history. Senior academic staff may have been NUI appointees up to 1997, and students still awarded NUI degrees, but neither identified strongly with the federal 'National' university in the way that they did with their home institution. One innovation proposed by the sub-committee and adopted by Senate was that Senate meetings (and a public NUI event in conjunction with it) should be held on a regular basis in each constituent university, and not always in Merrion Square. At the first ever Senate meeting in Cork in June 2005 (from which the host President absented him-self after giving a presentation on his plans for UCC), the Chancellor was urged to meet with the presidents to ascertain their views on the future of the NUI, reflecting mounting concern, particularly about the non-attendance of some presidents. This led to the establishment of a 'taskforce' to formulate the views of the universities, and this produced a document quite quickly. However, it was never given to Senate, because one of the presidents withdrew his consent.

While this report was awaited, the uneasy working consensus that had underpinned the work of the NUI since 1997 continued to be effective, despite occasional, non-specific complaints about NUI 'intrusion into the activities of the constituent universities', sometimes accompanied by assertions that the NUI universities had to be seen to be as independent as others in the IUA. This anxiety eventually focused on the issue of awarding honorary degrees, which after 1997 continued to be voted on by Senate. When some nominations by presidents were queried, the response (unlike on earlier occasions when this had happened) was an assertion of university autonomy. New procedures tightening up the process were approved by all, but UCD decided almost immediately to award a large number of honorary degrees in the K Club on the occasion of the Ryder Cup in September 2006, without reference to Senate or the Chancellor. UCD claimed (rather disingenuously, it later emerged) to have had strong legal advice on its competence to do this, and they were supported by the other presidents and registrars. The sense of crisis that had dogged the NUI for nine years was now acute, and public. The Chancellor and Senate continued to be conciliatory, effectively conceding the right of the universities to confer honorary degrees, while regretting the manner in which UCD had acted. For some members, such breaking of ranks seemed to be, in part, a consequence of the failure of Senate since 1997 to assert what it believed to be its statutory rights. Far from intruding into the internal affairs of the universities, it had given the impression that it would never challenge them.

At an Extraordinary Meeting of Senate, called to consider the issues arising from the UCD action, it was agreed that there was an urgent need for the NUI to obtain its own legal advice on this issue, and also on the implications of the 1997 Act generally. However, this was deferred, pending the production of a document by the registrars, which would 'finalise' the 'taskforce' report of January 2006. What they produced toned down the abrasive language of the original, but still asserted the independence of the universities, repeated (still unspecified) charges of 'intrusion' by the NUI, and proposed that all matters concerning academic standards be the sole concern of each university. It stressed that the universities 'wish to remain associated with [note – not 'part of'] the NUI', but even this very limited commitment was on the basis 'that the NUI transform itself to focus on a specific mission' – it might become, for example, 'an academy and educational trust dedicated to graduate education, research and scholarship in Irish language, literature and culture, with the potential to be a world leader in Irish Studies'.[3] In other words, the NUI could continue if it ceased to be, in any meaningful sense, the 'National University of Ireland'.

At this point, Senate finally decided to seek its own legal advice and it established a sub-committee to draw up a brief for senior counsel, and, in the light of the legal advice received, to report on the future of the NUI, the role of Senate and its relationship to the universities. Chaired by the Chancellor, it was composed of the registrars (or their nominees), Professor John Coolahan, Linda O'Shea Farren (member of Senate, Chair of Convocation, and a lawyer), Dr Séamus Mac Mathúna, and myself. The opinion of senior counsel, received in May 2007, was brutally frank, and devastating for those of us who had been arguing that the NUI continued to have statutory powers, especially in relation to the quality and comparability of NUI degrees. The legal opinion, instead, endorsed the view increasingly taken by the universities, its key findings being that, under the 1997 Act, the NUI had no statutory function in relation to degrees, had no power to ensure comparability, and while it could award honorary degrees, so could the constituent universities. In a nutshell, 'the [1997] Act has hollowed out the practical and functional jurisdiction of the NUI vis-à-vis the constituent universities, while leaving it in place as an institution'. The legal arguments put forward were so clear and compelling that the opinion was adopted unanimously by the sub-committee and later by the full Senate. The registrars agreed to draw up a new document in the light of the legal opinion, and of sub-committee and Senate discussions. This became the basis of the sub-committee report, once a series of amendments proposed by the Chancellor and others were accepted and incorporated.[4]

At a special meeting of Senate in September 2007, just before it went out of office, this report was welcomed and recommended to the incoming Senate for detailed consideration. The report was positive and conciliatory in tone, for the most part, envisaging a continuing role for the NUI by adapting the previous understanding of its remit to the new legal realities. It proposed 'a new relationship between the Senate and the constituent universities based on mutual respect', and acknowledged that both sides had 'at all times acted in good faith, based on different perceptions of the import of the Universities Act of 1997'. On the key issue, the report acknowledged a 'common interest in maintaining the high standards and comparability of NUI degrees' and recommended the setting up of a powerful education committee which would keep this under review and report regularly to Senate on this and other common academic interests. We also highlighted the issues on which legal advice had not yet been received, the most significant being matriculation, the relationship of the NUI with the recognised colleges, and its responsibilities in respect to statutory staff appointed before 1997. Unfortunately, the positive tone of the report was not echoed by the presidents when they spoke at the special meeting, though it had been our understanding that the document also represented their views.

During his speech when conferred with an honorary LLD by the NUI in October 2006, the Taoiseach, Bertie Ahern, stated that, 'the NUI Senate has been a strong binding force for the constituent universities down through the years, and its basic objectives are as relevant today as they were at its foundation'. Whether this can remain true into the future will depend, above all, on the attitude of the universities, and especially their presidents. They are under relentless pressure to deliver for their institutions in an ever more competitive and globalised environment, but they may come to realise that the NUI can offer a calm space for reflection, with colleagues from other universities, who have not only similar problems, but also common traditions and core values. Now that the contentious question of legal powers is resolved in their favour, and it is hoped that any basis of future conflict is removed, it is open to them to see the NUI as a resource rather than a restraint, especially in areas of academic development and co-operation, and as a valuable platform for their leadership role in Irish society, and in the search for international recognition. The opinion of senior counsel included the fact that Senate cannot simply transform itself by its own decision, for example into the academy or trust proposed at one stage by the universities. This, or abolition, would be a matter for government, who, in the process, would have an opportunity to revisit the 1997 Act, which the universities clearly do not want. If only for that reason, the NUI seems set to continue for the foreseeable future. The danger now, if a meaningful role is not developed and agreed over the lifetime of the next Senate, is that it will be allowed simply to wither on the vine, a travesty of a federal university, and a sad end to a century of significant achievement. Better far to wind the NUI up now with care and dignity.

At a time when universities in general are tied increasingly to government-imposed business models, this crisis in the NUI offers to its universities an opportunity to go back to the centuries-old proposition that a university should be, above all else, a *community* dedicated to scholarship and teaching. The NUI has been a distinctive, successful academic community for a century, based on a collaborative approach to achieving academic excellence and an international reputation for its members, both students and staff. With goodwill and imagination it can continue to be so, giving real 'added value', enhancing the 'NUI brand', adapting a great tradition to meet today's needs. That is the challenge facing the new Senate and I wish it well in the endeavour. It is, indeed, possible to envisage 'a dynamic future for the NUI' as the Taoiseach did in his address last year, but only if the opportunity that now offers is seized quickly and with enthusiasm.

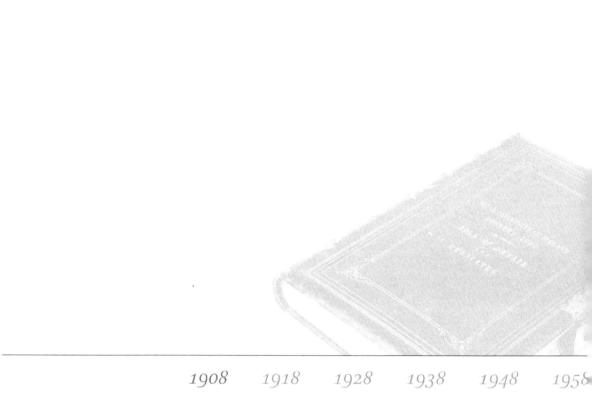

1908   1918   1928   1938   1948   1958

1968   1978   1988   1998   2008

Appendices

NATIONAL UNIVERSITY OF IRELAND NEW BUILDING.

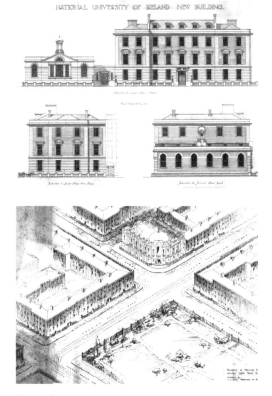

Figures 7,8 & 9 **The winning plans and artist's impression of the buildings proposed for the National University in 1914.**

APPENDIX I *NUI, 49 Merrion Square* ATTRACTA HALPIN

On its foundation, the National University of Ireland took over the buildings
of the Royal University in Earlsfort Terrace. In 1909, the Senate agreed to a
request from University College Dublin to make part of the building available
to the College;[1] before long the logic of UCD taking over the whole of the
Earlsfort Terrace building became apparent and ownership was transferred
to the College.[2] Numbers 48 and 49 Merrion Square were rented for the
National University of Ireland and the university relocated there in 1912.[3]
Initially this was intended as a temporary address and premises were acquired
in Upper Mount Street (numbers 55 to 62) and in Lower Fitzwilliam Street
(numbers 29 and 30) in 1914. Elaborate plans for a university building were
prepared and a competition for the design of extensive new premises on this
site was instituted, with Mr Charles J. McCarthy, city architect, as the assessor.[4] The scale of the proposed development (Senate Room of 1,800 square
feet and large meeting and examination hall of 5,000 square feet) reflects a
grandeur of vision not unlike that seen in the Senate House of the University of London. Interestingly, in light of the later controversy that would
surround the replacement of Georgian buildings in Fitzwilliam Street, it is
clear that the intention was to demolish and replace the houses purchased.
The instructions to competitors included the following:

> The style of the architecture and the materials to be employed are left to the
> discretion of the competitors, but it is essential that the building should be
> of good architectural character, expressive of its purpose and without
> unnecessary elaboration. It is desired that Irish materials shall be used as
> far as possible. The character of the surroundings generally should also be
> taken into account.

With the First World War casting its shadow, NUI agreed to a government
request to defer its building plans, even though a winner of the competition
had by then been selected (see plates opposite). In the changed circumstances

of the foundation of the Irish state and a reappraisal of the accommodation needs of the university, the plans for a new building were abandoned. The houses which had been purchased by the university were handed over to the state and the potential demolitions were avoided.[5]

In 1927, the Merrion Square premises were purchased by the National University of Ireland[6] and accordingly 49 Merrion Square became the permanent address of the university. NUI has been fortunate to have been housed since 1912 in such handsome Georgian buildings and in such a convenient central location.

Situated on the east side of the square, number 49 was built by George Kent some time between the 1790s and 1814. The house was leased in 1818 by Sir Robert Way Harty who was later elected Lord Mayor of Dublin. He is generally credited with having commissioned the mural paintings which are such an important feature of the house. Noting the 'elegant scheme of mural paintings in the two first-floor rooms *c*.1820', Christine Casey, in her authoritative study of the buildings of Dublin, comments that 'these are the most ambitious c19 painted interiors in Dublin'.[7] The murals completely cover the walls of the two rooms from the dado upwards, the mural or murals on each wall being set in illusionistic wooden frames.

A study of the paintings undertaken by Marguerite O'Farrell in 1976[8] shows that the sources and inspirations for the Italianate landscape scenes with classical and mythological references were works by a number of artists including Claude Lorrain and Rubens. Noting that the paintings were rediscovered in 1946, she identifies seven sources for the murals in the front room, as follows: on the north wall (plates 93 and 94), a scene in a panoramic Arcadian setting with dancers and musicians is based on the painting *Il Molino* by Claude Lorrain (1600–82), now in the Doria Pamphilj Gallery, Rome; on the south wall (plate 95), the mural again features musicians in a landscape and is based on the painting Pastoral Landscape also by Claude; the charming mural in one of the fireplace recesses showing a woman holding child under a tree (plate 96) is based on the work of Salvatore Rosa (1615–73); of two murals on the east wall, one of cattle at water (plate 97) is influenced by an engraving of The Watering Place by Peter Paul Rubens (1577–1640), now in the National Gallery, London while the other showing a group of soldiers in armour beside a lake (plate 98) is from a painting by Jacques Courtois in the series 'I Banditti'.

The two murals on the west wall are in a genre style, one (plate 99) from

Plates 96–112
Nineteenth-century murals of Italianate landscape scenes in the NUI building,
49 Merrion Square. See appendix I, pp. 291–3.

93

94

95

96

97

98

99

100

101

102

103

104

105

106

107

108

109

an engraving by Pierre Charles Canot of the painting *Le Soleil levant c.*1759 by Jean Baptiste Pillement (1728–1808) and the second mural (plate 100) is based on the work of Nicholaes Berchem (1620–83), engravings of whose work were widely circulated in the eighteenth century.

O'Farrell also identifies the sources of most of the eight murals in the back room. Again she associates – though not definitively – with Nicholaes Berchem the large mural that fills the north wall (plates 101 and 102), showing an Italian town with castelled buildings in a leafy setting by a river with fishing boats. The Italian landscape mural above the mantelpiece on the south wall (plates 103 and 104) is, according to O'Farrell, taken from the painting *Castel Gandolfo* by Gian Francesco Grimaldi (1606–80). In the recess beside the fireplace facing the door is a landscape with figures based on the style of Jan de Wynants (1625–84) (plate 105). O'Farrell notes that 'the foreground figures of this mural seem to be painted by a completely different hand to the rest of the cycle'.

In the other recess, the painting (plate 106) is based on *The Father of Psyche Sacrificing at the Temple of Apollo* by Claude. O'Farrell conjectures, based on some modifications of the original and stylistic similarities which the mural shares with a version of the work by the English engraver Richard Earlom (1743–1822), that the muralist worked from this version.

The mural on the right of the east wall window (plate 107) shows a landscape with figures, one on horseback and according to O'Farrell is similar in style to the work 'I Banditti' by Jacques Courtois in the same position in the front room as described above. The painting to the left of the window features classical figures in a hillside landscape. The surface shows the effects of water damage suffered in the early 1990s but was successfully conserved in 2001.

O'Farrell notes that two murals on the west wall on either side of the folding doors (plates 108 and 109) 'appear to be in the style of Jacques Courtois and to have Ovidian themes'.

In scale and quality, the cycle of mural paintings in 49 Merrion Square is unique in Dublin and is significant in terms of the Georgian heritage of interior decoration. Since they now form part of working offices, these paintings are largely hidden treasures. However, as far as is practicable, NUI is committed to granting access to these delightful works: visits are regularly arranged for art historians and other scholars and access for the general public is provided on particular occasions such as Heritage Week.

APPENDIX II *Chancellors 1908–present*

Upon the dissolution of the Royal University, the National University of Ireland came into being, established by Charter in 1908. The first Chancellor of the new University was appointed and Convocation, in accordance with University Statutes, has elected all subsequent chancellors.

His Grace the Most Revd William J. Walsh
DD, Archbishop of Dublin; appointed 2 December 1908; elected Chancellor 17 December 1908; died in office 9 April 1921.

Éamon de Valéra
BA, BSc, LLD, PhD, ScD, FRC, elected 19 December 1921; died in office 29 August 1975.

Thomas K. Whitaker
DEconSc, elected 5 May 1976; resigned 31 December 1996.

Garret FitzGerald
PhD, MRIA, elected 15 October 1997.

APPENDIX III *Vice-Chancellors 1909–present*

The Senate at its meeting on 10 December 1914 decided that the President of each of the Constituent Colleges (or Constituent Universities since 1997) should be elected to the position of Vice-Chancellor, in rotation every two years.

Sir Christopher Nixon, Bart. (subsequently a Privy Councillor), MD, LLD, 11 November 1909–19 July 1914.

Sir Bertram C. A. Windle, MA, MD, DSc, LLD, FRS, President, University College Cork, 10 December 1916–6 December 1918.

Alexander Anderson, MA, DSc, LLD, President, University College Galway; 10 December 1914–10 December 1916; 16 December 1920–31 December 1922; 1 January 1927–31 December 1928; 1 January 1933–resigned 10 October 1934.

Denis J. Coffey, MA, MB, BCh, BAO, DSc, LLD, FRCPI, President, University College Dublin; 16 December 1918–6 December 1920; 1 January 1925–31 December 1926; 1 January 1931–31 December 1932; 1 January 1937–31 December 1938.

Rt Revd Monsignor John Hynes, MA LLD BD (Mayn), President, University College Galway; 1 January 1939–31 December 1940.

Patrick J. Merriman, MA, LLD, President, University College Cork, 1 January 1923–31 December 1924; 1 January 1929–31 December 1930; 1 January 1935–31 December 1936; 1 January 1941–31 December 1942.

Arthur W. Conway, MA, DSc, ScD, LLD, FRS, President, University College Dublin; 1 January 1943–31 December 1944; and 1 January 1945 to 31 December 1945.

Alfred O'Rahilly, MA, DSc, DPhil, DLitt (subsequently Revd Alfred O'Rahilly), President, University College Cork; 1 January 1946–31 December 1947; 1 January 1952–31 December 1953.

Rt Revd Monsignor Patrick J. Browne, MA, DSc (*An Dr Pádraig de Brún*), President, University College Galway; 1 January 1948–31 December 1949; 1 January 1954–31 December 1955.

Michael Tierney, KSG, MA, DLitt, President, University College Dublin; 1 January 1950–31 December 1951; 1 January 1956–31 December 1957; 1 January 1962–30 September 1964.

Henry St. J. Atkins, DSc, President, University College Cork; 1 January 1958–31 December 1959; 1 January 1960 to 31 December 1960.

Máirtín Ó Tnúthail, DSc, President, University College Galway; 1 January 1961–31 December 1961; 1 January 1967–31 December 1968; 1 January 1973–31 December 1974.

John J. McHenry, MA (Cantab), DSc, FInstP,

MRIA, President, University College Cork,
1 October 1964–31 December 1966.

Jeremiah J. Hogan, KSS MA BLitt (Oxon) DLitt,
President, University College Dublin;
1 January 1969–31 December 1970.

Michael D. McCarthy, MA, PhD, DSc, LLD, President, University College Cork; 1 January 1971–
31 December 1972; 1 January 1977–4 June 1978.

Thomas Murphy, MD, FRCPI, President, University
College Dublin; 1 January 1975–31 December
1976, 1 January 1981–31 December 1982.

Tadhg Ó Ciardha, MA, PhD, President, University
College Cork; 13 July 1978–31 December
1978, 1 January 1983–31 December 1984.

Colm Ó hEocha, MSc, PhD, President, University
College Galway; 1 January 1979–31 December
1980; 1 January 1985–31 December 1986;
1 January 1991–31 December 1992.

Patrick Masterson, MA, PhD LLD, President,
University College Dublin; 1 January 1987–26
January 1989; 1 January 1993–3 February 1993.

Michael P. Mortell, MSc, PhD, President, University

College Cork: 26 January 1989–31 December
1990; 4 February 1993–31 December 1994.

Art Cosgrove, BA, PhD, President, University
College Dublin; 1 January 1995–31 December
1996; 1 January 2003–31 December 2003.

Patrick P. Fottrell, DSc, PhD, MRIA, President,
National University of Ireland, Galway;
1 January 1997–31 December 1998.

William J. Smyth, BA, PhD, President, National
University of Ireland, Maynooth; 1 January
1999–31 December 2000.

Gerard T. Wrixon, BE, MS (Caltech), PhD (Calif),
FREng, FIEEE, MRIA, President, UCC; 1 January
2001–31 December 2002.

Iognaid Ó Muircheartaigh, MA, PhD, President,
National University of Ireland, Galway;
1 January 2004–31 December 2005.

John G. Hughes, BSc, PhD, FBCS, President,
National University of Ireland, Maynooth;
1 January 2006–31 December 2007.

Michael Murphy, MD, FRCPI, President, University
College Cork; 1 January 2008–present.

APPENDIX IV *Pro-Vice-Chancellors 1909–present*

Each of the presidents of the Constituent
Colleges (or Constituent Universities since 1997)
acts as Pro-Vice-Chancellor for the University.

Sir Bertram C. A. Windle, MA, MD, DSc, LLD, FRS,
President, University College Cork; 22 December 1909–9 December, 1916; 6 December
1918–21 November 1919.

Rt Revd Monsignor J. F. Hogan, DD, President,
St. Patrick's College, Maynooth; 10 December
1914; resigned 18 October 1918.

Alexander Anderson, MA, DSc, LLD, President,
University College Galway; 22 December
1912–10 December 1914; 10 December 1916–
1 January 1921; 1 January 1923–31 December
1926; 1 January 1929–31 December 1932.

Rt Revd Monsignor James MacCaffrey, LLD,
President, St. Patrick's College, Maynooth;
12 December 1918–1 November 1935.

Denis J. Coffey, MA, MB BCh BAO, LLD, DSc,

FRCPI, President, University College Dublin;
6 December 1920–31 December 1924; 1 January
1927–31 December 1930; 1 January 1933–31
December 1936; 1 January 1939–31 March 1940.

Rt Revd Monsignor John F. D'Alton, MA, DLitt, DD
(Subsequently Most Revd John F. D'Alton, MA,
DLitt, DD, Archbishop of Armagh and Primate
of All-Ireland, later His Eminence, John F. Car-
dinal D'Alton), President, St. Patrick's College,
Maynooth; 22 October 1936–3 July 1942.

Patrick J. Merriman, MA, LLD, President, University College Cork; 16 December 1919–31 December 1922; 1 January 1925–31 December 1928;
1 January 1931–31 December 1934; 1 January
1937–31 December 1940; 1 January 1943.

Rt Revd Monsignor John Hynes, MA, LLD, BD,
President, UCG; 25 October 1934–31 December
1934; 1 January 1935–31 December 1936;
1 January 1937–31 December 1938.

Arthur W. Conway, MA, DSc, ScD, LLD, FRS,

President, UCD; 18 April 1940–31 December 1942; 1 January 1946–2 October 1947.

Rt Revd Monsignor Edward Kissane, DLitt, DD, LSS, LLD, President, St. Patrick's College, Maynooth; 22 October 1942–21 February 1959.

Alfred O'Rahilly, MA, DSc, DPhil, DLitt (subsequently Revd Alfred O'Rahilly), President, University College Cork; 28 October 1943–31 December 1945; 1 January 1948–31 December 1951; 1 January 1954–19 September 1954.

Rt Revd Monsignor Patrick J. Browne, MA, DSc (*An Dr Pádraig de Brún*), President, University College Galway; 18 April 1945–31 December 1947; 1 January 1950–31 December 1953; 1 January 1956–31 December 1959.

Michael Tierney, KSG, MA, DLitt, President, University College Dublin; 30 October 1947–31 December 1949; 1 January 1952–31 December 1955; 1 January 1958–31 December 1961.

Henry St J. Atkins, DSc, President, University College Cork; 28 October 1954–31 December 1957; 1 January 1962–17 October 1963.

Rt Revd Monsignor Gerard Mitchell, BA, DD, President, St. Patrick's College, Maynooth; 9 July 1959–27 November 1967.

Máirtín Ó Tnúthail, DSc, President, UCG; 7 July 1960–31 December 1960; 1 January 1962–31 December 1966; 1 January 1969–31 December 1972; 1 January 1975–1 September 1975.

John J. McHenry, MA (Cantab), DSc, FInstP, MRIA, President, UCC; 9 January 1964–30 September 1964; 1 January 1967–9 June 1967.

Jeremiah J. Hogan, KSS, MA, BLitt (Oxon), President, UCD; 29 October 1964–31 December 1968; 1 January 1971–21 April 1972.

Michael D. McCarthy, MA, PhD DSc, LLD, President, University College Cork; 1 September 1967–31 December 1970; 1 January 1973–31 December 1974; 1 January 1975–31 December 1976.

Rt Revd Monsignor Patrick J. Corish, MA, DD, President, St. Patrick's College, Maynooth; 11 January 1968–12 October 1968.

Rt Revd Monsignor Jeremiah Newman, MA, DPh, LLD, President, St. Patrick's College, Maynooth; 1 January 1969–21 June, 1974.

Thomas Murphy, MD, FRCPI, FRCSI, DSc, President, UCD; 13 July 1972–31 December 1974; 1 January 1977–31 December 1980; 1 January 1983–3 December 1985.

Rt Revd Monsignor Tomás Ó Fiaich, MA (subsequently Most Revd Tomás Cardinal Ó Fiaich, Archbishop of Armagh and Primate of all Ireland), President, St. Patrick's College, Maynooth; 11 July 1974–31 October 1977.

Tadhg Ó Ciardha, MA, PhD, LLD, President, UCC; 1 January 1979–31 December 1982; 1 January 1987–31 December 1988.

Colm Ó hEocha, MSc, PhD, President, UCG; 11 December 1975–31 December 1978; 1 January 1981–31 December 1984; 1 January 1987–31 December 1990; 1 January 1993–30 June, 1996.

Rt Revd Monsignor Michael G. Olden, DHistEccl, President, St. Patrick's College, Maynooth, co-opted 8 November 1977–21 March 1985.

Rt Revd Monsignor Mícheál Ledwith, BA, LPh, DD, President, St. Patrick's College, Maynooth; 5 June 1985–27 July 1994.

Patrick Masterson, MA, PhD, President, UCD; 30 January 1986–31 December 1986; 1 January 1989–31 December 1993.

Michael Mortell, MSc, PhD, President, University College Cork-National University of Ireland, Cork; 1 January 1991–31 December 1992; 1 January 1995–26 January 1999.

Art Cosgrove, BA, PhD, President, University College Dublin-National University of Ireland, Dublin; 1 January 1994–31 December 1994; 1 January 1997–31 December, 2002.

William J. Smyth, BA, PhD, Master, St. Patrick's College, Maynooth; 27 July, 1994–31 December 1998; appointed President, National University of Ireland, Maynooth, 16 June 1997–31 December 1998, 1 January 2001–21 June 2004.

Patrick P. Fottrell, DSc, PhD, MRIA, President, University College Galway; 1 July 1996–31 December 1996; 1 January 1999–31 July 2000.

Gerard T. Wrixon, BE, MS (Caltech), PhD (Calif), appointed President, University College Cork, 27 January 1999–31 December 2000;

1 January 2003–1 February 2007.

Iognáid Ó Muircheartaigh, MA, PhD appointed President, NUI, Galway, August 2000–31 December 2003; 1 January 2006–6 March 2008.

Hugh Brady, MB BCh BAO, BSC, PhD, MD, FRCPI, President, University College Dublin, 1 January 2004–31 December 2004.

John G. Hughes, BSc, PhD, FBCS *(from 21 June 2004)* President, National University of Ireland, Maynooth; 21 June 2004–31 December 2005; 1 January 2008–present.

Michael Murphy, MD FRCPI *(from 1 February 2007)* President, University College Cork; 1 February 2007–31 December 2007.

APPENDIX V *Registrars 1908–present*

Joseph McGrath (subsequently Sir Joseph McGrath), LLD, appointed 2 December 1908–15 March 1923.

Frederick H. Wiber, LLD, appointed by Senate, 1 February 1924–11 July 1936.

Alexander A. McCarthy, BA, LLD, appointed by Senate, 28 October 1937–3 August 1952.

Séamus Wilmot, BA, BComm, HDip in Ed, LLD, appointed by Senate, 11 December 1952–4 May 1972.

John Bourke, MComm, PhD, LLD appointed by Senate, 27 January 1972, appointed to date from 4 May 1972–9 June 1979.

Michael Gilheany, BA, BComm, MEconSc, LLD, appointed by Senate June 1979–24 January 1987.

John Nolan, MA, MPA, LLD, appointed by Senate 1 September 1987–27 February 2004.

Attracta Halpin, BA MSc (Dub), MBA (Lond), LLD, appointed by Senate 11 March 2004.

APPENDIX VI *Members of Senate 1908–present*

Current members of Senate are set in **Bold Italic**

Alton, Bryan G., MD, BSc, elected by Convocation, 10 October 1964; term of office expired 31 October 1972.

Anderson, Alexander, MA, DSc, LLD, President, University College Galway; appointed 2 December 1908; resigned 10 October 1934.

Andrews, Christopher S., BComm, DEconSc, nominated by the Government, 20 October 1959; re-nominated 28 October 1964; re-nominated 17 November 1972; resigned as from 25 July 1977.

Atkins, Henry St. J., BSc, elected by the Governing Body, University College Cork; 25 January 1944, *vice* Alfred O'Rahilly, MA DSc, DPhil, an *ex officio* member; re-elected 18 October 1944; re-elected 17 October 1949; re-elected 15 October 1954; appointed President, University College Cork; 28 October 1954;

retired from Presidency, 17 October 1963.

Bacon, John W., MA, elected by the Governing Body, University College Dublin, 13 October 1914; re-elected 16 October 1919; re-elected 17 October 1924; re-elected 16 October 1929; re-elected 17 October 1934.

Barniville, Senator Henry L., BA, MD, MCh, elected by Convocation, 13 October 1934; elected by the Governing Body, University College Dublin, 17 October 1939; elected by Convocation, 13 October 1944; re-elected 14 October 1949; re-elected 16 October 1954; re-elected 10 October 1959.

Barrett, Very Revd Michael Canon, DPhil, appointed *vice* Very Revd Andrew Canon Murphy, 5 August 1914; term of office expired 31 October 1914.

Barry, David T., MD, DSc, DPH, FRCS, Eng, elected by the Governing Body, University College Cork, *vice* the late John P. Molohan,

MA, 7 May, 1915; term of office expired
31 October 1919.

Barry, John D., BE, MSc, PhD, CEng, nominated
by the Government, 17 November 1972;
re-nominated 2 November 1977.

Barry, Patrick D., MSc, PhD, elected by the
Governing Body, University College Cork;
13 October 1977; term of office expired
October 1982.

Barton, The Hon. Mr Justice (subsequently
The Rt Hon. Sir Dunbar Plunket Barton, Bart.),
MA, appointed 2 December 1908; term of
office expired 31 October 1914; reappointed
by H.M. the King, 31 October 1914; reappointed
31 October 1919; resigned 7 January 1923.

Bhreathnach, Helen, BA, elected by Convocation, 15 October 1997, term of office expired
31 October 2002.

Boland, Maurice, DSc, MAgrSc, PhD; elected
by Governing Authority, UCD, 2007.

Bourke, Geoffrey J., MA, MD, FRCPI, FFCM,
FFCMI, elected by the Governing Body,
University College Dublin, 16 October 1987;
term of office expired 31 October 1992.

Bourke, John, MComm, PhD, LLD, appointed
Registrar of the University as from 4 May
1972; term of office expired 9 June 1979.

Bourke, His Honour Judge Matthew J., MA, KC,
Recorder of Cork, appointed *vice* Samuel H.
Butcher, LLD, M.P., 2 January 1912; term of
office expired 31 October 1914.

Boylan, Rt Revd Monsignor Patrick J., MA, DLitt,
DD, elected by Convocation, 13 October
1934; re-elected 13 October 1939; re-elected
13 October 1944; re-elected 14 October
1949; nominated by the Government,
27 October 1954; term of office expired
31 October 1959.

Boyle, Gerard, elected by the Governing Body,
National University of Ireland, Maynooth,
9 October 2002; resigned 5 December 2006.

Brady, Hugh, MB BCh BAO, BSC, PhD, MD,
FRCPI, appointed President of University
College Dublin-National University of
Ireland, Dublin, 1 January 2004.

Breatnach, Risteárd A., MA, MRIA, co-opted
by Senate, 9 January 1964, *vice* the late
James Hogan, DLitt, co-opted 13 November
1964; co-opted again 10 November 1972;
term of office expired 31 October 1977.

Brennan, Alderman Thomas, elected by the
Governing Body, University College Dublin,
11 October 1977; term of office expired
31 October 1982.

Brophy, Brendan, elected by the Governing
Body, University College Dublin, 17 October
1972; term of office expired 31 October
1977.

Browne, James, BE, MEngSc, PhD (Manc),
DSc (Manc), FIEI, Registrar, NUI, Galway;
elected by the Governing Body, National
University of Ireland Galway 1 February
2001. Re-elected 10 October 2002; re-elected
by the Governing Body, National University
of Ireland Galway, 2007.

Browne, Revd Michael J., BA, DD, DCL, LLD
(subsequently Most Revd Michael J.
Browne, Bishop of Galway), appointed by
the Executive Council, 23 October 1934;
nominated by the Government, 1 November
1939; renominated 17 November 1944;
renominated 22 October 1949; renominated
27 October 1954; renominated 20 October
1959; renominated 28 October 1964;
renominated 17 November 1972; resigned
2 August 1976.

Browne, Rt Revd Monsignor Patrick J., MA DSc
(*An Dr. Pádraig de Brún*), elected by Convocation, 7 October 1924; term of office expired
31 October 1929; re-elected 13 October
1934; re-elected 13 October 1939; term of
office expired 31 October 1944; appointed
President, University College Galway,
18 April 1945; retired from Presidency
13 October 1959; nominated by the
Government 20 October 1959.

Burnell, Ann, MSc, PhD. Elected by the Governing Body, National University of Ireland,
Maynooth, 9 October, 2002.

Busteed, John, MComm, elected by the

Governing Body, University College Cork, 27 June 1944, *vice* the late Joseph Downey, MComm, re-elected 18 October 1944; re-elected 17 October 1949; re-elected 15 October 1954; term of office expired 31 October 1959.

Butcher, Samuel H., LLD, MP, appointed 2 December 1908.

Butler, Michael, BA, ACIS, nominated by the Government, 10 November 1992; term of office expired 31 October 1997.

Butler, Sir William F. (subsequently a Privy Councillor), appointed 2 December 1908.

Butler, William F. T., MA, appointed 2 December 1908; resigned 2 November 1910.

Canny, Nicholas P., MA, PhD, co-opted as Member of Senate, 4 November 1987; term of office expired 31 October 1992.

Carr, Peter F., BSc, PhD, elected by Convocation, 15 October 1992; elected by the Governing Body, National University of Ireland, Maynooth, 29 October 1997; resigned January 2001.

Chance, Sir Arthur, FRCSI, appointed *vice* the late Rt Hon. Sir Christopher Nixon, Bart., MD, LLD, 19 August 1914; term of office expired 31 October 1914.

Coakley, James B., MSc, MD, elected by the Governing Body, University College Dublin, 17 October 1972; re-elected 11 October 1977; re-elected 18 October 1982; re-elected 16 October 1987; term of office expired 31 October 1992.

Coffey, Denis J., MA, MB, BCh, BAO, LLD, DSc, FRCPI, KCSS, President, University College Dublin; appointed 2 December 1908; retired from Presidency, 31 March 1940; elected by the Governing Body of University College Dublin, 25 June 1940; re-elected 17 October 1944.

Coffey, Patrick, ME, AMInstCE, elected by the Governing Body, University College Cork, 10 April 1964, *vice* Dr. John J. McHenry, who was appointed President, University College Cork; term of office expired 31 October 1964.

Comerford, Richard V., MA, PhD, elected by

the Governing Body, National University of Ireland, Maynooth, 29 October 1997, term of office expired 31 October 2002.

Coolahan, John, MA MEd PhD, co-opted as Member of Senate, 6 November 1997. Elected by the Governing Body, National University of Ireland, Maynooth 9 October 2002.

Concannon, Senator Helena, MA, DLitt, appointed by the Executive Council, 23 October 1934; nominated by the Government, 1 November 1939; re-nominated 17 November 1944; re-nominated 22 October 1949.

Conran, Matthew J., MA, DSc, elected by Convocation, 7 October 1924; re-elected 12 October 1929; term of office expired 31 October 1934.

Conway, Arthur W., MA, DSc, ScD, LLD, FRS, appointed 2 December 1908; term of office expired 31 October 1914; re-elected by the Governing Body, University College Dublin, 13 October 1914; re-elected 16 October 1919; re-elected 17 October 1924; re-elected 16 October 1929; re-elected 17 October 1934; re-elected 17 October 1939; appointed President of University College Dublin, 18 April 1940; retired from Presidency 2 October 1947.

Conway, Edward J., MD, DSc, FRCPI, FRS (*vice* Professor M. Tierney, appointed President, University College Dublin), elected by Convocation, 31 January 1948; re-elected 14 October 1949; re-elected 16 October 1954; term of office expired 31 October 1959.

Corcoran, Mary, PhD; co-opted November 2007.

Corcoran, Revd Timothy, SJ, DLitt, HDip in Ed, elected by the Governing Body, University College Dublin, 17 October 1924; re-elected 16 October 1929; re-elected 17 October 1934; re-elected 17 October 1939.

Corish, Rt Revd Monsignor Patrick J., MA, DD, President, St. Patrick's College, Maynooth, co-opted as Member of Senate *vice* Rt Revd Monsignor Gerard Mitchell, BA, DD, 11 January 1968; resigned, 12 October 1968.

Corry, Siobhán, nominated by the Government, 19 February 2008.

Cosgrove, Art, BA, PhD, elected by the Governing Body, University College Dublin, 16 October, 1987; re-elected 16 October 1992; appointed President, University College Dublin, 1 January 1994; retired from Presidency 31 December 2003.

Cox, Michael F., MD, LLD, FRCPI, appointed December 2nd, 1908; term of office expired 31 October 1914; re-appointed by H.M. the King, 31 October 1914; re-appointed 31 October 1919; re-appointed by the Executive Council, 25 November 1924.

Crawford, Revd William, MA, appointed 2 December 1908; term of office expired 31 October 1914.

Cronin, Very Revd Michael Canon, MA, DD (Subsequently Rt Revd Monsignor Cronin), appointed by the Executive Council *vice* the late Michael F. Cox., MD, LLD, FRCPI, 19 December 1928; re-appointed 18 July 1929; term of office expired 31 October 1934.

Cunningham, John F., MD, MAO, FRCOG, elected by Convocation, 10 October 1959; term of office expired 31 October 1964.

Curran, Michael P., MSc, elected by the Governing Body, University College Galway, 14 October 1977, re-elected 15 October 1982; term of office expired 31 October 1987.

Curtis, Ruth, MA, PhD, co-opted as Member of Senate, 15 January 1998. Elected by the Governing Body, National University of Ireland, Galway 10 October 2002 until 31 January 2005.

D'Alton, Very Revd E.A. Canon, LLD, elected by the Governing Body, UCG, 8 October 1914, resigned 9 January 1919.

D'Alton, Rt Revd Monsignor John F., MA, DLitt, DD (subsequently *His Grace Most Revd John F. D'Alton*, Archbishop of Armagh and Primate of All Ireland, later His Eminence, John F. Cardinal D'Alton), elected by Convocation, 7 October 1919; term of office expired 31 October 1924; appointed President of

St. Patrick's College, Maynooth, 1936; co-opted as Member of Senate *vice* the late Rt Revd Monsignor J. MacCaffrey, LLD, 22 October 1936; co-opted 16 November 1939; resigned 3 July 1942.

D'Arcy, Fergus, MA, PhD, FRHistS, elected by the Governing Body, University College Dublin, 19 December 1995; re-elected 15 October 1997; re-elected 16 October 2002.

de Bhaldraithe-Marsh, Clíona, BA, MA, elected by Convocation, 15 October 1997; elected by the Governing Body, University College Dublin–NUI Dublin 16 October 2002; elected by Convocation, 11 October 2007.

Delany, Revd William, SJ, LLD, appointed 2 December 1908; term of office expired 31 October 1914; co-opted as Member of Senate, 18 November 1914; term of office expired 31 October 1919.

Dempsey, Alexander (subsequently Sir Alexander Dempsey), MD, appointed 2 December 1908; term of office expired 31 October 1914.

de Valera, Éamon, BA, BSc, HDip in Ed, LLD, PhD, ScD, FRS, elected Chancellor, 19 December 1921.

de Valera, Ruaidhrí, MA, PhD, elected by Convocation, 12 October 1972; re-elected 13 October 1977.

Dinan, Thomas J., DipinEd, MSc, co-opted as Member of Senate, 26 November 1959; term of office expired 31 October 1964.

Donovan, Patrick F., MA, elected by the Governing Body, University College Dublin, 17 October 1944; re-elected 29 November 1949; term of office expired 31 October 1954.

Donovan, Robert, DLitt, elected by the Governing Body, University College Dublin, 13 October 1914; re-elected 16 October 1919; re-elected 17 October 1924; re-elected 16 October 1929; term of office expired 31 October 1934.

Doonan, Shawn, co-opted as Member of Senate, 4 November 1987; term of office expired 31 October 1992.

Dowdall, James C., LLD, elected by the Governing Body, University College Cork, June 1923; *vice* Daniel J. O'Connor, MA, MD, resigned; term of office expired 31 October 1924; re-elected 10 October 1924; re-elected 11 October 1929; re-elected 13 October 1934; died 27 June 1939.

Downes, Martin J., MAgrSc, PhD, elected by Convocation, 15 October 1997.

Downey, Joseph, MComm, elected by the Governing Body, University College Cork, 11 October 1929; re-elected 13 October 1934; re-elected 13 October 1939.

Doyle, Kay, MA, nominated by the Government 11 November 1997; term of office expired 31 October 2002.

Drudy, Sheelagh, MA, PhD, elected by the Governing Body, National University of Ireland, Maynooth, 29 October 1997; term of office expired 31 October 2002.

Drumm, James J., DSc, elected by Convocation, October 13th, 1934; re-elected 13 October 1939; re-elected 13 October 1944; re-elected 14 October 1949; re-elected 16 October 1954; term of office expired 31 October 1959.

Duggan, Miss Lucy, MA, PhD, nominated by the Government, 6 July 1952, *vice* the late Senator Helena Concannon, MA, DLitt, re-nominated 27 October 1954; re-nominated 31 October 1959; re-nominated 28 October 1964; term of office expired 31 October, 1972.

Duignan, Michael V., MA, elected by the Governing Body, University College Galway, 2 March 1971; re-elected 11 October 1972; term of office expired 31 October 1977.

Dundon, John, MB BCh BAO, FRCSI & E, elected by the Governing Body, University College Cork, 11 October 1929; re-elected 13 October 1934; term of office expired 31 October 1939.

Dunne, Thomas J., MA, PhD, co-opted as Member of Senate, 6 November 1997; co-opted as Member of Senate 7 November 2002.

Fahy, Edward F., MSc, PhD, elected by the Governing Body, University College Cork, 12 October 1972; term of office expired 31 October 1977.

Fanning, J. Ronan, BA; elected by Governing Authority, UCD, November 2007.

Fee, Revd Thomas J., MA, LicHistSc (Ó Fiaich, Monsignor Tomás S.). (subsequently His Eminence, Tomás Cardinal Ó Fiaich, Archbishop of Armagh and Primate of All Ireland), elected by Convocation, 10 October 1964; term of office expired 31 October 1972; President, St. Patrick's College, Maynooth, 1974; co-opted as Member of Senate 11 July 1974; term of office expired 31 October 1977.

Finlay, Revd Thomas A, SJ, MA, elected by Convocation, 6 October 1914; term of office expired 31 October 1919; co-opted as Member of Senate, 13 November 1919; term of office expired 31 October 1924.

FitzGerald, Denis P., BA, MB BCh BAO, elected by the Governing Body, University College Cork, March, 1920, *vice* P.J. Merriman, MA, elected President, University College Cork; term of office expired 31 October 1924.

FitzGerald, Garret, BA, PhD, TD, elected by Convocation, 12 October 1972; re-elected 13 October 1977; re-elected 14 October 1982; re-elected 16 October 1987; re-elected 15 October 1992; elected Chancellor of the University by Convocation, 15 October 1997.

Flavin, James N., MSc, PhD, elected by the Governing Body, University College Galway, 30 April 1980 *vice* Declan M. Larkin, MSc, PhD, resigned; re-elected 15 October 1982; re-elected 29 October 1987; term of office expired 31 October 1992.

Flood, Chris, nominated by the Government 14 February 2003; resigned 2006

Flood, John C., BA, BComm, MD, MCh, elected by Convocation, 13 October 1939; term of office expired 31 October 1944.

Fottrell, Patrick, DSc, PhD MRIA, elected by the Governing Body, University College Galway, 20 October 1987; re-elected 16 October 1992; appointed President, University College Galway, 1 July 1996; retired 31 July 2000.

Francis, Thomas, MA, nominated by the

Government, January 1989; term of office expired 31 October 1992; elected by Convocation, 15 October 1997; re-elected 16 October 2002; re-elected 11 October 2007.

Gallagher, Eamonn J., MAgrSc, PhD, elected by the Governing Body, University College Dublin, 16 October 1987; re-elected 16 October 1992; term of office expired 31 October 1997.

Gantly, Joe, BEng (Dub), MBA; elected by Governing Authority UCC, 2007.

Gavan-Duffy, Louise, MA, LLD, elected by Convocation, 7 October 1919; term of office expired 31 October 1924.

Gilheany, Michael, BA, BComm, MEconSc, LLD, appointed Registrar of the University, 10 June 1979.

Gill, Thomas P., appointed *vice* Rt Hon. Sir William F. Butler, GCB, 25 November 1910; term of office expired 31 October 1914.

Giller, Paul, BSc (Lond); Registrar, UCC; co-opted, 21 April 2005; co-opted November 2007

Gilmartin, His Grace The Most Revd Thomas P., DD, Archbishop of Tuam, elected by the Governing Body, University College Galway, *vice* Very Revd E.A. Canon D'Alton, LLD, 6 May 1919; term of office expired 31 October 1919; re-elected 14 October 1919; re-elected 10 October 1924; re-elected 16 October 1929; re-elected 14 October 1934.

Gwynn, Revd Aubrey, SJ, MA, BLitt (Oxon), elected by the Governing Body, University College Dublin, 16 October 1954; term of office expired 31 October 1959.

Gwynn, Stephen L., BA, DLitt, appointed 2 December 1908; resigned 12 January 1912.

Hackett, Felix E. W., MA, MSc, PhD, appointed by the Executive Council, 23 October 1934; nominated by the Government, 1 November 1939; re-nominated 17 November 1944; re-nominated 22 October 1949; term of office expired 31 October 1954.

Hall, William J., MSc, MD, PhD, co-opted as Member of Senate, 2 November 1992; term of office expired 31 October 1997.

Halpin, Attracta, BA, MSc (Dub), MBA (Lond), LLD *ex-officio*, appointed Registrar, NUI, 11 March 2004.

Hanafin, Mary, BA, TD, nominated by the Government, January 1989; re-nominated 10 November 1992; elected by the Governing Body, National University of Ireland, Maynooth, 29 October 1997.

Harrington, Sir Stanley, BA, appointed 2 December 1908; term of office expired 31 October 31 1914.

Hayden, Mary T., MA, appointed 2 December 1908; term of office expired 31 October 1914; re-appointed by H.M. the King, 31 October 1914; re-appointed 31 October 1919; term of office expired 31 October 1924.

Hayes, Senator Michael, MA, HDip in Ed, BL, nominated by the Government, 27 October 1954; co-opted as Member of Senate, 26 November 1959; co-opted 13 November 1964; term of office expired 31 October 1972.

Healy, His Grace The Most Revd John, DD, LLD, Archbishop of Tuam, appointed 2 December 1908; term of office expired 31 October 1914.

Hegarty, Anthony F., PhD, BSc, FRSC, MRIA, elected by the Governing Body, University College Dublin, 16 October 1992; re-elected 15 October 1997; re-elected 16 October 2002.

Herity, Michael, MA, PhD, elected by Convocation, 13 October 1977; term of office expired 31 October 1982; elected by the Governing Body, University College Dublin, 16 October 1987; re-elected 16 October 1992; term of office expired 31 October 1997.

Hoey-Heffron, Angela, BCL, LLB, elected by Convocation 16 October 2002

Hogan, James, BA, DLitt, co-opted by Senate, 16 November 1939; co-opted 17 November 1944; co-opted 7 December 1949; co-opted 12 November 1954; co-opted 26 November 1959.

Hogan, Jeremiah J., KSS, MA, BLitt (Oxon), DLitt, elected by Convocation, 13 October 1944; re-elected 14 October 1949; elected by the Governing Body, University College

Dublin, 16 October 1954; re-elected 17 November 1959; appointed President, University College Dublin, October 29th, 1964; retired April 21st, 1972.

Hogan, Very Revd John F. Canon, DD (subsequently Rt Revd Monsignor Hogan), President, St. Patrick's College, Maynooth; appointed *vice* His Grace, The Most Revd Daniel Mannix, DD, LLD, February 12th, 1913; term of office expired October 31st, 1914; co-opted as Member of Senate, November 18th, 1914; resigned October 18th, 1918.

Hogan, Michael A., BE, DSc, PhD, elected by the Governing Body, University College Dublin, October 16th, 1954; re-elected November 17th, 1959; re-elected January 5th, 1965.

Honan, Cathy, BComm, nominated by the Government, 11 November 1997; nominated by the Government, 14 February 2003.

Horgan, Michael C., BSc (Dub), MIE; Registrar, RCSI; co-opted November 2002; co-opted November 2007.

Horgan, Rt Revd Monsignor John D., MA, PhD, DD, elected by the Governing Body, University College Dublin, 22 October 1952, *vice* the late Professor John J. Nolan, MA, DSc; elected by Convocation, 16 October 1954; re-elected 10 October 1959; re-elected 10 October 1964; term of office expired 31 October 1972.

Houghton, James A., BSc, PhD, MFH, elected by the Governing Body of National University of Ireland, Galway, 10 October 2002; re-elected by the Governing Body of National University of Ireland, Galway, November 2007

Hughes, John G., BSc, PhD, FBCS (*from 21 June 2004*) President, National University of Ireland, Maynooth

Hurley, John Robert, BA, HDip in Ed; elected by Convocation, 11 October 2007

Hussey, E. Caroline, PhD, elected by Convocation, 14 October 1982; re-elected 14 October 1987; re-elected 15 October 1992; elected by the Governing Body, University College

Dublin-National University of Ireland, Dublin, 16 October 2002.

Hyde, Douglas, LLD, DLitt (subsequently President of Ireland), appointed 2 December 1908; term of office expired 31 October 1914; elected by Convocation, 6 October 1914; term of office expired 31 October 1919.

Hynes, Rt Revd Monsignor John, MA, BD, elected by the Governing Body, University College Galway, 14 October 1919; re-elected 10 October 1924; re-elected 16 October 1929; appointed President, University College Galway, 25 October 1934; retired from Presidency 5 January 1945.

Kearney, Philip, nominated by the Government, 19 February 2008.

Keenan, Edward, MD, co-opted 11 April 1957, *vice* the late Professor John McGrath, MD; elected by the Governing Body, University College Dublin, 17 November 1959.

Kelly, John, PhD, elected by the Governing Body, University College Dublin, 18 October 1982; co-opted as Member of Senate 4 November 1987; co-opted 2 November 1992; elected by Convocation, 15 October 1997; term of office expired 31 October 2002.

Kennedy, Maurice, MSc, PhD, elected by the Governing Body, University College Dublin, 17 October 1972; co-opted as Member of Senate, 8 November 1977; term of office expired 31 October 1982. *Kenny, Mr. Justice John J.*, MA, LLB, elected by Convocation, 10 October 1964; term of office expired 31 October 1972.

Kiely, Patrick, MD, MCh, BSc (Pádraig Ó Cadhla), elected by Convocation, 13 October 1934; re-elected 13 October 1939; re-elected 13 October 1944; re-elected 14 October 1949; elected by the Governing Body, University College Cork, 15 October 1954; re-elected 15 October 1959; re-elected 13 October 1964; term of office expired 31 October 1972.

Kissane, Rt Revd Monsignor Edward, DLitt, DD, LSS, President, St. Patrick's College, Maynooth, co-opted as Member of Senate,

16 July 1942, *vice* Most Revd John F. D'Alton, MA, DLitt, DD, Bishop of Meath, resigned; co-opted 17 November 1944; co-opted 7 December 1949; co-opted 12 November 1954; 21 February 1959

Larkin, Declan M., MSc, PhD, co-opted 15 January 1976; elected by the Governing Body, University College Galway, 14 October 1977; resigned 31 January 1980.

Lawton, Richard R., MA, elected by Convocation, 12 October 1929; term of office expired 31 October 1934.

Ledwith, Rt Revd Monsignor Mícheál, BA, LPh, DD, President, St. Patrick's College, Maynooth; co-opted as Member of Senate, 5 June 1985, *vice* Rt Revd Monsignor Michael G. Olden, resigned; co-opted as Member of Senate, 4 November 1987; co-opted 2 November 1992; resigned 27 July, 1994.

Lee, J. Joseph, MA, elected by Convocation, 15 October 1992; term of office expired 31 October 1997.

Lucey, Denis I. F., BAgrSc, MSc, PhD, elected by the Governing Body, University College Cork, 13 October 1977; re-elected 18 October 1982; re-elected 16 October, 1987; re-elected 15 October 1992; re-elected 14 October 1997; re-elected 13 November 2003.

Lynch, Mrs Celia, BA, BComm, nominated by the Government, 17 November 1972; re-nominated 2 November 1977; term of office expired 31 October 1982.

Lynch, Patrick, MA, elected by Convocation, 12 October 1972; term of office expired 31 October 1977.

MacAodhagáin, Revd Aindrias, CSSp, MA, elected by Convocation, 10 October 1959; re-elected 10 October 1964.

McArdle, John S., MCh, FRCSI, appointed 2 December 1908; term of office expired 31 October 1914.

MacCaffrey, Very Revd James Canon, LLD (subsequently Rt Revd Monsignor MacCaffrey) President, St. Patrick's College, Maynooth;

co-opted as Member of Senate *vice* Rt Revd Monsignor J.F. Hogan, DD, 12 December 1918; co-opted 13 November 1919; co-opted 13 November 1924; co-opted 14 November 1929; co-opted 13 November 1934.

McCann, John, appointed by the Executive Council *vice* the late Rt Hon. Laurence A. Waldron, 2 May 1924; term of office expired 31 October 1924; re-appointed 25 November 1924; re-appointed 18 July 1929; term of office expired 31 October 1934.

McCartney, Donal, MA, PhD, elected by the Governing Body, University College Dublin, 11 October 1977; re-elected 18 October 1982; re-elected 16 October 1987; term of office expired 31 October 1992.

McCarthy, Alexander A., BA, LLD, appointed Registrar of the University by Senate, 28 October 1937.

McCarthy, Matthew F., PhD, DSc, co-opted as Member of Senate, 2 November 1992; elected by the Governing Body, National University of Ireland, Galway, 28 October 1997; term of office expired 31 October 2002.

McCarthy, Michael D., MA, PhD, DSc, LLD, appointed President, University College Cork, 1 September 1967; retired 4 June 1978.

McCarvill, Eileen M. L. (*née* McGrane), MA, HDip in Ed, elected by Convocation, 7 October 1924; re-elected 12 October 1929; re-elected 13 October 1934; term of office expired 31 October 1939.

McClelland, John A., MA, DSc, FRS, appointed 2 December 1908; term of office expired 31 October 1914; elected by Convocation, 6 October 1914; term of office expired 31 October 1919; co-opted as Member of Senate, 13 November 1919.

MacCormac, Michael, MA, MComm, DEconSc, elected by the Governing Body, University College Dublin, 11 October 1977; re-elected 18 October 1982; term of office expired 31 October 1987.

McDermott, Edward N., BSc, MD, MCh, elected by the Governing Body, University College

Galway, 17 October 1959; re-elected
15 October 1964; term of office expired
31 October 1972.

McDonagh, Revd Michael E., BSc, LPh, DD,
elected by Convocation, 12 October 1972;
re-elected 13 October 1977; re-elected 14
October 1982; re-elected 14 October 1987;
re-elected 15 October 1992; term of office
expired 31 October 1997.

McDowell, J. Moore, BA, MA, elected by the
Governing Authority, UCD, November 2007.

Mac Enri, Seaghan P., MA, MD, elected by the
Governing Body, University College Galway,
vice the late Alfred Senier, MD, PhD, DSc,
15 October 1918; term of office expired
31 October 1919; re-elected 14 October 1919;
re-elected 10 October 1924; re-elected
16 October 1929.

McGilligan, Patrick, MA, DEconSc, HDip in Ed,
elected by Convocation, 7 October 1919; re-
elected 7 October 1924; re-elected 12 October
1929; term of office expired 31 October 1934.

MacGiollarnath, Proinnsias, MA, LLB, elected
by the Governing Body, University College
Galway, 11 October 1972; term of office
expired 31 October 1977.

McGrath, John, MSc, MD, elected by Convocation, 14 October 1949; co-opted 12 November
1954.

McGrath, Joseph (subsequently *Sir Joseph
McGrath*), LLD, Registrar; appointed
2 December 1908.

MacHale, Joseph P., BA, MComm, ACA, elected
by the Governing Body, University College
Dublin, 17 April 1962, *vice* the late Professor
Edward Keenan, MD; re-elected 5 January
1965; term of office expired 31 October 1972.

McHenry, John J., MA (Cantab), DSc, FInstP,
MRIA, elected by the Governing Body,
University College Cork, 17 October 1949;
re-elected 15 October 1954; re-elected
15 October 1959; appointed President,
University College Cork, 9 January 1964;
retired from Presidency, 9 June 1967.

McHugh, Roger J., MA, PhD, elected by

Convocation, 16 October 1954;
re-elected 10 October 1959; re-elected
10 October 1964; term of office expired
31 October 1972.

McKenna, Anne T., MPsychSc, PhD, nominated
by the Government, 5 November 1982; term
of office expired 31 October 1987.

McKenna, Brian, BE, MEngSc, CEng,
MIChemE, elected by the Governing Body,
University College Dublin, 16 October 1992;
term of office expired 31 October 1997.

McKenna Lawlor, Susan, MSc, PhD, elected
by Convocation, 15 October 1997; term of
office expired 31 October 2002.

McLaughlin, Revd Patrick J.I., MSc, DesSc,
elected by Convocation, 16 October 1954;
term of office expired 31 October 1959.

McLaughlin, Edward P., BA, MD, elected by
the Governing Body, University College
Dublin, 17 October 1934; re-elected
17 October 1939; term of office expired
31 October 1944.

MacNeill, John, BA, DLitt, appointed
2 December 1908; term of office expired
31 October 1914; elected by Convocation,
7 October 1919; term of office expired
31 October 1924.

McNulty, Paul B., BE, MSc, PhD, elected
by Convocation, 15 October 1992; term
of office expired 31 October 1997.

McWalter, James C., MA, MD, LLD, elected
by Convocation, 6 October 1914; term of
office expired 31 October 1919.

McWeeney, Henry C., MA, appointed 2 December
1908; term of office expired 31 October
1914; elected by Convocation, 6 October
1914; term of office expired 31 October
1919; co-opted as Member of Senate,
13 November 1919; co-opted 13 November
1924; co-opted 14 November 1929;
co-opted 13 November 1934.

Madden, Therese J., BSocSc, DASS, CQSW, MSW,
elected by Convocation 16 October 2002.

Magennis, Alexander J., MEconSc, FSAA,
elected by the Governing Body,

University College Cork, 13 October 1939; term of office expired 31 October 1944.

Magennis, William, MS, DLitt, KCSS, appointed 2 December 1908; term of office expired 31 October 1914; elected by the Governing Body, University College Dublin, 13 October 1914; re-elected 16 October 1919; re-elected 17 October 1924; re-elected 16 October 1929; re-elected 17 October 1934; term of office expired 31 October 1939; nominated by the Government, 14 October 1942, re-nominated 17 October 1944.

Maguire, Anita, BSc, PhD, elected by Governing Authority UCC, November 2007

Maguire, Thomas, appointed 2 December 1908; resigned 7 May 1913.

Maguire, William, BA, MD, FRCPI, DipMental Diseases, appointed *vice* Thomas Maguire, 17 June 1913; term of office expired 31 October 1914.

Malone, Revd John F., BA, elected by Convocation, 13 October 1977; term of office expired 31 October 1982.

Manning, Maurice, MA, DLitt, elected by Convocation, 14 October 1982; re-elected 14 October 1987; re-elected 15 October 1992; re-elected 15 October 1997; re-elected 16 October 2002; re-elected 11 October 2007.

Mannix, Rt Revd Monsignor Daniel, DD, LLD (subsequently Archbishop of Melbourne); appointed 2 December 1908; resigned 18 January 1913.

Martin, Augustine, MA, PhD, elected by Convocation, 14 October 1982; re-elected 14 October 1987; elected by the Governing Body, University College Dublin, 16 October 1992.

Masterson, Patrick P., MA, PhD, elected by Convocation, 12 October 1972; re-elected 13 October 1977; elected by the Governing Body, University College Dublin, 18 October 1982; appointed President, University College Dublin, 30 January 1986; retired 31 December, 1993.

Meenan, James F., MA, MRIA, FREconSc, BL,

elected by Convocation, 16 October 1954; re-elected 10 October 1959; elected by the Governing Body, University College Dublin, 5 January 1965, re-elected 17 October 1972; term of office expired 31 October 1977.

Meenan, Patrick N., MD, FCPath, elected by the Governing Body, University College Dublin, 11 October 1977; re-elected 18 October 1982; term of office expired 31 October 1987.

Meredith, James Creed, MA, DLitt, KC (subsequently Mr. Justice Meredith), appointed by the Executive Council, 18 July 1923, *vice* The Rt Hon. Sir D. Plunkett Barton, Bart, MA, KC, resigned; term of office expired 31 October 1924; re-appointed by the Executive Council, 25 November 1924; re-appointed 18 July 1929; re-appointed 23 October 1934; re-appointed 1 November 1939.

Merriman, Patrick J., MA, elected by Convocation, 16 October 1914; elected by the Governing Body, University College Cork, 11 October 1919; appointed President, University College Cork, 16 December 1919.

Mitchell, Rt Revd Monsignor Gerard, BA, DD, President, St. Patrick's College, Maynooth, co-opted as Member of Senate, *vice* the late Rt Revd Monsignor Edward Kissane, DLitt, DD, LSS, 9 July 1959; co-opted 26 November 1959; co-opted 13 November 1964; resigned 27 November 1967.

Mitchell, James, BE, BSc, FGS, LLD, elected by the Governing Body, University College Galway, 13 April 1937, *vice* the late Most Revd Thomas O'Doherty, DD, Bishop of Galway; re-elected 12 October 1939; re-elected 17 October 1944; re-elected 14 October 1949; re-elected 16 October 1954; re-elected 17 October 1959; re-elected 15 October 1964; term of office expired 31 October, 1972.

Molohan, John P., MA, appointed *vice* William F.T. Butler, MA, 25 November 1910; term of office expired 31 October 1914; elected by the Governing Body of University College Cork, 16 October 1914.

Monahan, Rosemary, BSc, MSc, elected by the Governing Authority, NUI, Maynooth, November 2007

Moran, M. Aidan, MSc, PhD, elected by the Governing Body, UCC, 15 October 1992; re-elected 14 October 1997; co-opted as Member of Senate 7 November 2002.

Morgan, Pat, BSc, PhD, elected by the Governing Body of National University of Ireland, Galway, 10 October 2002; re-elected by the Governing Authority of National University of Ireland, Galway, November 2007

Morrisroe, Most Revd Patrick, DD, Bishop of Achonry, elected by the Governing Body, University College Galway, January, 1940, *vice* His Grace the Most Revd Thomas P. Gilmartin, DD, Archbishop of Tuam, deceased; term of office expired 31 October 1944.

Mortell, Michael P., MSc, MS, PhD, co-opted as Member of Senate, 9 November 1982; elected by the Governing Body, University College Cork, 16 October 1987; appointed President, University College Cork, 26 January 1989; retired 26 January 1999.

Mulcahy, Máire F., MSc, PhD; elected by the Governing Body, University College Cork, 16 October 1987; term of office expired 31 October 1992.

Mulligan, Frank J., BSc, PhD, co-opted as Member of Senate, 7 November 2002; resigned November 2006

Murphy, Revd Andrew (subsequently Canon Murphy), appointed 2 December 1908.

Murphy, John A., MA, elected by Convocation, 14 October 1982; re-elected 14 October 1987; re-elected 15 October 1992; term of office expired 31 October 1997.

Murphy, Michael B., MB, BCH, BAO, MD, President, UCC, as of 1 February 2007

Murphy, Thomas, MD, DPH, BScPH, FRCPI, LLD, DSc, elected by Convocation *vice*, Senator H.L. Barniville, 15 April 1961; elected by the Governing Body, University College Dublin, 5 January 1965; appointed President, University College Dublin, 13 July 1972;

retired as President, 3 December 1985.

Nevin, Thomas E., DSc, elected by Convocation, 10 October 1959; elected by the Governing Body, University College Dublin, 5 January 1965; co-opted 10 November 1972; term of office expired, 31 October 1977.

Newman, Rt Revd Monsignor Jeremiah, MA, DPh, LLD (subsequently Most Revd Jeremiah J. Newman, Bishop of Limerick), President, St. Patrick's College, Maynooth, co-opted as Member of Senate *vice* Rt Revd Monsignor Patrick J. Corish, MA, DD, 4 November 1968, co-opted 10 November 1972; resigned 21 June 1974.

Ní Chinnéide, Máire, BA, appointed by the Executive Council, 25 November 1924; re-appointed 18 July 1929; term of office expired 31 October 1934.

Nixon, Sir Christopher, Bart. (subsequently a Privy Councillor), MD, LLD, appointed 2 December 1908.

Nolan, John A., MA, MPA, LLD, appointed Registrar of the University, 1 September 1987; retired 27 February 2004.

Nolan, John J., MA, DSc, elected by Convocation, 7 October 1924; term of office expired 31 October 1929; elected by the Governing Body, University College Dublin, 8 May 1939, *vice* the late John W. Bacon, MA; term of office expired 17 October 1939; re-elected 17 October 1944; re-elected 29 November 1949.

Nolan, Philip, MB BCh BAO, BSc, PhD, Registrar, UCD; co-opted November 2007

Nolan, Thomas J., BA, DSc, elected by the Governing Body, University College Dublin, 17 October 1944.

O'Beirne, Thomas C., MA, HDip in Ed (*Tomas C. O'Beirn*), elected by Convocation, 12 October 1929; term of office expired 31 October 1934.

Ó Briain, Liam, MA, DLitt, co-opted by Senate, 7 December 1949; co-opted 12 November 1954; term of office expired 31 October 1959.

O'Brien, Senator George A.T., DLitt, co-opted

15 April 1948, *vice* the late Professor J.M. O'Sullivan, MA, PhD, term of office expired 31 October 1949; elected by the Governing Body, University College Dublin, 16 October 1954; re-elected 17 November 1959; term of office expired 31 October 1964.

Ó *Broiméil, Sean A.*, BA, nominated by the Government, 5 November 1982; re-nominated January 1989; term of office expired 31 October 1992.

Ó *Buachalla, Senator Liam*, MComm, HDip in Ed, elected by Convocation, 13 October 1934; term of office expired 31 October 1939; elected by the Governing Body, University College Galway, 17 October 1959; re-elected 15 October 1964.

Ó *Cadhlaigh, Cormac*, MA, elected by Convocation, 13 October 1934; re-elected 13 October 1939; term of office expired 31 October 1944; elected by the Governing Body, University College Dublin, 26 June 1945; re-elected 29 November 1949; term of office expired 31 October 1954.

O'*Carroll, Joseph F.*, MD, MCh, LLD, FRCPI, appointed 2 December 1908; term of office expired 31 October 1914; co-opted as Member of Senate, 18 November 1914; term of office expired 31 October 1919.

Ó *Céidigh, Pádraig*, MSc, PhD; elected by the Governing Body, University College Galway, 20 October 1987; re-elected 16 October 1992; re-elected 29 January 1998; term of office expired 31 October 2002.

Ó *Cinnéide, Séamus*, BA, MSocSc, elected by Convocation, 16 October 2002.

Ó *Ciardha, Tadhg*, MA, PhD, LLD, elected by the Governing Body, University College Cork, 15 October 1959; re-elected 13 October 1964, re-elected 12 October 1972; re-elected 13 October 1977; appointed President, University College Cork, 13 July 1978; retired 31 December 1988.

Ó *Coileáin, Seán*, BA, MA, AM (Harv), PhD (Harv), MRIA, elected by the Governing Body, University College Cork, 15 October

1992; re-elected 14 October 1997; re-elected 13 November 2002; elected by Convocation 11 October 2007.

O'*Connell, Augustine J.*, MComm, elected by the Governing Body, University College Dublin, 26 June 1945; re-elected 28 November 1949; term of office expired 31 October 1954.

O'*Connell, Sir John R.*, MA, LLD, KCSG, elected by the Governing Body, University College Cork, 10 October 1924; term of office expired 31 October 1929.

O'*Connor, Charles A.*, MA, KC (subsequently Master of the Rolls), appointed 2 December 1908; term of office expired 31 October 1914.

O'*Connor, Daniel J.*, MA, MD, FRCPI, elected by the Governing Body, University College Cork, 16 October 1914; re-elected 9 October 1919; resigned 4 February 1923. O'*Connor, Geraldine F.*, BComm, Barrister-at-Law, elected by Convocation, 15 October 1997; term of office expired 31 October 2002.

O'*Connor, James M.*, BA, MD, DSc, elected by the Governing Body, University College Dublin, October 17th, 1944; re-elected November 29th, 1949; re-elected October 16th, 1954; term of office expired October 31st, 1959.

O'*Dea, Most Revd Thomas*, DD, Bishop of Galway, appointed *vice* Stephen Gwynn, BA, 30 December 1912; term of office expired 31 October 1914; re-elected by the Governing Body, University College Galway, 8 October 1914; re-elected 14 October 1919.

O'*Doherty, Most Revd T.*, BA, DD, Bishop of Galway, elected by the Governing Body, University College Galway, 11 October 1923, *vice* the late Most Revd T. O'Dea, DD; term of office expired 31 October 1924; re-elected 10 October 1924; re-elected 16 October 1929; re-elected 14 October 1934.

O'*Donnell, John*, ME, BSc, MIChemE, elected by the Governing Body, University College Dublin, 17 October 1972; term of office expired 31 October 1977.

O'*Donnell, Michael*, MEconSc, BE, nominated

by the Government, 14 December 1979, *vice* John D. Barry, BE, MSc, PhD, deceased; re-nominated 5 November 1982; term of office expired 31 October 1987.

O'Donovan, Daniel G., MSc, PhD, elected by the Governing Body, University College Cork, 18 October 1982; term of office expired 31 October 1987.

O'Donovan, James M., MSc, MD, FRCP, elected by the Governing Body, University College Cork, 13 October 1939; re-elected 18 October 1944; term of office expired 31 October 1949.

O'Dwyer, Edward M., MAO, FRCOG, elected by the Governing Body, University College Galway, 11 October 1972; co-opted as Member of Senate 8 November 1977; elected by the Governing Body, University College Galway, 15 October 1982; term of office expired 31 October 1987.

O'Farrelly, Agnes M. W. (Una Ní Fhaircheallaigh), MA, DLitt, elected by Convocation, 6 October 1914; term of office expired 31 October 1919; re-elected 7 October 1924; re-elected 12 October 1929; term of office expired 31 October 1934; re-elected by Convocation, 13 October 1944; term of office expired 31 October 1949.

Ó Fathaigh, Mairtín, BA, MEd, PhD, nominated by the Government, 11 November 1997; term of office expired 31 October 2002.

O'Flynn, Bartholomew, BA, BE, elected by the Governing Body, University College Cork, 16 October 1914; re-elected 9 October 1919; term of office expired 31 October 1924.

Ó hÉideáin, Revd Eustás, OP, MA, DD, elected by the Governing Body, University College Galway, 14 October 1977; co-opted as Member of Senate 9 November 1982; term of office expired 31 October 1987.

Ó hEocha, Colm, MSc, PhD, LLD, elected by the Governing Body, University College Galway, 20 January 1972; co-opted as Member of Senate 10 November 1972; appointed President, University College Galway, 11 December 1975; retired

30 June 1996; died 19 May, 1997.

O'Keeffe, Very Revd Denis Canon, MA, DD, elected by Convocation, 13 October 1939; re-elected 17 November 1944; re-elected 14 October 1949.

O'Keeffe, John D., BE, PhD, elected by the Governing Body, University College Galway, 11 October 1972; re-elected 14 October 1977; re-elected 15 October 1982; re-elected 20 October 1987; term of office expired 31 October 1992.

O'Kelly, William.D., MD, DPH, elected by Convocation, 7 October 1919; term of office expired 31 October 1924.

Olden, Rt Revd Monsignor Michael G., DHistEccl, President, St. Patrick's College, Maynooth, co-opted as Member of Senate 8 November 1977; co-opted 9 November 1982; resigned 21 March 1985.

O'Leary, Eleanor, PhD, FRSI, IACT, IAHIP, HDipinEd, elected by the Governing Body of University College Cork 13 November 2002.

O'Mahony, Revd Brendan, OFMCap, MA, PhD, co-opted as Member of Senate 8 November 1977; term of office expired 31 October 1982.

O'Mahony, Very Revd Edward, OFMCap, MA, DLitt, nominated by the Government, 8 July 1946; re-nominated 22 October 1949; term of office expired 31 October 1954; elected by the Governing Body, University College Cork, 26 January 1955, *vice* Dr. H. St. J. Atkins, an *ex-officio* member; re-elected 15 October 1959.

O'Mahoney, Dermot F., elected by Governing Authority UCC, November 2007

Ó Máille, Tomás, DLitt, elected by the Governing Body, University College Galway, 27 June 1930, *vice* the late Seaghan P. MacEnri, MA, MD: re-elected 14 October 1934.

O'Malley, Kevin, MD, PhD, DSc, FRCPF, FRCP (Glas), FRCPI, co-opted as Member of Senate, 6 November 1997; co-opted as Member of Senate 7 November 2002.

Ó Mathúna, Seán, MA, PhD, nominated by the Government, 2 November 1977; re-nominated

5 November 1982; re-nominated January
1989; re-nominated 10 November 1992;
term of office expired 31 October 1997.

O'Meara, John J., MA, DPhil (Oxon), elected by
Convocation, 10 October 1964; term of
office expired 31 October 1972.

Ó Muircheartaigh, Iognáid, MA, PhD, elected
by the Governing Body, University College
Galway, 6 December 1996; re-elected
28 October 1997; appointed President,
National University of Ireland, Galway
1 August, 2000.

Ó Muirithe, Diarmaid, PhD, elected by
Convocation, 14 October 1982; term
of office expired 31 October 1987.

O'Neill, Patrick J., elected by the Governing
Body, University College Dublin, 13 October
1914; re-elected 16 October 1919; term of
office expired 31 October 1924.

O'Rahilly, Alfred, MA, DSc, DPhil, DLitt (subsequently Revd Alfred O'Rahilly) elected by
Convocation, 7 October 1919; term of office
expired 31 October 1924; elected by the
Governing Body, University College Cork,
10 October 1924; re-elected 11 October 1929;
re-elected 13 October 1934; re-elected
13 October 1939; appointed President,
University College Cork, 28 October 1943;
retired from Presidency, 19 September 1954.

O'Regan, Ronan, MB BCh BAO, MD, BSc, PhD,
MRIA, elected by the Governing Body,
University College Dublin,15 March 1994;
re-elected 15 October 1997; term of office
expired 31 October 2002.

Ó Riain, Senator Eoin, BA, SC, nominated by
the Government, 21 September 1960, *vice*
the Rt Revd Monsignor Pádraig de Brún, BSc,
deceased; re-nominated 28 October 1964;
term of office expired 31 October 1972.

O'Riordan, Mary, MB BCh BAO, DCH, FPC,
MPH, elected by convocation, 11 October
2007.

Ó Rodaighe, Aodhagán, MSc, PhD, elected by
the Governing Body, UCG, 16 October 1992;
term of office expired 31 October 1997.

O'Shea Farren, Linda, BCL, elected by
Convocation 16 October 2002; re-elected
by Convocation 11 October 2007.

Ó Súilleabháin, Micheál, BA, BComm, BacScOec,
DrScPol, elected by the Governing Body,
University College Cork, 15 October 1992;
re-elected 14 October 1997. Elected by Convocation 16 October 2002.

O'Sullivan, Bernadine, BA, HDip in Ed; elected
by Convocation 11 October 2007.

O'Sullivan, Denis J., MD, FRCP, elected by the
Governing Body, University College Cork,
12 October 1972; term of office expired
31 October 1977.

O'Sullivan, Elizabeth M., MA, elected by
Convocation, 7 October 1919; term of office
expired 31 October 1924; co-opted as
Member of Senate, 13 November 1924;
co-opted 14 November 1929; co-opted
13 November 1934; term of office expired
31 October 1939.

O'Sullivan, John M., MA, PhD, co-opted by
Senate, *vice* the late Henry C. McWeeney, MA,
5 December 1935; co-opted 16 November
1939; co-opted 17 November 1944.

O'Sullivan, Patrick T., MD, BCh, MRCP
(Lond), appointed 2 December 1908; term
of office expired 31 October 1914; elected
by the Governing Body, University College
Cork, 16 October 1914; term of office
expired 31 October 1919; re-elected by the
Governing Body, University College Cork,
14 December 1923, *vice* Timothy Smiddy,
MA, resigned; re-elected 10 October 1924;
term of office expired 31 October 1929.

Ó Tuama, Seán, MA, PhD, elected by the
Governing Body, University College Cork,
16 October 1987; term of office expired
31 October 1992.

Ó Tuathaigh, Gearóid, MA, elected by the
Governing Body, University College Galway,
16 October 1992; re-elected 28 October 1997;
term of office expired 31 October 2002.

Ó Tnúthail, Máirtín, DSc, LLD, appointed
President, University College Galway, 7 July

1960; retired 1 September 1975.

Palles, The Rt Hon. Christopher, LLD, Lord Chief Baron of the Exchequer, appointed 2 December 1908; term of office expired 31 October 1919.

Pearson, Charles Y., MD, MCh, FRCS, Eng, appointed 2 December 1908; term of office expired 31 October 1914; co-opted as Member of Senate, 18 November 1914; term of office expired 31 October 1919.

Power, Michael, MA, BSc, elected by the Governing Body, University College Galway, 23 January 1935, *vice* Rt Revd Monsignor John Hynes, MA, BD; re-elected 12 October 1939; re-elected 17 October 1944; re-elected 14 October 1949; re-elected 16 October 1954; term of office expired 31 October 1959.

Purcell, Pierce F., MA, MAI (Dub), LLD, elected by the Governing Body, University College Dublin, 29 June 1943, *vice* the late Revd Timothy Corcoran, SJ, DLitt, HDip in Ed; re-elected 17 October 1944; co-opted 7 December 1949; term of office expired 31 October 1954.

Purcell, Pierce H., BA, elected by Convocation, October 14th, 1987; term of office expired 31 October 1992.

Pye, Joseph P., MD, MCh, DSc, appointed 2 December 1908; term of office expired 31 October 1914; re-elected by the Governing Body, University College Galway, 8 October 1914; term of office expired 31 October 1919.

Pyne, Gerald T., MSc, PhD, elected by the Governing Body, University College Cork, 30 October 1962, *vice* the late Very Revd Edward O'Mahony, O.F.M. Cap., MA, DLitt; re-elected 13 October 1964; term of office expired 31 October 1972.

Quinlan, Patrick M., BE, DSc, PhD, elected by Convocation, 10 October 1959; elected by the Governing Body, University College Cork, 13 October 1964; elected by Convocation, 12 October 1972; term of office expired 31 October 1977; elected by the Governing

Body as from 14 December 1978, in place of Tadhg Ó Ciardha , appointed President, University College Cork; re-elected by Convocation, 14 October 1982; re-elected by Convocation, 14 October 1987; term of office expired 31 October 1992.

Raftery, Thomas F., MAgrSc, elected by the Governing Body, University College Cork, 13 October 1977; re-elected 18 October 1982; term of office expired 31 October 1987.

Redmond, David, MSc, PhD (Illinois); elected by the Governing Authority, National University of Ireland, Maynooth, 12 February 2001; re-elected 9 October 2002; re-elected 11 October 2007.

Reid, Benedict, BA, MEd, nominated by the Government, 10 November 1992; re-nominated 11 November 1997. Nominated by the Government 14 February 2003; nominated by the Government, 19 February 2008.

Reilly, Joseph, MA, DSc, DESc, elected by the Governing Body, University College Cork, 3 February 1943, *vice* the late Alexander J. Magennis, MEconSc, FSAA.; term of office expired 31 October 1944.

Reilly, Patrick, BE, elected by the Governing Authority, NUI Galway, November 2005; re-elected by the Governing Authority, NUI. Galway, of November 2007

Risworth, Frank S., BA, BE, MAI (Dub), LLD, elected by the Governing Body, University College Galway, 12 October 1939; re-elected 17 October 1944; term of office expired 31 October 1949.

Roche, Sir George, appointed 2 December 1908; term of office expired 31 October 1914.

Roche, Louis P., MA, DèsL, elected by the Governing Body, University College Dublin, 29 November 1949; term of office expired 31 October 1954.

Roche, Tina, nominated by the Government, 14 February 2003.

Ryan, Hugh, MA, DSc, co-opted as Member of Senate, 22 October 1920, *vice* the late John A. McClelland, MA, DSc, FRS, term of office

expired 31 October 1924; re-elected by
Convocation, 7 October 1924; term of
office expired 31 October 1929.

Ryan, Norma, PhD, elected by the Governing
Authority, UCC, November 2007

Ryan, Paul, BComm, MBS, DPA, PhD (Lond),
ACA, elected by the Governing Body,
University College Dublin–National Univer-
sity of Ireland Dublin 16 October 2002.

Semple, Patrick, MA, appointed 2 December
1908; term of office expired 31 October
1914; elected by the Governing Body,
University College Dublin, 13 October 1914;
re-elected 16 October 1919; re-elected
17 October 1924; re-elected 16 October 1929;
re-elected 17 October 1934; re-elected
17 October 1939; term of office expired
31 October 1944.

Senier, Alfred, MD, PhD, DSc, appointed December 2nd, 1908; term of office expired 31 October 1914; elected by the Governing Body,
University College Galway, 8 October 1914.

Sexton, Michael C., MSc, PhD, elected by the
Governing Body, University College Cork,
18 October 1982; term of office expired
31 October 1987.

Shaw, Revd Francis J., SK, MA, elected by the
Governing Body, University College Dublin, 19 March 1963, *vice* the late Thomas
S. Wheeler, DSc; term of office expired
31 October 1964.

Shannon, Patrick M., BSc, PhD, elected by
Governing Authority, UCD, November 2007.

Shea, Stephen, MD, elected by the Governing
Body, University College Galway, 14 October
1949; re-elected 16 October 1954; term of
office expired 31 October 1959; co-opted as
Member of Senate, 13 November 1964;
term of office expired 31 October 1972.

Sigerson, George, MD, appointed 2 December
1908; term of office expired 31 October 1914;
elected by Convocation, 6 October 1914;
term of office expired 31 October 1919.

Smiddy, Timothy, MA, DEconSc, elected by
the Governing Body, University College Cork,

9 October 1919; resigned 30 September 1923.

Smyth, William J., BA, PhD, Master, St Patrick's
College, Maynooth, co-opted as Member of
Senate, 27 July 1994; appointed President,
National University of Ireland, Maynooth,
16 June 1997. Resigned 21 June 2004.

Stuart, Miss Norah, MA, elected by Convocation, 16 October 1954; term of office
expired 31 October 1959.

Teegan, John P., MSc, PhD, elected by the
Governing Body, University College Cork,
12 October 1972; term of office expired
31 October 1977.

Tierney, James J., MA, MRIA, elected by the
Governing Body, University College Dublin,
17 November 1959; re-elected 5 January 1965;
term of office expired 31 October 1972.

Tierney, Michael, KSG, MA, DLitt, elected by
Convocation, 7 October 1924; re-elected
12 October 1929; term of office expired
31 October 1934; re-elected 13 October
1939; re-elected 13 October 1944; appointed
President, University College Dublin,
30 October 1947; retired from Presidency,
30 September 1964.

Timoney, James R., MA, elected by Convocation,
10 October 1964, re-elected 12 October 1972;
re-elected 13 October 1977; term of office
expired 31 October 1982.

Ua Dochartaigh, Rt Revd Monsignor, Eamonn T.,
MA, BD, PhD, elected by Convocation,
12 October 1972, re-elected 13 October
1977; co-opted 9 November 1982; term
of office expired 31 October 1987.

van Sinderen-Law, Jean, BSc, PhD, elected by
the Governing Body of University College
Cork–National University of Ireland, Cork,
18 February 2003.

Waldron, Laurence A. (subsequently a Privy
Councillor) appointed 2 December 1908;
term of office expired 31 October 1914;
re-appointed by H.M. the King, 31 October
1914; re-appointed 31 October 1919.

Walsh, Edward M., BE, PhD, nominated by
the Government, 25 January 1977, *vice* the

Most Revd Michael Browne, resigned; re-nominated 2 November 1977; term of office expired 31 October 1982.

Walsh, Henry N., ME, elected by the Governing Body, University College Cork, 18 October 1944; re-elected 17 October 1949; term of office expired 31 October 1954.

Walsh, Jim, BA, MA, co-opted November 2002; elected by Governing Authority, NUI, Maynooth, 2007.

Walsh, His Grace the Most Revd Joseph, MA, DD, Archbishop of Tuam, elected by the Governing Body, University College Galway, 17 October 1944; re-elected 14 October 1949; re-elected 16 October 1954; re-elected 17 October 1959; re-elected 15 October 1964; retired 15 October 1971.

Walsh, Thomas, MA, BSc, MD, DPH, HDip in Ed, elected by Convocation, 7 October 1919; term of office expired 31 October 1924; co-opted as Member of Senate, 13 November 1924; co-opted 14 November 1929; co-opted 13 November 1934; co-opted 16 November 1939; co-opted 17 November 1944; term of office expired 31 October 1949.

Walsh, His Grace the Most Revd William J., DD, Archbishop of Dublin, appointed 2 December 1908; elected Chancellor of the University, 17 December 1908.

Watson, Richard O., BSc, MSc, PhD elected by the Governing Authority, NUI Maynooth, November 2007.

Wheeler, Thomas S., DSc, PhD, FRCScI, elected by the Governing Body, University College Dublin, 16 October 1954; re-elected 17 November 1959.

Whitaker, Thomas K., DEconSc, elected Chancellor of the University, 5 May 1976; resigned 31 December 1996.

Wiber, Frederick H., LLD, appointed Registrar of the University by Senate, 1 February 1924.

Williams, Thomas D., MA, elected by the Governing Body, University College Dublin, 18 December 1971; re-elected 17 October 1972; re-elected 11 October 1977; term of office expired 31 October 1982.

Williams, William J., MA, HDip in Ed, elected by Convocation, 12 October 1929; term of office expired 31 October 1934.

Wilmot, Séamus, BA, BComm, HDip in Ed, LLD, appointed Registrar of the University by Senate, 11 December 1952; term of office expired 4 May 1972.

Windle, Bertram C.A., MD, DSc, LLD, FRS (subsequently Sir Bertram C. A. Windle), President, University College Cork; appointed 2 December 1908; resigned 21 November 1919.

Wrixon, Gerard T., BE, MS (Caltech), PhD (Calif), appointed President, University College Cork-National University of Ireland, Cork, 27 January 1999.

A Senate election due to take place in October 1969 was postponed for one year by Government order, and again in 1970 and 1971.

Timeline of NUI Appointments, 1908–2008

Year	Chancellor	Registrar	Vice-Chancellor	Pro-Vice-Chancellor (UCC)
1908	William J. Walsh	Joseph McGrath		
1909	William J. Walsh	Joseph McGrath	Christopher Nixon	
1910	William J. Walsh	Joseph McGrath	Christopher Nixon	
1911	William J. Walsh	Joseph McGrath	Christopher Nixon	
1912	William J. Walsh	Joseph McGrath	Christopher Nixon	
1913	William J. Walsh	Joseph McGrath	Christopher Nixon	
1914	William J. Walsh	Joseph McGrath	Christopher Nixon / Alexander Anderson	Bertram Windle
1915	William J. Walsh	Joseph McGrath	Alexander Anderson	Bertram Windle
1916	William J. Walsh	Joseph McGrath	Alexander Anderson / Bertram Windle	Bertram Windle
1917	William J. Walsh	Joseph McGrath	Bertram Windle	
1918	William J. Walsh	Joseph McGrath	Bertram Windle / Denis J. Coffey	Bertram Windle
1919	William J. Walsh	Joseph McGrath	Denis J. Coffey	Patrick Merriman
1920	William J. Walsh	Joseph McGrath	Denis J. Coffey	Patrick Merriman
1921	William J. Walsh / Eamon de Valera	Joseph McGrath	Alexander Anderson	Patrick Merriman

Pro-Vice-Chancellor (UCD)	Pro-Vice-Chancellor (NUIG)*	Pro-Vice-Chancellor (NUIM)†
Denis J. Coffey	Alexander Anderson	J.F. Hogan
Denis J. Coffey		J.F. Hogan
Denis J. Coffey	Alexander Anderson	J.F. Hogan
Denis J. Coffey	Alexander Anderson	J.F. Hogan
Denis J. Coffey	Alexander Anderson	J.F. Hogan / James Mac Caffrey
	Alexander Anderson	James Mac Caffrey
	Alexander Anderson	James Mac Caffrey
Denis J. Coffey	Alexander Anderson	James Mac Caffrey

* Following its designation as a constituent university in 1997, University College
  Galway was renamed as the National University of Ireland, Galway.
† St Patrick's College, Maynooth became a constituent university of the National
  University in 1997 and was named the National University of Ireland, Maynooth.

Year	Chancellor	Registrar	Vice-Chancellor	Pro-Vice-Chancellor (UCC)
1922	Eamon de Valera	Joseph McGrath	Alexander Anderson	Patrick Merriman
1923	Eamon de Valera	Joseph McGrath	Patrick Merriman	
1924	Eamon de Valera	Frederick H. Wiber	Patrick Merriman	
1925	Eamon de Valera	Frederick H. Wiber	Denis J. Coffey	Patrick Merriman
1926	Eamon de Valera	Frederick H. Wiber	Denis J. Coffey	Patrick Merriman
1927	Eamon de Valera	Frederick H. Wiber	Alexander Anderson	Patrick Merriman
1928	Eamon de Valera	Frederick H. Wiber	Alexander Anderson	Patrick Merriman
1929	Eamon de Valera	Frederick H. Wiber	Patrick Merriman	
1930	Eamon de Valera	Frederick H. Wiber	Patrick Merriman	
1931	Eamon de Valera	Frederick H. Wiber	Denis J. Coffey	Patrick Merriman
1932	Eamon de Valera	Frederick H. Wiber	Denis J. Coffey	Patrick Merriman
1933	Eamon de Valera	Frederick H. Wiber	Alexander Anderson	Patrick Merriman
1934	Eamon de Valera	Frederick H. Wiber	Alexander Anderson	Patrick Merriman
1935	Eamon de Valera	Frederick H. Wiber	Patrick Merriman	
1936	Eamon de Valera	Frederick H. Wiber	Patrick Merriman	

Pro-Vice-Chancellor (UCD)	Pro-Vice-Chancellor (NUIG)*	Pro-Vice-Chancellor (NUIM)†
Denis J. Coffey		James Mac Caffrey
Denis J. Coffey	Alexander Anderson	James Mac Caffrey
Denis J. Coffey	Alexander Anderson	James Mac Caffrey
	Alexander Anderson	James Mac Caffrey
	Alexander Anderson	James Mac Caffrey
Denis J. Coffey		James Mac Caffrey
Denis J. Coffey		James Mac Caffrey
Denis J. Coffey	Alexander Anderson	James Mac Caffrey
Denis J. Coffey	Alexander Anderson	James Mac Caffrey
	Alexander Anderson	James Mac Caffrey
	Alexander Anderson	James Mac Caffrey
Denis J. Coffey		James Mac Caffrey
Denis J. Coffey	John Hynes	James Mac Caffrey
Denis J. Coffey	John Hynes	James Mac Caffrey
Denis J. Coffey	John Hynes	John F. D'Alton

* Following its designation as a constituent university in 1997, University College
Galway was renamed as the National University of Ireland, Galway.
† St Patrick's College, Maynooth became a constituent university of the National
University in 1997 and was named the National University of Ireland, Maynooth.

Year	Chancellor	Registrar	Vice-Chancellor	Pro-Vice-Chancellor (UCC)
1937	Eamon de Valera	Alexander A. McCarthy	Denis J. Coffey	Patrick Merriman
1938	Eamon de Valera	Alexander A. McCarthy	Denis J. Coffey	Patrick Merriman
1939	Eamon de Valera	Alexander A. McCarthy	Mon. John Hynes	Patrick Merriman
1940	Eamon de Valera	Alexander A. McCarthy	Mon. John Hynes	Patrick Merriman
1941	Eamon de Valera	Alexander A. McCarthy	Patrick Merriman	
1942	Eamon de Valera	Alexander A. McCarthy	Patrick Merriman	
1943	Eamon de Valera	Alexander A. McCarthy	Arthur W. Conway	Patrick Merriman / Alfred O'Rahilly
1944	Eamon de Valera	Alexander A. McCarthy	Arthur W. Conway	Alfred O'Rahilly
1945	Eamon de Valera	Alexander A. McCarthy	Arthur W. Conway	Alfred O'Rahilly
1946	Eamon de Valera	Alexander A. McCarthy	Alfred O'Rahilly	
1947	Eamon de Valera	Alexander A. McCarthy	Alfred O'Rahilly	
1948	Eamon de Valera	Alexander A. McCarthy	Patrick J. Browne	Alfred O'Rahilly
1949	Eamon de Valera	Alexander A. McCarthy	Patrick J. Browne	Alfred O'Rahilly
1950	Eamon de Valera	Alexander A. McCarthy	Michael Tierney	Alfred O'Rahilly
1951	Eamon de Valera	Alexander A. McCarthy	Michael Tierney	Alfred O'Rahilly

Pro-Vice-Chancellor (UCD)	Pro-Vice-Chancellor (NUIG)*	Pro-Vice-Chancellor (NUIM)†
	John Hynes	John F. D'Alton
	John Hynes	John F. D'Alton
Denis J. Coffey		John F. D'Alton
Denis J. Coffey / Arthur Conway		John F. D'Alton
Arthur W. Conway		John F. D'Alton
Arthur W. Conway		John F. D'Alton / Edward Kissane
		Edward Kissane
		Edward Kissane
	Patrick J. Browne	Edward Kissane
Arthur W. Conway	Patrick J. Browne	Edward Kissane
Michael Tierney	Patrick J. Browne	Edward Kissane
Michael Tierney		Edward Kissane
Michael Tierney		Edward Kissane
	Patrick J. Browne	Edward Kissane
	Patrick J. Browne	Edward Kissane

* Following its designation as a constituent university in 1997, University College Galway was renamed as the National University of Ireland, Galway.

† St Patrick's College, Maynooth became a constituent university of the National University in 1997 and was named the National University of Ireland, Maynooth.

Year	Chancellor	Registrar	Vice-Chancellor	Pro-Vice-Chancellor (UCC)
1952	Eamon de Valera	Alexander A. McCarthy / Seamus Wilmot	Alfred O'Rahilly	
1953	Eamon de Valera	Seamus Wilmot	Alfred O'Rahilly	
1954	Eamon de Valera	Seamus Wilmot	Patrick J. Browne	Alfred O'Rahilly / Henry St J. Atkins
1955	Eamon de Valera	Seamus Wilmot	Patrick J. Browne	Henry St J. Atkins
1956	Eamon de Valera	Seamus Wilmot	Michael Tierney	Henry St J. Atkins
1957	Eamon de Valera	Seamus Wilmot	Michael Tierney	Henry St J. Atkins
1958	Eamon de Valera	Seamus Wilmot	Henry St J. Atkins	
1959	Eamon de Valera	Seamus Wilmot	Henry St J. Atkins	
1960	Eamon de Valera	Seamus Wilmot	Henry St J. Atkins	
1961	Eamon de Valera	Seamus Wilmot	Máirtín Ó Tnúthail	Henry St J. Atkins
1962	Eamon de Valera	Seamus Wilmot	Michael Tierney	Henry St J. Atkins
1963	Eamon de Valera	Seamus Wilmot	Michael Tierney	Henry St J. Atkins
1964	Eamon de Valera	Seamus Wilmot	Michael Tierney / John J. McHenry	John J. McHenry
1965	Eamon de Valera	Seamus Wilmot	John J. McHenry	
1966	Eamon de Valera	Seamus Wilmot	John J. McHenry	

Pro-Vice-Chancellor (UCD)	Pro-Vice-Chancellor (NUIG)*	Pro-Vice-Chancellor (NUIM)†
Michael Tierney	Patrick J. Browne	Edward Kissane
Michael Tierney	Patrick J. Browne	Edward Kissane
Michael Tierney		Edward Kissane
Michael Tierney		Edward Kissane
	Patrick J. Browne	Edward Kissane
	Patrick J. Browne	Edward Kissane
Michael Tierney	Patrick J. Browne	Edward Kissane
Michael Tierney	Patrick J. Browne	Edward Kissane / Gerard Mitchell
Michael Tierney	Máirtín Ó Tnúthail	Gerard Mitchell
Michael Tierney		Gerard Mitchell
	Máirtín Ó Tnúthail	Gerard Mitchell
	Máirtín Ó Tnúthail	Gerard Mitchell
Jeremiah J. Hogan	Máirtín Ó Tnúthail	Gerard Mitchell
Jeremiah J. Hogan	Máirtín Ó Tnúthail	Gerard Mitchell
Jeremiah J. Hogan	Máirtín Ó Tnúthail	Gerard Mitchell

* Following its designation as a constituent university in 1997, University College Galway was renamed as the National University of Ireland, Galway.
† St Patrick's College, Maynooth became a constituent university of the National University in 1997 and was named the National University of Ireland, Maynooth.

Year	Chancellor	Registrar	Vice-Chancellor	Pro-Vice-Chancellor (UCC)
1967	Eamon de Valera	Seamus Wilmot	Máirtín Ó Tnúthail	John J. McHenry / Michael D. McCarthy
1968	Eamon de Valera	Seamus Wilmot	Máirtín Ó Tnúthail	Michael D. McCarthy
1969	Eamon de Valera	Seamus Wilmot	Jeremiah J. Hogan	Michael D. McCarthy
1970	Eamon de Valera	Seamus Wilmot	Jeremiah J. Hogan	Michael D. McCarthy
1971	Eamon de Valera	Seamus Wilmot	Michael D. McCarthy	
1972	Eamon de Valera	Seamus Wilmot / John Bourke	Michael D. McCarthy	
1973	Eamon de Valera	John Bourke	Máirtín Ó Tnúthail	Michael D. McCarthy
1974	Eamon de Valera	John Bourke	Máirtín Ó Tnúthail	Michael D. McCarthy
1975	Eamon de Valera	John Bourke	Thomas Murphy	Michael D. McCarthy
1976	Thomas K. Whitaker	John Bourke	Thomas Murphy	Michael D. McCarthy
1977	Thomas K. Whitaker	John Bourke	Michael D. McCarthy	
1978	Thomas K. Whitaker	John Bourke	Michael D. McCarthy / Tadhg Ó Ciardha	
1979	Thomas K. Whitaker	John Bourke / Michael Gilheany	Colm Ó hEocha	Tadhg Ó Ciardha
1980	Thomas K. Whitaker	Michael Gilheany	Colm Ó hEocha	Tadhg Ó Ciardha
1981	Thomas K. Whitaker	Michael Gilheany	Thomas Murphy	Tadhg Ó Ciardha

Pro-Vice-Chancellor (UCD)	Pro-Vice-Chancellor (NUIG)*	Pro-Vice-Chancellor (NUIM)†
Jeremiah J. Hogan		Gerard Mitchell
Jeremiah J. Hogan		Patrick J. Corish
	Máirtín Ó Tnúthail	Jeremiah Newman
	Máirtín Ó Tnúthail	Jeremiah Newman
Jeremiah J. Hogan	Máirtín Ó Tnúthail	Jeremiah Newman
Jeremiah J. Hogan / Thomas Murphy	Máirtín Ó Tnúthail	Jeremiah Newman
Thomas Murphy		Jeremiah Newman
Thomas Murphy		Jeremiah Newman / Tomás Ó Fiaich
	Máirtín Ó Tnúthail / Colm Ó hEocha	Tomás Ó Fiaich
	Colm Ó hEocha	Tomás Ó Fiaich
Thomas Murphy	Colm Ó hEocha	Tomás Ó Fiaich / Michael G. Olden
Thomas Murphy	Colm Ó hEocha	Michael G. Olden
Thomas Murphy		Michael G. Olden
Thomas Murphy		Michael G. Olden
	Colm Ó hEocha	Michael G. Olden

* Following its designation as a constituent university in 1997, University College Galway was renamed as the National University of Ireland, Galway.
† St Patrick's College, Maynooth became a constituent university of the National University in 1997 and was named the National University of Ireland, Maynooth.

Year	Chancellor	Registrar	Vice-Chancellor	Pro-Vice-Chancellor (UCC)
1982	Thomas K. Whitaker	Michael Gilheany	Thomas Murphy	Tadhg Ó Ciardha
1983	Thomas K. Whitaker	Michael Gilheany	Tadhg Ó Ciardha	
1984	Thomas K. Whitaker	Michael Gilheany	Tadhg Ó Ciardha	
1985	Thomas K. Whitaker	Michael Gilheany	Colm Ó hEocha	Tadhg Ó Ciardha
1986	Thomas K. Whitaker	Michael Gilheany	Colm Ó hEocha	Tadhg Ó Ciardha
1987	Thomas K. Whitaker	Michael Gilheany / John Nolan	Patrick Masterson	Tadhg Ó Ciardha
1988	Thomas K. Whitaker	John Nolan	Patrick Masterson	Tadhg Ó Ciardha
1989	Thomas K. Whitaker	John Nolan	Michael P. Mortell	
1990	Thomas K. Whitaker	John Nolan	Michael P. Mortell	
1991	Thomas K. Whitaker	John Nolan	Colm Ó hEocha	Michael P. Mortell
1992	Thomas K. Whitaker	John Nolan	Colm Ó hEocha	Michael P. Mortell
1993	Thomas K. Whitaker	John Nolan	Patrick Masterson / Michael P. Mortell	
1994	Thomas K. Whitaker	John Nolan	Michael P. Mortell	
1995	Thomas K. Whitaker	John Nolan	Art Cosgrove	Michael P. Mortell
1996	Thomas K. Whitaker	John Nolan	Art Cosgrove	Michael P. Mortell

Pro-Vice-Chancellor (UCD)	Pro-Vice-Chancellor (NUIG)*	Pro-Vice-Chancellor (NUIM)†
	Colm Ó hEocha	Michael G. Olden
Thomas Murphy	Colm Ó hEocha	Michael G. Olden
Thomas Murphy	Colm Ó hEocha	Michael G. Olden
Thomas Murphy		Michael G. Olden / Mícheál Ledwith
Patrick Masterson		Mícheál Ledwith
	Colm Ó hEocha	Mícheál Ledwith
	Colm Ó hEocha	Mícheál Ledwith
Patrick Masterson	Colm Ó hEocha	Mícheál Ledwith
Patrick Masterson	Colm Ó hEocha	Mícheál Ledwith
Patrick Masterson		Mícheál Ledwith
Patrick Masterson		Mícheál Ledwith
Patrick Masterson	Colm Ó hEocha	Mícheál Ledwith
Art Cosgrove	Colm Ó hEocha	Mícheál Ledwith / William J. Smyth
	Colm Ó hEocha	William J. Smyth
	Colm Ó hEocha / Patrick P. Fottrell	William J. Smyth

* Following its designation as a constituent university in 1997, University College Galway was renamed as the National University of Ireland, Galway.
† St Patrick's College, Maynooth became a constituent university of the National University in 1997 and was named the National University of Ireland, Maynooth.

Year	Chancellor	Registrar	Vice-Chancellor	Pro-Vice-Chancellor (UCC)
1997	Garret FitzGerald	John Nolan	Patrick P. Fottrell	Michael P. Mortell
1998	Garret FitzGerald	John Nolan	Patrick P. Fottrell	Michael P. Mortell
1999	Garret FitzGerald	John Nolan	William J. Smyth	Michael P. Mortell / Gerard T. Wrixon
2000	Garret FitzGerald	John Nolan	William J. Smyth	Gerard T. Wrixon
2001	Garret FitzGerald	John Nolan	Gerard T. Wrixon	
2002	Garret FitzGerald	John Nolan	Gerard T. Wrixon	
2003	Garret FitzGerald	John Nolan	Art Cosgrove	Gerard T. Wrixon
2004	Garret FitzGerald	John Nolan / Attracta Halpin	Iognaid Ó Muircheartaigh	Gerard T. Wrixon
2005	Garret FitzGerald	Attracta Halpin	Iognaid Ó Muircheartaigh	Gerard T. Wrixon
2006	Garret FitzGerald	Attracta Halpin	John G. Hughes	Gerard T. Wrixon
2007	Garret FitzGerald	Attracta Halpin	John G. Hughes	Gerard T. Wrixon
2008	Garret FitzGerald	Attracta Halpin	Michael Murphy	

Pro-Vice-Chancellor (UCD)	Pro-Vice-Chancellor (NUIG)*	Pro-Vice-Chancellor (NUIM)†
Art Cosgrove		William J. Smyth
Art Cosgrove		William J. Smyth
Art Cosgrove	Patrick P. Fottrell	
Art Cosgrove	Patrick P. Fottrell / Iognáid Ó Muircheartaigh	
Art Cosgrove	Iognaid Ó Muircheartaigh	William J. Smyth
Art Cosgrove	Iognaid Ó Muircheartaigh	William J. Smyth
	Iognaid Ó Muircheartaigh	William J. Smyth
Hugh Brady		William J. Smyth / John G. Hughes
Hugh Brady		John G. Hughes
Hugh Brady	Iognaid Ó Muircheartaigh	
Hugh Brady	Iognaid Ó Muircheartaigh	
Hugh Brady	Iognaid Ó Muircheartaigh / James Browne	John G. Hughes

* Following its designation as a constituent university in 1997, University College Galway was renamed as the National University of Ireland, Galway.

† St Patrick's College, Maynooth became a constituent university of the National University in 1997 and was named the National University of Ireland, Maynooth.

APPENDIX VIII *NUI Awards and Scholarships*

Since its foundation in 1908, the National University of Ireland has been fortunate to receive a number of generous trusts and bequests. These funds have been invested and the income generated has been used to finance scholarships and prizes in accordance with the wishes of the benefactors of the university. In addition, the university – from its own resources – continues to offer annually a number of valuable and prestigious studentships and bursaries for competition amongst the graduates of the university. The combined annual value of NUI awards is now in excess of €1 million.

NUI Fellowships
Three NUI Fellowships have been established at post-doctoral level and one at postgraduate level for competition amongst NUI graduates at home or abroad. The main purpose of the fellowships is to encourage and support graduates of proven academic excellence to advance their scholarly research and to contribute to the learning culture in the constituent institutions.

Post-Doctoral Fellowship in the Humanities (€80,000)
This Post-Doctoral Fellowship in the Humanities, funded by a special NUI fund, was first offered for competition amongst NUI graduates in 1999.

Post-Doctoral Fellowship in the Sciences (€80,000)
This Post-Doctoral Fellowship in the Sciences, funded by a special NUI fund, was first offered for competition amongst NUI graduates in 1999.

Comhaltacht Iar-Dhochtura i Léann na Gaeilge/an Léann Ceilteach (€80,000 over two years)
Tairgeadh an Chomhaltacht seo, a íoctar as Ciste Adam Boyd Simpson agus Eleanor Boyd, chun iomaíochta idir céimithe d'Ollscoil na hÉireann ag baile nó thar lear i 2003. Is í aidhm don Chomhaltacht spreagadh agus tacaíocht a thabhairt do scoláire iar-dhochtúra den chéad scoth a c(h)uid taighde a chur ar aghaidh i gComh-Ollscoil de chuid Ollscoil na hÉireann. This post-doctoral fellowship, funded by the Adam Boyd Simpson and Eleanor Boyd Fund, was offered for competition amongst NUI graduates in 1999.

The E. J. Phelan Postgraduate Fellowship in International Law (€51,000 over two years)
This fellowship, funded by a special bequest from the late Mr and Mrs Edward J. Phelan was first awarded in 2002, and is offered in alternate years. The fellowship is intended to encourage and support a postgraduate student of proven academic excellence to advance his/her scholarly research in the field of International Law.

NUI Awards for Graduates
Throughout the history of the NUI, one of its principal objectives has been to provide opportunities for its most able graduates by means of scholarships, prizes and awards. 'Awards for Graduates' comprises scholarships funded by bequests to the university or funded through the university's own resources.

NUI Travelling Studentships (€42,000, over three years)
The Travelling Studentship Scheme, funded by the University from its own resources, has been in existence since 1910. The scheme encourages the most able students in the NUI federal system to undertake doctoral research abroad, which in turn will further enrich the learning community within NUI.

Dr Mary L. Thornton / NUI Scholarship in Education (€5,000)
This is a scholarship in education. It is funded by a bequest from the late Dr Thornton and is awarded annually. The Scholarship, which is open to NUI graduates, is intended to encourage postgraduate research within NUI in the field of education.

Irish Historical Research Prize (€5,000)
This prestigious Prize was originally offered by NUI in conjunction with the Travelling Studentship Scheme (Travelling Studentship in History) until 1921 when the Senate drew up separate regulations for the prize, which has been offered since that time in alternate years. The prize is for the best original work of Irish historical research, published for the first time by a student or graduate of the National University of Ireland.

The Denis Phelan Scholarships and Prizes (overall value, c. €14,000)
The Denis Phelan Scholarships were established in 2003 and are funded by the NUI Robemakers, Phelan Conan Limited. The awards are made annually and are open for competition among students of the constituent universities and recognised colleges achieving the highest marks in a range of subjects (determined each year by the Senate) in the relevant NUI primary degree examinations.

NUI Art and Design Prize (€2,500)
This prize is offered annually for a piece of work by a graduate of the National College of Art and Design (NCAD) who has distinguished him or herself in Fine Art.

Mansion House Fund Scholarship and Prize in Irish (€2,000 and €1,300)
Scolaireacht agus Duais Chiste Theach an Ardmheara sa Ghaeilge
The Mansion House Fund is designed to promote 'the study of Irish Language, Literature and History'. These awards are based on the results of the degree examinations in Irish (Modern, Early, Medieval and Classical, or any combination of these) for the BA Honours degree throughout the Constituent Universities.

Mansion House Fund Scholarship and Prize in Irish History (€2,000 and €1,300)
Scolaireacht agus Duais Chiste Theach an Ardmheara sa Stair Gaeilge
Traditionally, the Mansion House Fund has been used to finance the Scholarship and Prize in Irish. In addition, the Senate has established an annual Scholarship and Prize in Irish History. These awards are based on the results of the degree examinations in Irish History for the BA degree examination in the Constituent Universities.

Pierce Malone Scholarships in Engineering and Philosophy
Pierce Malone made provision in his will for the establishment and endowment by the National University of Ireland of Annual Scholarships in Philosophy, and in Engineering. The Scholarships are awarded annually and are called the Pierce Malone Scholarships.

The Pierce Malone Scholarship in Engineering (€2,000)
This scholarship is awarded in connection with the NUI Travelling Studentships in the Sciences and is awarded to an Engineering graduate based on
the recommendation of the interview panel for the competition for the four
travelling studentships in the sciences.
The Pierce Malone Scholarship in Philosophy (€2,000)
This Scholarship is awarded to the top student in Philosophy based on a
corpus of written work presented for the BA degree examination in each of
the NUI constituent universities.

French Government Medals and Prizes for Proficiency in French

In 1926, the French Government presented a medal to the university to be
awarded in that year for proficiency in French. The medal was offered annually until 1956, when the French Government increased the number of medals
to three, for competition amongst students of the then Constituent Colleges.
In 1962, a fourth Medal was added to include the then Recognised College,
St Patrick's College, Maynooth. These Medals are awarded annually in each
of the four NUI constituent universities. NUI also awards a cash prize of
Đ1000 to each recipient.

NUI Awards for Undergraduates

The Senate has reviewed the range and scope of scholarships and prizes
available to undergraduates. As a result, the university has been able to expand
the number of Scholarships and Prizes available to undergraduates, and
awarded on merit.

Dr Henry Hutchinson Stewart Scholarships and Prizes (€2,300, €1,200, €560)

The Dr H. H. Stewart Scholarships scheme was re-structured in 1998 and
the number of Scholarships was increased, to provide for seven Literary
Scholarships and seventeen Medical Scholarships.
Dr H. H. Stewart Literary Scholarships and Prizes
Each year, a scholarship, second and third place Prizes, are awarded in each of
the following subjects: English, French, German, Irish, Italian, Latin, Spanish
and are based on the results of First Arts and First Commerce International
Examinations within the constituent universities.

Dr H. H. Stewart Medical Scholarships and Prizes
Each year, a scholarship, second and third place Prizes, are awarded in each
of the following subjects: Anatomy, Biochemistry, Dentistry (*scholarship and
second prize only*), Diagnostic Imaging (*scholarship and second prize only*),
General Practice, Gynaecology & Obstetrics, Medical Microbiology, Medicine,
Nursing, Paediatrics, Pathology, Pharmacology, Physiology, Physiotherapy
(*scholarship and second prize only*), Psychiatry, Public Health, Surgery. The
awards are based on the results of the examinations in those subjects in the
Faculties of Medicine and Health Sciences of the Constituent Universities
and the Royal College of Surgeons in Ireland and also, in the case of Nursing,
the Department of Nursing, St. Angela's College of Education, Sligo.

The O'Brien Bequest Awards
Dr Daniel P. O'Brien completed his medical studies in the Catholic University
School of Medicine, St. Cecilia Street, Dublin and he obtained the qualification
of LRCP & SI in 1895, the Fellowship of the Royal College of Surgeons in 1897
and in 1911, he passed the MB BCh BAO Degrees Examination of the National
University of Ireland. He was in active practice in Rockhampton, Queens-
land, Australia for nearly forty years and bequeathed £3,320 in 1947 to the
National University of Ireland. This bequest is used to fund awards as follows:
*The NUI Award Scheme for Students with Disabilities (€11,000 available
overall; individual awards granted)*
Under this scheme, which is in operation since 1981, awards with a total value
of €10,000 are provided for new entrant undergraduate students who have
serious physical disabilities and who propose to pursue Primary Degree
courses in the National University of Ireland.
The NUI Equal Educational Opportunities Scheme (overall value, €12,000)
NUI is committed to promoting greater social equity in Irish higher education
through securing increased participation in the Constituent Universities
by economically disadvantaged students.
   The sum of €8,000 is available each academic year – €2,000 in each constituent university – to support a student or students in economically disadvantaged circumstances.

The NUI Club London Scholarship (€2,000)
In February 1929, a dining club for graduates of the National University of

Ireland (including the Royal University of Ireland) was formally established. This club provided a centre in London for Irish graduates during the Second World War and postwar periods and continued successfully for a further sixty years. In November 2003, the members – acknowledging that the club membership had been declining steadily during the previous 15 years – approved a recommendation that the club should be dissolved and its assets offered as a gift to the NUI for the purpose of establishing an NUI Club London Memorial Scholarship.

This scholarship, introduced for the first time in 2004–5, is placed on offer for competition amongst students registered in a different faculty/college each year as determined by the Senate.

NUI Grants towards Publications (individual grants of up to €3,000)
The university has traditionally provided a small number of grants-in-aid annually towards scholarly publications by staff of the NUI constituent universities, on the basis of individual applications to the Senate. The scheme is open to full-time and part-time staff of NUI constituent universities and recognised colleges.

NUI Grant to the Constituent Universities (The Thomas Crawford Hayes Awards–€209,507)
In 1922, Miss Isabelle Hayes bequeathed £27,600 to the National University of Ireland in memory of her late brother Dr Thomas Crawford Hayes, a graduate of Trinity College Dublin and Fellow of the Royal College of Physicians, London, for the purpose of founding or aiding a chair of biology in the university and also for the furtherance and promotion of natural knowledge. The scheme has been modified to the effect that the income from the fund is now applied in the broad area of the biological sciences, where each of the four NUI constituent universities receive an annual grant.

NOTES

Chapter 1
From Royal to National University,
1879–1908

1 Hansard HC (series 4) vol. 193, col. 626 (28 July 1908).

2 *An Act to Promote the Advancement of Learning and to Extend the Benefits Connected with University Education in Ireland*, 1879, 42 & 43 Vict. c. 65.

3 Susan Parkes, 'Higher education, 1793–1908', *A New History of Ireland*, vol. VI (Oxford: Clarendon Press, 1996), pp. 539–70, 562.

4 T. W. Moody and J. C. Beckett, *Queen's Belfast, 1845–1949* (London: Faber and Faber, 1959), p. 297.

5 A Scholar of the Catholic University of Ireland, *The Queen's Colleges and the Royal University of Ireland* (Dublin: Browne & Nolan, 1883). See Aidan J. O'Reilly, 'The role of Archbishop W. Walsh in the resolution of the Irish university question' (PhD thesis, NUI Maynooth, 2001 for evidence of Walsh's authorship), p. 50, 51.

6 *Queen's Colleges (Ireland) Commission*, HC 1884–5 (C 4313), XXV.

7 O'Reilly, 'The role of Archbishop Walsh', pp. 134–61.

8 Hansard, HC (series 3) vol. 340, cols. 743–54.

9 William J. Walsh, *Statement of the Chief Grievances of Irish Catholics in the Matter of Education, Primary, Intermediate and University* (Dublin: Browne & Nolan, 1890).

10 William J. Walsh, *The Irish University Question: The Catholic Case* (Dublin: Browne & Nolan, 1897).

11 T. W. Moody, 'The Irish university question in the nineteenth century', *History* 43 (1958), pp. 104–5.

12 Andrew Gailey, *Ireland and the Death of Kindness: Constructive Unionism 1890–1905* (Cork: Cork University Press, 1987), p. 127.

13 Ibid., pp. 128–31.

14 Thomas J. Morrissey, SJ, *Towards a National University: William Delany SJ: An Era of Initiative in Irish Education* (Dublin: Wolfhound, 1983), p. 170.

15 *Royal Commission on University Education in Ireland Final Report*, HC 1903 (Cd 1483), XXXII.

16 O'Reilly, 'The role of Archbishop Walsh', p. 305.

17 *Royal Commission on University Education, Final Report.*

18 O'Reilly, 'The role of Archbishop Walsh', pp. 328–42.

19 Moody and Beckett, *Queen's Belfast*, p. 359 and O'Reilly, 'The role of Archbishop Walsh', p. 336.

20 O'Reilly, 'The role of Archbishop Walsh', pp. 340–1.

21 *Royal Commission on Trinity College and the University of Dublin*, HC 1906 (Cd 3174, 31786), LVI.

22 David W. Miller, *Church, State and Nation in Ireland, 1898–1921* (Dublin: Gill & Macmillan, 1973), pp. 177–80, and O'Reilly, 'The role of Archbishop Walsh', pp. 376–7.

NOTES TO PAGES 14–27

NOTES TO PAGES 14–27

23 'Catholic Graduates and Undergraduates Association', *The University Situation and the National Convention* (Dublin: Browne & Nolan, 1907), p. 14.

24 O'Reilly, 'The role of Archbishop Walsh', pp. 408–10.

25 Ibid., pp. 424–7.

26 Hansard HC (series 4) vol. 847 CLXXXVIII.

27 O'Reilly, 'The role of Archbishop Walsh', p. 436.

28 Ibid., p. 437.

29 Irish Universities Act, 1908 (8 Edw. VII, *c*. 38).

30 DDA, file 375/6 (18 Dec. 1908).

31 Patrick J. Corish, *Maynooth College, 1795–1995* (Dublin: Gill & Macmillan, 1995), p. 263.

32 Moody, 'Irish university question', pp. 99–109.

33 Hansard HC (series 4) vol. 193, col. 646.

Chapter 2
Achieving Equality: Women and the Foundation of the National University of Ireland

1 Helen Blackburn, Obituary of Isabella Tod, *Englishwomen's Review*, no. 3 (1897), p. 61; Anne V. O'Connor, 'Education in nineteenth-century Ireland', in Angela Bourke et al. (eds), *The Field Day Anthology of Irish Writing, Volume v: Irish Women's Writing and Traditions* (Cork: Cork University Press, 2002), p. 652.

2 Isabella Tod, 'Higher education of women in Ireland', *Englishwomen's Review*, LXXXVII (1880), p. 291.

3 Anon, 'Women's higher education in Ireland', *Lyceum*, VI (1893), pp. 142–3.

4 Diary of Mary Hayden, 15 Sept. 1880 (NLI, MS 16,269).

5 G. O'Flynn, 'Some aspects of the education of Irish women through the years', *Capuchin Annual* (1977), p. 176.

6 Evidence of Thomas Hamilton, Royal Commission on University Education (Ireland), *British Parliamentary Papers (BPP)*, vol. 31 (1902), p. 60.

7 'Obituary of Mary Aherne, BA', *Cork University Record* 11 (1947), p. 1, and John A. Murphy, *The College: A History of Queen's/University College Cork, 1845–1995* (Cork: Cork University Press, 1996), p. 173.

8 M. D. McCarthy, 'Some university statistics', *Cork University Record* 4 (1945), p. 15.

9 Murphy, *The College*, p. 129.

10 Ibid.

11 S. Geraghty, 'The first women engineer', *Engineers Journal* 52 (1998), p. 31.

12 *UCG*, vol. II (Nov., 1903), p. 18 and vol. III, Nov. 1904, pp. 17, 32.

13 Seán Tobin, 'Mathematics' in T. Foley (ed.), *Queen's College to National University: Essays on the Academic History of QCG/UCG/NUI* (Dublin: Four Courts, 1999), p. 173.

14 Frances Moffett, *I also am of Ireland* (Bath: Chivers, 1986), pp. 189–90.

15 M. D. O'Sullivan, 'The centenary of Galway College', *Journal of the Galway Archaeological and Historical Society*, 51 (1999), p. 33.

16 Margaret Tierney Downes, *The Case of the Catholic Lady Students of the Royal University of Ireland Stated* (Dublin, 1888), p. 13.

17 Murphy, *The College*, p. 130.

18 Fathers of the Society of Jesus, *A Page of Irish History: The Story of University College, Dublin, 1883–1909* (Dublin: Talbot, 1930), p. 279.

19 *St Stephen's* (UCD student journal), vol. I (1902), p. 114.

20 Ibid.

21 IAWGCG to A. McDonnell, 28 Feb. 1902, (UCD: Minutes of the National University Women's Graduate Association (NUWGA), 1/39).

22 A. Clery, *Dublin Essays* (Dublin: Maunsel, 1919), p. 55.

23 *St Stephen's*, vol. I (1902), p. 114.

24 *St Stephen's* (1901), p. 75.

25 Fathers of the Society of Jesus, *Page of Irish History*, p. 279.

26 *St Stephen's*, Nov. (1901), p. 33 and Dec. (1903), p. 13.

27 Educational Endowments (Ireland) Commission, 1885–6, *BPP*, vol. 26 (1886), p. 789.

28 Francis Sheehy Skeffington to William Delany, 1904, Sheehy Skeffington papers (NLI, MS, 21641/1).

29 Hanna Sheehy Skeffington, 'Women and the university commission', *New Ireland Review* XVII (1902), p. 151.

30 *St Stephen's*, Mar. (1902), p. 66.

31 Royal Commission on University Education in Ireland, 'Third Report of the Commissioners', *BPP*, vol. 32 (1902), pp. 318–21.

32 Ibid, pp. 319, 320.

33 E. Breathnach, 'Charting new waters: women's experience in higher education, 1879–1908', in Mary Cullen (ed.), *Girls Don't Do Honours: Irish Women and Education in the Nineteenth and Twentieth Centuries* (Dublin: Women's Education Bureau, 1987), pp. 73–5.

34 Mary Hayden and Hanna Sheehy Skeffington, 'Women in university: a reply', *New Ireland Review*, vol. I (1908).

35 Letter to UCD Governing Body, 16 Apr. 1910, (UCD: NUWGA papers, 1/3 8).

36 Meeting of NUI Senate, Friday, 14 July 1911 (NUI minutes, vol.I, 17 Dec. 1908–14 July 1911), pp. 276–7 and Meeting of Senate, Friday, 27 Oct. 1911 (NUI minutes, vol. II, 27 Oct. 1911–13 Dec. 1912), p. 310.

37 Meeting of Senate, Friday, 14 July 1911 (NUI minutes vol. I), p. 279.

38 Murphy, *The College*, p. 129.

39 Professor Mary Ryan, MA, 'Random recollections', Cork University Record 5 (1945), pp. 15–19.

40 Ibid., pp. 15–16, and 'The first woman professor', *QCC* VII (Mar. 1911), p. 92.

41 Senia Pašeta, *Before the Revolution: Nationalism, Social Change and Ireland's Catholic Elite, 1879–1922* (Cork: Cork University Press, 1999), pp. 90–1 and Mary

Macken, 'In memoriam: Mary T. Hayden', *Studies* 31 (Sept. 1942) and Fathers of the Society of Jesus, *Page of Irish History*, pp. 454–5.

42 Mary Clancy, ' . . . it was our joy to keep the flag flying: A study of the women's suffrage campaign in County Galway', *UCG Women's Studies Centre Review* 3 (1995), pp. 98–9.

43 *Galway Express*, 10 May 1913.

44 NUWGA, Memorandum on the Status of Women, 23 May 1937 (NAI, D/T) and NUWGA, Report of the Joint Committee of Women's Societies and Social Workers, 1935–42, (UCD: NUWGA papers, 1/60); and S. Paseta, 'Women and civil society: feminist responses to the Irish constitution of 1937' in J. Harris (ed.), *Civil Society in British History: Ideas, Identities, Institutions* (Oxford: Oxford University Press, 2005), pp. 213–29.

45 Murphy, *The College*, p. 131.

Chapter 3
The Position of the Irish Language

1 Fergal McGrath, 'The university question', in Patrick Corish (ed.), *A History of Irish Catholicism*, v, fascicule 6 (Dublin: Gill & Macmillan, 1972).

2 The most accessible accounts of the controversy may be found in Tomás Ó Fiaich, 'The great controversy', in Seán Ó Tuama (ed.), *The Gaelic League Idea* (Cork: Mercier Press, 1972), pp. 63–75; Proinsias Mac Aonghusa, *Ar Son na Gaeilge: Conradh na Gaeilge 1893–1993* (Baile Átha Cliath: Conradh na Gaeilge, 1993), pp. 72–98; Donncha Ó Súilleabháin, *Cath na Gaeilge sa Chóras Oideachais 1893–1911* (Baile Átha Cliath: Conradh na Gaeilge, 1988).

3 The context is explored in Patrick Maume, *The Long Gestation: Irish Nationalist Life 1891–1918* (Dublin: Gill & Macmillan, 1999); Senia Pašeta, *Before the Revolution: Nationalism, Social Change and Ireland's Catholic*

Elite 1879–1922 (Cork: Cork University Press, 1999); and P. J. Mathews, *Revival: The Abbey Theatre, Sinn Féin, the Gaelic League and the Co-operative Movement* (Notre Dame, Indiana: University of Notre Dame Press, 2003). For intimacy of reference, see Douglas Hyde, *Language, Lore and Lyrics*, ed. Breandán Ó Conaire (Dublin: Irish Academic Press, 1986).

4 Máirtín Ó Murchú, *Cumann Buan-Choimeádta na Gaeilge: Tús an Athréimnithe* (Baile Átha Cliath: Cois Life Teoranta, 2001) is the definitive account.

5 Máirín Ní Mhuiríosa, *Réamh-Chonraitheoirí* (Baile Átha Cliath: Clódhanna Teoranta, 1968); also Tomás Ó hAilín, 'Irish revival movements', in Brian Ó Cuív (ed.), *A View of the Irish Language* (Dublin: Stationery Office, 1969), pp. 91–100.

6 Clare O'Halloran, *Golden Ages and Barbarous Nations: Antiquarian Debate and Cultural Politics in Ireland, c.1750–1800* (Cork: Cork University Press in association with Field Day, 2004); Joep Leerssen, *Remembrance and Imagination. Patterns in the Historical and Literary Representation of Ireland in the Nineteenth Century* (Cork: Cork University Press in association with Field Day, 1996); Damien Murray, *Romanticism, Nationalism and Irish Antiquarian Societies, 1840–80* (Maynooth: National University of Ireland, Department of Old and Middle Irish, 2000).

7 Ó Fiaich, 'The great controversy', p. 64.

8 Ibid., p. 65, but these figures do not include schools run by the Christian Brothers outside the state system. For a detailed study, see Thomas A. O'Donoghue, *Bilingual Education in Ireland, 1904–1922* (Perth: Murdoch UP, 2000).

9 Ó Fiaich, 'The great controversy', p. 67; for Mahaffy, see W. B. Stanford and R. B. McDowell, *Mahaffy. A Biography of an Anglo-Irishman* (London: Routledge & Kegan Paul, 1971).

10 Janet Egleson Dunleavy and Gareth W. Dunleavy, *Douglas Hyde: A Maker of Modern Ireland* (Berkeley: University of California Press, 1991); Risteárd Ó Glaisne, *Dúbhglas de h-Íde: Ceannródaí Cultúrtha 1860–1910* (Baile Átha Cliath: Conradh na Gaeilge, 1991).

11 See note 3 above. Also Patrick Maume, *D. P. Moran* (Dundalk: Dundalgan Press, 1995).

12 Ó Fiaich, 'The great controversy', p. 70.

13 Of course, the contemplation of some form of 'Home Rule all round' was the most explicit acknowledgment of this distinctiveness; see J. Kendle, *Ireland and the Federal Solution: The Debate over the United Kingdom Constitution, 1870–1921* (Kingston: McGill-Queen's University Press, 1989). Also Gearóid Ó Tuathaigh, 'The state, sentiment and the politics of language', in Bruce Stewart (ed.), *Hearts and Minds: Irish Culture and Society under the Act of Union* (Gerrards Cross, Bucks.: Colin Smythe, 2002), pp. 71–89.

14 Mac Aonghusa, *Ar Son na Gaeilge*, p. 85; Ó Fiaich, 'The great controversy', p. 70.

15 The atmosphere was already soured by trenchant criticism by the Gaelic League of the inadequate provision for Irish in the teaching and formation of priests at Maynooth College; see, Gearóid Ó Tuathaigh, 'Maigh Nuad agus Stair na Gaeilge', in Etaín Ó Síocháin (ed.), *Maigh Nuad: Saothrú na Gaeilge 1795–1995* (Maigh Nuad: An Sagart, 1995), pp. 13–35.

16 Thomas J. Morrissey, *Towards a National University: William Delany (1835–1924)* (Dublin: Wolfhound, 1983).

17 Eoin MacNeill, *Irish in the National University of Ireland* (Dublin: An Cló-Cumann, 1909); see Michael Tierney, *Eoin MacNeill: Scholar and Man of Action 1867–1945* (Oxford: Clarendon Press, 1980) and F. X. Martin and F. J. Byrne (eds), *The Scholar Revolutionary: Eoin MacNeill, 1867–1945, and the Making of the New Ireland* (Shannon: Irish University Press, 1973).

18 Ó Fiaich, 'The great controversy', p. 72; see also for an extended of O'Hickey's interven-

tion, Mac Aonghusa, *Ar Son na Gaeilge*, pp. 88–96. For a sympathetic biography, see Pádraig Eric Mac Fhinn, *Mícheál P. Ó hIceadha* (Baile Átha Cliath: Sáirséal agus Dill, 1974).

19 *Ollscoil na hÉireann/National University of Ireland. Calendar 1995–1996*, pp. 34, 40.

20 Between 1944 and 1970 the Catholic Archbishop of Dublin sought to enforce a 'ban' on Catholics entering Trinity; see Donal McCartney, *UCD: A National Idea* (Dublin: Gill & Macmillan, 1999).

21 This view is implicit in later expressions of anxiety at changes in Irish education policy: 'the position of Irish within the identity and social meaning of systems of middle class groups is becoming fragmented. The emergence of more instrumentally oriented educational objectives within some post-primary schools, and of a third-level sector which does not impose an Irish requirement to entrants, has facilitated a situation in which high educational and occupational achievement does not necessarily include high competence in Irish'. Advisory Planning Committee, *Irish and the Education System: An Analysis of Examination Results* (Dublin: Bord na Gaeilge, 1986), pp. 75–6.

22 The two original NIHE institutions are now the University of Limerick and Dublin City University, while the RTCs are now the Institutes of Technology.

Chapter 4
University College Cork

I wish to thank Ms Nóirín Moynihan, NUI; Ms Caitríona Mulcahy, archivist UCC; Caitríona Crowe, National Archives; UCC President Emeritus Michael Mortell; and the Boole Library UCC staff, for their help in the preparation of this paper.

1 For otherwise unattributed references in the Windle part of this paper, see John A. Murphy, *The College: A History of Queen's/*

University College Cork (Cork: University Press, 1995), ch. 7 and endnotes; and Monica Taylor, *Sir Bertram Windle* (London: Longmans, 1932).

2 Hansard, HC vol. 188, col. 849 (11 May 1908).

3 *Cork Examiner*, 27 Apr. 1908. See also, *President's Report*, 1907–8 (App. A), p. 10.

4 College Council minutes, 27 May 1908.

5 Bertram Windle to the secretaries, Royal University of Ireland, 10 Nov. 1909 in UCC Archives (UCC, Officers 8/83).

6 NUI Senate minutes, 6 May 1910.

7 Senate minutes, 29 Jan. 1909.

8 Senate minutes, 8 July 1915.

9 Bertram Windle to Baron Pallas, 8 Dec. 1909 (UC, Council 12/53).

10 Bertram Windle to Sir Christopher Nixon, 2 Mar. 1910 (UC, Council 12/134(2)).

11 Ibid.

12 Bertram Windle to Joseph McGrath, 26 Nov. 1909 (UC, Council 12/109).

13 *Cork Examiner*, 26 May 1910.

14 *Cork Examiner*, 30 Mar. 1912. To a modern reader 'Home Rule' might more appropriately describe the constituent college status UCC had enjoyed since 1908. But in popular usage it was a sufficiently flexible concept (in pre-'republic' political rhetoric) to extend to independence.

15 *Cork Constitution*, 14 May 1912.

16 See *President's Report*, 1909–10, 1911–12, 1913–14.

17 *The Times*, Special Irish Number, 4 Nov. 1919.

18 The *Cork Examiner* was an enthusiastic advocate of the demand for independence (see its lengthy opinion column, 26 Mar. 1918), the (Protestant) *Cork Constitution*, perhaps understandably, less so: cf. *Cork Constitution*, 27 Mar. 1918.

19 *Statement of the Governing Body ... separate University of Munster* (Cork 1918: Munster University Pamphlets (MUP)), Boole Library, UCC; Governing Body Resolution, 9 Mar. 1918).

20 For what follows, see Murphy, *The College*, pp. 204 ff.; J. Anthony Gaughan, *Alfred*

O'Rahilly I – Academic (Dublin: Kingdom
Books, 1986), pp. 65 ff; Newspaper cuttings
file, UC Archives.

21 Senate minutes, 21 May 1919.

22 *Irish Independent*, 26 Apr. 1919.

23 Bertram Windle to Arthur W. Samuels, Irish
attorney general, 21 Feb. 1919 (MUP, 1919);
Taylor, *Windle,* pp. 274-5.

24 Bertram Windle to McGrath, 5 Mar. 1919
(MUP, 1919).

25 *Cork Examiner*, 26 Mar. 1918.

26 Senate minutes, 28 Feb. 1918.

27 MUP, 27 Mar. 1919.

28 Gaughan, *O'Rahilly I*, p. 70. For NUI
opposition, see *Irish Independent*,
6 Mar, 24 May 1919.

29 *Freeman's Journal, Irish Times, Cork Examiner,*
7 June 1919.

30 Murphy, *The College*, p. 207.

31 Senate minutes, 24 Oct. 1919.

32 A special meeting of the Governing Body
endorsed Statute IX (2 May 1917). A Senate
meeting of 6 July 1917 petitioned the Lords
Justices in Council to disallow the statute,
which was duly done on 10 Dec. 1917. Nearly
half a century later, Jim Hurley, Secretary
UCC, writing to his UCD counterpart, J. P.
McHale on 23 Nov. 1961, says he never
heard 'any satisfactory reason for the
Senate's opposition. It could not have
been because of the Revolution in Russia,
as the first reading was in Feb. 1917' (File
no. 966, Secretary's Office filing, UCC).

33 Murphy, *The College*, p. 207.

34 *The Times*, Special Irish Number, 4 Nov. 1919.

35 For Merriman, see Murphy, *The College*,
ch. 8, pp. 214 ff.

36 See Senate minutes, 8 July 1976: professorship of electrical engineering, UCC.

37 For O'Rahilly, see Murphy, *The College*, ch.
X, pp. 267 ff.

38 *Cork University Record*, no. 4, Summer
1945, pp. 8-18.

39 *Cork University Record*, no. 11, Christmas
1947, p. 23.

40 *Cork University Record*, no. 2, Christmas

1944, pp. 2-3.

41 J. Anthony Gaughan, *Alfred O'Rahilly III:
Catholic Apologist* (Dublin: Kingdom
Books, 1993), part 2, p. 180.

42 *Commission on Higher Education 1960-1967:*
Report vol. I (Dublin: 1967), pp. 405; 408-9;
414-19.

43 *Report on University Re-organisation*
(Dublin: 1972) (App. I), pp. 68-76; (App.
III), pp. 83-6.

44 Ibid., 17 Dec. 1974 (App II); Dáil Éireann,
Parliamentary Debate vol. 277, cols 733,
739 (22 Jan. 1975).

45 Dáil Éireann Debate – Analysis of some
statements by Dr Garret FitzGerald, 6 June
1975 (NAI, s 18644).

46 National University of Ireland/Higher
Education Authority corr. 1984-2004, no.
10, Michael Gilheaney, 23 Apr. 1985 (NUI
Archives).

47 University College Cork/Oral History
Archives, Tadhg Ó Ciardha, 21 May 1991.

48 Michael P. Mortell, interview with author,
25 Oct. 2006.

49 Aloys Fleischmann, letter to author, 9 July
1992.

50 Senate minutes, 25 Jan. 1996.

51 Governing Body, 11 June 1996.

52 Chancellor, Senate minutes, 3 Oct. 1996.

53 Senate minutes, 25 Apr. 1996.

54 Seanad Éireann Parliamentary Debates,
vols 150, 151; index sub (Universities Bill).

55 Universities Act 1997, Acts of the
Oireachtas, no. 24 of 1997, pp. 975-1015.

56 Seanad Éireann, vol. 150, cols 1565-6 (16
Apr. 1997).

57 *Evening Echo*, 28 Nov. 1995.

58 *The NUI Federal University in an Era of
Transition*, National University of Ireland.
(7 Nov. 2002).

Chapter 5
National University of Ireland, Galway

1 College submission to the Minister of
Education on 2 Feb. 1923.

2   The quotations are from Governing Body minutes, except where noted.

3   The Presidents of the College/University for the period in question were: Professor Alexander Anderson (1899–1934), Rt Rev. Mgr John Hynes (1934–45), Rt Rev. Mgr Pádraig de Brún (1945–59), Dr Martin J. Newell (1960–75), Dr Colm Ó hEocha (1975–96), Dr Patrick F. Fottrell (1996–2000), Dr Iognáid Ó Muircheartaigh (2000–8).

4   Source: Christopher Townley (former Librarian).

5   Dáil Éireann Report, 11 July 1924.

6   Dáil Éireann Report, 21 July 1924.

7   Ibid.

8   *Conference on Galway University College: Report on the Conference, 1926*, from which the following material is also drawn.

9   Dáil Éireann Report, 24 Oct. 1929.

10 NUI Calendars.

11 Letter of 8 Aug. 1995 to the Department of Education.

Chapter 6
University College Dublin

1   Healy to Walsh, 8 June 1908 (P. J. Walsh, *William J. Walsh* (Dublin and Cork: Talbot Press, 1928), p. 562).

2   Hansard (series 4) vol. CLXXXVII, col. 392 (31 March 1908).

3   Ibid., cols 339–40.

4   Ibid., vol. CLXXXVIII, col. 849 (11 May 1908).

5   Ibid., vol. CLXXXVII, col. 393 (31 March 1908).

6   Ibid., col. 383 (31 March 1908).

7   Windle to McGrath, 24 Mar. 1910 (NUIA, McGrath papers).

8   O'Rahilly to Tierney, 23 Apr. 1951 (UCDA, PO2/51).

9   *An Claidheamh Soluis*, 8 Feb. 1908.

10 NUI Senate minutes, 23 June 1910, I, 114.

11 Windle to McGrath, 20 Jan. 1912; 12 Jan. 1913 (NUIA, McGrath papers).

12 Windle to McGrath, 26 June 1910; 12 Jan.,

13 Oct. 1912; 10, 12, 28 Nov., 11 Dec. 1914 (NUIA, McGrath papers).

13 NUI Senate minutes, 16 May 1940, Appendix D.

14 Ibid.

15 John A. Murphy, *The College: A History of Queen's/University College Cork, 1845–1995* (Cork: Cork University Press, 1995), p. 205.

16 NUI Senate minutes, 28 Feb. 1919.

17 Ibid., 7 May 1919.

18 Ibid., 21 May 1919.

19 Michael Ennis JP, of Monkstown, Dublin, was elected to the Governing Body by the General Council of County Councils. Agnes O'Farrelly, a lecturer in the Department of Modern Irish and prominent in the Gaelic League, was elected to the Governing Body by the graduates.

20 UCD Governing Body minutes, 26 June 1919.

21 Michael Tierney, 'The university after thirty years' (UCDA, Tierney papers, LA30/207, pp. 5, 17–24). This article, written in 1940 or 1941, was intended for *Studies* but does not appear to have been published.

22 Michael Tierney, 'Memorandum on university question, no. 1', Jan. 1951 (UCDA, PO7/2).

23 UCDA, PO7/3.

24 Tierney to de Brun, 25 Jan. 1951 (UCDA, PO2/51/52).

25 *Irish Independent*, 17 Apr. 1951.

26 *Catholic University of Ireland, 1854: Centenary Celebrations* (Dublin: University College Dublin, 1954), pp. 4, 24.

27 Denis Gwynn and James Hogan, 'Some afterthoughts on the Newman centenary celebrations', *University Review*, I: 2 (autumn 1954), pp. 3–9.

28 James Meenan diary, 10 Dec. 1954 (UCDA); Meenan to Tierney, 12 Dec. 1954 (Tierney papers, UCDA, LA30/164).

29 James Meenan diary, 10 Dec. 1954 (UCDA).

30 NUI Senate minutes, 23 Oct. 1968.

31 UCD Governing Body minutes, 29 Apr. 1969.

32 Ibid., 14 Mar. 1989.

Chapter 7
*National University of Ireland,
Maynooth*

I am indebted to Ms Nóirín Moynihan for
assistance with the archival sources held by
the National University of Ireland. Breeda
Behan, Peter Carr, Pat Dalton and Frank
Mulligan from NUI Maynooth helped make
the compilation of this institutional story
possible. My task was made considerably
easier by the very fine record of the College's
development contained within Patrick J.
Corish, *Maynooth College, 1795–1995*
(Dublin: Gill & Macmillan, 1995).

1   Personal letter of the Chief Secretary,
    Augustine Birrell, to the President of
    Maynooth, Mgr Hogan, 27 Nov. 1914
    (Maynooth College Archives).
2   The foundation of Maynooth in 1795
    had been a pragmatic act that provided
    state support for the education of priests
    three decades before the enactment of
    Catholic Emancipation in 1829. The row
    over the role of religion and identity
    within university education found its
    fullest expression in the debate over the
    'Godless colleges' established in Belfast,
    Cork and Galway in 1845, in the establish-
    ment of the Catholic University in Dublin
    in 1854, and in the responses to a series of
    failed Parliamentary initiatives stretching
    from Gladstone to Balfour.
3   Patrick J. Corish, *Maynooth College 1795–1995*
    (Dublin: Gill & Macmillan, 1995), p. 264.
4   The Robertson Commission had been
    established in 1901 but it attracted little
    support for its final recommendations
    which failed to deal with the issue of
    Maynooth and its Theology Faculty.
    The Fry Commission established in 1906
    removed the question of Trinity College,
    Dublin from its discussions but it too failed
    to offer concrete recommendations for
    the future of Maynooth.

5   Charles Craig, Hansard, HC, vol. CXCIII,
    col. 386 (23 July 1908).
6   Augustine Birrell to President of Maynooth,
    14 Jan. 1914 (Maynooth College Archives).
    He suggested that 'Maynooth men will
    soon swell the Senate and manage Univ-
    ersity affairs'. In the event representatives
    of Maynooth never acquired more than
    two of the four seats reserved for
    Convocation.
7   Dr Hazel, Hansard, HC, vol. CXCIII,
    col. 524 (24 July 1908).
8   The role of Fr Delaney in briefing the
    leader of the Irish party is described in
    some detail in *A Page of Irish History: Story
    of University College, Dublin 1883–1909*,
    Compiled by the Fathers of the Society
    of Jesus (Dublin: Talbot Press, 1930),
    pp. 560–1.
9   John Redmond, Hansard, HC, vol. CXCIII,
    col. 530 (24 July 1908).
10 Dr Hazel, Hansard, HC, vol. CXCIII,
    col. 518 (24 July 1908).
11 John Redmond, Hansard, HC,
    vol. CLXXXVIII, col. 790 (11 May 1908).
12 Dr Hazel, Hansard, HC, vol. CXCIII,
    col. 521 (24 July 1908).
13 Ibid., col. 522.
14 Correspondence of Daniel Mannix to
    Archbishop Walsh, 20 July 1906 (Maynooth
    College Archives).
15 Corish, *Maynooth College*, p. 262.
16 Birrell, Hansard, HC, vol. CXCIII, col. 548
    (24 July 1908).
17 Mannix's handwritten submission was
    less than impressive in composition with
    sections scribbled out and insertions
    squeezed in. It has all the hallmarks of
    a hastily written document that was sub-
    mitted in adherence to the required for-
    malities. The copy laid before senate was
    professionally printed.
18 Maynooth lore has it that Mannix, when
    asked for a reference by a departing stu-
    dent, refused saying, 'Being known as a

student of Maynooth is sufficient reference for anyone'.

19 Application for the recognition of the College as a 'Recognised College' of the University, submitted by Dr Mannix to the 27 July 1909 senate (NUIA).

20 His Grace the Archbishop of Dublin, Chancellor of the National University of Ireland, in reference to Division of Funds of the Late Royal University of Ireland, 23 Feb. 1911 (NUIA, Box 52).

21 Corish, *Maynooth College*, p. 263.

22 In 1914 the government approved a Supplemental and Amending Charter for the University and made provision for the President of a Recognised College to be an ex-officio member of the General Board of Studies, 'if the Senate should in the case of any such recognised College so decide'. The senate had earlier requested that specifically the President of Maynooth should be made an *ex-officio* member of the Board but Birrell refused to agree to such a named position, requiring a generic description instead (NUIA, Senate minutes).

23 On 18 November 1914 the Registrar of the University wrote to the Chancellor informing him that Rt Rev. Monsignor J. F. Hogan DD was one of four co-opted to senate, he having earlier been appointed by royal warrant to the outgoing senate (NUIA, Box 1).

24 NUI Senate minutes, Feb. 1911.

25 NUI Senate minutes, July 1911.

26 Chief Secretary to Registrar of the National University, 20 Dec. 1913 (NUIA, Box 1).

27 Chief Secretary Birrell to Mgr Hogan, President of Maynooth, 14 Jan. 1914 (Maynooth College Archives).

28 Birrell to Hogan, 27 Nov. 1914 (Maynooth College Archives).

29 Corish, *Maynooth College*, p. 364.

30 Ibid., p. 368.

31 By way of comparison, the original campus of Cork was no more than 49 acres in extent.

32 Corish, *Maynooth College*, p. 383.

33 The proposals of the Commission on Higher Education were not immediately acted on as the issue of university legislation became embroiled in proposals for a merger of Trinity College and University College Dublin.

34 Correspondence, 20 June 1984 (NUIA, B84-144).

35 Chancellor to President Olden, 26 June 1984 (NUIA).

36 Legal Opinion of Mr G. Stapleton, 19 July 1984 (NUIA).

37 Minutes of Meeting of Standing Committee, 7 Nov. 1984.

38 NUI Senate minutes, 24 March 1988.

39 Report of President to the Trustees, June 1990 (Maynooth College Archives).

40 Submission by the President of St Patrick's College, Maynooth to the Special Meeting of Senate, 10 Dec. 1990 (NUIA).

41 Chancellor to Mrs Mary O'Rourke, Minister for Education, 5 Mar. 1991 (NUIA).

42 Meeting of Senate, 9 July 1992.

43 Report of President to the Trustees, October 1992. Maynooth College Archives.

44 The detailed proposals for legislative change made by the senate to the minister in July 1992, including the relevant sections dealing with the Governing Body for National University Maynooth and the special provisions for the selection of the Maynooth president were discussed and accepted by the trustees at their meeting in June 1992 (Maynooth College Archives).

45 Recognition of the public standing of Maynooth was further evidenced when 153 university presidents attended the CRE conference in the college in May 1993.

46 The strategic planning exercise was to find expression in the publication in 1995 of *Maynooth, Towards The Next Century* (Maynooth College Archives).

47 At a reunion meeting, held in Maynooth in May 2004, of the university presidents and provost in office at the time of the passage

of the University Act, the former minister confirmed this interpretation of events.

48 Under the perceptive guidance of the college's first lay Bursar, Pat Dalton, the accounts and budgets of the College had been divided into separate accounts for each of the seminary, pontifical, and recognised college units. Staff paid from the annual state grant were likewise separately accounted for except in the case of a number of officers with overlapping intra-institutional responsibilities. This separation which had been put in place in the 1970s greatly facilitated the 1994 division of the College and the legal separation of 1997.

49 The initial meeting between the Master and Dr Art Cosgrove, President of University College Dublin, occurred in July 1994 and the proposal to senate was made in July 1995.

50 The title of master ceased with the implementation of the legislation and the incumbent had the choice of the title of president or provost or whatever other title might be decided upon by the governing authority. In conformity with the practice in the other three constitutent universities, the title President was chosen.

51 Membership of the Commission was William J. Smyth, President, Peter Carr, Registrar, Art Cosgrove representing the Chancellor, and John Hayden representing the Chairman of the Higher Education Authority.

52 Archbishop Desmond Connell and Ms Mary Hanafin were both members of the first Governing Authority.

Chapter 8
William J. Walsh, 1908–21

I am very grateful to Ms Noelle Dowling, Dublin Diocesan Archivist; Ms Nóirín Moynihan, National University of Ireland Archivist, Ms Vera Orschel, Archivist, Irish College Rome, and to Fr Thomas Morrissey SJ, Archbishop Walsh's biographer, for their help in the preparation of this essay.

1 *Irish Independent*, 9 April 1921.
2 Francis Cruise O'Brien, *The Leader*, 14 May 1910, p. 296.
3 Myles V. Ronan, *The Most Rev. W. J. Walsh: Archbishop of Dublin* (Bray: The Associate Magazine, 1927), p. 1.
4 Thomas J. Morrissey, *William J. Walsh: Archbishop of Dublin, 1841–1921* (Dublin: Four Courts, 2000), p. 5.
5 Michael Davitt, *The Fall of Feudalism in Ireland* (London, 1904), pp. 551–60.
6 Ronan, *The Most Rev. W. J. Walsh*, p. 3.
7 Morrissey, *William J. Walsh*, p. 124
8 Ibid., p. 353.
9 P. J. Walsh, *William J. Walsh* (Dublin and Cork: Talbot Press, 1928, p. 95.
10 *The Tablet*, 16 April 1921.
11 David C. Sheehy, 'William J. Walsh', *Oxford DNB* (2004).
12 James Joyce, *Portrait of the Artist as a Young Man* (London: Chancellor Press), p.138.
13 Morrissey, *William J. Walsh*, pp. 352–3.
14 William Walsh to Joseph McGrath, 29 Jan. 1915 (NUI, Chancellor's Correspondence/107 [NUI/CC])
15 Ronan, *The Most Rev. W. J. Walsh*, p. 7.
16 Sheehy, *DNB*; Mary A. Bolster, *Carysfort 1877–1977: Two Centenary Lectures* (Dublin, 1981); Carla King, 'The early years of the College, 1875–1921', in James Kelly (ed.), *St Patrick's College Drumcondra: A History* (Dublin: Four Courts, 2006), pp. 91–133; John Coolahan, *Irish Education: History and Structure* (Dublin: Institute of Public Administration, 1981), pp 53–4.
17 Ronan, *The Most Rev. W. J. Walsh*, p. 7.
18 *Manchester Guardian*, 11 Apr. 1921.
19 Francis Cruise O'Brien, *The Leader*, 14 May 1910, p. 296.
20 See chapter 1 above, pp. 3–18; Aidan J. O'Reilly, 'The Role of Archbishop W. Walsh in the Resolution of the Irish University Question' (PhD thesis, NUI Maynooth, 2001).
21 Augustine Birrell to William Walsh, 8 July 1908 (DDA, Walsh papers).

22 T. M. Healy to William Walsh, 8 June 1908 (DDA, Walsh papers).

23 Donal McCartney, *The National University of Ireland and Eamon de Valera* (Dublin: University Press of Ireland, 1983), p. 11.

24 Walsh, *William J. Walsh*, p. 563.

25 V. T. H. Delaney, *Christopher Palles* (Dublin, A. Figgis, 1960).

26 Ronan Keane, 'Christopher Palles', *Oxford DNB* (2004).

27 Delaney, *Palles*, p. 152.

28 Walsh, *William J. Walsh*, p. 56.

29 *Freeman's Journal*, 9 Apr. 1921,

30 McCartney, *The National University*, p. 13.

31 Morrissey, *William J. Walsh*, p. 234.

32 William Walsh to Joseph McGrath, [N.D. 22 Nov. 1911?] (NUI/CC, 51).

33 John O'Donnell, Arthur O'Hagan, Solicitors, to William Walsh, 10 Apr. 1911 (DDA, Walsh papers/NUI/2).

34 McCartney, *National University*, p. 12.

35 Donal McCartney, *UCD: A National Idea* (Dublin: Gill & Macmillan, 1999), p. 79.

36 Mary Hayden to William Walsh, 8 June 1909 (DDA, Walsh papers/NUI/6).

37 Mary Hayden to William Walsh, 10 June 1909 (DDA, Walsh papers/NUI/6).

38 W. F. Butler to William Walsh, 10 Jan. 1910 (DDA, Walsh papers/NUI/4); William Walsh to Joseph McGrath, 3 Nov. 1913 (NUI/CC/84).

39 William Magennis to William Walsh, 1 Apr. 1908 (DDA, Walsh papers/NUI/1); G. C. Ashlin to William Walsh, 29 Jan. 1909 (DDA, Walsh papers/NUI/6); Hugh Lane to William Walsh, 11 Oct. 1909 (DDA, Walsh papers/NUI/11).

40 'Bishops' Scholars' to William Walsh, Oct. 1910 (DDA, Walsh papers/NUI/4).

41 Charles Casey to William Walsh, 24 Oct. 1908 (DDA, Walsh papers/NUI/13).

42 Morrissey, *William J. Walsh*, p. 236.

43 Timothy Corcoran, *The National University Handbook: 1908–31* (Dublin: NUI, 1932), pp. 24–5; McCartney, *The National University*, p. 13.

44 'JD' to John Hagan, 15 Jan. 1909 (Irish College Archives, Rome, HAG 1/1909/1).

45 Cathy Hays, 'Joseph McGrath (1858–1923)', *Dictionary of Irish Biography*.

46 William Walsh to Joseph McGrath, 1 June 1905 (NUI/CC/2).

47 Joseph McGrath to William Walsh, 16 Sept. 1913, NUI McGrath papers; David C. Sheehy, 'The "Brick Palace" at Drumcondra: Archbishop Walsh and the building of Archbishop's House', in James Kelly and Daire Keogh (eds), *History of the Catholic Diocese of Dublin* (Dublin, Four Courts, 2000), pp. 313–31; William Walsh to Joseph McGrath, 9 Jan. 1915 (NUI/CC/2).

48 William Walsh to Joseph McGrath, 27 Oct. 1914 (NUI/CC/107).

49 Ibid.

50 William Walsh to Joseph McGrath, 14 Sept. 1909 (NUI/CC/31).

51 *Freeman's Journal*, 24 May 1921.

52 A. P. McGill, Dublin Castle, to William Walsh, 28 Feb. 1914 (DDA, Walsh papers/ NUI/1).

53 William Walsh to Joseph McGrath, 8 Dec. 1909 (NUI/CC/2).

54 William Walsh to Joseph McGrath, 16 June 1911 (NUI/CC/52); 12 Dec. 1912, (NUI/CC/5); 15 Apr. 1910 (NUI/CC); 15 Apr. 1910 (NUI/ CC/31).

55 Joseph McGrath to Wiliam Walsh, 20 Apr. 1910 (NUI/McGrath papers).

56 McCartney, *UCD: A National Idea*, pp. 32–3.

57 Morrissey, *William J. Walsh*, p. 231.

58 William Walsh to William Delany, 7 Aug. 1909 (DDA, Walsh papers/NUI/6).

59 John O'Donnell to William Walsh, 23 Oct. 1912 (DDA, Walsh papers/NUI/2); Corcoran, *The National University Handbook*, pp. 106–7; The archbishop was personally hostile to Fr Finlay, and indeed his brother Thomas Finlay SJ, but his stated objection to the appointment was due to uncertainty which remained surrounding the draft deed of foundation, William

Walsh to John O'Donnell, 22 Oct. 1912 (NUI/CC/51).

60 Bertram Windle to William Walsh, 29 Dec. 1908 (DDA, Walsh papers/NUI/12).

61 McCartney, *UCD: A National Idea*, p. 33.

62 Ibid., pp. 33–5.

63 *Freeman's Journal*, 9 Apr. 1921.

64 John [Eoin] MacNeill to William Walsh, 14 Dec. 1908 (DDA, Walsh papers/NUI/12).

65 Thomas J. Morrissey, *Towards a National University: William Delany SJ (1835–1924)* (Dublin: Wolfhound, 1983), pp. 321 ff.

66 Bertram Windle to William Walsh, 15 July 1909 (DDA, Walsh papers/NUI/6).

67 Ibid.

68 'JD' to John Hagan, 15 Jan. 1909 (Irish College Archives, Rome, HAG 1/1909/1).

69 William Walsh to Joseph McGrath, 15 Apr. 1910 (NUI/CC/31).

70 Breandan Ó Madagáin, 'Irish: a difficult birth', in Tadhg Foley (ed.), *From Queen's College to National University* (Dublin: Four Courts, 1999), p. 354.

71 John A. Murphy, *The College: A History of Queen's/University College Cork* (Cork: Cork University Press, 1995), p. 183.

72 William Walsh to Augustine Birrell, 6 Jan. 1908 (DDA, f. 14).

73 William Walsh to Joseph McGrath, 9 June 1912 (NUI/CC/51).

74 William Walsh to Joseph McGrath, 20 June 1912 (NUI/CC/51).

75 Bertram Windle to Joseph McGrath, 7 May 1913 (NUI/McGrath papers).

76 William Walsh to Joseph McGrath, 5 Dec. 1913 (NUI/CC/84).

77 William Walsh to Joseph McGrath, 24 Jan. 1915 (NUI/CC/107); Bertram Windle to Joseph McGrath, 27 Jan. 1915 (NUI/McGrath).

78 David C. Sheehy, 'William J. Walsh', *DNB*.

79 Bertram Windle to William Walsh, 19 Jan. 1910; C. J. Nixon to William Walsh, 20 Jan. 1910 (DDA, Walsh papers/NUI/4); William Walsh to Joseph McGrath, 9 Dec. 1909 (NUI/CC/2).

80 William Walsh to Joseph McGrath, 6 Oct. 1914 (NUI/CC/107).

81 William Walsh to Joseph McGrath, 15 Apr. 1915 (NUI/CC/107).

82 Bertram Windle to William Walsh, 21 Jan. 1910 (DDA, Walsh papers/NUI/4).

83 Bertram Windle to Joseph McGrath, 12 Jan. 1913 (NUI/McGrath).

84 Bertram Windle to William Walsh, 21 Jan. 1910 (DDA, Walsh papers/NUI/4).

85 Murphy, *The College*, pp. 201–7.

86 Bertram Windle to Joseph McGrath, 3 Oct. 1912; 13 Oct. 1915 (NUI/McGrath papers).

87 William Walsh to Joseph McGrath, 30 May 1913 (NUI/CC/84).

88 Augustine Birrell to William Walsh, 10 Dec. 1914 (DDA, Walsh papers, NUI/1).

89 Address to Winborne (NUI/CC/135).

90 Morrissey, *William J. Walsh*, pp. 340–1.

91 Cited in ibid., p. 352.

92 T. P. O'Connor, *Daily Telegraph*, 11 Apr. 1921.

93 *Irish Independent*, 14 April 1921.

94 NUI Senate minutes, 19 April 1921, VIII, 3102.

95 Resolution of Governing Body of UCD, 7 May 1921 (DDA, Walsh papers, 380/8).

Chapter 9
Eamon de Valera, 1921–75

1 Donal McCartney, *The National University of Ireland and Eamon de Valera* (Dublin: University Press of Ireland, 1983), p. 25.

2 'My Selection as Chancellor' (UCDA, de Valera papers, P150/93).

3 Michael F. Cox to Eamon de Valera, 20 July 1921 (UCDA, de Valera papers, P150/93).

4 De Valera to Cox, 20 July 1921 (UCDA, de Valera papers, P150/93).

5 McCartney, *The NUI and Eamon de Valera*, p. 36.

6 *An Seansailéir ag caint leis na micléinn*, pp. 1–2 (UCDA, de Valera papers, P150/93).

7 Interview with Dr Garret FitzGerald, Aug. 2006.

8 NUI Senate minutes, Special Election Meeting, 19 Dec. 1921, VIII, p. 203.

9 Kathleen O'Connell to the Registrar, 2 Mar. 1922, 21 June 1922 (NUIA, Box 214).

10 NUI Senate minutes, IX, 5 Dec. 1924, pp. 323-9.

11 O'Connell to the Registrar, 17 July 1936 (NUIA, Box 368).

12 NUI Senate minutes, 16 May 1940, XVIII, Appendix D, p. 151, Text of Speech by Eamon de Valera, LLD, PhD, TD, An Taoiseach, Chancellor of the University, 11 Apr. 1940.

13 McCartney, *The NUI and Eamon de Valera*, p. 36

14 Ibid., pp. 36-45.

15 NUI, Senate minutes, 8 Apr. 1954, XXVII, p. 351.

16 NUI, Senate minutes, 10 Mar. 1932, XIII, p. 97.

17 Ibid.

18 NUI, Senate minutes, 19 May 1938, XVII, p. 8.

19 Maurice Moynihan to Alex McCarthy, 28 July 1938, p. 1 (NUI, Box 419).

20 Ibid.

21 Ibid., pp. 1-2.

22 *Report of the Commission on Accommodation Needs of the Constituent Colleges of the National University of Ireland* (Dublin, 1959), p. 128.

23 Ibid.

24 Ibid., p. 1.

25 Michael Tierney to Eamon de Valera, 13 April 1959 (NAI, D/T s.16289).

26 Dáil Debates, vol. 180, col. 939 (23 Mar. 1960); Seán O'Connor, *A Troubled Sky: Reflections on the Irish Education Scene, 1957-1968* (Dublin: Education Research Centre, 1986), p. 46.

27 'Gift to Chancellor', *Irish Press*, 4 Dec. 1958 (UCDA, de Valera papers, P150/98).

28 *University College Dublin and the Future* (Dublin: Tuairim, 1959), pp. 11-12

29 *Report of the Commission on Accommodation Needs*, p. 128.

30 Tierney to de Valera, 13 April 1959 (NAI, D/T s.16289).

31 Maurice Moynihan to Tarlach Ó Raifeartaigh, 29 Apr. 1959 (NAI, D/T s.16289).

32 Statement by the Government Information Bureau on behalf of the Department of Education, 2 June 1959 (CAB 2/19, G.C.8/191, Cabinet minutes, 26 May 1959, p. 2).

33 Tierney to de Valera, 4 June 1959 (NAI D/T s.16289).

34 'Archbishop to be University Chancellor', *Sunday Dispatch*, 18 Jan. 1959 (UCDA, de Valera papers, P150/98).

35 Ibid.

36 'Report refuted by Taoiseach', *Irish Press*, 21 Jan. 1959 (UCDA, de Valera papers, P150/93).

37 NUI Senate minutes, 9 July 1959, XXXII, p. 75.

38 Ibid.

39 McCartney, *The NUI and Eamon de Valera*, p. 34.

40 Ibid., NUI Senate minutes, Extraordinary Meeting, 18 Sept. 1975, 75-15, pp. 113-14.

41 Circular by the Chancellor to members of the University Senate, 27 July 1961 (NUIA, Box 536).

42 'President's 50 Years as Chancellor', *Irish Press*, 11 Dec. 1971 (UCDA, de Valera papers, P150/98).

43 NUI Senate minutes, Extraordinary Meeting, 17 July 1975, 75-14, pp. 110-12.

44 NUI Senate minutes, Extraordinary Meeting, 18 Sept. 1975, 75-15, pp. 113-14.

45 Ibid.

Chapter 10
T. K. Whitaker, 1976-96

I am indebted to Nóirín Moynihan and to Dr John Nolan for their help and advice in regard to the archives of the NUI.

1 NUI Archives (hereafter NUIA), box of papers labelled 'Documentation from former Chancellor Dr T. K. Whitaker' (hereafter cited as 'TKW docs').

2 Henry Robinson, *Memories: Wise and Otherwise* (London: Cassell & Co., 1923), p. 292. The civil servant in question was John Anderson, subsequently Viscount Waverly,

permanent under-secretary in Dublin
Castle in 1920–1.

3 T. K. Whitaker, *Retrospect: 2006–1916*
(Dublin: Institute of Public
Administration, 2006), pp. 1, 11–13.

4 Donal McCartney, *The National University
of Ireland and Eamon de Valera* (Dublin:
University Press of Ireland, 1983), pp. 35–6.

5 T. K. Whitaker (hereafter TKW) to John
Bourke, Registrar of the NUI, 8 June 1976,
summarising his remarks on the occasion
of his installation – printed as appendix 'C'
to Senate minutes of 8 July 1976 (NUIA,
box 599).

6 Author's interview with Dr T. K. Whitaker,
29 May 2007.

7 Ibid.

8 NUI Senate minutes, 26 Nov. 1976, pp.
167–9.

9 Author's interview with TKW, 29 May 2007.

10 John Coolahan, 'Higher education, 1908–84'
in J. R. Hill (ed.), *A New History of Ireland: VII
Ireland, 1921–84* (Oxford: Oxford University
Press, 2003), p. 287.

11 *Dáil Debates*, vol. 350, 12, col. 1979, 24 May
1984.

12 Michael Olden, President of Maynooth, to
Dr T. K. Whitaker, 18 June 1984 (NUI, TKW
docs).

13 Gemma Hussey, *At the Cutting Edge:
Cabinet Diaries 1982–1987* (Dublin: Gill &
Macmillan, 1990), pp. 67–8 – entry for 9
Nov. 1983.

14 *Programme for Action in Education, 1984–1987*
(Dublin, 1984).

15 Confidential draft letter from TKW to the
Registrar of the NUI, 6 June 1984 (NUIA,
box 1). It should be noted that this account
and the other records of the NUI are at
variance with the account in Garret
FitzGerald, *All in a Life: An Autobiography*
(Dublin: Gill & Macmillan, 1991), p. 578,
which implies that the initiative for the
award of the degree to President Reagan
came from the NUI.

16 TKW to Garret FitzGerald ['Dear Garret'],
18 May 1984 (NUIA, TKW docs).

17 Garret FitzGerald to Ken Whitaker, 18 June
1984 (NUIA, TKW docs).

18 Text of letter from NUI Senate to Dept.
of Education, 14 Mar. 1986, NUI, Senate
minutes, 13 Mar. 1986, p. 10. The Carysfort
buildings and grounds eventually became
part of the UCD campus.

19 TKW to Mgr Micheál Ledwith, President
of Maynooth, 20 Nov. 1989 (NUIA, box 34).

20 John Nolan 'for Chancellor' to Mgr
Micheál Ledwith, President of Maynooth,
8 Jan. 1990 (NUIA, box 46).

21 NUI Senate minutes, 28 Jan. 1988.

22 Author's interview with Dr Art Cosgrove,
former President of UCD, 1 June 2007.

23 'Future of matriculation examination –
Note from the Chancellor to members of
the Senate', March 1989 (NUIA, TKW docs).

24 NUI Senate minutes, 26 Jan. 1989, 4.8.

25 NUI Senate minutes, 6 Apr. 1989, 5.

26 TKW to Declan Brennan, Secretary, Dept.
of Education, 12 Apr. 1989 (NUIA, box 34).

27 'Report on the meeting between the
Minister for Education and the National
University of Ireland on Thursday, 25 May
1989 at 3.00 p.m. in Leinster House' (NUIA,
TKW docs).

28 Private information.

29 NUI Senate minutes, 13 July 1989.

30 TKW to the Registrar, John Nolan, 19 July
1989 (NUIA, box 34).

31 TKW to Registrar NUI, 18 Oct. 1989 (NUIA,
box 24).

32 NUI Senate minutes, 16 Nov. 1989, pp. 29–31.

33 *Irish Press*, 17 Nov. 1989.

34 See 'Colleges prepare for legal battle to
break up NUI', *Sunday Tribune*, 26 Nov. 1989.

35 NUI Senate minutes, 25 Jan. 1990, pp. 16–17.

36 NUI minutes of special meeting of Senate,
10 Dec. 1990.

37 NUI Senate minutes, 24 Jan. 1991, p. 31.

38 NUI minutes of special meeting of Senate,
7 Feb. 1991.

39 Author's interview with Dr Art Cosgrove, former President of UCD but then an ordinary member of the Senate, 1 June 2007.

40 Private information.

41 'Record of the meeting between the NUI and the Minister for Education', 19 June 1991 (NUIA, TKW docs); see also Senate minutes, 11 July 1971, for the Chancellor's report of the meeting.

42 'A background note tracing the sequence of development s in relation to NUI legislation, during the period 1991 to 1996', appendix 1 (NUIA, TKW docs).

43 'Briefing note for the NUI officers in preparation for their bi-lateral meeting with the Department of Education on 30 Jan. 1996' (NUIA, TKW docs).

44 Minister for Education's press release, 30 July 1996.

45 NUI, Senate minutes, 3 Oct. 1996, pp. 2, 4. Whitaker felt particularly strongly about the threatened staffing controls to which he returned in winding up the debate, arguing that 'it would be inappropriate to detract from the prerogative of management by requiring advance approval of the numbers and grades of staff. A respectable body should be entitled to recruit the number and categories of personnel it deemed necessary to realize its management objectives. It should also be acceptable that there should be some provision for *post-factum* audit, which could take the form of a periodic review requiring the relevant body to substantiate its judgements. In view of the powers in the 1971 Act, the existence of a well-established consultative process between the HEA and individual universities on budgetary matters and the new provision for a budgeted term of years programme, it is clear that the public interest is sufficiently safeguarded and, accordingly, that many of the provisions in this Bill are unnecessarily specific and detract from legitimate management freedom.'

46 See the two files marked 'University Bill 1996 Information Pack A and B' (NUIA, TKW docs).

47 Chancellor to the Registrar of the NUI, 18 Sept. 1996, file marked 'University Bill 1996 Information Pack B' (NUIA, TKW docs).

48 NUI, Senate minutes, 7 Nov. 1996, pp. 2, 37–8.

Chapter 11
Garret FitzGerald, 1997–

1 Garret FitzGerald, *All in a Life* (Dublin, Gill & Macmillan, 1991), p. 1.

2 *Irish Times*, 20 Oct. 2007.

3 *The NUI Federal University in an Era of Transition* (Dublin, Nov. 2002).

4 *Report of Governing Authority subcommittee on the NUI*, Registrar's Office UCD (12 June 2007).

5 Ibid., para. 13.

Chapter 12
The Senate and the Changing Role of the Registrar

1 Irish Universities Act, 1908, 8 Edw. VII, c 28.

2 NUI Senate minutes, 17 Dec. 1908, I, p. 1.

3 NUI Senate minutes, 17 Dec. 1908, I, pp. 1–2.

4 NUI Senate minutes, 14 July 1911, I, p. 285.

5 NUI Senate minutes, 17 Dec. 1908, p. 1.

6 NUI Senate minutes, 24 Feb. 1910, I, p. 69.

7 NUI Senate minutes, 26 Mar. 1914, III, p. 325.

8 Letter dated 19 Apr. 1909 (NUIA).

9 NUI Senate minutes, 19 May 1916, V, pp. 111, 116.

10 NUI Senate minutes, 1 Feb. 1924, IX, p. 204.

11 NUI Senate minutes, 26 Oct. 1923, IX, p.138.

12 NUI Senate minutes, 3 May 1929, XI, p. 289.

13 NUI Senate minutes, 9 July 1936, XV, p. 229.

14 NUI Senate minutes, 3 Dec. 1936, XVI, p. 9.

15 NUI Senate minutes, 8 Apr. 1937, XVI, pp. 89–97.

16 NUI Senate minutes, 28 Oct. 1937, XVI, pp. 196–8

17 NUI Senate minutes, 11 Dec. 1952, p. 7.

18 NUI Senate minutes, 23 Mar. 1972, p. 24.

19 NUI Senate minutes, 8 July 1976, Appendices B and C.

20 NUI Senate minutes, 26 Nov. 1976, p. 167.

21 NUI Senate minutes, 25 Jan. 1979, p. 3.

22 NUI Senate minutes, 5 Apr. 1979, p. 26.

23 Ibid. 16 July 1987, p. 14

24 NUI Charter ch. v.

25 NUI Senate minutes, 21 Apr. 2004, p. 12.

26 A. Sloman, *A University in the Making* (Reith Lectures, 1963) (London: BBC, 1964).

27 NUI Statutes, ch. xxxv of Statute LXXXVI.

28 James Joyce, *Ulysses: A Reader's Edition* (London, Picador, 1997), p. 303; T. J. Morrissey SJ, *Towards a National University: William Delany S.J. and Era of Initiative in Irish Education* (Dublin: Wolfhound, 1983).

29 See C. Kiernan, *Daniel Mannix and Ireland* (Dublin: Gill & Macmillan, 1984).

30 Universities Act 1997, Section 45 (2) pp. 32–3.

31 M. Shattock (2006) *Managing Good Governance in Higher Education* (Maidenhead: Open University Press/ McGraw-Hill Education, 2006), p. 149.

32 NUI Charter XI.

33 Universities Act 1997, Section 47, p. 34.

34 S. Rowland, *The Enquiring University Compliance and Contestation in Higher Education* (Maidenhead: Open University Press, 2006), p. 5.

35 Shattock, *Managing Good Governance*, p. 1.

36 R. Barnett, *Realizing the University in an Age of Supercomplexity* (Buckingham: Society for Research into Higher Education and Open University Press, 2000).

37 *Review of National Policies for Education: Review of Higher Education in Ireland Examiners' Report* (OECD EDU/EC (2004) 14), p. 64.

38 Shattock, *Managing Good Governance*, p. 65.

39 National University of Ireland, *The NUI Federal University in an Era of Transition* (Dublin: NUI, 2002).

40 Shattock, *Managing Good Governance*, p. 78.

41 P. Gumport and B. Sporn, *Institutional Adaptation: Demands for Management and University Administration*. National Center for Postsecondary Improvement School of Education Stanford University NCPI Technical Report no. 1–07, 1999, p. 3.

42 *European University Association Creativity in Higher Education Report on the EUA Creativity Project 2006–2007* (Brussels: European University Association), p. 34.

43 *Extern Examiners in the National University of Ireland NUI Senate Policy Document* published in 1998 and updated annually.

44 *NUI Awards* published annually by NUI gives details of the fellowships, studentships, scholarships and other awards made by the Senate.

45 *Seanad Éireann Register of Electors National University of Ireland Constituency Seanad Electoral (University Members) Act, 1937* published annually by NUI.

46 *Iris Oifigiúil*, 10 Aug. 2007, p. 8.

47 The current arrangements are set to change under plans announced by the Minister for the Environment Mr John Gormley TD (*Irish Times*, 23 Nov. 2007) to create a single constituency in Seanad Éireann elections and enfranchise all graduates.

48 D. Holmes, 'Some personal perspectives on the role of university administrators and managers in British universities', *Perspectives* 2: 4 (1998), pp. 110–17.

Chapter 13
The Recognised Colleges

This is an abridged version of a more detailed paper which is available from the NUI office. I am very grateful for the helpful archival and administrative assistance provided at the NUI Central Office by Ms Nóirín Moynihan, Senior Administrative Officer, and Ms Ann Milner, Secretary to the Registrar, during the preparation of this article.

Chapter 14
The Role of Convocation

I am grateful to Ms Nóirín Moynihan and Mr Eddie Smyth for their assistance with the archival sources held by the NUI, from which much of the research for this chapter was derived. I am also grateful to Ms Máire Harris of Gael Linn for her assistance in relation to the period when Dónall Ó Móráin was Chairman of Convocation.

Chapter 16
The National University of Ireland and the Changing Structure of Irish Higher Education, 1967–2007

1 James, Meenan, 'The Universities – III', *Statistical Social Inquiry Society Journal*, XVIII (1950), p. 351 and *Commission on Higher Education Report* (PR.9389) (Dublin: Stationery Office, 1967), I, table 17, p. 31.
2 *Investment in Education* (PR. 8311) (Dublin: Stationery Office, 1966), p. 175.
3 Commission on Higher Education, *Presentation and Summary of the Report* (PR. 9326) (Dublin, Stationery Office, 1967), pp. 22–3.
4 *Report of the Commission on Accommodation Needs of the Constituent Colleges of the NUI* (PR.5089) (Dublin, 1959), p. 126.
5 Ibid., p. 125.
6 Steering Committee on Technical Education, *Report on Regional Technical Colleges* (Prl. 371) (Dublin: Stationery Office, 1967), pp. 39–41.
7 Higher Education Authority, *First Report* (Dublin: Stationery Office, 1969), p. 46.
8 Press Release from Minister Richard Burke on new government proposals, 16 Dec. 1974.
9 Department of Education, *A Programme for Action in Education, 1984–87* (Dublin: Stationery Office, 1984).
10 Tony White, *Investing in People: Higher Education in Ireland, 1960–2000* (Dublin: Institute of Public Administration, 2001), Appendix 1, pp. 282–3.
11 Department of Education, *Statistical Report for the year 2000–1* (Dublin: Stationery Office).
12 Department of Education *Green Paper: Education for a Changing World* (PL. 8969) (Dublin: Stationery Office, 1992), p. 203.
13 *Report of the International Review Group to the HEA* (Dublin: HEA, 1998).
14 Report of the Steering Committee to the HEA, *The Future Development of Higher Education* (Dublin: HEA, 1995).
15 Department of Education, *White Paper: Charting our Education Future* (PN. 2009) (Dublin: Stationery Office, 1995), p. 87.
16 Figures supplied by the HEA, 14 Feb. 2007.
17 OECD, *Reviews of National Policies of Education: Higher Education in Ireland* (Paris: OECD, 2006).

Chapter 17
Coming to Terms with the 1997 Act: The National University of Ireland Senate, 1997–2007

My account, as a former member of Senate and a participant in the events and discussions outlined, is simply that – my account. It is not to be read as representing views other than my own.

1 'The Future of the National University of Ireland and the Role of the NUI Senate', p. 2.
2 *The NUI Federal University in an Era of Transition* (Dublin: NUI, 2002).
3 'The future of the National University of Ireland: the consensus view of the NUI Registrars', quote, p. 2.
4 'The future of the National University of Ireland, the role of the NUI Senate and Executive and the relationship with the constituent universities'.

Appendix 1
NUI, 49 Merrion Square

1 NUI Senate minutes 27 July 1909, I, p. 17.
2 NUI Senate minutes, 28 Feb.1911, I, p. 201
3 NUI Senate minutes, 12 May 1911, I, p. 248
4 NUI Senate minutes, 26 March 1914, III, p. 324
5 NUI Senate minutes, 26 March 1926, X, p. 29
6 NUI Senate minutes, 4 Nov. 1927, XI, p. 29
7 Christine Casey, *Dublin: The City within the Grand and Royal Canals and the Circular Road*

with the *Phoenix Park* (New Haven and London: Yale University Press, 2005), p. 587.
8 M. O'Farrell, 'A cycle of late Georgian mural paintings in the Senate of the National University of Ireland', MA thesis UCD, 1976. The conclusions of Ms O'Farrell's study are contained in a booklet *Murals in the Senate Room of the National University of Ireland* available from NUI.

Index

Wimborne, Baron 133
Windle, Bertram, Pres. of QCC and
  UCC
  and federal NUI xvii, 51–2, 91, 133
  and 1908 Act 280
  promotes independence for UCC 47–8,
    50–1, 53–4, 88, 132
  and University of Munster 47, 53, 80
  drafts NUI Statutes 48
  view of Dublin-centred NUI 49
  travel to Dublin 48
  and UCD 89–90
  and Catholic Church 128–9
  and name of university 50, 61

retirement 53–4
Windsor Castle 124
Women's Graduate Association *see*
  Irish Association of Women
  Graduate and Candidate Graduates
Wood Quay issue 165
World Bank 147
World War I *see* First World War
World War II *see* Second World War
Wrixon, Gerry, President of UCC 62,
  169
Wyndham, George, Chief Secretary for
  Ireland 3, 11, 12
Wyndham's Land Bill 11